Thomas Traherne

CENTURIES, POEMS, AND THANKSGIVINGS

it self: for unless it be of it self it is not Lov. Constraint is Destructive & opposit to its Nature. The Lov from wch it floweth, is the fountain of & Lov wch Streameth from it, & Communicateth it self, & & Lov wch resteth in & object is & Lov wch Streameth to it. So & in all Lov & Trinity is Clear. By secret passages without Stirring it proceedeth to its Object, & is as Powerfully present as if it did not proceed at all. & Lov & lieth in & Bosom of & Lover, being & Lov & is perceived in & Spirit of & Beloved: y is, & same in Substance, tho in & Maner of substance, or Subsistence, different. Lov in & Bosom is & Parent of Lov. Lov in & Stream is & Lov seen, or Dwelling in & Object proceedeth from Both. yet are all three one & & self same Lov: the three loves.

4-1

Lov in & fountain, & Lov in & Stream are Both & same. And therfore are they Both Equal in Time & Glory. for Lov comunicateth it self by Being: And therfore Lov in & fountain is & very Lov comunicated to its Object. Lov in & fountain is Lov in & Stream, & Lov in & Stream Equaly Glorious wth Lov in & fountain. Tho it Streameth to its Object it abideth in & Lover, & is & Lov of & Lover.

4-2

where Lov is & Lover, & Lover Lov streaming from & Lover, is & Lover Lov is Lover Streaming from Himself: & existing in another person.

4-3.

This person is & Son of GOD: Who as He is & Wisdom of & father, so is He & Lov of & father. for & Lov of & father is & Wisdom of & father. And this Person did GOD by loving us beget, y He might be & Means of all our Glory.

4-4.

This person differs in nothing from & father but only in this y He is Begotton of Him. He is Eternal wth & father, as Glorious & as Intelligent. He is of & same Mind in every thing in all worlds, loveth & same Objects in a infinit a Measure. It & Means by wch & father Loveth, doeth, Createth Redeemeth governeth & Perfecteth all things. And & Means also by w we Lov & Lov & father: our Strength & our Eternity. He is y Mediator between GOD & His Creatures. God therfore being willing to redeem us by His own Blood (Act 20.) by Him redeemed us, & in His person died for us.

4-5

How Wonderfull is it, y GOD by being Lov should Spare a Redeemer to Die for us! But how much more Wonderfull, y by this means Himself should be: & be GOD by being LOV! By this means also He refineth our Nature, & enableth us to purge out &

From THE SECOND CENTURY

(see pp. 78–80)

Thomas Traherne

CENTURIES, POEMS, AND THANKSGIVINGS

EDITED BY

H. M. MARGOLIOUTH

Volume I

INTRODUCTION AND
CENTURIES

OXFORD
AT THE CLARENDON PRESS

Oxford University Press, Ely House, London W. 1

GLASGOW NEW YORK TORONTO MELBOURNE WELLINGTON
CAPE TOWN IBADAN NAIROBI DAR ES SALAAM LUSAKA ADDIS ABABA
DELHI BOMBAY CALCUTTA MADRAS KARACHI LAHORE DACCA
KUALA LUMPUR SINGAPORE HONG KONG TOKYO

© *Oxford University Press 1958*

First published 1958
Reprinted from corrected sheets of the first edition
1965, 1972

Printed in Great Britain
at the University Press, Oxford
by Vivian Ridler
Printer to the University

CONTENTS

Contents

VOLUME II

* F version of a poem in D or C (see Abbreviations, p. 335).

Contents

** Poems found only in F (see Abbreviations, p. 335).

Contents

Contents

Contents

Contents

ABBREVIATIONS

C   Centuries (Bodleian MS. Eng. th. e. 50)

CYB   The Church's Year Book, called by Dobell 'The Book of Private Devotions' (Bodleian MS. Eng. th. e. 51)

D   Dobell Folio (Bodleian MS. Eng. poet. c. 42)

F   *Poems of Felicity* (British Museum MS. Burney 392)

PNB   Philip Traherne's Notebook (Bodleian MS. Lat. misc. f. 45)

W   *The Poetical Works of Thomas Traherne*, ed. Gladys I. Wade, 1932

Wade   *Thomas Traherne, A Critical Biography*, by Gladys I. Wade, 1944 (second printing, 1946)

*   F version of a poem in D or C

**   Poem found only in F

INTRODUCTION

Purpose and Contents of this edition

Except for a few comparatively unimportant poems, this edition contains writings already published, viz:

(1) The *Centuries*, published in a modernized text by Dobell in 1908, reprinted 1927, 1934, 1948, and 1950, the last with an introduction by John Hayward. There were a few pages of notes and references. In the present edition Traherne's spelling, capitalization, and punctuation are retained. The numerous changes he made in his text are recorded in the notes, which also aim at giving as many references as possible.

(2) The *Poems*. Those in Dobell's manuscript were first published by him in a modernized text in 1903 and reprinted in 1906. Those in Burney MS. 392 in the British Museum were published by H. I. Bell in 1910 in a page-by-page reproduction. The two were combined in 1932 in Miss G. I. Wade's edition, which (like Dobell's) also contained other poems by Traherne from manuscript and printed sources. Miss Wade abandoned Dobell's modernization of his part of the text. The present edition differs in three ways from Miss Wade's. (i) The poems contained in the third *Century* are not reprinted among the *Poems* (but, for easy reference, they are included in the index of titles and the index of first lines). (ii) Poems from Bodleian MS. Lat. misc. f. 45 are printed for the first time. (iii) I have adopted an entirely different arrangement of the poems, the chief object being to make it easy for the reader to assess the amount of alteration made in Traherne's poems by his brother Philip.

(3) The *Thanksgivings*. These were first published in 1699 and were reprinted in 1941 by R. Daniells. Miss Wade, following Dobell, included three passages of rhymed poetry, but the whole work was written by Traherne not as prose but as

unconventional poetry, influenced to some extent by the rhythms of the English versions of the Psalms. The *Thanks-givings* are highly characteristic of Traherne and cannot properly be excluded from an edition of all his extant poetry.

The Centuries

These are contained in a notebook (Bodleian MS. Eng. th. e. 50), which, with the Dobell manuscript of the poems, was picked up for a few pence on a London street bookstall by W. T. Brooke in the winter of 1896–7. Neither contained any note of authorship, and both were some years later ascribed to Traherne by Bertram Dobell after a clever combination of flair and detective work.

The book is bound in old brown leather to which Grosart, through whose hands it passed, added the lettering 'MSS. of Henry Vaughan Silurist'. Grosart died in 1899 before his pro-jected new edition of Vaughan, with what he thought was this new Vaughan material, could be produced.

There are 140 leaves measuring 6·7 by 4·3 inches (17 by 11 cm.). The contents are as follows:

1^r and 1^v Notes by Dobell.

2^r Traherne's presentation quatrain and a few jottings (perhaps trying a pen).

2^v Notes by Traherne on Blessedness, a series of headings with no special connexion with the *Centuries*.

3^r A title 'Centuries of Meditations', in a hand which may be seventeenth-century but is certainly not Traherne's.

3^v, 4^r, 4^v Blank.

5^r–91^r The *Centuries*. The bottom two-thirds of 87 is cut away, leaving the words 'The fifth Century' on the recto. The verso is blank.

91^v A heading '11'.

92–140 Blank.

Traherne gave the book no title, and, though many of his sec-tions can be properly described as meditations, many cannot. The purpose of his writing was not to put his meditations on paper, but to instruct his friend in the way of Felicity: he would fill the book with 'Profitable Wonders'. What the manuscript suggests is that he started writing his paragraphs or sections (there are paragraph breaks in only two sections) and numbering them. At number 101 he decided not to head it '101' but to head it 'The Second Century' (or hundred) and so to start the numbering again with '1'. Though the beginning of this second *Century* reverts to the main topic, which was last specially touched on in I. 65, there is no real break in subject-matter between I and II. On the other hand II. 100 reaches a climax which might well have concluded the work. By this time, however, Traherne was conscious that he was writing *Centuries*. He also wished to support his instruction in Felicity by an account of his own personal experience of it. So he started the third *Century* with autobiography, the last third of this *Century* explaining how Traherne had found a kindred spirit in the Psalmist. In the fourth *Century* he set out to expound the 'principles' of Felicity, and concluded with a summary. He started a fifth *Century* on the theme of the identity of God and the Way and Object of Felicity, and in V. 10 reached a climax with which the *Centuries* happily and fitly conclude. Yet it is clear from '11' at the top of the next page that Traherne, at one time at any rate, thought of going on. Instead he revised what he had written.

In this edition, as in Dobell's, Traherne's revised text is given except that two fairly long deleted passages (in II. 36 and II. 60), which Dobell relegated to his notes, are here printed in the text in square brackets. Dobell himself printed I. 81, through the whole of which Traherne drew lines, and I do the same. It should be noted that there are comparatively few erasures in the *Centuries*, nearly always deletions, and that there is very seldom any difficulty in reading the deleted words.

The *Centuries* as first written in the manuscript are not in the main a fair copy. The poems form an exception, and I think it highly probable that the prayers and some of the paragraphs which are strictly meditations were, like the poems, already in existence and judged by Traherne to be suitable for insertion in this work. But the great body of instruction about Felicity seems to have been written *currente calamo*; there are some confirmatory facts such as the inadvertent numbering as '89' in the second *Century* of the section following 87.

The Poems

I. The Dobell manuscript (Bodleian MS. Eng. poet. c. 42) is of folio size and contains 97 original leaves measuring approximately 11·8 by 7·6 inches or 30 by 19 cm. It has been bound, probably in the earlier part of the nineteenth century, in boards with leather back and corners and lettered on the back 'Ledbury Manuscript'. Thicker paper, added with the binding, accounts for No. 1 of the Bodleian foliation and for a blank leaf after the foliation. The recto of folio 2, the first page of the manuscript, is darkened with age and suggests that there was no earlier binding.

All the writing is in double columns. That of the poems, a fair copy, is large and careful: that of the rest of the manuscript is often small and less careful, more like that of some of the corrections and additions to the *Centuries*.

The contents are as follows:

Inside front cover⎫ Notes by Dobell, of which that on 1ʳ is reprinted by
    1ʳ   1ᵛ ⎭ Wade, pp. 250–1.

2ʳ, 3ᵛ–16ʳ Fair copies of poems. These include two leaves foliated 9*a* and 9*b*, of which the second is imperfect: see note on *The Estate*. The poems end on the left-hand column of 16ʳ, the right-hand column being blank.

2ᵛ, 3ʳ   Blank.

16ᵛ–96ʳ (except 18 and 84) This, the greater part of the manuscript, is sometimes referred to as the Commonplace Book. It is not exactly that, but consists of extracts and notes arranged in alphabetical order beginning with 'Aristotles Philosophie' and ending with 'Virtue'. These notes had probably been started, with the first half of A, in some other manuscript book, as appears from the heading 'Astronomie vid Admiration': 'Admiration' is alphabetically too early for this volume.

There are two leaves 48 (48*a* and 48*b*), the latter being one column only as 9*b*. There are several other excisions in this part of the book and many blank spaces. The latter one would expect since entries in alphabetical order could otherwise not be made as the work of research progressed.

Bound in between leaves 17 and 19 is leaf 18, which is a fragment of someone's 'Incident Expences 1746'. It begins with four shillings 'To Sus. Treherne Spin:'. The last complete entry is of two shillings for expenses at Ledbury.

Similarly bound in between leaves 83 and 85 is leaf 84, an eighteenth-century fragment containing recipes against deafness, toothache, &c.

The handwriting of the Commonplace Book has been much debated. Dobell's notes are printed by Miss Wade (see above). Miss Wade decided that the whole was in Traherne's hand, but Miss Angela Russell reports in an unpublished thesis that two leading experts agree with her in finding two hands. Traherne wrote all the headings, but an 'amanuensis' made or completed many of the entries. Since the entries excerpt from the last part of Gale's *Court of the Gentiles* (published 1677), this finding seems final.

This book, like that of the *Centuries*, contains no note of authorship. The full story of Bertram Dobell's ascription to Traherne is given in the introduction to the editions of 1903, 1906, and 1932. He started by disbelieving Grosart's ascription to Vaughan. W. T. Brooke, the original finder of the manuscripts, knew the anonymous *Serious and Pathetical Contemplation*, which contains Traherne's *Thanksgivings*, and copied out for Dobell the rhymed pieces in it. Dobell was convinced that the author was also the author of the poems in his manuscripts. The Address 'To the Reader' of the *Thanksgivings* stated that the author was chaplain to Sir Orlando Bridgeman. Wood served to identify him as Thomas Traherne, author of *Roman Forgeries* and *Christian Ethicks*. *Christian Ethicks* contained the verse excerpt beginning 'As in a Clock', most of which is also found with some variations in *Century* III. 21. A beautiful piece of detection founded on flair was thus triumphantly completed, and a new name was added to the list of English poets of the seventeenth century.

An important point is that the poems come first in the manuscript book. They must therefore have been complete, i.e. been considered a completed selection, so that the rest of the book was available for what we might now call research notes. It is possible, as Miss Wade says (p. 254), that the collection of this material was begun as preliminary work for *Christian Ethicks*.

Since all this work was done after the transcription of the poems, it follows that that transcription cannot have been made very near the end of Traherne's life. It was, however, later than the writing of the *Centuries*, since the text of the poem, *The Approach*, which occurs in both, is in an earlier form in the *Centuries* than in the Dobell manuscript.

After Thomas's death his brother Philip made some changes in some of the poems. He also inserted from another selection, of which the manuscript has not been recovered, headings of other poems in various places where he thought they might come in a published volume.

II. This, however, was quite tentative and incomplete and bears no close relation to the volume which Philip did prepare for the press with the title *Poems of Felicity*. It did not achieve publication until 1910. This volume (Burney MS. 392) had been acquired by the British Museum in 1818. The manuscript title-page gives the author as 'Tho: Traheron. B.D. Author of the *Roman Forgeries*, & *Christian Ethiks*', but it was not until some years after Dobell had introduced Traherne the poet that anyone noticed this volume.

It opens with three prefatory poems, *The Dedication* by Philip, *The Author to the Critical Peruser* (running title *The Præface*) by Thomas, and *The Publisher To the Reader* by Philip. After that, on the verso facing the first of the poems proper, *The Salutation*, Philip quoted from Psalm 51^{15}, 'O Lord, open thou my Lips, and my Mouth shall shew forth Thy Prais'. Characteristically this is the Bible not the Prayer Book version, and characteristically Philip introduces what I imagine to be his pet spelling system.

The poems proper are headed '*Divine Reflections* On The Native Objects of 𝔞n 𝔍nfant-𝔈y' and begin with the same poem as the Dobell manuscript. They number sixty-one in all, counting as two each the six pairs of poems with a single heading (*Bells, Churches, Right Apprehension, The Inference, Insatiableness, The Review*). Of these sixty-one D contains twenty-two and also two stanzas (*Blisse*) of another (*The Apostacy*). It is noteworthy that these twenty-two are the first twenty-two in D: fourteen poems which, together with *Blisse*, conclude D are omitted *en bloc*. It is possible that Philip judged these poems inferior, but also possible that he reserved them for a second volume. We know that, besides these fourteen, there were others which he might have so used: four at least of the titles he inserted in D cannot be identified with any known poem.

Philip keeps the order of the first ten and the last five of these twenty-two poems, but alters the order of the seven which come between the tenth (*The Approach*) and the eighteenth (*Speed*). He inserts two fresh poems between the fourth (*Innocence*) and the fifth (*The Præparative*), sixteen between the eighth (*The Rapture*) and the ninth (*The Improvment*), two between *The Improvment* and the tenth (*The Approach*), a new *Right Apprehension* before that from D, one new poem[1] between the twentieth (*The Person*) and the twenty-first (*The Estate*), and one new poem between the twenty-first (*The Estate*) and the twenty-second (*The Enquiry*). After that come sixteen fresh poems. The fact that this last group takes the place of the excluded D group is an argument against the suggestion that a second volume was intended. There is more of the 'Infant-Ey' and less arguing in this F group than in the excluded D group.

Philip's arrangement of the poems is on the whole a good one. His editing and changing of the text is a disaster. A comparison of the twenty-two poems which are found in both D and F show what he did, and make it certain that the other thirty-nine poems in F are not altogether as Thomas left them. Further evidence is provided by the further changes made in manuscript F itself.

In spite, therefore, of the excellence of Philip's order I have here used a different one to facilitate a comparison of Thomas's text and Philip's. After Thomas's *The Author to the Critical Peruser* I print the first twenty-two D poems in the D order on left-hand pages, and opposite them on right-hand pages I print the same poems as they appear in F. After that come the remainder of the F poems and then the remainder of the D poems. Two poems in F do not have Thomas's available version facing Philip's, i.e. *News*, found as *On News* in *Century* III. 26, and the two stanzas of *The Apostacy* found as *Blisse* in D.

I have made one important change from previous editions.

[1] *The Image*, which he subsequently deleted.

Philip made a certain number of changes in D itself. Both Dobell and Miss Wade print the poems with Philip's changes, though Miss Wade records Thomas's original in her notes. This is quite wrong, and I have everywhere restored Thomas's own text. In a few places Thomas himself made changes. I have sometimes preferred what he first wrote, recording his change in the notes.

If only I could also have restored Thomas's own text through' out the poems found only in F! That is impossible, but there are many places where Philip changed the text from what he first wrote down. There is a strong presumption that what he first wrote down is generally a transcription of Thomas: sometimes, of course, it may be a version of his own on which he later thought he could improve. But I have felt justified in printing the first F version where it can be done without ruining metre or rhyme. Where we could restore a first line of Thomas's but, for what should be the rhyming line, have only a line of Philip's which does not rhyme with it, there is nothing to do but print Philip's two rhyming lines and record in the notes what is recoverable of the original.

III. After this great bulk of the metrical poems there follow two smaller groups, those from printed sources and those from manuscripts other than D and F. The printed sources are *Christian Ethicks*, published in 1675, the year after Traherne's death, and the six from *Hexameron*, or, *Meditations on the Six Days of Creation*, published in 1717. No question arises about those from *Christian Ethicks*, except of the possibility of retouching while the book was going through the press after Thomas's death. This is, how' ever, unlikely, especially as Philip did not get back to England from Smyrna until some time in 1675. The ascription to Thomas of *Hexameron* and the included poems for each day of the Creation was first made by Miss Wade in the Preface, pp. xii–xx, to her 1932 edition. Her arguments are strong. She judges it an early work on stylistic grounds. It must certainly be that, if only because we have so much from Traherne's last few years that there is hardly room for anything more. Moreover youth is just possibly suggested by a sentence on p. 37, 'As I grow in Years make me grow in Grace'. I accept Miss Wade's ascription with only a little hesitation, though I find that such a rhyme as 'rend . . . Command' (*Second Day* 13–14) does not occur elsewhere in Traherne.

The second smaller group is that from manuscripts CYB and PNB. These two manuscripts call for a fuller description than has hitherto been available.

The Church's Year-Book

Dobell called this 'The Book of Private Devotions', which will doubtless persist as an alternative title, but it does not describe the scheme and purpose of the book.

The notebook (Bodleian MS. Eng. th. e. 51) contains 133 leaves measuring approximately 6·7 by 4·2 inches or 17 by 10·8 cm. (almost the same as C). It is in contemporary leather binding, as are C and PNB. There is a fly-leaf (foliated 'ii' by the Bodleian); leaves 1–57, 68–113, foliated in ink with 68 following 57, perhaps by Thomas Traherne or his brother, contain writing; leaves 114–42, foliated by the Bodleian, are blank, as is the inside of the back cover, foliated '143' by the Bodleian.

The contents, in Thomas Traherne's writing, are a series of meditations, prayers, &c., on chief days in the Church's year from Easter to All Saints' Day. It is highly probable that it is the second part of a work of which the first is lost. Traherne would have started with the beginning of the Church's year in Advent and got as far, in a preceding notebook, as Good Friday. We noted that there may have been a similar, though smaller, loss of a beginning in another notebook of the research notes which occupy the greater part of D.

The following is a brief table of the main contents of CYB:

ff. 1–13ᵛ 'Meditations and Devotions upon the Resurrection of our Savior.'

13ᵛ–14ʳ Poem: 'Unto the Spring of Purest Life' (a translation mainly unoriginal).

14ᵛ–15ʳ 'Prayers upon the Resurrection.'

15ʳ 'Exultations.'

15ᵛ–16ʳ 'An Advertisement Concerning Paschal Time' (the period between Easter and Ascension Day).

16ᵛ–17ʳ 'Meditations and Devotions for St. Marks Day' (25 April).

ff. 17ᵛ–22ʳ 'Meditations upon the Festival of St Philip and James' (1 May).

22ᵛ–24ʳ 'Rogation Week' (the week containing Ascension Day).

24ʳ–27ʳ 'Acts of Adoration and Thanksgiving.'

27ᵛ–28ʳ 'Intercessions.'

28ʳ–30ʳ 'Confession of Sins, Collected chiefly out of Bishop Andrews', with, near the end, the poem 'Com Holy Ghost Eternal God' (a translation).

30ʳ–31ʳ A Litany to be used in these or any other Days of Devotion or Humiliation.'

31ʳ–40ᵛ 'Meditations and Devotions for Ascension Day', including (39ᵛ) 'A Prayer Most of which was taken out of Dr. Featley for Ascension Day'.

41ʳ–41ᵛ 'Expectation Week' (i.e. for Whitsun).

41ᵛ–42ʳ 'A Soliloquie with our own Souls.'

42ʳ–42ᵛ 'Aspirations.'

42ᵛ–43ʳ 'Motivs to Hope.'

43ʳ–56ʳ 'Of the Coming of the Holy Ghost.'

56ᵛ–68ʳ 'For Trinity Sunday' (leaves 58–67 cut out).

68ʳ–70ʳ 'Devotions on St Barnabas Day' (11 June).

70ᵛ–75ᵛ 'Devotions on St John Baptists Day' (24 June), including (75ʳ) a 'Prayer for S. John Baptists Day, taken out of Dr Taylor' ('O Holy and most Glorious . . . Jesus Christ Amen').

75ᵛ–79ʳ 'Meditations and Devotions for St Peters Day' (29 June).

79ᵛ–82ʳ 'On St James his Day' (25 July).

82ᵛ–84ᵛ 'on St Bartholomews Day' (24 August), ending with 'An Hymne upon St Bartholomews Day'.

85ʳ–88ᵛ 'Meditations and Devotions on St Matthews Day' (21 September), including (88ʳˑᵛ) 'A short Meditation upon our Vocation'.

89ʳ–97ᵛ 'Meditations and Devotions on St Michaels Day' (29 September).

98ʳ–99ᵛ 'Meditations and Prayers For St Lukes Day' (18 October).

100ʳ–103ᵛ 'Meditations and Devotions on the Festival of St Simon and St Jude' (28 October).

104ʳ–113ʳ 'Upon All Saints Day' (1 November), including 'A Hymne to all Saints out of Herbert' (i.e. *To all Angels and Saints*, Oxford English Texts, p. 77). (p. 113 is not in Traherne's hand.)

The work was probably written with a view to eventual publication. There are some later corrections and additions in a darker ink, and some technique of emphasis or quotation by spacing letters in some headings and elsewhere.

The most probable date is 1673, i.e. the lost beginning started in Advent 1672.

There are two arguments for this. First, the Litany (30ʳ–31ʳ) suggests that Traherne was worried about public affairs. His patron, Sir Orlando Bridgeman, ceased to be Lord Keeper on 17 November 1672 owing to his disagreement with the king's policy. Note the appeals on 30ᵛ,

'From all the Evils of State Good Lord Deliver us.'

'From Deifying of Kings', &c.

'From Flattering of the People', &c., and the reference on 31ʳ to 'sleepless Nights'.

Secondly, the relation of the Saints' Days to the Sundays rules out several years. If we take the years 1660–74, we can rule out 1668 because in that year Lady Day came after Easter but no Lady Day (Annunciation of the Blessed Virgin Mary, 25 March) comes in this work: we can rule out 1660, 1663, 1671, and 1674 because in those years Trinity Sunday came after St. Barna‑ bas's Day (11 June): 1674 is also ruled out because Traherne died in early October of that year, i.e. before St. Luke, SS. Simon and Jude, and All Saints' Day. It is probable that the absence of St. Andrew's Day (30 November) can be used as evidence. If that day came before Advent, it would fall at the end of the Church year and we should expect it to conclude Traherne's book. It does not do so. The Year Book should therefore belong to a calendar year in which St. Andrew's Day did not precede Advent. This rules out 1660, 1661, 1665, 1666, 1667, 1671, and 1672, in all of which St. Andrew's Day preceded Advent.

We are left with 1662, 1664, 1669, 1670, and 1673. Even if the last argument is not accepted, the political allusions seem to limit the choice to 1672 and 1673. The Declaration of Indulgence of March 1672 might account for them and permit a 1672 date, but would Sir Orlando pass on his worries to his chaplain before his resignation? Easter to All Saints' Day 1673 remains the most probable time for the composition of this work, of which the first part is lost.

The work is not entirely original. The excerpts from Andrews, Featley, Taylor, and Herbert and the largely borrowed translation of the first poem have been mentioned already. Collects for St. Matthew's Day, St. Michael's Day, and St. James's Day are from the Book of Common Prayer. It is more than possible that an intensive study of the relevant religious literature would reveal other borrowings or adaptations.

Philip Traherne's Notebook

This, the smallest of the four Bodleian manuscripts (Lat. misc. f. 45), contains vi+388 *pages* measuring approximately 5·7 by 3·7 inches or 14·5 by 9·5 cm. It is in contemporary leather binding. It has an original pagination in ink of pp. 1–55 (Philip's part) and 67–168 (Thomas's first part), the latter being a misnumbering of 69–170.

Miss Wade had not seen the book, but, under the heading 'A Collection of Early Verse', gave an account based on information supplied by Mr. P. J. Dobell (Wade, pp. 247–50).

The chief contents are as follows (Bodleian pagination):

Pages
    i (first fly-leaf) Doodles and odd words including signatures by Thomas.
    ii A passage in cipher.
    iii (second fly-leaf) Inscription and date—'Philip Traherne is the true owner of this booke Amen Anno Domini 1655'.
    iv Latin quotation from Bacon.
    v An elaborate title-page by Philip.
    vi Blank.
  1–5 Latin exercises.
    6 Blank.
  7–32 and 41–55 Very neatly written notes on Ethics, Geometry, and History. This is all Philip's, but a short later insertion on p. 21 may be Thomas's.
33–40 and 56–68 Blank.
69–170 Miscellaneous quotations, notes, &c., by Thomas, mostly in Latin. There are many blanks (76–84, 102–12, 126, 152, 162, 164, 166, 168) because each subject is kept separate. On p. 148 is the signature 'Thomas Traherone'.

Pages

171–83 Blank.

184–211 Poetry (see below).

212 Blank.

213–34 More notes by Thomas. These are in Latin.

235 English note by Thomas (quoted in Notes, ii, p. 348).

236 Blank.

237–40 A quotation in very careful handwriting from Thomas Burnet's *Theoria Sacra* (published 1681), which suggests that Philip had re-acquired the book after Thomas's death.

241–338 Blank.

339–41 Latin notes by Thomas.

342–73 Blank.

374–5 Poetical translation by Thomas.

376–end Blank.

The poetry section contains the following:

Page

184 'What e're I have from God alone I have.'
'Oh how injurious is this wall of sin.'

185 'As fragrant Mirrhe within the bosom hid.'

186–8 Blank.

189 'To bee a Monarch is a glorious thing.'

190 Blank.

191 On the Bible.

192–6 Blank.

197 Epitaphium ('Hic situs est Haeres Mundi').

199, 8 'Rise noble soule & come away', which begins on 199.

200 Latin elegiac version of p. 201

201 Strode's 'I saw fair Chloris'.

202 'Stet quicunque volet potens', &c., from Seneca, *Thyestes*, lines 391–403.

203 A very poor verse translation of p. 202. At the top in darker ink is written 'Philip'. I take it that this is Philip's translation copied out by Thomas.

204 Blank.

205 Epitaphium Annae Cholmeley sacrum.

206 Blank.

207 Memento mori.

208 Blank.

209 a Serious and a Curious night Meditation.

Pages

210 Blank.

211 In Obitum viri optimi J: C. Eirenarchae.

212 Blank except for a reference to Leviticus 27^{10}.

Finally, by itself,

374 'Nescitis Cupidi Arcium' from Seneca, *Thyestes*, line 342 and sixteen other lines ending with line 390.

375 Translation of p. 374, 'Yee that Towers so much prize'.

Both CYB and PNB were acquired by the Bodleian from Messrs. Dobell. The latter had bought PNB at a London sale-room in 1935, and CYB had been an earlier purchase. It had been in Grosart's library unrecognized.

The Thanksgivings

The volume containing these is a duodecimo of prefatory matter and 148 pages: the numbers 99, 102, 141, 142 are each given to two pages, so that the last page is numbered 144. The volume is entitled *A Serious and Pathetical Contemplation of the Mercies of God, in several most Devout and Sublime Thanksgivings for the same.* It was 'Published By the Reverend Doctor HICKS, At the request of a Friend of the Authors. *LONDON*; Printed for ☙amuel ฿eble at the *Turks-head Fleet Street*, over against *Fetter-lane-end*, 1699'.

It was reprinted by the University of Toronto Press (ed. R. Daniells) in 1941.

It is not likely that it follows Traherne's manuscript in all minutiae, e.g. the spelling 'than' is not Traherne's. The biblical references inserted from time to time are also not his, if one is to judge by their extreme rarity in his extant manuscripts. It looks as if the editor inserted them occasionally when he knew them, but did not go to the trouble of identifying others.

There is no reason to suppose that Traherne wrote the long-winded title, nor, of course, was he responsible for the frontis-piece, a rather poor engraving of men and angels adoring God. The 'Friend of the Authors' is undoubtedly Susanna Hopton, for whom see below. The non-juror George Hickes (1642–1715, see *DNB*) came into possession of other manuscripts when Mrs. Hopton died in 1709: the question of their authorship, single or composite, is discussed by Miss Wade at length. Hickes may have been imperfectly informed. These *Thanksgivings*, however, he definitely ascribes to Traherne in all but name: see *To The Reader*, printed below. Even without that ascription no one familiar with Traherne's other writings could fail to recognize them immediately as his.

Materials for Traherne's Biography

There is much biographical material in the *Poems* and *Centuries*, especially Century III. The following list does not include them or anything from Traherne's own writings except under (13).

(1) Wood (ed. Bliss, 1813–20)

(i) *Athenae Oxonienses*

THOMAS TRAHERNE, *a shoemaker's son of Hereford** (**A Herefordshire man born*. First edit.) was entred a commoner of Brasen-n. college on the first day of March 1652, took one degree in arts, left the house for a time, entred into the sacred function, and in 1661 he was actually created master of arts. About that time he became rector of Credinhill commonly called Crednell near to the city of Hereford, afterwards domestic chaplain to S. Orlando Bridgman lord Keeper of the great seal, and minister of Tuddington, called by some Teddington, near Hampton Court in Middlesex, and in 1669 bach. of divinity. He hath written,

Roman Forgeries: or, a true Account of false Records discovering the Impostures and counterfeit Antiquities of the Church of Rome. Lond. 1673. oct. [Bodl. 8vo. B. 294. Th.]

Christian Ethics: or divine Morality, opening the Way to Blessedness, by the Rules of Virtue and Reason. Lond. 1675. oct. [Bodl. 8vo. G. 65. Th.] He died at Teddington before-mention'd, in the house of S. Orl. Bridgman, and was buried on the tenth day of October in the church there, under the reading desk, in sixteen hundred seventy and four. This person, who always led a single and a devout life, was well read in primitive antiquity as in the councils, fathers, &c.

(ii) *Fasti*

13 October 1656 'Tho. Traherne of Brasen. coll.', B.A.
6 November 1661 'Tho. Traherne of Brasen. coll.', M.A.
11 December 1669 'Tho. Traherne. of Brasen. coll.', B.D.

(2) 'Brasenose College Register, 1509–1901' (Oxford, 1909)

1652/3 Traherne, Thomas. [Herefs.] Adm. pleb. 1 Mar. 1652/3, aged 15; matr. 2 Apr. 1653; B.A. 13 Oct. 1656; cr. M.A. 6 Nov. 1661; readm. 9 Dec; B.D. 1669.

(3) Brasenose Buttery Books, available for the first time in the autumn of 1957

There are gaps in the sixth decade of the century. Traherne's name appears as an undergraduate in the fourth quarter of 1653. It is absent from extant books for 1658 (third quarter), 1659 (third and fourth quarters), 1660 (the whole.)

(4) 'The Brasenose Book of Benefactors' (Oxford, 1909)

1664 Thomas Traherne Rector de Credenhill in Comitatu Herefordiensi nuper hujus Collegii commensalis donavit viginti solidos. [Brasenose was at this time building chapel, cloister, and library.]

(5) Lambeth Palace Library MS. 998

(i) *Thomas Traherne*, clerk, admitted 30 Dec., 1657, by the Commissioners for the Approbation of Public Preachers to the Rectory of Crednell, alias Creddenhill, Co. Hereford: patron Amabella Countess Dowager of Kent.

(ii) Thomas Traherne, cl. Admitted the 30th Day of December 1657 to the R. of Crednell, als. Creddenhill in the County of Hereford Upon a Pres: exhib the 23th day of Decr 1657, from Amabella Countesse Dowager of Kent the Patronesse thereof. And Certificates from Wm. Voile Wm. Lowe Sam Smith Geo Primrose Rob Breton Ben Baxter of Upton upon Seaverne Jo Cholmley.

(6) Bodleian MS. Oxford Diocesan Papers, d. 106

Octob. 20 Nomina ordinatorum per Robertum divina providentia
1660   Oxon. Episcopum, apud Launton comitatu et diocese Oxon. Vicesimo die mensis Octobris, 1660.

> Isaac Wright, Coll. Wadham. Art. Magister, diaconus et presbyter.
> Thomas Traherne, Coll. Aen: Nasi Art. Bacc. diaconus et Presbyter.

(7) W. H. Cooke, 'County of Hereford' (1892)

Parish of Credenhill:

Patron	Date	Rector
Gilbert, 7th Earl of Salop	1606	Roger Breynton, M.A.
Hereford Parliamentary Committee	1646	George Primrose, *vac.*
„	1650	Edmund Quarrell
The King, through lapse	1660	William Carpenter, M.A. vacated for Staunton-on-Wye
Anthony, Earl of Kent	1661	Thomas Traherne, D.D.
„	1674	John Clarke, M.A.

(8) Contemporary Transcripts of Credenhill Parish Registers

These are preserved in the Booth Porch Muniment room in Hereford Cathedral. Miss Angela Russell, who has examined them, reported as follows in an article 'The Life of Thomas Traherne' (*Review of English Studies*, January 1955, pp. 34–43):

The only contemporary records of Traherne's years at Credenhill are some transcripts, dating from 1662, of the Parish Registers, which were presented to the Bishop every year. Those for the years 1662 and 1663 were written and signed by George Gwillim, the churchwarden. Those for 1664, 1665, and 1666 are signed by 'Tho. Traherne Rector', or 'Tho Traherne Rr'; those for 1667 and 1668 are written and signed in Traherne's own hand. The transcripts for 1669 and 1670 are written and signed by William Payne, churchwarden; that of 1671 by Francis Browne, churchwarden. Traherne signed that of 1672 (although the signature is barely decipherable). A churchwarden wrote out and signed the transcript for 1673, while that of 1674 is signed by Traherne's successor, 'John Clerke Rector'.

The transcripts show that the parish of Credenhill was small, or sparsely populated. In 1662 there were five burials and one baptism; the most lively year, 1667, showing two baptisms, three marriages, and three burials; one burial being of a certain 'Edward Traherne Late of the City of Herefford'. 1665 shows one baptism only; 1666, one baptism and one burial; 1672, one baptism, one marriage, and one burial.

(9) Traherne's Will (reprinted from Dobell's editions)

THE WILL OF THOMAS TRAHERNE,
AS REGISTERED IN THE
PREROGATIVE COURT OF CANTERBURY

Memorandum that Thomas Traherne late of Teddington in the County of Midd Clerk deceased in the time of the sickness whereof he dyed and vpon or about the Seaven and Twentyth of September 1674 having sent for John Berdo Gent to come to him the said Thomas Traherne then lying sick at the Lady Bridgmans house in Teddington and the said Mr Berdo being come vnto him he the said Thomas Traherne being then of perfect mind and memory vsed these or the like words to the said Mr. Berdo vizt. I haue sent for you to make my Will for mee or to that effect Whereupon the said Mr Berdo asked of him the said Mr Thomas Traherne whether he would haue it made in Writing To which the said Thomas Traherne answeared in these or the like words vizt. Noe I haue not so much but that I can dispose of it by Word of Mouth or to that effect And the said Thomas Traherne being then of perfect mind and memory by Word of Mouth with an intent to make his Will and to settle and dispose of his Goods and Estate did vtter and speake these or the like words vizt. I desire my Lady Bridgman and her daughter the Lady Charlott should haue each of them a Ring And to you (speaking to the said Mr. Berdo) I give Tenn Pounds and to Mrs Cockson Tenn shillings and to Phillipp Landman ffyve shillings and to John Rowland the Gardiner ffyve shillings and to Mary the Laundry maid ffyve shillings and to all the rest of the servants half a crowne apeece. My best Hatt I give it to my brother Phillipp And sister (speaking to Mrs Susan Traherne the wife of his brother Phillipp which Susan was then present) I desire you would keepe it for him And all the rest of my Clothes that is worth your acceptance I give to you And for those that are not worth your accepting I would have you to giue them to Phillipp Landman or to whome you please with my old Hatt All my Books I give to my brother Phillipp And (still speaking to the said Mrs Susan then present) I make you and my brother Phillipp my whole Executors which words or the like in effect The said Thomas Traherne being then of perfect mind and memory did then utter Animo testandi and with an intent that the same should stand and be as and for his last Will and Testament in the presence and hearing of John Berdo Alice Cockson and Mary Linum.

John Berdo Alice Cockson The Mark of Mary Linum.

Proved at London 22 Oct 1674 by Susan Traherne, one of the Executors, to whom administration was granted, power being reserved of making the like grant to Philip Traherne, the other executor, should he ask for the same.

(10) His property in Hereford

(i) Adjoining *Symond's Hospital*, or alms-house, are five other tenements, which were given A.D. 1683 [*sic*], by Thomas Traherne, B.D. to the successive ministers and churchwardens of the parish of All-Saints, for the use of as many poor persons, belonging to that parish.

Duncumb's *Hereford* (1804), i. 410 [Erroneous, as (ii) shows].

(ii) The following extract 'from the report of the Charity Commissioners investigating the Herefordshire charities between 1819–1837' was kindly supplied by Mr. A. Shaw Wright, County Librarian, Hereford:

TRAHERON'S CHARITY

By indenture, bearing date 28th June 1677, and made between Philip Traheron, of Hinton Martell, in the county of Dorset, brother and heir of Thomas Traheron, then late of Teddington, in the county of Middlesex, deceased, of the one part, and the mayor, aldermen, and citizens of Hereford of the other part, after reciting that the said Thomas Traheron had often declared in his lifetime, that he would settle the houses and tenements thereinafter mentioned on the said mayor, aldermen and citizens for ever, it was witnessed that the said Philip Traheron, with a desire to fulfil the wishes and intentions of his said brother, did enfeoff release and confirm to the said mayor, aldermen, and citizens, and their successors, those five houses adjoining to each other with the gardens thereto belonging, in Widemarsh-street, in the parish of All Saints, in the suburbs of the city of Hereford, near to a brook called The Tan Brook, to hold the same on trust, that the mayor and justices of the peace of the said city for the time being, or the major part of them, the mayor to be one, should settle the persons then in possession of four of the said houses and gardens to continue in the same for their respective lives, and should, within one month after the date thereof, admit into the other house and garden such poor person as the said Philip Traheron should nominate and appoint the same person to continue therein during his or her life. And that for ever from thenceforth the said mayor and justices, in case of the death or expulsion of any of the persons so settled in the said houses or thereafter to be admitted and settled therein, should admit a poor person of the parish of All Saints, whom they should think to be the fittest object of charity, in the place and stead of the person so dead or expelled as aforesaid; provided that no person should be admitted or settled who did not conform to the liturgy, discipline and doctrine of the church of England, and attend divine service in the parish church of All Saints aforesaid, unless prevented by sickness or other lawful cause; and lest the said houses should become ruinous and decayed, so as not to serve for con-venient habitations, the said mayor, aldermen, and citizens did, for them-selves and their successors, covenant with the said Philip Traheron that they would, at their own proper cost and charge, at all times well and suffi-ciently repair, uphold, and sustain the five several houses aforesaid, and any of them, with their appurtenances.

This deed was found among the muniments of the corporation, but the town-clerk was altogether ignorant of its existence, and, though he knew the almshouses, was not aware that the founder had placed them under the management of the corporation. It appeared upon inquiry that, having no endowment, they had been suffered to fall into the hands of the officers of All Saints' parish, who had occasionally repaired them. The houses are five in number, and the inmates are selected from the poor of All Saints' parish, but the right of selection and the liability to repair are vested in the corporation and not in the parish.

[I do not know how Traherne came to own these houses, but one may suppose that the rents helped towards his education and apparent indepen-dence after taking his B.A.]

(11) Immediate references to Traherne's death

(i) Teddington Parish Register. 10 October 1674. Burial entry.

(ii) Sir Edward Harley of Brampton Bryan, Herefordshire, in a 'Retro-spect on The Completion of his Fiftieth Year' (*Letters of Lady Brilliana Harley*, ed. T. T. Lewis, Camden Society, 1854, p. 249).

'In August, my dear neice Frances Fitzjames of the small-pox. Since that, my worthy friend Mr. Thomas Treherne and my cosin Reads wife, both dead in the same day! and now my sister Palmer; while I, poor unprofitable worm, am still spared.'

(iii) Thomas Good, Master of Balliol, formerly prebend of Hereford, to William Thomas, Dean of Worcester (see *Times Literary Supplement*, 27 Oct. 1927).

'I believe it is not news to you that Tom Traherne is dead, one of the most pious ingenious men that ever I was acquainted with.'

(12) Aubrey's 'Miscellanies' (1696)

Mr. Traherne, B.D. (chaplain to Sir Orlando Bridgman, Lord Keeper), a learned and sober person, was son of a shoemaker in Hereford; one night as he lay in bed, the moon shining very bright, he saw the phantom of one of the apprentices sitting in a chair in red waistcoat and headband about his head, and strap upon his knee, which apprentice was really in bed and asleep with another fellow-apprentice, in the same chamber, and saw him. The fellow was living, 1671. Another time, as he was in bed, he saw a basket sailing in the air, along by the valence of his bed; I think he said there was fruit in the basket; it was a phantom. From himself.

(13) 'Roman Forgeries'

The following passage, which concludes 'An Advertise-ment to the Reader' prefixed to *Roman Forgeries*, shows Traherne at his research work at Oxford:

I shall add one passage which befel me in the *Schools*, as I was studying these things and searching the most Old and Authentick Records in pur-suance of them. One Evening, as I came out of the *Bodleian Library*, which is the Glory of *Oxford*, and this Nation, at the Stairs-foot I was saluted by a Person that has deserved well both of Scholars and Learning, who being an intimate Friend of mine, told me there was a Gentleman his Cosen, pointing to a Grave Person, in the Quadrangle, a man that had spent many thousand pounds in promoting Popery, and that he had a desire to speak with me. The Gentleman came up to us of his own accord: We agreed, for the greater liberty and privacy, to walk abroad into the *New-Parks*. He was a notable man, of an Eloquent Tongue, and competent Reading, bold, forward, talkative enough: He told me, that the Church of *Rome* had Eleven Millions of *Martyrs*, Seventeen *Oecumenical Councils*, above an Hundred *Provincial Councils*, all the *Doctors*, all the *Fathers*, *Unity*, *Antiquity*, *Consent*, &c. I desired him to name me *One* of his *Eleven Millions of Martyrs*, excepting those that died for Treason in Queen *Elizabeths*, and King *James* his days: For the *Martyrs* of the *Primitive times*, were Martyrs of the *Catholick*, but not of the *Roman* Church: They only being Martyrs of the *Roman Church*, that die for *Transubstantiation*, the *Popes Supremacy*, the Doctrine of *Merits*, *Purgatory*, and the like. So many he told me they had, but I could not get him to name one. As for his *Councils*, *Antiquities*, and *Fathers*, I asked him what he would say, if I could clearly prove, that the Church of *Rome* was guilty of *forging* them, so far, that they had published *Canons* in the *Apostles* names, and invented *Councils* that never were; forged *Letters* of Fathers, and *Decretal Epistles*, in the name of the first Bishops and Martyrs of *Rome*, made 5, 6, 700 years after they were dead, to the utter disguizing and defacing of Antiquity, for the first 400 years next after our Saviour? *Tush, these are nothing but lyes,* quoth he, *whereby the Protestants endeavour to disgrace the*

Papists. Sir, answered I, you are a Scholar, and have heard of *Isidore, Mer-cator, James Merlin, Peter Crabbe, Laurentius Surius, Severinus Binius, Labbè, Cossartius,* and the *Collectio Regia,* Books of vast Bulk and Price, as well as of great Majesty and Magnificence: You met me this Evening at the *Library door*; if you please to meet me there to morrow morning at eight of the Clock, I will take you in; and we will go from Class to Class, from Book to Book, and there I will first shew in *your own Authors,* that you publish such Instruments for good *Records,* and then prove, that those *Instruments* are downright frauds and *forgeries,* though cited by you upon all occasions. He would not come; but made this strange reply; *What if they be Forgeries? what hurt is that to the Church of* Rome? No! (cryed I, amazed) Is it no hurt to the *Church of Rome,* to be found guilty of *forging Canons* in the *Apostles* names, and *Epistles* in the *Fathers* names, which they never made? Is it nothing in *Rome* to be guilty of *counterfeiting Decrees* and *Councils,* and *Records* of *Antiquity? I have done with you!* whereupon I turned from him as an obdurate person. And with this I thought it meet to acquaint the Reader.

(14) 'A Serious and Pathetical Contemplation' (1699)

(i) George Hickes

A LETTER

Concerning this Book from the PUBLISHER to the BOOKSELLER.

Mr. *Keble*

When I desired you to Print these excellent Papers, I told you they were recommended to me by a devout Person, who was a great Judge of Books of Devotion, having given the World one already, which had been well received in three Impressions, and would in time furnish it with more. And when I promis'd you to write a *Preface* before them, I knew not of any other Person that designed to do it, but since *I* have received one from the hand of a worthy Gentleman of the Authors acquaintance, who had a desire to pay his respects to his pious Friends Memory in a *Preface* to his noble Remains. And indeed he had a much better title to write a *Preface* before them, than a stranger, who can only tell how greatly the Author of them wrote, but knew not how *greatly* he lived. *I* will therefore intreat you to accept of his *Preface* for mine and to send me twenty Copies of the Book well Bound, as soon as you can, and at as easy rates as you can afford them. *I* believe *I* shall have occasion for a greater number, for the Book in every thing answers to its title, and as *I* have received great delight and benefit in reading of it: So *I* shall recommend it to persons of parts and pious inclinations, as *I* shall find Opportunities. *I* wish all Booksellers would employ the Press so much for Gods Honour, and the publick Good, as you do, for besides other Peices which are written with great force and eloquence to chastise the Vices of the Age, you have printed many good Books of Devotion, which made me desire that you should print this. Had the Author liv'd to Publish it, it would have come abroad with greater advantages; for there are some places, which seem to require the hand of the same Architect who made them, to reform 'em, but they are but few, and such as only need to be made a little more correct or plain, and we must not wonder that there are some uncorrect, and obscure Passages in a Book which is so full of Thoughts, and composed in *Numbers*, or numerous Periods, which tho of the *freer* sort, are not so easy for an Author to express his thoughts in, as plain and unconfined Prose. *I* wish you a very happy New year, and remain

Your faithful Friend
and Servant

Jan. 2d. 169/⅞.

George Hickes.

(ii) Unsigned Preface

TO THE READER

Tho the unhappy decay of true Piety, and the Immoralities of the Age we live in, may be a discouragement to the multiplying such Books as this, yet on the other hand this degeneracy of Manners, and too evident contempt of Religion, makes it (it may be) the more necessary to endeavour to retreive the Spirit of Devotion, and the sacred Fires of Primitive Christianity. And since 'tis hop'd this ensuing Treatise may somewhat conduce to these noble Ends: It is thought to be no unprofitable Undertaking to commit it to the Press, it being part of the Remains of a very devout Christian, who is long since removed to the Regions of Beatified Spirits, to sing those Praises and Hallelujahs, in which he was very vigorously employ'd, whilst he dwelt amongst us; and since somewhat of *Preface* is become as it were a necessary part of every *Book*, instead of any particular *Dedication* (which is commonly overstuft with Flattery and Complements) I will only give thee some account of the *Author*. To tell thee who he was, is I think, to no purpose: And therefore I will only tell thee what he was, for that may possibly recommend these following Thanksgivings, and Meditations to thy use. He was a Divine of the *Church of England,* of a very comprehensive Soul, and very acute Parts, so fully bent upon that Honourable Function in which he was engaged; and so wonderfully transported with the Love of God to Mankind, with the excellency of those Divine Laws which are prescribed to us, and with those inexpressible Felicities to which we are entitled by being created in, and redeemed to, the Divine Image, that he dwelt continually amongst these thoughts, with great delight and satisfaction, spending most of his time when at home, in digesting his notions of these things into writing, and was so full of them when abroad, that those that would converse with him, were forced to endure some discourse upon these subjects, whether they had any sense of Religion, or not. And therefore to such he might be sometimes thought troublesome, but his company was very acceptable to all such as had any inclinations to Vertue, and Religion.

And tho he had the misfortune to come abroad into the World, in the late disordered Times when the Foundations were cast down, and this excellent Church laid in the dust, and dissolved into *Confusion* and *Enthusiasme*; yet his Soul was of a more refin'd allay, and his Judgment in discerning of things more solid, and considerate then to be infected with that Leaven, and therefore became much in love with the beautiful order and *Primitive* Devotions of this our excellent Church. Insomuch that I beleive, he never failed any one day either publickly or in his private Closet, to make use of her publick Offices, as one part of his devotion, unless some very unavoidable business interrupted him. He was a man of a cheerful and sprightly Temper, free from any thing of the sourness or formality, by which some great pretenders of Piety rather disparage and misrepresent true Religion, than recommend it; and therefore was very affable and pleasant in his Conversation, ready to do all good Offices to his Friends, and Charitable to the Poor almost beyond his ability. But being removed out of the Country to the service of the late Lord Keeper *Bridgman*, as his Chaplain, he died young, and got early to those blissful Mansions, to which he at all times aspir'd.

Philip Traherne senior (1566–1645)

He was of St. Peter's parish, Hereford, an innkeeper and prominent citizen. He was Mayor in 1622 and 1645, the latter year that of the siege of Hereford by the Scotch. Philip Traherne, a strong royalist, left sons named Philip and John.

His relationship to Thomas Traherne is unknown, but that he was a relation is highly probable. Thomas's brother was named Philip. Thomas in writing of his childhood speaks familiarly of an inn and 'the Mayor's Gown' (*Poverty*** 1–14, *Solitude*** 11, 111). Someone must have made provision for Thomas and his brother to be well educated. It can hardly have been anyone but the innkeeper and mayor.

Philip, brother of Thomas (? 1635–1723)

See H. I. Bell's Introduction to *Poems of Felicity*, pp. ix–xx.

Angela Russell (*Review of English Studies*, Jan. 1955, p. 36) quotes an entry in the parish register of Lugwardine, near Hereford, 'Philip the son of Thos. Treherne and Mary, his wife, baptized Aug. 9th 1635', the name 'Thomas' being struck through and 'Philip' substituted.

If this is Thomas Traherne's brother, he was by two years the elder. The reference to Lugwardine in 'To the same purpos'** 9 makes the identification probable. Miss Russell also notes 'that Philip Traherne's son, Thomas, fellow of King's College, Cambridge, gave as his arms those of the Traherne family as emblazoned in Lugwardine church'. It is possible, however, that this Philip died in infancy and was succeeded by another. There are some reasons for supposing Thomas was the elder of the two. Philip seems in 1664 to have been only recently ordained (H. I. Bell, Introduction, pp. x, xi). If Thomas had a sympathetic elder brother, it is surprising that there is no mention of him in the *Centuries* or elsewhere.

Though there is no record of Philip having had a University education, PNB shows that in 1655 he was engaged in just that sort of study. By 23 May 1664 he was in holy orders; on 19 June 1666 he was admitted as perpetual curate of St. Botolph's, Aldersgate; on 15 November 1669 the Court Book of the Levant Company notes that the Solicitor-General (Sir Heneage Finch) had recommended 'one Mr. Traherne to goe Minister to Smyrna'.

In consequence of this he was created B.D., Cambridge. On 30 December 1669 (*S.P. Dom.*, p. 630) the king wrote to the Vice-Chancellor and Senate of Cambridge: 'The Turkey Company having appointed Phil. Traheron their preacher at Smyrna, have requested our letter for him to be created B.D. without performing the usual exercises, which we grant for his encouragement.'

On 1 September 1670 (*S.P. Dom.*, p. 412) the Levant Company wrote to Consul Ricaut at Smyrna: 'you are . . . to furnish an inventory of the company's books to Philip Treherne, who is coming out as minister'.

Philip evidently went out in the early autumn of 1670. He stayed for just four years, resigning on 21 October 1674. He could hardly by then have heard of his brother's death. The fact that his wife Susan, niece of Susanna Hopton, was already in England on 27 September when Thomas made his nuncupative will suggests that he may already have intended to resign. He did not, however, actually return to England until 1675, too late to have anything to do with the publication in that year of Thomas's *Christian Ethicks*, which had been licensed on 25 November 1674.

From 1675 to his death in 1723 he was rector of Hinton Martell in Dorset, and from 1684 a minister of Wimborne Minster in the same county. He published in 1685 *The Soul's Communion With her Savior. or, The History of our Lord Jesus Christ, Written by the Four Evangelists, Digested into Devotional Meditations. The First Part.* This was an abridgement of a work, probably by Thomas, which was later published in full as *Meditations and Devotions Upon the Life of Christ*, Part II of *A Collection of Meditations and Devotions in Three Parts* published by Nathaniel Spinckes in 1717.

Philip seems to have started spelling his name Traheron soon after 1664.

Susanna Hopton (1627–1709)

See Wade, pp. 79–88, &c., and *DNB*.

Susanna Harvey of Staffordshire was a royalist who, after the king's execution, became a Roman Catholic but rejoined the Church of England at the Restoration. Shortly before that she had married Richard Hopton, a former Parliamentarian officer who had turned royalist after the king's execution. After the Restoration they lived at Kington in Herefordshire, some fifteen miles from Credenhill. There Mrs. Hopton became the centre of a religious society which included Thomas Traherne. For her or for this society much of Traherne's work was probably written, the *Centuries* certainly. Her niece married his brother. Thomas's manuscripts, which achieved publication in the seventeenth, eighteenth, or twentieth century, or which are still unpublished, were some of them in his brother's possession and some in Mrs. Hopton's. Their anonymity led some of them to be ascribed after her death to Mrs. Hopton herself.

Hickes's earliest account of her is in the preface to *A Second Collection of Controversial Letters* (1710).

The Credenhill Problem

The question is, When was Traherne actually in residence as rector of Credenhill? As was shown above he was appointed both in 1657 under the Commonwealth and in 1661 after the Restoration.

(1) The Hereford Parliamentary Committee, taking over in 1646 from the patron, the Earl of Shrewsbury, ejected Roger Breynton and put in George Primrose. Primrose vacated in 1650 and the Committee put in Edmund Quarrell, who was turned out at the Restoration. The Crown, not the previous patron, appointed William Carpenter, who in 1661 vacated for Staunton-on-Wye. A new patron, the Earl of Kent, then put in Thomas Traherne. Traherne held the living until his death, but spent the last five years of his life in London and Teddington as domestic chaplain to Bridgeman and as 'minister' at Teddington. Someone else must have acted as minister at Credenhill.

Dobell and succeeding writers say that Traherne became Bridgeman's chaplain in 1667. There is no evidence at all for this. The date must have been chosen simply because in that year Bridgeman became Lord Keeper. The transcripts of the Credenhill registers for 1667 and 1668 are written and signed by Traherne. Those for 1669 and succeeding years are not, except that that for 1672 is signed, not written, by Traherne. The inference is that by the beginning of 1670, when the 1669 transcript would be made, Traherne was out of residence. It must have been some time in 1669 that he became Bridgeman's chaplain. I should connect it with his taking the B.D. degree on 11 December 1669. It cannot have been before 1669, since on 16 April 1669 Hezekiah Burton was made D.D. Cambridge by royal mandate 'being then chaplain to Lord Keeper Bridgman' (footnote in Wood's *Fasti*, ii. 185, ed. Bliss, 1820).

(2) On 30 June 1654 the Commissioners for Approbation of public preachers appointed as incumbent of Credenhill James Warwicke (or Warrocke) on the presentation of William, Mar-quis of Hertford, John, Earl of Rutland, William, Earl of Devon, and Henry, Lord Beauchamp (A. Russell, *ut supra*, supplemented by information from Lambeth).

On 30 December 1657 the same Commissioners admitted Traherne, the patron this time being Amabella, Dowager Coun-tess of Kent.

It looks very much as if there was a disagreement between, on the one hand, the local Parliamentary Committee, whose man Quarrell stayed on and, according to Walker (*Sufferings of the Clergy*, ii. 201), objected strongly to being ejected at the Restora-tion, and, on the other hand, the successors to the Earl of Shrews-bury as patrons. Warwicke's patrons are a committee in themselves, but Traherne's is the mother of the young Earl of Kent, who in 1661 acted on his own behalf. His father had been a sound Parliamentarian, which explains why under the Commonwealth his widow was allowed to acquire the patronage.

There is no evidence that either Warwicke or Traherne resided as rector under the Commonwealth. Traherne, though he 'left the house for a time', presumably spent some time at Oxford between graduating as B.A. in 1656 and M.A. in 1661,[1] even though he was 'created' M.A. The third *Century* does not necessarily suggest that his absence from Oxford followed immediately on his taking the first degree: he may have been in residence at Oxford in 1657. It is possible that after 1657 his studies, wherever he was, were financed from the Credenhill revenues, Quarrell being in effect minister: but this is guess-work.

[1] The meeting of Convocation, at which the Decree was passed permitting Traherne to take the degree of M.A., was held on 12 Sept. 1661 (Oxford Univer-sity Archives, *Register of Convocation*, Ta 27, p. 131). The Decree covered five other persons who were allowed to take degrees in Theology, Medicine, or Law. There is no record of the particular lack of qualification (residence or exercises) which rendered this procedure necessary if the degree was to be granted at that time, but it is highly improbable that none of the required residence had been kept. The reason for the Decree was, I imagine, that Traherne might enter on the incumbency of Credenhill as a Master of Arts.

Miss Russell (*ut supra*, p. 39) suggests that Quarrell was never incumbent of Credenhill but only of Staunton-on-Wye. But Walker states definitely that Breynton held the two livings in plurality. So did Carpenter, who in 1661 kept the Staunton living only, Traherne going to Credenhill. The curious doubling of appointments during the Commonwealth may have been an effort to do away with the plurality, but it is not evident that it succeeded.

Summary biography

Traherne was born in 1637, before but perhaps not long before 20 October. The evidence is (1) that he was already 15 on 1 March 1653, (2) that he was episcopally ordained on 20 October 1660. Since he was then ordained both deacon and priest, it can be safely assumed that he had reached the canonical age of 23 for deacon's orders. He cannot have reached the canonical age, 24, for priests orders. It is improbable that he waited longer than necessary for ordination. The lapse of nearly five months since the Restoration suggests that he did not reach 23 till October.

His father, a shoemaker of Hereford, was of Lugwardine origin. His name was Thomas (Wade, pp. 31–32). It is possible that both he and his wife died while their two sons, Thomas and Philip, were infants. We hear nothing of them, nor of more children. This fits in with the probability amounting to certainty that the boys were more or less adopted by the rich and important innkeeper, Philip Traherne senior. Young Thomas, however, was able to remember his original poverty-stricken home as well as the inn. There is no evidence that either boy went to Hereford Cathedral School, but both had a good education.

Thomas came up to Brasenose in 1652–3, took his B.A. in 1656, was away from Oxford for part of the time between then and 1661 when he was made M.A. by Decree: he resided at Credenhill as rector from 1661 to 1669. There he became a member of the religious circle centring on Susanna Hopton at Kington. It is probable that he also from time to time travelled the 80 miles to Oxford to work in the Bodleian on *Roman Forgeries*. On p. 90 of that book he mentions a work in the possession of

Dr. Barlow, Provost of Queen's and Margaret Professor of Divinity. He does not call him Bodley's Librarian. Barlow, Bodley's Librarian 1642–60, became Provost of Queen's in 1657 and Margaret Professor in 1660. A further link between Traherne and Oxford in the first decade of the restored monarchy is provided by his gift to Brasenose in 1664, a gift which shows he was in touch with the University. It is indeed quite likely that he was at work with a view to his B.D. and that *Roman Forgeries*[1] is the seventeenth-century equivalent of the modern B.D. thesis. For all its touches of controversial scorn and even humour the first half of it has, to one accustomed to such things and in spite of the lapse of three centuries, a distinct smell of the thesis. That half deals with forged insertions in the Canons of the Councils, the second half with the False Decretals and the Donation of Constantine.

In 1669 he took his B.D. and—no coincidence this—became Sir Orlando Bridgeman's chaplain. By what must be a mere coincidence his brother Philip was made B.D. at Cambridge less than a month later.

From 1669 to his death in October 1674 he was in London and Teddington. His literary work must have been intense. He published *Roman Forgeries* and wrote and sent to the press *Christian Ethicks*. He wrote the *Centuries*, the *Church's Year Book*, the *Thanksgiving and Prayer for the Nation*, and perhaps the other *Thanksgivings*. He must also have made the D fair copy of his *Poems*, and compiled the notes in D. Bridgeman may have stimulated him to write, but we owe the *Centuries* at least to his absence from Herefordshire and from Susanna Hopton's circle.

Traherne's rhymes

Traherne has a great many rhymes which are now defective. It is probable that some of them were defective in his day, having once been good rhymes but remained as traditional rhymes after pronunciation had changed. Many, however, such as the well-known mine/joyn or great/compleat types, were exact rhymes. These include sounds/wounds, have/brave, stones/ones, and many

---

[1] Entered on the Stationers' Register, 25 Sept. 1673.

others for an explanation of which recourse may be had to
H. C. K. Wyld, *Studies in English Rhymes* (1923). Wyld does
not, however, explain one peculiarity of Traherne, his consistent
rhyming of 'joy' with 'ay' or 'ey'. He has joy/convey, joy/away,
joy/lay, joys/prais, enjoys/ways, enjoyd/obeyd, joy/display, joy/day.
Dr. E. J. Dobson tells me that he has noticed a few sixteenth-
century examples of this rhyme, and that its frequency in Traherne
is remarkable. He does not think that it indicates a dialectal
pronunciation by Traherne.

There is another oddity in Traherne's rhyming technique. He
very frequently uses an *m/n* assonance, and occasionally an *m/ng*
or *n/ng* assonance. I have counted about thirty such assonances,
some of them triple. *The Salutation* opens with one (Limmes/
begins). Others taken at random are Forms/adorns (*My Spirit*
33, 34), Inns/Things (*Christendom*** 44, 46), Wing/Swim (*On
Leaping over the Moon*** 23, 24).

A very few other assonances taking the place of rhyme may be
found—together/Sever (*The Anticipation* 84, 85, too late for a true
rhyme of which Wyld gives earlier examples); sound/town/
ground/crown'd (*On Christmas-Day*** 109, 112, 113, 114);
Philip is responsible for Lips/mix (*The Author to the Critical
Peruser* 47, 48).

Traherne the Writer

Traherne, both in the *Poems* and in the *Centuries*, is the poet of
Felicity. He tells of his Felicity as an infant, of his temporary loss
of it and of his Paradise regained ('He called his Hous the Hous
of Paradice', C IV. 22, lines 3-4). It was regained with a richness unknown in infancy. The child among 'his new-born
blisses' (it is impossible to read Traherne without thinking of
Wordsworth's *Ode*) had singleness of eye and keenness of sense-
perception unblunted by reflexion or knowledge of evil. The
'gleam' (Wordsworth again) was on everything he saw. This was
lost awhile because neither his companions nor his educators had
right values; but Traherne became a child again in the sense in
which that is necessary for entering the Kingdom of Heaven
(*Innocence* 60).

Yet to an adult who is 'Heir of the World', to whom the whole phenomenal world is given as his Garden in Eden, two things are added, and, unless they are added, there is no Felicity for him. First, he must be conscious of his happiness: he not only enjoys the World but loves the 'Beauty of Enjoying it' (C I. 31, line 2). This consciousness of Felicity is an enrichment not possible for the infant, and from it spring a whole mental development and creation—for Traherne his *Poems* and *Centuries*. Secondly, the adult is aware that the phenomenal world is not all: it is not even primary or infinite. Primary and infinite is Spirit, that is God, a Trinity of Love. There is nothing conventional, second-hand, or merely 'orthodox' about Traherne's Christianity. That is clear from the great sections on Love in the middle third of the second *Century*. His consciousness of Spirit and of his contact therewith and part therein is described in *My Spirit*. It may or may not be right to attribute[1] to Traherne actual mystical experience, but he had that living and permanent awareness of Spirit which is necessary for Felicity in the adult.

This double awareness, of enjoying the phenomenal world and of belonging to a spiritual life, is the foundation of Traherne's philosophy as seen, for example, in *The Circulation* and *Amendment*. I am Heir of the World. That is God's bounty. But everything in the World is the better for being enjoyed by me. In this way I make a return to God for his bounty. I return his gifts to him with interest. God enjoys the World through me.

> Thy Soul, O GOD, doth prize
> The Seas, the Earth, our Souls, the Skies,
> As we return the same to Thee;
> They more delight thine Eys,
> And sweeter be,
> As unto Thee we Offer up the same,
> Then as to us, from Thee at first they came.
>
> (*Amendment* 36-42.)

That is Traherne. Is he a great poet? What are his limitations? He had nothing of the dramatist: he has not attempted to create

---

[1] As I do: *My Spirit*, first note.

a single character. He is not a poet of detailed 'observation of nature': he counts the streaks of no tulips. Even if he wished to count them, he might be dazzled by the gleam. He is not a poet of wide-ranging esemplastic imagination: he reaches no Xanadu. He can make the mistake of arguing in verse, and in complicated stanzaic verse at that, and the result is not poetry.

> The End Compleat, the Means must needs be so.
> By which we plainly Know,
> From all Eternitie,
> The Means wherby God is, must perfect be.
>
> (*The Anticipation* 46–49.)

He is, of course, an ecstatic poet. He has fine openings ('How like an Angel came I down', *Wonder* 1): even *The Anticipation* opens finely. No one—not Vaughan, not Wordsworth—is more vivid or convincing about his felicity as an infant. No one, in my limited experience, has so married the worlds of sense and spirit, leaving the objects of sense undimmed and showing the potencies of spirit as 'all Act'.

He was a conscious and deliberate artist in prose and verse. He never repeats a stanza form in a second poem. He excises unnecessary little words from the *Centuries*. There is no drab worn-out verbiage. Many a modern writer, 'involved' in his 'cases' and 'factors', his circumlocutions and half-meaningless words, might do well to study Traherne for his style, as well as for his pure and percipient soul.

I am indebted to several Oxford scholars for help with some of the more recondite allusions in the *Centuries*, and to Professor N. Sykes for help with the Lambeth entries.

THE CENTURIES

This book unto the friend of my best friend
As of the Wisest Love a Mark I send
That she may write my Makers prais therin
And make her self therby a Cherubin.

1

An Empty Book is like an Infants Soul, in which any Thing may be Written. It is Capable of all Things, but containeth Nothing. I hav a Mind to fill this with Profitable Wonders. And since Love made you put it into my Hands I will fill it with those Truths you Love, without Knowing them: and with those 5 Things which, if it be Possible, shall shew my Lov; To you, in Communicating most *Enriching Truths;* to Truth, in Exalting Her Beauties in such a Soul.

2

Do not Wonder that I Promise to fill it, with those Truths you love, but know not: For tho it be a Maxime in the Scholes, That there is no Lov of a thing unknown; yet I hav found, that Things unknown have a Secret Influence on the Soul: and like the Centre of the Earth unseen, violently Attract it. We lov we know 5 not what: and therfore evry Thing allures us. As Iron at a Distance is drawn by the Loadstone, there being some Invisible Communications between them: So is there in us a World of Lov to somwhat, tho we know not what in the World that should be. There are Invisible Ways of Conveyance by which some Great 10 Thing doth touch our Souls, and by which we tend to it. Do you not feel yourself Drawn with the Expectation and Desire of som Great Thing?

3

I will open my Mouth in Parables: I will utter Things that have been Kept Secret from the foundation of the World. Things Strange yet Common; Incredible, yet Known; Most High, yet Plain; infinitly Profitable, but not Esteemed. Is it not a Great Thing, that you should be Heir of the World? Is it not a very 5 Enriching Veritie? In which the Fellowship of the Mystery, which from the beginning of the World hath been hid in GOD, lies concealed! The Thing hath been from the Creation of the World, but hath not so been Explained, as that the interior Beauty should be understood. It is my Design therfore in such a Plain maner to unfold it, that my Friendship may appear, in making you Possessor of the Whole World.

4

I will not by the Nois of Bloody Wars, and the Dethroning of Kings, advance you to Glory: but by the Gentle Ways of Peace and Lov. As a Deep Friendship meditats and intends the Deepest Designes for the Advancement of its Objects, so doth it shew it self in Chusing the Sweetest and most Delightfull Methods, wherby not to Weary, but Pleas the Person, it desireth to advance. Where Lov administers Physick, its Tenderness is exprest in Balms and Cordials. It hateth Corrosives, and is Rich in its Administrations. Even so God, Designing to shew his Lov in exalting you hath chosen the Ways of Eas and Repose, by which you should ascend. And I after his Similitude will lead you into Paths Plain and Familiar. Where all Envy, Rapine, Bloodshed, Complaint, and Malice shall be far removed; and nothing appear but Contentment and Thanksgiving. Yet shall the End be so Glorious, that Angels durst not hope for so Great a One till they had seen it.

5

The fellowship of the Mystery that hath been hid in God, since the Creation is not only the Contemplation of his Lov in the Work of Redemption: Tho that is Wonderfull: But the End, for which we are Redeemd: A Communion with Him in all His Glory. for which caus, S Peter saith The God of all Grace, hath called us unto His Eternal Glory by Jesus Christ. His Eternal Glory by the Methods of His Divine Wisdom being made ours: and our Fruition of it, the End for which our Savior suffered.

6

True Lov, as it intendeth the Greatest Gifts, intendeth also the
Greatest Benefits. It contenteth not it self in Shewing Great
Things unless it can make them Greatly Usefull. For Lov
greatly Delighteth in seeing its Object continualy seated in the
Highest Happiness. Unless therfore I could advance you Higher 5
by the uses of what I give, my Lov could not be satisfied, in
Giving you the Whole World. But becaus when you Enjoy it,
you are Advanced to the Throne of God, and may see His Lov;
I rest well Pleased in Bestowing it. It will make you to see your
own Greatness, the Truth of the Scriptures, the Amiableness of 10
Virtu, and the Beauty of Religion. It will enable you also, to
contemn the World, and to overflow with Praises.

7

To Contemn the World, and to Enjoy the World, are Things
contrary to each other. How then can we contemn the World
which we are Born to Enjoy? Truly there are two Worlds. One
was made by God, the other by Men. That made by GOD, was
Great and Beautifull. Before the Fall, It was Adams Joy, and the 5
Temple of his Glory. That made by men is a Babel of Confu-
sions: Invented Riches, Pomps and Vanities, brought in by Sin.
Giv all (saith Thomas a Kempis) for all. Leav the one that you
may enjoy the other.

8

What is more Easy and Sweet then Meditation? yet in this hath
God commended his Lov, that by Meditation it is Enjoyed. As
Nothing is more Easy then to Think, so nothing is more Difficult
then to Think Well. The Easiness of Thinking we received from
God, the Difficulty of thinking Well, proceedeth from our selvs. 5
Yet in Truth, it is far more Easy to think well then Ill, becaus
Good Thoughts be sweet and Delightfull: Evil Thoughts are full
of Discontent and Trouble. So that an Evil Habit, and Custom
hav made it Difficult to think well, not Nature. For by Nature,
nothing is so Difficult as to Think amiss. 10

9

Is it not Easy to conceiv the World in your Mind? To think the
Heavens fair? The Sun Glorious? The Earth fruitfull? The Air
Pleasant? The Sea Profitable? And the Giver Bountifull? Yet
these are the things which it is difficult to retain. For could we
5 always be Sensible of their Use and Value; we should be always
Delighted with their Wealth and Glory.

10

To think well is to serv God in the Interior Court: To hav a
Mind composed of Divine Thoughts, and set in frame, to be
Like Him within. To Conceiv aright and to Enjoy the World, is
to Conceiv the Holy Ghost, and to see His Lov; Which is the
5 Mind of the Father. And this more Pleaseth Him then Many
Worlds, could we Creat as fair and Great as this. For when you
are once acquainted with the World, you will find the Goodness
and Wisdom of God, so manifest therin, that it was Impossible
another, or Better should be made. Which being made to be
10 Enjoyed, Nothing can Pleas or serv Him more then the Soul
that enjoys it. For that Soul doth accomplish the End of His
Desire in Creating it.

11

Lov is Deeper then at first it can be thought. It never ceaseth but
in Endless Things. It ever Multiplies. Its Benefits and its Designes
are always Infinit. Were you not Holy Divine and Blessed in
Enjoying the World, I should not care so much to Bestow it.
5 But now in this you accomplish the End of your Creation, and
serv God best, and Pleas Him most: I rejoyce in Giving it. For to
Enable you to Pleas GOD, is the Highest Service a Man can do
you. It is to make you Pleasing to the King of Heaven, that you
may be the Darling of His Bosom.

12

Can you be Holy without Accomplishing the End for which you are Created? Can you be Divine unless you be Holy? Can you Accomplish the End for which you were Created, unless you be Righteous? Can you then be Righteous, unless you be Just in rendering to Things their Due Esteem? All Things were made 5 to be yours. And you were made to Prize them according to their value: which is your Office and Duty, the End for which you were Created, and the Means wherby you Enjoy. The End for which you were Created is that by Prizing all that God hath don, you may Enjoy your self and Him in Blessedness. 10

13

To be Holy is so Zealously to Desire, so vastly to Esteem, and so Earnestly to Endeavour it, that we would not for millions of Gold and Silver, Decline, nor fail, nor Mistake in a Tittle. For then we Pleas God when we are most like Him. we are like Him when our Minds are in Frame. our Minds are in Frame when our 5 Thoughts are like his. And our Thoughts are then like his when we hav such Conceptions of all objects as God hath, and Prize all Things according to their value. For God doth Prize all Things rightly. Which is a Key that Opens into the very Thoughts of his Bosom. It seemeth Arrogance to pretend to the Knowledg of his 10 Secret Thoughts. But how shall we hav the Mind of God, unless we Know his Thoughts? Or how shall we be led by his Divine Spirit, till we hav his Mind? His Thoughts are Hidden: but he hath revealed unto us the Hidden Things of Darkness. By his Works and by his Attributs we know His Thoughts. And by 15 Thinking the same are Divine and Blessed.

14

When Things are ours in their Proper Places, nothing is needfull but Prizing to Enjoy them. God therfore hath made it infinitly Easy to Enjoy, by making evry Thing ours, and us able so Easily to Prize them. Evry thing is ours that serves us in its Place. The

5 Sun servs us as much as is Possible, and more then we could
imagine. The Clouds and Stars Minister unto us, the World
surrounds us with Beauty, the Air refresheth us the Sea revives
the Earth and us. The Earth it self is Better then Gold becaus it
produceth fruits and flowers. And therfore in the Beginning, was
10 it made Manifest to be mine, becaus Adam alone was made to
Enjoy it. By making One, and not a Multitud, God evidently
shewed One alone to be the End of the World, and evry one its
Enjoyer. for evry one may Enjoy it as much as He.

15

Such Endless Depths lie in the Divinity, and the Wisdom of
God, that as He maketh one, so He maketh evry one the end of
the World: the Supernumerary Persons being Enrichers of his
Inheritance. Adam and the World are both mine. And the
5 Posterity of Adam enrich it Infinitly. Souls are Gods Jewels.
Evry one of which is worth many Worlds. They are his Riches
becaus his Image. and mine for that reason. So that I alone am
the End of the World. Angels and Men being all mine. And if
others are so, they are made to Enjoy it for my further Advance-
10 ment. God only being the Giver, and I the Receiver. So that
Seneca Philosophized rightly, when he said, *Deus me dedit solum
toti Mundo, et totum Mundum mihi soli.* God gave me alone to all the
World, and all the World to me alone.

16

That all the World is yours, your very Senses and the Inclinations of your Mind declare. The Works of God manifest, his
Laws testify and his Word doth Prove it. His Attributes most
sweetly make it evident. The Powers of your Soul confirm it. So
5 that in the midst of such rich Demonstrations, you may infinitly Delight in God as your Father Friend and Benefactor, in
your self as his Heir Child and Bride, in the Whole WORLD,
as the Gift and Token of His Lov. Neither can any thing but
Ignorance Destroy your Joys. for if you know your self, or God,
10 or the World, you must of Necessity Enjoy it.

17

To know GOD is Life Eternal. There must therfore some Exceeding Great Thing be always attained in the Knowledge of Him. To Know God is to Know Goodness; It is to see the Beauty of infinit Lov: To see it attended with Almighty Power and Eternal Wisdom; and using both those in the Magnifying 5 of its Object. It is to see the King of Heaven and Earth take infinit Delight in *Giving*. Whatever Knowledge els you hav of God, it is but Superstition. Which Plutarch rightly Defineth, *to be an Ignorant Dread of his Divine Power, without any Joy in his Goodness*. He is not an Object of Terror, but Delight. To know 10 Him therfore as He is, is to frame the most Beautifull Idea in all Worlds. He Delighteth in our Happiness more then we: and is of all other the most Lovly Object. An infinit Lord, who having all Riches Honors and Pleasures in his own Hand, is infinitly Willing to give them unto me. Which is the fairest Idea that can 15 be Devised.

18

The WORLD is not this little Cottage of Heaven and Earth. Tho this be fair, it is too small a Gift. When God made the WORLD, He made the Heavens and the Heavens of Heavens, and the Angels and the Celestial Powers. These also are Parts of the World: so are all those infinit and Eternal Treasures that are 5 to abide for ever, after the Day of Judgement. Neither are these, some here, and some there, but all evry where, and at once to be Enjoyed. The WORLD is unknown, till the Value and Glory of it is seen: till the Beauty and the Serviceableness of its Parts is Considered. When you enter into it, it is an illimited feild of 10 Varietie and Beauty: where you may lose your self in the Multitude of Wonders and Delights. But it is an Happy Loss to lose one self in Admiration at ones own Felicity: and to find GOD in exchange for oneself. Which we then do when we see Him in His Gifts, and Adore his Glory.　　15

19

You never Know your self, till you Know more then your Body.
The Image of God was not seated in the features of your face, but
in the Lineaments of your Soul. In the Knowledg of your
Powers, Inclinations and Principles, the Knowledg of your self
5 cheifly consisteth. Which are so Great that even to the most
Learned of men their Greatness is Incredible; and so Divine, that
they are infinit in Value. Alass the WORLD is but a little
Centre in Comparison of you. Suppose it Millions of Miles from
the Earth to the Heavens, and Millions of Millions above the
10 Stars, both here and over the heads of our Antipodes: it is surrounded with infinit and Eternal Space: And like a Gentlemans
house to one that is Travelling; It is a long time before you com
unto it, you passe it in an Instant, and leave it for ever. The Omnipresence and Eternity of God are your Fellows and Companions.
15 And all that is in them ought to be made your familiar Treasures.
Your Understanding comprehends the World like the Dust of a
Ballance, measures Heaven with a Span and esteems a thousand
yeers but as one Day. So that Great Endless Eternal Delights are
only fit to be its Enjoyments.

20

The Laws of GOD, which are the Commentaries of his Works,
shew them to be yours: becaus They teach you to lov God with
all your Soul, and with all your Might. Whom if you lov with all
the Endless Powers of your Soul, you will lov Him in Him self, in
5 His Attributs, in His Counsels, in all his Works, in all His Ways:
and in evry Kind of Thing wherin He appeareth, you will Prize
Him, you will Honor Him, you will Delight in Him, you will
ever desire to be with him and to pleas Him. For to lov Him includeth all this. You will feed with Pleasure upon evry Thing that
10 is His. So that the World shall be a Grand Jewel of Delight unto
you: a very Paradise; and the Gate of Heaven. It is indeed the
Beautifull Frontispiece of Eternitie. the Temple of God, the
Palace of his children. The Laws of God Discover all that is
therin to be Created for your sake. For they command you to lov

all that is Good, and when you see well, you enjoy what you lov. 15
They apply the Endless Powers of your Soul to all their Objects:
and by ten thousand Methods make evry Thing to serv you.
They command you to lov all Angels and Men, They command
all Angels and Men to lov you. When you lov them, they are
your Treasures; when They lov you, to your great advantage you 20
are theirs. All things serv you for serving them whom you lov,
and of whom you are Beloved. The Enterance of His Words
giveth Light to the Simple. You are Magnified among Angels
and Men: Enriched by them, and Happy in them.

21

By the very Right of your Sences you Enjoy the World. Is not the
Beauty of the Hemisphere present to your Ey? Doth not the Glory
of the Sun pay Tribut to your Sight? Is not the Vision of the
WORLD an Amiable Thing? Do not the Stars shed Influences to
Perfect the Air? Is not that a marvellous Body to Breath in? To 5
visit the Lungs: repair the Spirits: revive the Sences: Cool the
Blood: fill the Empty Spaces between the Earth and Heavens; and
yet giv Liberty to all Objects? Prize these first: and you shall
Enjoy the Residue. Glory, Dominion, Power, Wisdom, Honor,
Angels, Souls, Kingdoms, Ages. *Be faithfull in a little, and you* 10
shall be Master over much. if you be not faithfull in esteeming these,
who shall put into your Hands the true Treasures. If you be
Negligent in Prizing these, you will be Negligent in Prizing all.
there is a Diseas in Him who Despiseth present mercies, which
till it be cured, he can never be Happy. He esteemeth nothing that 15
he hath, but is ever Gaping after more: which when he hath He
despiseth in like manner. Insatiableness is Good, but not Ingratitud.

22

It is of the Nobility of Mans Soul that He is Insatiable. for he hath a
Benefactor so Prone to Give, that He delighteth in us for Asking.
Do not your Inclinations tell you that the WORLD is yours?
Do you not covet all? Do you not long to hav it; to Enjoy it; to

5 Overcom it? To what End do Men gather Riches, but to
Multiplie more? Do they not like Pyrrhus the King of Epire, adde
hous to hous and Lands to Lands, that they may get it all? It is
storied of that Prince, that having conceived a Purpose to invade
Italy, he sent for Cineas, a Philosopher and the Kings friend: to
10 whom he communicated his Designe, and desired his Counsel.
Cineas asked him to what Purpose he invaded Italie? He said, To
Conquer it. And what will you do when you hav Conquerd it?
Go into France said the King, and Conquer that. And what
will you do when you have Conquerd France? Conquer Ger-
15 many. And what then? said the Philosopher. Conquer Spain. I
perceive said Cineas, you mean to conquer all the World. What
will you do when you have conquerd all? Why then said the
King we will return, and Enjoy our selvs at Quiet in our own
Land. So you may now said the Philosopher without all this adoe.
20 Yet could he not Divert him till he was ruind by the Romans.
Thus men get one Hundred Pound a year that they may get
another; and having two covet Eight, and there is no End of all
their Labor; becaus the Desire of their Soul is Insatiable. Like
Alexander the Great they must hav all: and when they hav got
25 it all be quiet. And may they not do all this before they begin?
Nay it would be well, if they could be Quiet. But if after all, they
shall be like the stars, that are seated on high, but hav no Rest,
what gain they more, but Labor for their Trouble? It was wittily
fained that that Yong man sate down and Cried for more Worlds.
30 so insatiable is Man that Millions will not Pleas him. They are no
more then so many Tennis-Balls, in Comparison of the Greatness
and Highness of his Soul.

23

The Noble Inclination wherby Man thirsteth after Riches and
Dominion, is his Highest Virtu, when rightly Guided: and
Carries him as in a Triumphant Chariot, to his Soveraign
Happiness. Men are made Miserable only by abusing it. Taking
5 a fals way to Satisfy it they Persue the Wind: Nay labor in the
very fire, and after all reap but Vanitie. Wheras, as Gods Lov,

which is the fountain of all, did cost us Nothing: so were all other
Things prepared by it, to satisfy our Inclinations in the Best of
Manners. freely, without any cost of ours. Being therfore all
Satisfactions are near at hand, by going further we do but leav 10
them: And Wearying our selvs in a long way round about, like
a Blind man, forsake them. They are immediatly near to the very
Gates of our Sences. It becometh the Bounty of God to prepare
them freely: to make them Glorious, and their Enjoyment Easy.
For becaus His Lov is free so are his Treasures. He therfore that 15
will Despise them becaus he hath them is Marvellously Irrational.
The Way to Possess them is to Esteem them. And the true Way of
Reigning over them, is to break the WORLD all into Parts, to
examine them asunder. And if we find them so Excellent that
Better could not Possibly be made, and so made that they could 20
not be more ours, to rejoyce in all with Pleasure answerable to the
Merit of their Goodness. We being then Kings over the Whole
World, when we restore the Pieces to their Proper Places, being
Perfectly Pleased with the whole Composure. This shall giv you
a thorow grounded Contentment, far beyond what troublesom 25
Wars, or Conquests can acquire.

24

Is it not a sweet Thing to hav all Covetousness and Ambition
satisfied, Suspicion and infidelity removed, Courage and Joy in⁄
fused? Yet is all this in the fruition of the World attained. for
therby God is seen in all His Wisdom, Power, Goodness, and
Glory.

25

Your Enjoyment of the World is never right, till you so Esteem it,
that evry thing in it, is more your Treasure, then a Kings Ex⁄
chequer full of Gold and Silver. And that Exchequer yours also
in its Place and Service. Can you take too much Joy in your
fathers Works? He is Himself in evry Thing. som Things are little 5
on the outside, and Rough and Common. but I remember the

Time, when the Dust of the Streets were as precious as Gold to
my Infant Eys, and now they are more precious to the Ey of
Reason.

26

The Services of Things, and their Excellencies are Spiritual: being
Objects not of the Ey, but of the Mind: And you more Spiritual
by how much more you Esteem them. Pigs eat Acorns, but
neither consider the Sun that gav them Life, nor the Influences of
5 the Heavens by which they were Nourished, nor the very Root
of the Tree from whence they came. This being the Work of
Angels Who in a Wide and Clear Light see even the Sea that
gave them Moysture. And feed upon that Acorn Spiritualy, while
they Know the Ends for which it was Created and feast upon all
10 these, as upon a World of Joys within it: while to Ignorant Swine
that eat the Shell, it is an Empty Husk of no Taste nor Delightfull
Savor.

27

You never Enjoy the World aright, till you see how a Sand
Exhibiteth the Wisdom and Power of God: And Prize in evry
Thing the Service which they do you, by Manifesting His Glory
and Goodness to your Soul, far more then the Visible Beauty on
5 their Surface, or the Material Services, they can do your Body.
Wine by its Moysture quencheth my Thirst, whether I consider it
or no: but to see it flowing from his Lov who gav it unto Man.
Quencheth the Thirst even of the Holy Angels. To consider it,
is to Drink it Spiritualy. To Rejoice in its Diffusion is to be of a
10 Publick Mind. And to take Pleasure in all the Benefits it doth
to all is Heavenly. for so they do in Heaven. To do so, is to be
Divine and Good. and to imitat our Infinit and Eternal Father.

28

Your Enjoyment of the World is never right, till evry Morning
you awake in Heaven: see your self in your fathers Palace: and
look upon the Skies and the Earth and the Air, as Celestial Joys:

having such a Reverend Esteem of all, as if you were among the
Angels. The Bride of a Monarch, in her Husbands Chamber, 5
hath no such Causes of Delight as you.

29

You never Enjoy the World aright, till the Sea it self floweth in
your Veins, till you are Clothed with the Heavens, and Crowned
with the Stars: and Perceiv your self to be the Sole Heir of the
whole World: and more then so, becaus Men are in it who are
evry one Sole Heirs, as well as you. Till you can Sing and Rejoyce 5
and Delight in GOD, as Misers do in Gold, and Kings in
Scepters, you never Enjoy the World.

30

Till your Spirit filleth the whole World, and the Stars are your
Jewels, till you are as Familiar with the Ways of God in all Ages
as with your Walk and Table: till you are intimatly Acquainted
with that Shady Nothing out of which the World was made: till
you lov Men so as to Desire their Happiness, with a Thirst equal 5
to the zeal of your own: till you Delight in GOD for being Good
to all: you never Enjoy the World. Till you more feel it then your
Privat Estate, and are more present in the Hemisphere, Considering the Glories and the Beauties there, then in your own Hous.
Till you remember how lately you were made, and how wonder- 10
full it was when you came into it: and more rejoyce in the Palace
of your Glory, then if it had been made but to Day Morning.

31

Yet further, you never Enjoy the World aright, till you so lov the
Beauty of Enjoying it, that you are Covetous and Earnest to
Persuade others to Enjoy it. And so perfectly hate the Abominable
Corruption of Men in Despising it, that you had rather suffer
the flames of Hell then willingly be Guilty of their Error. There 5
is so much Blindness and Ingratitud, and Damned folly in it.

The World is a Mirror of infinit Beauty, yet no Man sees it. It is a
Temple of Majesty yet no Man regards it. It is a Region of Light
and Peace, did not Men Disquiet it. It is the Paradice of God. It is
10 more to Man since he is faln, then it was before. It is the Place of
Angels, and the Gate of Heaven. When Jacob waked out of His
Dream, he said, *God is here and I wist it not. How Dreadfull is this
Place! This is none other, then the Hous of God, and the Gate of Heaven.*

32

Can any Ingratitud be more Damned then that which is fed by
Benefits? Or folly Greater then that which bereaveth us of infinit
Treasures? They Despise them meerly becaus they hav them: And
invent Ways to make them selvs Miserable in the Presence of
5 Riches. They Study a thousand New fangled Treasures, which
God never made: and then Griev and Repine that they be not
Happy. They Dote on their own Works, and Neglect Gods.
Which are full of Majesty Riches and Wisdom. And having fled
away from them becaus they are Solid Divine and True Greedily
10 persuing Tinsild vanities, they walk on in Darkness, and will not
understand. They do the Works of Darkness, and Delight in
the Riches of the Prince of Darkness, and follow them till they
com into Eternal Darkness. According to *that of the* Psalmist *All
the foundations* of the Earth are out of course.

33

The Riches of Darkness are those which Men hav made, during
their Ignorance of God Almightie's Treasures. That lead us from
the Lov of all, to Labor and Contention Discontentment and
Vanity, The Works of Darkness are Repining, Envy, Malice,
5 Covetousness, fraud, Oppression, Discontent and Violence: All
which proceed from the Corruption of men and their mistake in
the Chois of Riches: For having refused those which God made,
and taken to themselvs Treasures of their own, they invented
scarce and Rare, Insufficient, Hard to be Gotten, litle, movable
10 and useless Treasures. Yet as violently Persue them as if they

were the most Necessary and Excellent Things in the whole
World. And tho they are all Mad, yet having made a Combination they seem Wise; and it is a hard matter to persuade them
either to Truth or Reason. There seemeth to be no Way, but
theirs: wheras God Knoweth They are as far out of the Way of 15
Happiness, as the East is from the West. For by this means, they
hav let in Broyls and Dissatisfactions into the World, and are
ready to Eat and Devour one another, Particular and feeble
Interests, fals Proprieties, Insatiable Longings, fraud, Emulation,
Murmuring and Dissension being evry where seen, Theft and 20
Pride and Danger and cousenage envy and contention Drowning
the Peace and Beauty of Nature as Waters cover the sea. O how
they are ready to sink always under the Burden and Cumber of
Devised Wants! Verily, the Prospect of their Ugly Errors, is able
to turn ones Stomach: they are so Hideous and Deformed.   25

34

Would one think it Possible for a man to Delight in Gauderies
like a Butterflie, and Neglect the Heavens? Did we not daily see
it, it would be Incredible. They rejoyce in a Piece of Gold more
then in the Sun: and get a few little Glittering Stones and call
them Jewels. And Admire them becaus they be Resplendent like 5
the stars, and Transparent like the Air, and Pellucid like the sea.
But the stars them selvs which are ten thousand Times more usefull
Great and Glorious, they Disregard. Nor shall the Air it self be
Counted any Thing, tho it be worth all the Pearls and Diamonds
in ten thousand Worlds, a WORK so Divine by reason of 10
its Precious and Pure Transparency, that all Worlds would be
worth Nothing without such a Treasure.

35

The Riches of the Light are the Works of God, which are the
Portion and Inheritance of his sons, to be seen and enjoyed in
Heaven and Earth, the Sea, and all that is therin. the Light and
the Day. Great, and fathomless in use and Excellency, True,

5 Necessary. Freely Given, Proceeding wholy from his Infinit Lov As Worthy as they are Easy to be Enjoyed. Obliging us to lov Him, and to Delight in Him, filling us with Gratitud, and mak⸗ ing us to over flow with Praises and Thanksgivings. The Works of Contentment and Pleasure are of the Day. So are the Works

10 which flow from the Understanding of our Mutual Serviceable⸗ ness to each other: Arising from the Sufficiency and Excellency of our Treasures, Contentment, Joy, Peace, Unitie, Charity &c. wherby we are all Knit together, and Delight in each others Happiness. For while evry one is Heir of all the World, and all

15 the rest his Superadded Treasures. all the World servs Him in Himself, and in them as his Superadded Treasures.

36

The Common Error which makes it difficult to believ all the World to be wholy ours, is to be shund as a Rock of Shipwrack: or a Dangerous Quicksands. For the Poyson which they Drank hath infatuated their fancies and now they Know not, neither

5 will they understand, they walk on in Darkness. *All the founda⸗ tions of the Earth are out of Cours.* It is safety not to be with them. And a Great Part of Happiness to be freed from their Seducing and Enslaving Errors. That while Others liv in a Golgotha or Prison, we should be in Eden, is a very Great Mystery. And a

10 Mercy it is that we should be Rejoycing in the Temple of Heaven, while they are Toyling and Lamenting in Hell, for the World is both a Paradice and a Prison to different Persons.

37

The Brightness and Magnificence of this World, which by reason of its Height and Greatness is hidden from Men, is Divine and Wonderfull. It Addeth much to the Glory of that Temple in which we live. Yet it is the Caus why men under⸗

5 stand it not. They think it too Great and Wide to be Enjoyed. But since it is all filled with the Majesty of His Glory who Dwelleth in it: and the Goodness of the Lord filleth the World,

and His Wisdom shineth evry where within it and about it; and
it aboundeth in an infinit Varietie of Services; we need nothing
but open Eys, to be Ravished like the Cherubims. Well may we 10
bear the Greatness of the World, since it is our Storehous and
Treasurie. That our Treasures should be Endless is an Happy
Inconvenience: that all Regions should be full of Joys: and the
Room infinit wherin they are Seated.

38

You never Enjoy the World aright, till you see all things in it so
perfectly yours, that you cannot desire them any other Way: and
till you are Convinced, that all Things serv you Best in their
Proper Places. For can you desire to Enjoy any thing a Better
Way then in Gods Image? *It is the Height of Gods Perfection that* 5
hideth His Bounty: And the Lowness of your Base and Sneaking
Spirit, that make you Ignorant of his Perfection. (Evry one hath
in Him a Spirit, with which he may be Angry.) Gods Bounty is
so Perfect that *He giveth all Things in the Best of Manners:* making
those to whom He Giveth so Noble, Divine and Glorious, that 10
they shall Enjoy in His Similitude. Nor can they be fit to Enjoy
in His presence, or in Communion with Him, that are not truly
Divine and Noble. So that you must hav Glorious Principles
implanted in your Nature; a clear Eye able to see afar off, A
Great and Generous Heart, Apt to Enjoy at any Distance: a 15
Good and Liberal Soul Prone to Delight in the Felicity of all, and
an infinit Delight to be their Treasure: Neither is it any Prejudice
to you that this is required. for *there is Great Difference between a*
Worm and a Cherubim. And it more concerneth you to be an
Illustrious Creature, then to hav the Possession of the whole 20
World.

39

Your Enjoyment is never right, till you esteem evry Soul so Great
a Treasure as our Savior doth: and that the Laws of God are
sweeter then the Hony and Hony Comb becaus they command
you to lov them all in such Perfect Maner. For how are they Gods

5 Treasures? Are they not the Riches of His Lov? Is it not his
Goodness that maketh Him Glorious to them? Can the Sun or
Stars serv Him any other Way, then by serving them? And how
will you be the Son of God, but by having a Great Soul like unto
your Fathers. *The Laws of God command you to live in His Image.*
10 *and to do so, is to live in Heaven.* God commandeth you to lov
all like Him, becaus He would hav you to be his Son, all them
to be your Riches, you to be Glorious before them, and all the
Creatures in serving them to be your Treasures, while you are his
Delight, like him in Beauty, and the Darling of his Bosom.

40

Socrates was wont to say, *They are most Happy and neerest the Gods
that needed Nothing.* And coming once up into the Exchange at
Athens, where they that Traded Asked Him, What will you
Buy; what do you lack? After he had Gravely Walkt up into the
5 Middle, spreading forth his Hands and turning about, *Good Gods,*
saith he, *who would hav thought there were so many Things in the
World which I do not want!* And so left the Place under the Reproach of Nature. He was wont to say, *That Happiness consisted
not in Having Many, but in Needing the Fewest Things: for the Gods
10 Needed Nothing at all, and they were most like them that least Needed.*
We Needed Heaven and Earth, our Sences, Such Souls and
Such Bodies, with infinit Riches in the Image of God to be Enjoyed: Which God of his Mercy having freely prepared, they are
most Happy that so live in the Enjoyment of those, as to need no
15 Accidental Trivial Thing. No Splendors, Pomps and Vanities.
Socrates perhaps being an Heathen, knew not that all Things
proceeded from God to Man, and by Man returned to God: but
we that know it: must need All Things as God doth that we may
receiv them with Joy, and liv in His Image.

41

As Pictures are made Curious by Lights and Shades, which without Shades, could not be: so is Felicitie composed of Wants and

Supplies, without which Mixture there could be no Felicity. Were there no Needs, Wants would be Wanting themselvs: And Supplies Superfluous. Want being the Parent of Celestial Treasure. It is very Strange; Want itself is a Treasure in Heaven: And so Great an one, that without it there could be no Treasure. GOD did infinitly for us, when He made us to Want like GODS, that like GODS we might be satisfied. The Heathen DIETIES wanted nothing, and were therfore unhappy; For they had no Being. But the LORD GOD of Israel the Living and True GOD, was from all Eternity, and from all Eternity Wanted like a GOD. He Wanted the Communication of His Divine Essence, and Persons to Enjoy it. He Wanted Worlds, He wanted Spectators, He wanted Joys, He wanted Treasures. He wanted, yet he wanted not, for he had them.

42

This is very strange that GOD should Want. for in Him is the Fulness of all Blessedness: He overfloweth Eternaly. His Wants are as Glorious as Infinit. Perfectiv needs that are in His Nature, and ever Blessed, becaus always Satisfied. He is from Eternity full of Want: Or els He would not be full of Treasure. Infinit Want is the very Ground and Caus of infinit Treasure. It is Incridible, yet very Plain: Want is the Fountain of all His Fulness. Want in GOD is a Treasure to us. For had there been no Need He would not hav Created the World, nor Made us, nor Manifested his Wisdom, nor Exercised his Power, nor Beautified Eternity, nor prepared the Joys of Heaven. But He Wanted Angels and Men, Images, Companions. And these He had from all Eternitie.

43

Infinit Wants Satisfied Produce infinit Joys; And, in the Possession of those Joys are infinit Joys themselvs. *The Desire Satisfied is a Tree of Life*. Desire imports somthing absent: and a Need of what is Absent. GOD was never without this Tree of Life. He did Desire infinitly. yet He was never without the Fruits of this

Tree, which are the Joys it produced. I must lead you out of this, into another World, to learn your Wants. For till you find them you will never be Happy. Wants themselvs being sacred Occasions and Means of Felicitie.

44

You must Want like a GOD, that you may be Satisfied like GOD. Were you not made in His Image? He is infinitly Glorious, becaus all His Wants and Supplies are at the same time in his Nature from Eternity. He had, and from Eternity He was
5 without all His Treasures. From Eternity He needed them, and from Eternity He enjoyed them. For all Eternity is at once in Him. both the Empty Durations before the World was made, and the full ones after. His Wants are as Lively as His Enjoyments: And always present with Him. For His Life is Perfect, and He feels
10 them both. His Wants put a Lustre upon His Enjoyments and make them infinit. His Enjoyments being infinit Crown his Wants, and make them Beautifull even to GOD Himself. His Wants and Enjoyments being always present, are Delightfull to each other, stable Immutable Perfectiv of each other, and
15 Delightfull to Him. Who being Eternal and Immutable, Enjoyeth all His Wants and Treasures together. His Wants never Afflict Him, His Treasures never Disturb Him. His Wants always Delight Him, His Treasures never Cloy Him. The Sence of His Wants is always as Great, as if his Treasures were removed: and as
20 lively upon Him. The Sence of His Wants, as it Enlargeth His Life, so it infuseth a Valu, and continual Sweetness into the Treasures He Enjoyeth.

45

This is a Lesson long enough: which you may be all your Life in Learning, and to all Eternity in Practising. *Be Sensible of your Wants, that you may be sensible of your Treasures.* He is most like GOD that is sensible of evry Thing. Did you not from all
5 Eternity Want som one to give you a Being? Did you not Want

one to give you a Glorious Being? Did you not from all Eternity
Want som one to giv you infinit Treasures? And som one to give
you Spectators, Companions, Enjoyers? Did you not Want a
Dietie, to make them Sweet and Honorable by His infinit Wisdom? What you wanted from all Eternity, be sensible of to all 10
Eternity. Let your Wants be present from Everlasting. Is not this
a Strange Life to which I call you? Wherin you are to be present
with Things that were before the World was made? And at once
present even like GOD with infinit Wants and infinit Treasures:
Be present with your Want of a Diety, and you shall be present 15
with the Dietie. You shall Adore and Admire Him, Enjoy and
Prize Him; Believ in Him, and Delight in Him: See Him to be
the Fountain of all your Joys. and the Head of all your Treasures.

46

It was His Wisdom made you Need the Sun. It was His Goodness made you need the sea. Be sensible of what you need, or
Enjoy neither. Consider how much you need them. For thence
they Derive their Value. Suppose the Sun were Extinguished: or
the Sea were Drie. There would be no Light, no Beauty, no 5
Warmth, no Fruits, no Flowers, no Pleasant Gardens, Feasts, or
Prospects. No wine no Oyl no Bread, no Life, no Motion.
Would you not give all the Gold and Silver in the Indies for
such a Treasure? Prize it now you have it, at that Rate, and you
shall be a Grateful Creature: Nay you shall be a Divine and 10
Heavenly Person. For they in Heaven do Prize Blessings when
they hav them. They in Earth when they hav them Prize them not,
They in Hell Prize them, when they hav them not.

47

To hav Blessings and to Prize them is to be in Heaven; To hav
them, and not to Prize them, is to be in Hell, I would say upon
Earth: To prize them and not to hav them, is to be in Hell.
Which is Evident by the Effects. To Prize Blessings while we
hav them is to Enjoy them, and the effect therof is Contentation 5

Pleasure Thanksgiving Happiness. To Prize them when they are gone Produceth Envy, Covetousness, Repining, Ingratitud, Vexation, Miserie. But it was no Great Mistake to say, That to hav Blessings, and not to Prize them is to be in Hell. For it maketh them ineffectual, as if they were Absent. Yea in som respect it is Worse then to be in Hell. It is more vicious, and more Irrational.

48

They that would not upon Earth see their Wants from all Eternity, shall in Hell see their Treasures to all Eternity. Wants here may be seen and Enjoyed, Enjoyments there shall be seen, but wanted. Wants here may be Blessings, there they shall be Curses. Here they may be fountains of Pleasure and Thanksgiving, there they will be fountains of Wo and Blasphemie. No Miserie is Greater then that of Wanting in the Midst of Enjoyments, Of Seeing and Desiring yet never Possessing. Of beholding others Happy, being seen by them ourselvs in Misery. They that look into Hell here may avoid it herafter. They that refuse to look into Hell upon Earth, to consider the maner of the Torments of the Damned; shall be forced in Hell to see all the Earth, and remember the Felicities which they had when they were Living. Hell it self is a Part of GODs Kingdom, to wit His Prison. It is fitly mentioned in the Enjoyment of the World: And is it self by the Happy Enjoyed, as a Part of the world.

49

The Misery of them who hav and Prize not, Differeth from theirs, who Prize and hav not. The one are more Odious and less sensible; more foolish, and more vicious: The sences of the other are Exceeding Keen and Quick upon them; yet are they not so foolish and Odious as the former. The one would be Happy and cannot, the other may be Happy and will not. The one are more vicious, the other more Miserable. But How can that be? Is not he most Miserable that is most vicious? Yes, that is true. But they that

Prize not what they hav are Dead; their sences are laid asleep, and
when they com to Hell they wake: And then they begin to feel 10
their Misery. He that is most Odious is most Miserable, and he
that is most Pervers is most Odious.

50

They are Deep Instructions that are taken out of Hell, and
Heavenly Documents that are taken from abov. Upon Earth we
learn nothing but Vanitie. Where People Dream, and Loyter and
Wander, and Disquiet themselvs in vain, to make a vain shew;
but do not Profit becaus they prize not the Blessings they have 5
received. To Prize what we hav is a Deep and Heavenly Instruction. It will make us Righteous and Serious, Wise and Holy,
Divine and Blessed. It will make us escape Hell and attain
Heaven. For it will make us Carefull to pleas Him from whom
we hav received all. that we may liv in Heaven.   10

51

Wants are the Bands and Cements between God and us. Had
we not Wanted, we could never hav been Obliged. Wheras
now we are infinitly Obliged, becaus we Want infinitly. From
Eternity it was requisit that we should Want. We could never els
have Enjoyed any Thing: Our own Wants are Treasures. And if 5
Want be a Treasure, sure evry Thing is so. Wants are the Liga-
tures between God and us. The Sinews that convey Sences from
him into us: wherby we liv in Him, and feel his Enjoyments. For
had we not been Obliged by having our Wants Satisfied, we
should not hav been created to lov Him. And had we not been 10
Created to lov Him, we could never have Enjoyed his Eternal
Blessedness.

52

Lov has a marvellous Property of feeling in another. It can
Enjoy in another, as well as Enjoy Him. Lov is an infinit Treasure
to its Object, and its Object is so to it. GOD is LOV, and you

are His Object. You are Created to be his Lov: and He is yours.
5 He is Happy in you, when you are Happy: as Parents in their
Children. He is Afflicted in all your Afflictions. And whosoever
toucheth you toucheth the Apple of His Ey. Will not you be
happy in all his Enjoyments? He feeleth in you, will not you feel
in Him? He hath Obliged you to lov Him. And if you lov Him
10 you must of necessity be Heir of the World, for you are Happy in
Him. All His Praises are your Joys, all his Enjoyments are your
Treasures, all His Pleasures are your Enjoyments. In GOD you
are Crowned, in GOD you are concerned. In Him you feel, in
Him you liv, and mov and hav your Being. in Him you are
15 Blessed. Whatsoever therfore serveth Him serveth you and in Him
you inherit all Things.

53

O the Nobility of Divine Friendship! Are not all his Treasures
yours, and yours His? Is not your very Soul and Body His; Is not
His Life and Felicity yours: Is not His Desire yours? Is not His
Will yours? And if His will be yours, the Accomplishment of it
5 is yours, and the end of all is your Perfection. you are infinitly
Rich as He is: Being Pleased in evry thing as He is. And if His
Will be yours, yours is His. for you will what He Willeth, which
is to be truly Wise and Good and Holy. And when you Delight
in the same Reasons that moved Him to Will, you will Know it.
10 He willed the Creation not only that He might Appear but be:
wherin is seated the Mystery of the Eternal Generation of his Son.
Do you will it as He did, and you shall be Glorious as he is. He
Willed the Happiness of Men and Angels not only that He might
appear, but be Good and Wise and Glorious. And He willed it
15 with such infinit Desire, that He is infinitly Good: infinitly Good
in Him self, and infinitly Blessed in them. Do you will the
Happiness of Men and Angels as He did, and you shall be
Good, and Infinitly Blessed as He is. All their Happiness shall be
your Happiness as it is His. He willed the Glory of all Ages, and
20 the Government and Welfare of all Kingdoms and the Felicity
also of the Highest Cherubims. Do you extend your Will like

Him, and you shall be Great as He is, and concernd and Happy
in all these. He willed the Redemption of Mankind, and therfore
is His Son Jesus Christ an infinit Treasure. Unless you will it
too, He will be no Treasure to you. Verily you ought to will these 25
Things so Ardently: that GOD Himself should be therfore
your Joy because He Willed them. Your Will ought to be
United to His in all Places of His Dominion. Were you not
Born to hav Communion with Him? And that cannot be without this Heavenly Union. Which when it is what it ought is 30
Divine and Infinit. You are GODs Joy for Willing what he
willeth. For He loves to see you Good and Blessed. And will
not you lov to see Him Good? Verily if ever you would enjoy
God, you must enjoy His Goodness. All His Goodness to all
His Hosts in Heaven and Earth. And when you do so, you are 35
the Universal Heir of God and All Things. GOD is yours and
the Whole World. You are His, and you are all; Or in all, and
with all.

54

He that is in all, and with all, can never be Desolat. All the Joys
and all the Treasures, all the Counsels and all the Perfections all
the Angels and all the Saints of GOD are with Him. All the
Kingdoms of the World and the Glory of them are continualy in
his Ey: The Patriarchs Prophets and Apostles are always before 5
Him. The Counsels and the fathers, the Bishops and the Doctors
minister unto Him. All Temples are Open before Him, The
Melodie of all Quires reviveth Him, the Learning of all Universities doth employ him, the Riches of all Palaces Delight him,
The Joys of Eden Ravish Him, The Revelations of S. John 10
Transport Him, The Creation and the Day of Judgment pleas
Him, The Hosannas of the Church Militant, and the Hallelujahs
of the Saints Triumphant fill Him, The Splendor of all Corona-
tions entertain Him, The Joys of Heaven surround Him, And
our Saviors Cross like the Centre of Eternity is in Him, It taketh up 15
his Thoughts, and exerciseth all the Powers of his soul, with
Wonder Admiration Joy and Thanksgiving. The Omnipotence
of God is His Hous, and Eternity his Habitation.

55

The Contemplation of Eternity maketh the Soul Immortal. Whose Glory it is, that it can see before and after its Existence into Endless Spaces. Its Sight is its Presence. And therfore is the Presence of the understanding endless, becaus its Sight is so. O
5 what Glorious Creatures should we be, could we be present in Spirit with all Eternity! How Wise, would we esteem this presence of the understanding, to be more real then that of our Bodies! When my Soul is in Eden with our first Parents, I my self am there in a Blessed Maner. When I walk with Enoch, and see
10 his Translation, I am Transported with Him. The present Age is too little to contain it. I can visit Noah in His Ark, and swim upon the Waters of the Deluge. I can see Moses with his Rod, and the children of Israel passing thorow the Sea. I can Enter into Aarons Tabernacle, and Admire the Mysteries of the Holy Place.
15 I can Travail over the Land of Canaan, and see it overflowing with Milk and Hony; I can visit Solomon in his Glory, and go into his Temple, and view the sitting of His servants, and Admire the Magnificence and Glory of his Kingdom. No Creature but one like unto the Holy Angels can see into all Ages. Sure this
20 Power was not given in vain. but for some Wonderfull Purpose; worthy of itself to Enjoy and fathom. Would Men consider what GOD hath don, they would be Ravished in Spirit with the Glory of His Doings. For Heaven and Earth are full of the Majesty of His Glory. And how Happy would Men be could
25 they see and Enjoy it! But abov all these our Saviors Cross is the Throne of Delights. That Centre of Eternity, That Tree of Life in the midst of the Paradice of GOD!

56

There are we Entertained with the Wonder of all Ages. There we enter into the Heart of the Univers. There we Behold the Admiration of Angels. There we find the Price and Elixar of our Joys. As on evry side of the Earth all Heavy things tend to the
5 centre; so all Nations ought on evry Side to flow in unto it. It is

not by going with the feet, but by Journeys of the Soul, that we
Travail thither. By withdrawing our Thoughts from Wandering
in the Streets of this World, to the Contemplation and Serious
Meditation of his Bloody Sufferings. Where the Carcase is
thither will the Eagles be Gathered together. Our Eys must be 10
towards it, our Hearts set upon it, our Affections Drawn and our
Thoughts and Minds united to it. When I am lifted up saith the
Son of man I will draw all Men unto me. As fishes are Drawn
out of the Water, as Jeremie was Drawn out of the Dungeon, as
S. Peters Sheet was Drawn up into heaven; so shall we be Drawn 15
by that Sight from Ignorance and Sin and Earthly vanities, idle
sports Companions Feasts and Pleasures, to the Joyfull Contemplation of that Eternal Object. But by what Cords? The Cords of a
Man, and the Cords of Lov.

57

As Eagles are Drawn by the Sent of a Carcais, As Children are
Drawn together by the Sight of a Lion, As People flock to a
Coronation, and as a Man is Drawn to his Beloved Object, so
ought we. As the Sick are Drawn by the Credit of a Physician, as
the Poor are Drawn by the Liberality of a King, as the Devout 5
are Drawn by the fame of the Holy, and as the Curious are
Drawn by the Nois of a Miracle so ought we. As the stones were
Drawn to the Building of Thebes by the Melodie of Amphion,
as the Hungry are Drawn with the Desire of a Feast, and the
Pitifull Drawn to a Wofull Spectacle so ought we. What 10
Visible Chains or Cords draw these? What Invisible Links
allure? They follow all, or flock together of their own accord. And
shall not we much more? Who would not be Drawn to the Gate
of Heaven, were it open to receiv him? Yet nothing compels Him,
but that which forceth the Angels. Commoditie and Desire. For 15
these are Things which the Angels desire to look into. And of
Men it is Written, They shall look on Him whom they hav
Peirced. Verily the Israelites did not more Clearly see the Brazen
Serpent upon the Pole in the Wilderness, then we may our
Savior upon the Cross. The Serpent was seen with their Eys, the 20

Slayer of the Serpent is seen with our Souls. They had less need to see the one, then we to see the other.

58

The Cross is the Abyss of Wonders, the Centre of Desires, the Schole of Virtues, the Hous of Wisdom, the Throne of Lov, the Theatre of Joys and the Place of Sorrows; It is the Root of Happiness, and the Gate of Heaven.

59

Of all the Things in Heaven and Earth it is the most Peculiar. It is the most Exalted of all Objects. It is an Ensign lifted up for all Nations, to it shall the Gentiles seek, His Rest shall be Glorious: the Dispersed of Judah shall be gathered together to it, from the
5 four Corners of the Earth. If Lov be the Weight of the Soul, and its Object the Centre. All Eys and Hearts may convert and turn unto this Object: cleave unto this Centre, and by it enter into Rest. There we might see all Nations Assembled with their Eys and Hearts upon it. There we may see Gods Goodness Wisdom
10 and Power: yea his Mercy and Anger displayed. There we may see Mans Sin and infinit value. His Hope and Fear, his Misery and Happiness. There we might see the Rock of Ages, and the Joys of Heaven. There we may see a Man Loving all the World, and a GOD Dying for Mankind There we may see all Types
15 and Ceremonies, figures and Prophesies. And all Kingdoms Adoring a Malefactor: An Innocent Malefactor, yet the Greatest in the World. There we may see the most Distant Things in Eternity united: all Mysteries at once couched together and Ex-plained. The only reason why this Glorious Object is so Publickly
20 Admired by Churches and Kingdoms, and so little thought of by Particular men, is becaus it is truly the most Glorious. It is the Root of Comforts, and the Fountain of Joys. It is the only Supreme and Soveraign Spectacle in all Worlds. It is a Well of Life beneath in which we may see the face of Heaven abov: and
25 the only Mirror, wherin all things appear in their Proper Colors. that is sprinkled in the Blood of our Lord and Savior.

60

The Cross of Christ is the Jacobs ladder by which we Ascend into the Highest Heavens. There we see Joyfull Patriarchs, Expect✓ ing saints, and Prophets Ministering, Apostles Publishing and Doctors Teaching. All Nations concentering, and Angels Prais✓ ing. That Cross is a Tree set on fire with invisible flame, that 5 Illuminateth all the World. The Flame is Lov. The Lov in His Bosom who died on it. In the light of which we see how to possess all the Things in Heaven and Earth after His Similitud. For He that Suffered on it, was the Son of GOD as you are: tho He seemed a Mortal Man. He had Acquaintance and Relations as 10 you hav, but He was a Lover of Men and Angels. Was He not the Son of GOD and Heir of the Whole World? To this poor Bleeding Naked Man did all the Corn and Wine and Oyl, and Gold and Silver in the World minister in an Invisible Maner, even as he was exposed Lying and Dying upon the Cross. 15

61

Here you learn all Patience, Meekness, Self Denial, Courage, Prudence, Zeal, Lov, Charity, Contempt of the World, Joy, Penitence, Contrition, Modestie, Fidelity, Constancy Perseve✓ rance, Holiness, Contentation and Thanksgiving. With whatso✓ ever els is requisit for a Man, a Christian or a King. This Man 5 Bleeding here was Tutor to King Charles the Martyr: and Great Master to S. Paul the Convert who learned of Him Activity, and Zeal unto all Nations. Well therfore may we take up with this Prospect, and from hence behold all the Things in Heaven and Earth. Here we learn to imitat Jesus in his Lov unto all. 10

62

LORD JESUS what Lov shall I render unto Thee, for thy Lov unto me! Thy eternal Lov! Oh what fervor, what Ardor, what Humiliation, what Reverence, what Joy, what Adoration, what Zeal, what Thanksgiving! Thou that art Perfect in Beauty,

5 Thou that art the King of Eternal Glory, Thou that reignest in the Highest Heavens camest down from Heaven to Die for me! And shall not I liv unto Thee? O my joy! O my Sovereign Friend! O my Life, and my All! I beseech Thee let those Trickling Drops of Blood that run down Thy flesh drop upon me. O let Thy 10 Lov enflame me. Which is so deep and infinit, that Thou didst suffer the Wrath of GOD for me: And Purchase all Nations and Kingdoms to be my Treasures. O Thou that Redeemedst me from Hell, and when Thou hadst Overcom the Sharpness of Death didst open the Kingdom of Heaven to all Believers; What 15 shall I do unto Thee? What shall I do for Thee, O Thou Preserver of Men. Liv, Lov, and Admire; and learn to becom such unto Thee as Thou unto me. O Glorious Soul! whose Comprehensiv understanding at once contains all Kingdoms and Ages! O Glorious Mind! Whose Lov extendeth to all 20 Creatures! O miraculous and Eternal GODhead, now suffer- ing on the cross for me: As Abraham saw thy Day and was Glad, so didst Thou see me and this Day from all Eternitie, and see- ing me wast Gracious and Compassionat Towards me. (All Transeunt Things are Permanent in God) *Thou settest me before* 25 *Thy Face forever.*) O let me this day see Thee, and be united to Thee in Thy Holy Sufferings. Let me learn O GOD such Lessons from Thee, as may make me Wise, and Blessed as an Angel of GOD!

63

Why Lord Jesus dost Thou lov men; why are they thy Treasures? What Wonder is this, that Thou shouldst esteem them so as to Die for them? Shew me the Reasons of thy Lov, that I may Lov them too. O Goodness ineffable! they are the Treasures of thy 5 Goodness. who so infinitly lovest them that Thou gavest thy self for them. Thy Goodness delighted to be communicated to them whom thou hast saved. O Thou who art most Glorious in Good- ness, make me Abundant in this Goodness like unto Thee, That I may as Deeply pitty others Miserie, and as Ardently 10 Thirst their Happiness as Thou doest. Let the same mind be in me that is in Christ Jesus. For He that is not led by the Spirit of Christ is none of His. Holy Jesus I Admire thy Lov unto me also. O that I could see it through all those Wounds! O that I could feel it in all those Stripes! O that I could hear it in all those Groans! O that I could Taste it beneath that Gall and Vinegre! 15 O that I could smell the Savor of thy sweet Oyntments, even in this Golgotha or Place of a Skull. I Pray Thee teach me first thy Lov unto Me, and then unto Man Kind! But in thy Lov unto Mankind I am Beloved.

64

These Wounds are in themselvs Orifices too small to let in my Sight, to the vast Comprehensions of thine Eternal Lov. These Wounds Engraven in thy Hands but Shady Impressions; unless I see the Glory of thy Soul, in which the fulness of the GOD-HEAD Dwelleth Bodily. These Bloody Characters are too 5 Dim to let me read it, in its Lustre and Perfection. Till I see thy Person: and Know thy Ways! O Thou that Hangest upon this Cross before mine Eys, Whose face is Bleeding, and coverd over with Tears and filth and Blows! Angels Adore the GLORY of Thy GODHEAD in the Highest Heavens! Who in evry Thought, 10 and in evry Work didst Glorious Things for me from Everlasting. What Could I O my Lord Desire more then such a World! Such Heavens and such an Earth! Such Beasts and Fowls and fishes made for me. All these Do Homage unto me, and I hav Dominion over them from the Beginning! The Heavens and the 15 Earth Minister unto me, as if no Man were Created but I alone. I willingly Acknowledg it to be thy Gift! Thy Bounty unto Me! How many thousand Ways do Men also minister unto me! O what Riches hast Thou prepared out of Nothing for me! All Creatures labor for my sake, and I am made to Enjoy all thy 20 Creatures. O what Praises shall I return unto Thee, the Wisdom of the father, and the Brightness of the Glory of his Eternal Good-ness! Who didst make all for me before thou didst redeem me.

65

Had I been alive in Adams steed, how should I hav Admired
the Glory of the world! What a Confluence of Thoughts and
Wonders and Joys and Thanksgivings would hav replenished
me in the sight of so Magnificent a Theatre, so Bright a Dwelling
5 Place; so Great a Temple, so Stately a Hous replenished with all
Kind of Treasure, raised out of Nothing Created for me and for
me alone. shall I now Despise them? When I consider the
Heavens which Thou hast made, the moon and stars which are
the Works of thy Fingers; what is Man that Thou art Mindfull
10 of Him, or the Son of Man, that Thou Visitest Him! Thou hast
made Him a little lower then the Angels and Crowned him with
Glory and Honor! O what Lov must that needs be, that pre'
pared such a Palace! Attended with what Power! With what
Wisdom Illuminated! Abounding with what Zeal! And how
15 Glorious must the King be, that could out of Nothing Erect such
a Curious, so Great, and so Beautifull a Fabrick! It was Glorious
while new: and is as new as it was Glorious.

66

But this is Small. What O my Lord could I desire to be which
Thou hast not made me! If Thou hast exprest Thy Lov in
furnishing the Hous. How Gloriously doth it Shine in the
Possessor! My Lims and Members when rightly Prized, are Com'
5 parable to the fine Gold; The Topaz of Ethiopia and the Gold
of Ophir are not to be compared to them. What Diamonds are
Equal to my Eys; What Labyrinths to mine Ears; What Gates
of Ivory, or Rubie Leaves to the Double Portal of my Lips and
Teeth? Is not Sight a Jewel? Is not Hearing a Treasure? Is not
10 Speech a Glory! O my Lord Pardon my Ingratitud and pitty
my Dulnes, who am not Sensible of these Gifts. The freedom of
thy Bounty hath deceived me. These things were too near to be
considered. Thou preventedst me with thy Blessings, and I was
not aware. But now I giv Thanks and Adore and Prais Thee for
15 these Inestimable favors. I believ Thou lovest me, becaus Thou

hast endued me, with these Sacred and Living Treasures. Holy
Father, hence forth I more Desire to esteem them, then Palaces of
Gold! yea tho they were given me by Kings. I confess unto Thee
that I am Richer in them. O what Joy, what Delight and Jubilee
should there always be, would men Prize the Gifts of God accord⁄ 20
ing to their Value!

67

But what Creature could I desire to be which I am not Made?
There are Angels and Cherubim. I rejoyce O Lord in their
Happiness; and that I am what I am by thy Grace and favor.
Suppose O my Soul there were no Creature made at all, And
that GOD making Thee alone offered to make Thee what Thou 5
wouldst. What couldst Thou Desire; or what wouldst Thou
wish, or Crave to be? Since GOD is the most Glorious of all
Beings, and the most Blessed, couldst thou wish any more then
to be His IMAGE! O my Soul, He hath made His Image. Sing
O ye Angels, and Laud His Name ye Cherubims: Let all the 10
Kingdoms of the Earth be Glad, and let all the Hosts of Heaven
rejoyce. for He hath made His Image, the Likeness of himself, his
own Similitude. What Creature what Being what Thing more
Glorious could there be! GOD from all Eternity was infinitly
Blessed and desired to make one infinitly Blessed. He was infinit 15
LOV, and being Lovly in being so, Would prepare for Himself
a Most Lovly Object. having Studied from all Eternity, He saw,
none more Lovly then the Image of His Lov, His own Similitude.
O Dignity Unmeasurable! O Exaltation Passing Knowledge!
O Joy Unspeakable! Triumph O my Soul and Rejoyce for ever! 20
I see that I am infinitly Beloved. For *infinit Lov hath exprest and
pleased it self in Creating an Infinit Object.* GOD is LOV, and my
Soul is Lovely! God is Loving, and His Image Amiable. O my
Soul these are the Foundations of an Eternal Friendship between
GOD and Thee. He is infinitly Prone to Lov, and Thou art 25
Like Him. He is infinitly Lovly and Thou art Like Him. What
can more Agree then that which is infinitly Lovly, and that which
is infinitly Prone to lov! Where both are so Lovly, and so Prone

to lov, what Joys and Affections will be Excited between them!
30 What infinit Treasures will they be to each other! O my GOD
Thou hast Glorified thy self, and thy Creature infinitly, in making
thine Image! It is fitted for the Throne of GOD! It is meet to be
thy Companion! It is so Sublime and Wonderfull and Amiable,
that all Angels and Men were Created to Admire it. As it was
35 Created to Admire Thee, and to liv in Communion with Thee
for ever.

68

Being made alone, O my Soul, thou wouldst be in thy Body like
GOD in the World, an Invisible Mysterie, too Great to be Com-
prehended by all Creatures. Thou wouldst have all the Goodness
of God towards Thee to enjoy, in that thy Creation. Whatever is
5 in Him would be thy Treasure. But had He Determined to
Creat no more: there had been no Witnesses of thy Glory. No
Spectators of thy Communion with GOD. No other Treasures
beside GOD and Thou. One would think those were Sufficient.
But Infinit Goodness loves to Abound. And to overflow in-
10 finitly with Infinit Treasures. Lov lovs to do somwhat for its
Object more then to Creat it. It is always more stately being surrounded with Power, and more Delightfull being Inaccessible in
a Multitude of Treasures, and more Honorable in the midst of
Admirers: and more Glorious when it reigneth over many
15 Attendants. Lov therfore hath prepared all these for it self and its
Object. And becaus it is always more Great by how much the
Greater they are that minister unto it, It maketh its Attendants, the
most Glorious that can be, and infinitly Delighteth in giving
them all with all its Treasures to its Beloved. Had GOD Created
20 Thee alone, He had not been so Good as He is. He is Good to
Innumerable Millions now whom he Createth besides, And
more good unto thee, infinitly and [?] He Glorifieth His Eternal
Wisdom, in making His Goodness unto all Them Wholy thine,
25 and wholy infinit unto each of them yet wholy and soly thine in
all. Friendship will Manifest it self in doing all it can for its
Beloved. Since therfore GOD will make some other Creatures,
what kind of Creatures doth thy Soul Desire. *Wish Wisely thou*

shalt receiv a Grant. Since Lov is so sweet. and Thou art by GODs Lov so infinitly exalted: What canst Thou Desire but Creatures like unto thy Creator? Behold therfore Angels and Men 30 produced by his Goodness and made to Delight Thee.

69

O Adorable *Trinity*! What hast Thou don! Thou hast made me the End of all Things, and all the End of me. I in all, and all in Me. In evry Soul whom Thou hast Created, Thou hast given me the Similitude of thy self, to Enjoy! Could my Desires hav Aspired unto such Treasures? Could my Wisdom have Devised 5 such Sublime Enjoyments! Oh! Thou hast don more for us then we could ask or think. I prais and Admire and rejoyce in Thee: who art infinitly infinit in all thy Doings.

70

But what Laws O my Soul wouldst Thou desire? By which the Lives of those Creatures, should be Guided towards Thee? A Friend commandeth all in His Jurisdiction to lov his Friend: And therin Supremely manifesteth his Lov. GOD Himself Exalteth Thee and causeth Thee to Reign in His Soul. He Exalteth Thee 5 by His Laws and causeth Thee to reign in all others. the World. And souls are like his thy Heavenly Mansions The Lawgiver of Heaven and Earth Employeth all His Authority for Thee He Promoteth Thee in His Eternal Palace, and maketh Thee His Friend, and telleth His Nobles and all His Subjects. Whatsoever 10 ye do unto Him ye do unto Me. Joseph was not so great in Pharoahs Court, Nor Haman in the Court of Ahasuerus, as Thou art in Heaven. He Tendereth Thee as the Apple of His Ey. He hath set His Heart upon Thee, Thou art the sole Object of His Ey, and the End of all His Endeavors. 15

71

But what Life wouldst Thou lead? And by what Laws wouldst Thou thy self be guided? For none are so Miserable as the Lawless

and Disobedient. Laws are the Rules of Blessed Living. Thou
must therfore be guided by som Laws. What wouldst Thou
5 chuse? Surely since thy Nature and GODs are so Excellent, the
Laws of Nature, are the most Pleasing as the Laws of Blessedness.
GOD loved Thee with an infinit Lov, and became by doing so
thine infinit Treasure. Thou art the End unto Whom He liveth
For all the Lines of His Works and Counsels end in Thee, and
10 in thy Advancement. Wilt not Thou becom to Him an Infinit
Treasure, by loving Him according to His Desert. It is impossible
but to lov Him that loveth. Lov is so Amiable that it is Irresistible.
There is no Defence against that Arrow, nor any Deliverance in
that War, nor any Safeguard from that Charm. Wilt Thou not
15 liv unto Him? Thou must of Necessity liv unto som Thing. And
what so Glorious as His Infinit Lov? Since therfore Laws are
requisit to lead Thee, what Laws can thy Soul desire, then those
that Guid thee in the most Amiable Paths to the Highest End?
By lov alone is GOD Enjoyed By Lov alone Delighted in, by
20 Lov alone approached or Admired. His Nature requires Lov.
Thy Nature requires Lov. The Law of Nature Commands Thee
to lov Him. The Law of His Nature, and the Law of thine.

72

There is in Lov two Strange Perfections, that make it infinit in
Goodness. It is infinitly Diligent in doing Good; And it infinitly
Delighteth in that Goodness. It taketh No Pleasure Comparable
in any thing to that it taketh in Exalting and Blessing. And ther'
5 fore hath it made Thee a Comprehension infinit to see all Ages,
and an Affection Endless to lov all Kingdoms, and a Power
fathomless to Enjoy all Angels. And a Thirst unsatiable to desire
and Delight in them. And a never Wearied faculty alsufficient to
see, number take in Prize, and Esteem all the Varieties of Creatures
10 and their Excellencies in all Worlds that Thou mayst Enjoy them
in Communion with Him. It is all Obligation, that He requires
it. What Life wouldst Thou lead? wouldst Thou lov God alone?
GOD alone cannot be Beloved. He cannot be loved with a
finit Lov, becaus He is infinit. Were He Beloved alone, His Lov

would be limited. He must be Loved in all with an Illimited 15
Lov, even in all His Doings, in all His friends, in all His
Creatures. Evry where in all Things Thou must meet His Lov.
And this the Law of Nature Commands. And it is thy Glory
That Thou art fitted for it. His Lov unto thee is the Law and
Measure of thine unto him, his Lov unto all others the Law and 20
Obligation of thine unto all.

73

His Nature requireth that Thou lov all those whom He loveth.
And receiv Him in all those Things wherin He giveth Him self
unto Thee. Their Nature loveth to be Beloved and being Amiable
require Lov; as well as Delight in it. They require it both by
Desert and Desire. Thy Nature urgeth it. for without Loving 5
thou art Desolat, and by Loving Thou Enjoyest. Yea by Loving
Thou Expandest and Enlargest thy self. And the more Thou
lovest art the more Glorious. Thou lovest all thy friends Friends;
and needest not to fear any Dearth of Lov or Danger of In
sufficiency. For the more Thou lovest thy Friend, thy Soveraign 10
friend, the more Thou lovest all his. Which showeth the Endless
Proneness of Lov to increas and never to Decay. O my Soul
Thou livest in all those whom Thou lovest: and in them Enjoyest
all their Treasures.

74

Miraculous are the Effects of Divine Wisdom. He loveth evry one,
maketh evry one infinitly Happy: and is infinitly Happy in evry
one. He giveth all the World to one, He giveth it to evry one, He
giveth it to evry one in giving it to all, and Giveth it wholy to me
in giving it to evry one for evry ones sake. He is infinitly Happy 5
in Evry one, as many Times therefore as there are Happy Persons
He is infinitly Happy. Evry one is infinitly Happy in evry one,
Evry one therfore is as many Times infinitly Happy as there are
Happy Persons. He is infinitly Happy abov all their Happiness in
Comprehending all. And I Comprehending His and theirs, am, 10

Oh how Happy! Here is Lov! Here is a Kingdom! Where all are Knit in infinit Unity. all are Happy in each other. all are like Dieties. Evry one the End of all Things evry one supreme, evry one a Treasure and the Joy of all, and evry one most infinitly
15 Delighted in being so. All things are ever Joys for evry ones sake, and infinitly Richer to evry one for the sake of all. The same Thing is Multiplied by being Enjoyed. And He that is Greatest is most my Treasure. This is the Effect of Making Images. And by all their Lov is evry Image infinitly Exalted. Comprehending in his
20 Nature all Angels all Cherubims all Seraphims all Worlds all Creatures, and GOD over all Blessed for ever.

75

Being to lead this Life within I was Placed in Paradice without with som Advantages which the Angels hav not. And being Designed to Immortality and an Endless Life, was to Abide with GOD from everlasting to everlasting in all His Ways. But I
5 was Deceived by my Appetite, and fell into Sin. Ingratefully I despised Him that gav me my Being. I offended in an Apple against Him that gave me the whole World: But Thou O Savior art here upon the Cross suffering for my Sins. What shall I render unto Thee for so Great a Mercy! All Thanksgiving is too
10 Weak. And all Expression too feeble. I giv Thee my self my Soul and Body I offer unto Thee. It is unworthy of Thee, but Thou lovest me. Wash me with thy Blood from all my Sins: And fill me with Thy Holy Spirit that I may be like unto Thee. So shall I Prais Thy Name Acceptably for ever more. Amen.

76

And now, O Lord, Heaven and Earth are infinitly more valuable then they were before. being all bought with thy Precious Blood. And Thou O Jesus art a Treasure unto me far Greater then all those. At what Rate or Measure shall I Esteem Thee! Thou hast
5 restored me again to the Friendship of GOD, to the Enjoyment of the World, To the Hope of Eternal Glory, To the Lov of

Angels Cherubims and Men. To the Enjoyment and Obedience of Thy Holy Laws: which alone are sweeter to me then the Hony and the Hony Comb, and more precious then Thousands of Gold and Silver. Thou hast restored me abov all to the Image 10 of GOD. And Thou hast Redeemed all Ages and Kingdoms for me alone! Who am commanded to lov them as Thou doest. O that I might be unto them as Thou art! O that I might be unto Thee as Thou art to Me. As glorious and as Rich in Lov! O that I might Die for Thee! O that I might ever live unto Thee! In 15 evry Thought, in evry Action of my Life, in evry Moment I Bless Thee for Renewing the old commandment; upon New Obliga⁄ tions among Sinners, *As I hav loved you, so do ye also lov one another.* O let Thy Lov be in me. that thy Joy may be fulfilled in me for evermore. 20

77

Now O Lord I see the Greatness of Thy Lov wherwith Thou Diest. And by thy Actions more then by thy sufferings Admire Thee. But henceforth I will more Admire Thee by Thy sufferings. for considering that such Actions went before; what lov must move Thee to com into the Place of Guilty Sinners!

78

Lord I lament, and Abhor my self that I hav been the Occasion of these thy Sufferings. I had never known the Dignity of my Nature, hadst not Thou esteemed it: I had never seen, nor Under⁄ stood its Glory, hadst not Thou Assumed it. Be Thou Pleased to unite me unto Thee in the Bands of an Individual Lov, that I 5 may evermore liv unto Thee, and Liv in Thee. And by how much the more Vile I hav been, let my lov be so much O Lord the more Violent Henceforth and fervent unto Thee. O Thou who wouldst never hav permitted sin, hadst Thou not known how to Bring good out of Evil, hav Pitty upon me: Hear my 10 Prayer. O my GOD since Pitty Enbalmes Lov, let thine com Enricht, and be more precious to me Miserable Sinner. Let the

Remembrance of all the Glory wherin I was Created make me
more Serious and Humble, more Deep and Penitent more Pure
15 and Holy before Thee. And since the World is Sprinkled with
thy Blood, and Adorned with all Kingdoms and Ages for me:
which are Heavenly Treasures and vastly Greater then Heaven
and Earth. Let me see thy Glory in the Preparation of them, and
thy Goodness in their Government. Open unto me the Gate of
20 Righteousness, that I may enter in to the New Jerusalem.

79

My Lord, Thou Head of the Holy Catholic Church. I Admire
and Prais Thee for Purchasing to thy self such a glorious Bride:
and for Uniting us all by the Blood of thy Crosse. I beseech Thee
let my Lov unto all be Regular like thine, and Pure, and Infinit.
5 Make it Divine, and make it Holy. I confess I can see. but I cannot
Moderat, nor Lov as I ought. I Pray Thee for thy Loving kind´
ness sake supply my Want in this Particular. And so make me to
lov all, that I may be a Blessing to all. and welpleasing to Thee in
all. Teach me Wisdom, How to Expend my Blood Estate Life
10 and Time in thy service for the Good of all, and make all them
that are round about me Wise and Holy as Thou art. That we
might all be Knit together in GODly Lov, and united in thy
service to Thy Honor and Glory.

80[1]

My Excellent friend, you see that there are Treasures in Heaven
and Earth fit to be Enjoyed, besides those of Kings Courts and
Taverns. The Joys of the Temple are the Greatest Joys were they
understood; they are the most Magnificent Solemn and Divine.
5 There are Glorious Entertainments in this Miserable World,
could we find them out. What more Delightfull can be imagined,
then to see a Savior at this Distance Dying on the Cross to
Redeem a man from Hell, and to see one self the Beloved of GOD
and all Kingdoms, yea the Admired of Ages, and the Heir of

---

[1] This section is crossed through for deletion in the manuscript.

the whole World? Hath not His Blood united you and me, 10
Cannot we see and Lov and Enjoy each other at 100 Miles
Distance? In Him is the only Sweet and Divine Enjoyment. I
Desire but an Amiable Soul in any Part of all Eternity, and can
lov it unspeakably: And if lov it, Enjoy it. For Lov implies
Pleasure, becaus it is ever pleased with what is Beloved. Lov 15
GOD and Jesus Christ and Angels and Men, which you are
made to do as naturaly as the Sun is made to shine, and the
Beauty of the Holy Ghost Dwelling in you will make you my
Delight, and the Treasure of the Holy Angels. You will at last
be seen by me and all others, in all your Thoughts and in all your 20
Motions. In the mean time Delight only in the Lov of JESUS
and Direct all your Lov unto Him. Adore Him. Rejoyce in
Him, Admire His Lov and Prais Him, Secretly and in the
Congregation. Enjoy His Saints that are round about you, make
your self Amiable that you may be Admitted to their Enjoyment, 25
by Meekness Temperance, Modesty, Humility Charity Chastitie
Devotion Cheerfulness Gratitude Joy Thanksgiving. Retire from
them that you may be the more Precious, and com out unto them
the more Wise. So shall you make the Place wherin you live a
Nest of Sweet Perfumes, and evry Soul that is round about you 30
will be a Bed of Honor and Sweet Repose unto you.

81

My Goodness extendeth not to Thee O Lord, but to Thy Saints,
and to the Excellent in the Earth in whom is all my Delight.
To Delight in the Saints of God is the Way to Heaven. One
would think it Exceeding easy and reasonable to Esteem those
whom Jesus purchased with his precious Blood. And if we do 5
so how can we chuse but inherit all Things. All the Saints of all
Ages and all Kingdoms are his Inheritance, his Treasures, his
Jewels. Shall they not be yours since they are His whom you love
so infinitly? There is not a cup of cold Water given to a Disciple
in the name of a Disciple, but He accepteth it as don to Himself. 10
Had you been with Mary Magdalen, would you not hav annointed
his feet, and washed them in tears and wiped them with the Hairs

of your head? His poor Servants, his Contemptible and Dis⟨
guised members here upon Earth are his Feet, yea more the Apple
15 of His Ey: yea more, for He gave his Eys and Heart and Hands
and feet for them. O therfore universaly in all places tender them
and at all times be ready and Willing to Minister unto them. And
that with infinit Joy, Knowing the Excellency of your Duty. for
you are Enjoying the World, and Communicating your self like
20 God unto them. You are laying up Treasure in Heaven and
Enlarging your Soul, Beautifying your Life, and Delighting the
Holy Angels, Offering up sacrifices unto God, and perfuming
the World; Embracing Jesus Christ, and caressing your Savior
while you are Dispensing Charities among them. Every Alms
25 Deed is a Precious Stone in the Crown of Glory.

82

But there are a sort of Saints meet to be your Companions, in
another maner. But that they lie concealed. You must therfore
make your self exceeding Virtuous, that by the very Splendor of
your Fame you may find them out. While the Wicked are like
5 Heaps of Rubbish, these few Jewels lie buried in the Ruins of
Mankind: and must Diligently be Digd for. You may Know
them by their Lustre. and by the very Desire and Esteem they
hav of you when you are virtuous. For as it is the Glory of the Sun
that Darkness cannot approach it, becaus it is always encom⟨
10 passed with its own Beams; so it is the Priviledge of Holy Souls,
that they are always secure in their own Light, which driveth
away Divels and Evil Men: And is accessible by none, but
Lovers of Virtue. Beginners and Desirers will give you the
Opportunity of infusing your self and your Principles into them.
15 Practicers and Growers will mingle souls and be Delightfull
Companions, The Sublime and Perfect, in the Lustre of their
Spirit will shew you the Image of Almighty God and the Joys
of Heaven. They will Allure Protect Encourage Comfort Teach
Honor and Delight you But you must be very Good, for that is
20 the way to find them And very Patient to endure som time, and
very Diligent to observ where they are.

83

They will Prais our Savior with you and turn the World into Heaven. And if you find those of Noble and Benevolent Natures, Discreet and Magnanimous, Liberal and Cheerfull, Wise and Holy as they ought to be, you will hav in them Treasures Greater then all Relations, whatsoever. They will Exchange Souls with 5 you, Divide Estates, Communicate Comforts, Counsels and Honors, And in all Tenderness Constancy Fidelity and Lov be more yours then their own. There are exceeding few such Heavenly Lovers as Jesus was, who imparted his own Soul unto us. Yet som may Doubtlessly be found. And half a Dozen such as these 10 wisely chosen will represent unto us the New Jerusalem: Enter⸗ tain us always with Divine Discourses, Pleas us always with Heavenly Affections, Delight us always with Melodie and Praises. and ever make us near unto our Savior.

84

Yet you must Arm yourself with Expectations of their Infirmities, and resolv nobly to forgive them: not in a sordid and Cowardly maner, by taking no notice of them: nor in a Dim and Lazy maner, by letting them alone: but in a Divine and Illustrious maner by chiding them meekly, and vigorously rendering and 5 showering down all kind of Benefits. Cheerfully continuing to do Good, and whatever you suffer by your Piety and charity, Con⸗ fidence or Lov, to be like our Savior, Unwearied: who when he was abused, and had often been evil intreated among men, pro⸗ ceeded couragiously through all Treacheries and Deceits to die 10 for them. So shall you turn their very Vices, into Virtues to you, and as our Savior did make of a Wreath of Thorns, a Crown of Glory. But set the Splendor of Virtues before you, and when some fail, think with your self, there are some Sincere and Excellent, And why should not I be the most Virtuous? 15

85

With all their Eys behold our Savior, with all their Hearts Adore
Him, with all their Tongues and Affections praise him. See how
in all Closets, and in all Temples; in all Cities and in all feilds;
in all Nations and in all generations they are lifting up their
5 hands and Eys unto his Cross; and Delight in all their Adorations. This will Enlarge your Soul and make you to Dwell in all
Kingdoms and Ages: Strengthen your Faith and Enrich your
Affections: fill you with their Joys and make you a Lively Par-
taker in Communion with them It will make you a Possessor
10 Greater then the World. Men do mightily wrong themselvs:
when they refuse to be present in all Ages: and Neglect to see the
Beauty of all Kingdoms, and Despise the Resentments of evry
Soul, and Busie them selvs only with Pots and cups and things at
home, or shops and Trades and things in the street But do not
15 liv to God Manifesting Himself in all the World. nor care to
see, (and be present with Him, in) all the Glory of his Eternal
Kingdom. By seeing the Saints of all Ages we are present with
Them. By being present with them becom too Great for our own
Age, and near to our Savior.

86

O Jesu, Thou King of Saints, whom all Adore: and the Holy
Imitat, I Admire the perfection of thy Lov in evry soul! Thou
lovest evry one Wholy as if Him alone: Whose Soul is so Great
an Image of thine Eternal Father, that Thou camest down from
5 Heaven to die for Him, and to Purchase Mankind that they
might be his Treasures. I Admire to see thy Crosse in evry
Understanding, thy Passion in evry Memory, thy Crown of
Thorns in evry Ey, and thy Bleeding, Naked Wounded Body in
evry Soul. Thy Death liveth in evry Memory, thy Crucified
10 Person is Enbalmed in evry Affection, thy pierced feet are Bathed
in evry ones Tears, thy Blood all droppeth on evry soul: Thou
wholy Communicatest thy self to evry Soul in all Kingdoms, and
art wholy seen in every saint and wholy fed upon by evry

Christian. It is my Priviledge that I can enter with Thee into evry Soul, and in evry Living Temple of thy Manhood and thy 15 Godhead, behold again, and Enjoy thy Glory.

87

O how do thine Affections extend like the Sun Beams unto all the stars in heaven and to all the Kingdoms in the World. Thine at once Enlighten both Hemispheres. Quicken us with Life, Enable us to digest the Nourishment of our Souls, caus Us to see the Greatness of our Nature, the Lov of God, and the Joys of 5 Heaven: Melt us into Tears, Comfort and Enflame us, and do all in a Celestial maner, that the Sun can do in a Terrene and Earthly. O Let me so long Eye Thee, till I be turned into Thee, and look upon me till Thou art formed in me, that I may be a Mirror of thy Brightness, an Habitation of thy Lov and a Temple 10 of thy Glory. That all thy Saints might live in me, and I in them: enjoying all their felicities Joys and Treasures.

88

O Thou Sun of Righteousness, Ecclypsed on the Cross, overcast with sorrows, and covered with the shadow of Death, remov the vail of thy flesh that I may see thy Glory. Those cheeks are shades, those Lims and Members clouds, that hide the Glory of thy Mind, thy Knowledg and thy Lov from us. But were they re- 5 moved those inward Excellencies would remain Invisible. As therfore we see thy Flesh with our fleshly Eys, and handle thy Wounds with our Bodily Sences, let us see thy Understanding with our Understandings, and read thy Lov with our own. Let our Souls hav Communion with thy Soul, and let the Ey of our 10 Mind enter into thine. Who art Thou who Bleeding here causest the Ground to Tremble and the Rocks to rend, and the Graves to Open? Hath thy Death Influence so high as the Highest Heavens? That the Sun also Mourneth and is Clothed in Sables? Is thy Spirit present in the Temple, that the vail rendeth in twain at 15 thy Passion? O let me leav Kings Courts to com unto Thee, and

chuse rather in a Cave to serve Thee, then on a Throne to despise
Thee. O my Dying Gracious Lord, I perceiv the virtu of thy
Passion evry where: Let it I beseech Thee enter into my Soul, and
20 rent my Rocky Stony Heart, and tear the vail of my flesh that I
may see into the Holy of Holies! O Darken the Sun of Pride and
Vain Glory. Yea let the Sun it self be Dark in Comparison of
thy Lov! And open the Grave of my flesh, that my Soul may
arise to Prais Thee. Grant this for thy Mercy sake. Amen!

89

Is this He that was transfigured upon Mount Tabor! Pale,
Withered! Extended! Tortured! Soyld with Blood and Sweat
and Dust! Dried! Parched! O Sad! O Dismal Spectacle! All
His Joynts are dissolved, all His Blood is shed: to the last Drop! All
5 his Moysture is consumed! What is here but a Heap of Desola-
tions! a Deformed Carcais! a Disfigured Countenance! A Mass of
Miseries; and silent Footsteps of Innumerable Sufferings! Can this
be a Joy! Can this be an Entertainment! Can this Delight us!
O JESUS the more vile I here behold Thee, the more I Admire
10 Thee. Into what Low Abysses didst thou Descend; in what
Depths of misery dost Thou now lie! Oh what Contusions, what
Stripes and Wounds, what Desolations and Deformities didst
Thou suffer for our sakes! In all the Depths of thy Humiliation
I here Adore Thee! I prize and Desire always to see these Stripes
15 and these Deformities. It is sweeter to be with Thee in thy
Sufferings, then with Princes on their Thrones, and more do
I rejoyce with Thee in thy Miseries, then in all their Solemnities.
I Tremble also to see thy Condescentions. The Great Effects and
Expressions of thy Lov! Thou wast slain for me: and shall I leav
20 thy Body in the feild O Lord? Shall I go away and be Merry,
while the Love of my Soul and my only Lover is Dead upon the
Cross. Groans here, in the sight and Apprehension of thy Lov,
are beyond all Melodie, and the solemn sorrows of a loving Soul,
a faithfull Friend, a Tender Spouse, a Deep and Compassionat
25 Tru Lover, beyond all the Entertainments in the World. Thine
O Jesus will I ever be while I hav any Being.

90

This Body is not the Cloud, but a Pillar assumd to manifest His Lov unto us. In these Shades doth this Sun break forth most Oriently. In this Death is His Lov Painted in most lively colours. GOD never shewd Himself more a GOD, then when He appeared Man. Never gained more Glory then when He lost all Glory. Was never more Sensible of our Sad Estate, then when He was bereaved of all Sence. O let thy Goodness shine in me! I will lov all O Lord by thy Grace Assisting as Thou doest: And in Death it self, will I find Life, and in Conquest Victory. This Sampson by Dying Kild all His Enemies: And then carried the Gates of Hell and Death away, when being Dead, Himself was born to his Grave. Teach me O Lord these Mysterious Ascensions By Descending into Hell for the sake of others, let me Ascend into the Glory of the Highest Heavens. Let the Fidelity and Efficacy of my Lov appear, in all my Care and Suffering for Thee.

91

O Jesu Lord of Lov. and Prince of Life! who even being Dead, art Greater then all Angels Cherubims and Men. Let my Lov unto Thee be as Strong as Death: and so Deep that No Waters may be able to Drown it. O let it be ever Endless and Invincible! O that I could realy so lov Thee, as rather to suffer with S. Anselm the Pains of Hell then to Sin against Thee. O that no Torments, no Powers in Heaven or Earth, no Stratagems no Allurements might Divide me from Thee Let the Length and Bredth and Height and Depth of my Love unto Thee be Like Thine unto me. Let undreinable fountains, and unmeasurable Abysses be hidden in it. Let it be more vehement then flame, more Abundant then the sea, more Constant then the Candle in Aarons Tabernacle that burned day and night. Shall the sun shine for me; and be a Light from the Beginning of the World to this very day that never goeth out, and shall my Lov ceas, or intermit, O Lord, to shine or burn. O Let it be a Perpetual fire on the Altar of my Heart, and let my Soul it self be thy Living Sacrifice.

92

It is an inestimable Joy that I was raised out of Nothing, to see and Enjoy this Glorious World: It is a Sacred Gift wherby the children of Men are made my Treasures, but O Thou who art fairer then the Children of Men, how great and unconceivable is
5 the Joy of thy Lov! That I who was lately raised out of the dust, hav so Great a Friend, that I who in this life am born to mean Things according to the world should be called to inherit such Glorious Things in the way of heaven: Such a Lord, so Great a Lover, such Heavenly Mysteries, such Doings, and such suffer-
10 ings, with all the Benefit and pleasure of them in thy Intelligible Kingdom: it amazeth, it transporteth and ravisheth me. I will leave my fathers house and com unto Thee; For Thou art my Lord, and I will Worship Thee. That all Ages should appear so visibly before me, and all thy Ways be so lively Powerfull and present
15 with me, that the Land of Canaan should be so near, and all the Joys in Heaven and Earth so sweet to comfort me! This O Lord declareth thy Wisdom, and sheweth thy Power. But O the Riches of thine infinit Goodness in making my Soul an Inter-minable Temple, out of which nothing can be, from which
20 Nothing is removed, to which nothing is afar off; but all things immediatly near, in Real true and lively maner. O the Glory of that Endless Life, that can at once extend to all Eternity! Had the Cross been 20 Millions of Ages further, it had still been equaly near, nor is it possible to remov it, for it is with all Distances in my
25 Understanding, and tho it be removed many thousand Millions of Ages more is as clearly seen and Apprehended. This Soul for which Thou diedst, I desire to Know more perfectly, O my Savior. That I may prais thee for it, and believ it worthy, in its Nature, to be an Object of thy Lov; tho unworthy by reason of
30 sin: and that I may use it in thy Service, and Keep it pure to thy Glory.

93

As my Body without my Soul is a Carcase, so is my Soul without thy Spirit. A chaos, a Dark Obscure Heap of Empty faculties:

Ignorant of it self, unsensible of thy Goodness, Blind to thy
Glory: Dead in Sins and Trespasses. Having Eys I see not, having
Ears I hear not, having an Heart I understand not the Glory of 5
thy Works and the Glory of thy Kingdom. O Thou who art the
Root of my Being, and the Captain of my Salvation, look upon
me. Quicken me O Thou Life-giving and Quickening Seed.
Visit me with thy Light and thy Truth, let them lead me to thy
Holy Hill: and make me to see the Greatness of thy Lov in all its 10
Excellencies, Effects, Emanations Gifts and Operations. O my
Wisdom! O my Righteousness, Sanctification and Redemption;
let thy Wisdom Enlighten me, let thy Knowledg illuminat me,
let thy Blood redeem me, wash me and Cleans me, let thy Merits
justify me, O Thou who art Equal unto GOD, and didst suffer 15
for me. Let thy Righteousness clothe me. Let thy Will imprint
the Form of itself upon mine; and let my Will becom Conformable to thine: that thy Will and mine, may be united, and made
one for evermore.

94

Thy Will O Christ and thy Spirit in Essence are one. As therfore
thy Human Will is conformable to thy Divine; let my Will be
conformable to thine. Thy Divine Will is all Wisdom, Goodness,
Righteousness, Holiness, Glory and Blessedness. It is all Light and
Life and Love. It extendeth to all Things in Heaven and Earth, It 5
illuminateth all Eternity, it Beautifies the Omnipresence of GOD
with Glory without Dimensions. It is infinit in Greatness and
Magnifieth all that are united to it. Oh that my Will being made
Great by thine, might becom Divine, Exalted, Perfected! O Jesu
without Thee I can do nothing. O Thou in whom the fulness 10
of the GODhead Dwelleth I desire to learn of Thee, to becom
in Spirit like unto Thee. I desire not to learn of my Relations,
Acquaintance, Tradesmen Merchants or Earthly Princes to be
like unto them; but like unto Thee the King of Glory, and to
those who are thy Sons and Friends in another World. Grant 15
therfore, O Thou of whom the whole Family in Heaven and
Earth is named, that being Strengthened with Might by thy

Spirit in the Inner Man, I may be able to Comprehend with all
Saints, what is the Bredth and Length and Depth and Heighth,
20 and to know that Lov of Christ which Passeth Knowledg, that
I may be filled with all the fulness of GOD.

95

O Thou who Ascendedst up on High, and ledst Captivity Cap-
tiv, and gavest Gifts unto Men, as after thy Ascention into
Heaven thou didst send thy Holy Spirit down upon thine
Apostles in the form of a Rushing Mighty Wind, and in the
5 shape of cloven fiery Tongues; send down the Holy Ghost upon
me: Breath upon me, Inspire me, Quicken Me, Illuminat me,
Enflame me, fill me with the Spirit of GOD; that I may overflow
with Praises and Thanksgivings as they did. fill me with the
Riches of thy Glory, that Christ may Dwell in my Heart by faith,
10 that I being rooted and Grounded in Lov may speak the Wonderfull Works of GOD. Let me be Alive unto them: let me see them
all, let me feel them all, let me enjoy them all: that I may Admire
the Greatness of thy Lov unto my Soul, and rejoyce in Communion with Thee for evermore. How Happy O Lord am I,
15 Who am called to a Communion with GOD the father Son
and Holy Ghost, in all their Works and Ways, in all their Joys,
in all their Treasures, in all their Glory! Who hav such a Father,
having in Him the Fountain of Immortality Rest and Glory, and
the Joy of seeing Him Creating all Things for my sake! Such a
20 Son, Having in Him the Means of Peace and felicity, and the Joy
of seeing Him redeeming my Soul, by his sufferings on the Cross,
and doing all things that pertain to my salvation between the
father and Me: Such a Spirit and such a Comforter dwelling in
me to Quicken, Enlighten and Enable me, and to awaken all
25 the Powers of my Soul, that night and day the same Mind may be
in me that was in Christ Jesus!

96

O Thou who hast Redeemed me to be a Son of God, and called
me from vanity to inherit All Things, I Prais Thee, that having

Loved me, and Given thy self for me, Thou commandest us saying, As I hav loved you, so do ye also love one another. Wherin Thou hast commanded all Men, so to lov me, as to lay down their Lives for my Peace and Welfare. Since Lov is the End for which Heaven and Earth was made, enable me to see and discern the Sweetness of so great a Treasure. And since Thou hast Advanced me into the Throne of GOD, in the Bosom of all Angels and Men; commanding them by this Precept, to giv me an Union and Communion with Thee in their Dearest Affec⁄ tion; in their Highest Esteem; and in the most near and inward Room and Seat in their Hearts: Give me the Grace which S. Paul prayed for, that I may be Acceptable to the Saints; fill me with thy Holy Spirit, and make my Soul and Life Beautifull. make me all Wisdom Goodness and Lov, that I may be Worthy to be Esteemed and Accepted of them. That being Delighted also with their Felicity, I may be Crowned with thine, and with their Glory.

97

O Jesu, who having prepared all the Joys in Heaven and Earth for me, and redeemed me to Inherit thy Fathers Treasures; hast prepared for me the most Glorious Companions, in whose presence and Society I may Enjoy them: I Bless Thee for the Communion of Saints; and for thy Adorning the same, with all maner of Beauties, Excellencies, Perfections and Delights. O what a Glorious Assembly is the Church of the First Born, How Blessed and Divine! What Perfect Lovers! How Great and Honorable! How Wise! How sweet and Delightfull! Evry one being the End, evry one the King of Heaven; evry one the Son of GOD in Greatness and Glory; evry one the Intire and Perfect Friend of all the Residu; evry one the Joy of each others Soul; evry one the Light and Ornament of thy Kingdom; evry one thy Peculiar Friend, yet Loving evry one as thy Peculiar friend: and rejoycing in the Pleasures and Delights of evry one! O my God, make me one of that Happy Assembly. And let me lov evry one for whom Christ died, with a Lov as Great and Lively as His. That I may Dwell in Him, and He in me. and that

we all may be made perfect in one, even as Thou O Jesus art
20 in the Father and the Father is in Thee: that thy Lov may be in
us, and Thou in me for evermore.

98

Wisely O Jesu, didst Thou tell thy Disciples, when Thou
Promisedst them the Comforter, that the World cannot receiv
the Spirit of Truth: becaus it seeth Him not neither Knoweth
Him. But ye Know Him, for He Dwelleth with you, and shall
5 be in you. O let the Spirit of Truth dwell with me, and then little
matter for any other Comforter. When I see my self Beloved of the
Father: when I know the Perfection of thy Love, when the Father
and the Son loveth me, and both manifest themselvs unto me;
when they are near unto me and Abide with me for ever and
10 ever: little Harm can death do, or Sickness and Poverty. I can
never be alone becaus the Father and Son are with me. No
Reproaches can Discomfort me, no Enemies can hurt me. O let
me Know Thee Thou Spirit of Truth, be Thou always with me,
and Dwell within me. How is it Possible, but Thou shouldst
15 be an infinit Comforter; Who givest me a Being as Wide as
Eternity; a Well Being as Blessed as the Dietie, a Temple of
Glory in the Omnipresence of GOD, and a Light wherin to
Enjoy the New Jerusalem! An unmovable Inheritance, and an
Everlasting Kingdom that cannot be shaken! Thou art He who
20 shewest me all the Treasures in Heaven and Earth, who enablest
me to turn Afflictions into Pleasures, and to Enjoy mine Enemies:
Thou Enablest me to lov as I am Beloved, and to be Blessed in
GOD: Thou sealest me up unto the Day of Redemption, and
givest me a foretast of Heaven upon Earth. Thou art my God
25 and my Exceeding Joy, my Comforter and my Strength for evermore. Thou representest all things unto me, which the Father and
the Son hath don for me. Thou fillest me with Courage against all
Assaults and Enablest me to overcom in all Temptations; Thou
makest me Immovable by the very Treasures and the Joys which
30 Thou shewest to me. O Never leav me nor forsake me, but remain with me, and be my Comfort forever.

99

Wisely doth S. John say, We are the Sons of God; but the World knoweth us not becaus it knew Him not. He that Knoweth not the Spirit of God, can never Know a Son of GOD, nor what it is to be His Child. He made us the sons of GOD in Capacity by giving us a Power, to see Eternity, to Survey His 5 Treasures, to love his children, to know and to lov as He doth, to becom Righteous and Holy as He is; that we might be Blessed and Glorious as He is. The Holy Ghost maketh us the Sons of God in Act, when we are Righteous as He is Righteous, and Holy as He is Holy. When we prize all the Things in Heaven and 10 Earth, as He Prizeth Him, and make a Conscience of doing it as He doth after His similitude; then are we actualy present with them, and Blessed in them, being Righteous and Holy, as He is. then the Spirit of GOD dwelleth in us, and then are we indeed the Sons of God, a Chosen Generation, a Royal Priesthood, an 15 Holy Nation, a Peculiar People, Zealous of Good Works, shew⁄ ing forth the Praises of Him, who hath called us out of Darkness, into His Marvellous Light.

100

Christ Dwelling in our Hearts by Faith is an infinit Mystery. which may thus be understood. An Object Seen, is in the Faculty seeing it, and by that in the Soul of the Seer, after the Best of Maners. Wheras there are eight maners of In⁄being, the In⁄ being of an Object in a Faculty is the Best of all. Dead Things are 5 in a Room containing them in a vain maner; unless they are Objectivly in the Soul of a Seer. The Pleasure of an Enjoyer, is the very End why Things placed are in any Place. The Place and the Thing Placed in it, being both in the Understanding of a Spectator of them. Things Dead in Dead Place Effect nothing. 10 But in a Living Soul, that seeth their Excellencies, they Excite a Pleasure answerable to their value, a Wisdom to Embrace them, a Courage not to Forsake them, a Lov of their Donor, Praises and Thanksgivings; and a Greatness and a Joy Equal to their

15 Goodness. And thus all Ages are present in my Soul, and all Kingdoms, and GOD Blessed forever. And thus Jesus Christ is seen in me and dwelleth in me, when I believ upon Him. And thus all Saints are in me, and I in them. And thus all Angels and the Eternity and Infinity of GOD are in me for evermore. I being

20 the Living TEMPLE and Comprehensor of them. Since therfore all other ways of In-being would be utterly vain, were it not for this: And the Kingdom of God (as our Savior saith, this Way) is within you; let us ever think and Meditat on Him, that His conception Nativity Life and Death may be always within us.

25 Let Heaven and Earth Men and Angels, God and his Creatures be always within us. that is in our Sight, in our Sence, in our Lov and Esteem: that in the Light of the Holy Ghost we may see the Glory of His Eternal Kingdom, and Sing the Song of Moses, and the Song of the Lamb saying, Great and Marvellous

30 are thy Works Lord GOD Almighty, Just and true are thy Ways Thou King of Saints.

THE SECOND CENTURY

1

The Services which the World doth you, are transcendent to all
Imagination. Did it only sustain your Body and preserv your
Life, and Comfort your sences, you were bound to valu it as
much as those services were worth: but it Discovers the Being
of GOD unto you, It opens His Nature, and shews you his 5
Wisdom Goodness and Power, It Magnifies His Lov unto you,
It serves Angels and Men for you, It entertains you with many
Lovely and Glorious Objects, It feeds you with Joys, and be-
comes a Theme that furnishes you with perpetual Praises and
Thanksgivings, It enflameth you with the Lov of God, and is 10
the Link of your Union and Communion with Him. It is the
Temple wherin you are Exalted to Glory and Honor, and the
visible Porch or Gate of Eternitie. A sure Pledge of Eternal Joys,
to all them that Walk before God and are Perfect in it.

2

If you desire Directions how to enjoy it, Place yourself in it as if
no one were Created besides your self. And consider all the services
it doth, even to you alone. Prize those services with a Joy answerable to the value of them, be Truly Thankfull, and as Gratefull
for them, as their Merit deserves. And remember always how 5
Great soever the World is, it is the Beginning of Gifts. The first
Thing which GOD bestows to evry Infant, by the very Right
of His Nativity. Which becaus Men are Blind they cannot see;
and therfore know not that GOD is Liberal. from that first Error
they proceed, and multiply their Mistaking all along. They know 10
not themselvs nor their own Glory, they understand not His
Commandments, they see not the Sublimity of Righteous Actions,

they know not the Beauty of Truth, nor are acquainted with the Glory of the Holy Scriptures.

3

Till you see that the World is yours, you cannot weigh the Great⁄nes of Sin, nor the Misery of your fall, nor Prize your Redeemers Lov. one would think these should be Motives Sufficient to stir us up, to the Contemplation of GODs Works, wherin all the
5 Riches of His Kingdom will appear. For the Greatness of Sin proceedeth from the greatness of His Lov whom we hav offended from the Greatness of those Obligations which were laid upon us, from the Great Blessedness and Glory of the Estate wherin we were Placed, none of which can be seen, till Truth is
10 seen, a great Part of which is That the World is ours. So that indeed the Knowledg of this is the very real Light, wherin all Mysteries are Evidenced to us.

4

The Misery of your fall ariseth Naturaly from the Greatness of your Sin. For to Sin against infinit Lov is to make one self infinitly Deformed: To be infinitly Deformed, is to be infinitly Odious in His Eys, whose Lov of Beauty is the Hatred of Deformity. To be
5 infinitly odious in His Eys who once loved us with infinit Lov: to hav sind against all Obligations, and to hav faln from infinit Glory and Blessedness is infinit Misery: But cannot be seen, till the Glory of the Estate from which we are faln is Discerned. To be infinitly Odious in His Eys who infinitly loved us, maketh us
10 unavoidably Miserable: becaus it bereaveth us of the End for which we were Created, which was to Enjoy his Lov: and of the End also of all the Creatures which were made only to Manifest the same. For when we are bereaved of these, we liv to no purpose: and having lost the End to which we were Created, our Life is
15 cumbersom and irksom to us.

5

The Counsel which our Savior giveth in the Revelation, to the Church of Ephesus, is by all Churches, and by every Soul diligently to be observed. *Remember from whence thou art faln, and Repent.* Which intimates our Duty of Remembering our Happiness in the Estate of Innocence. For without this we can never 5 Prize our Redeemers Lov: He that Knows not to what He is redeemed cannot Prize the Work of Redemption. The Means cannot there be valued, where the End is despised. Since therfore by the Second Adam, we are restored to that we lost in the first: unless we valu that we lost in the first, we cannot truly rejoyce in 10 the second. But when we do, then all things receiv an infinit Esteem, and an Augmentation infinitly infinit, that follows after. Our Saviors Lov, His Incarnation, His Life and Death, His Resurrection, His Ascension into Heaven, His Intercession for us &c being then seen, and infinitly prized in a Glorious Light: as 15 also our Deliverance from Hell, and our Reconciliation unto God.

6

The Consideration also of this Truth, that the World is mine confirmeth my Faith. GOD having placed the Evidences of Religion in the Greatest and Highest Joys. For as long as I am Ignorant that the World is mine, the Lov of GOD is Defectiv to me. How can I believ that He gave His Son to die for me, who 5 having Power to do otherwise gave me nothing but Rags and Cottages? But when I see once that He gave Heaven and Earth to me, and made me in His Image to Enjoy them in His Similitude, I can easily believ that He gave His Son also for me. Especialy since He commanded all Angels and Men to lov me as 10 Him self: And so highly Honoreth me, that whatsoever is don unto me, He accounteth don unto Him.

7

Place yourself therfore in the midst of the World as if you were alone: and Meditat upon all the Services which it doth unto you.

Suppose the Sun were absent, and conceiv the World to be a
Dungeon of Darkness and Death about you: you will then find
5 His Beams more Delightfull then the Approach of Angels: and
loath the Abomination of that Sinfull Blindness, wherby you see
not the Glory of so Great and Bright a Creature, becaus the Air
is filled with its Beams. Then you will think that all its Light
shineth for you, and Confesse that GOD hath manifested Him⁄
10 self indeed, in the Preparation of so Divine a Creature. You will
abhor the Madness of those who esteem a Purs of Gold more
then it. Alass, what could a Man do with a Purse of Gold in an
Everlasting Dungeon? And shall we prize the sun less then it,
which is the Light and fountain of all our Pleasures? You will
15 then abhor the preposterous Method of those, who in an evil
sence are Blinded with its Beams, and to whom the presence of the
Light is the Greatest Darkness. For they who would repine at
GOD without the Sun, are unthankfull, having it: and therfore
only despise it, becaus it is Created.

8

It raiseth Corn to supply you with food, it melteth Waters to
Quench your Thirst, It infuseth Sence into all your Members, It
illuminates the World to entertain you with Prospects, It sur⁄
roundeth you with the Beauty of Hills and Valleys, It moveth and
5 laboreth Night and Day for your Comfort and Service; It
sprinkleth flowers upon the Ground for your Pleasure, and in all
these Things sheweth you the Goodness and Wisdom of a GOD
that can make one Thing so Beautifull, Delightfull, and Serviceable
having ordained the same to Innumerable Ends. It concocteth
10 Minerals, raiseth Exhalations, begetteth Clouds, sendeth down the
Dew and Rain and Snow, that refresheth and repaireth all the
Earth. And is far more Glorious in its Diurnal Motion, then if
there were two suns to make on either side a Perpetual Day: the
Swiftness wherby it moves in 24 hours about so vast an Universe
15 manifesteth the Power and Care of a Creator, more then any
station or Quiet could do. And producing innumerable Effects it
is more Glorious, then if Millions of Agents diversly did do them.

9

Did the Sun stand still that you might hav a perpetual Day, you would not know the sweetness of Repose: the Delightfull vicissitudes of Night and Day, the Early Sweetness and Spring of the Morning the Perfume and Beauty in the cool of the Evening, would all be swallowed up in Meridian Splendor: all which now 5 entertain you with Delights. The Antipodes would be empty, perpetual Darkness and Horror there, and the Works of God on the other side of the World in vain.

10

Were there two suns, that day might be alike in both Places, standing still, there would be nothing but Meridian Splendor under them and nothing but continual morning in other places, they would absume and Dry up all the Moysture of the Earth, which now is repaired as fast as it Decayeth, And perhaps when 5 the Nature of the Sun is Known, it is impossible there should be Two: At least it is impossible they should be more Excellent then this one: that we might Magnify the Diety and rest satisfied in Him, for making the Best of all possible Works for our Enjoyment. 10

11

Had the Sun been made one infinit Flame, it had been worse then it is. for there had been no Living; it had filled all Space, and devoured all other Things. So that it is far better being finit, then if it were infinit.

> Even as the Sea within a finit Shore 5
> Is far the Better 'caus it is no more.

Whence we may easily perceiv the Divine Wisdom hath atcheived things more then infinit in Goodness and Beauty. As a sure Token of their Perfect Excellency.

12

Entering thus far into the Nature of the Sun, we may see a little
Heaven in the Creatures. And yet we shall say less of the rest in
Particular: tho evry one in its Place be as Excellent as it: and this
without these cannot be sustained. Were all the Earth filthy
5 Mires, or Devouring Quicksands; firm Land would be an unspeakable Treasure. Were it all Beaten Gold it would be of no
value. It is a Treasure therfore of far Greater valu to a noble
Spirit, then if the Globe of the Earth were all Gold. A Noble
Spirit being only that which can Survey it all, and Comprehend
10 its Uses. The Air is Better, being a living Miracle as it now is, then
if it were Cramd and fild with Crowns and Scepters The Mountains are better then solid Diamonds, and those Things which
Scarcity maketh Jewels (when you enjoy these) are yours in their
Places. Why should you not render Thanks to God for them all?
15 You are the Adam, or the Eve that Enjoy them. Why should you
not Exult and Triumph in His Lov who hath done so Great
Things for you? Why should you not rejoyce and sing His
Praises? Learn to Enjoy what you hav first, and covet more if you
can afterwards.

13

Could the seas serv you were you alone, more then now they do?
Why do you not render Thanks for them? They serv you better
then if you were in them: evry thing serving you best in its Proper
Place. alone you were Lord over all: and bound to Admire His
5 Eternal Lov who raised you out of Nothing into this Glorious
World which He Created for you. To see infinit Goodness
Wisdom and Power making the Heavens and the Earth the
Seas, the Air the Sun and Stars! what Wonder, what Joy, what
Glory, what Triumph, what Delight should this afford! It is
10 more yours then if you had been made alone.

14

The Sun is but a little Spark of His infinit Lov. The Sea is but one
Drop of His Goodness. But what flames of Lov ought that Spark

to Kindle in your Soul; what Seas of Affection ought to flow for
that Drop in your Bosom! The Heavens are the Canopy and the
Earth is the footstool of your Throne: who reign in Communion 5
with GOD: or at least are called so to do. How lively should his
Divine Goodness appear unto you; how continualy should it rest
upon you; how deeply should it be impressed in you. Verily its
Impressions ought to be so deep, as to be always remaining always
felt, always Admired, always seen, and rejoyced in. You are never 10
truly Great till all the World is yours: and the Goodness of the
Donor so much your Joy, that you think upon it all day long.
Which King David, the Royal Man well understood, when He
said; My Lips shall be filled with thy Prais, and thy Honor all the
Day. I will make Mention of thy Loving Kindness in thy Holy 15
Temple.

15

The world servs you, as in serving those Cattle which you feed
upon, so in serving those Men, that Build and Plow, and Plant,
and Govern for you. It servs you in those that Pray and Adore and
Prais for you, that fill the World with Beauty and vertue; that are
made to lov. and Honor, to Pleas and Advance you with all the 5
Services that the Art of man can devise. So that you are alone in
the World, tho there are Millions in it beside. You are alone to
Enjoy and rejoyce in all, being the Adequat Object of His
Eternal Lov, and the End of all. Thus the world servs to promote
and Advance you.   10

16

These services are so Great, that when you enter into them, they
are ample fields and Territories of Joy: tho on the outside, they
seem so contemptible, that they promise Nothing. The Magnified
Pleasures of this corrupted World, are like the Egyptian Temples
in old time, that were Magnifica in frontispicio Ridicula in 5
Penetrali: They hav a Royal Frontispiece, but are Ridiculous
when you com in. These Hidden Pleasures: becaus they are Great
Common and Simple, are not understood.

17

Besides these immediat Pleasures here beneath, there are many Sublime and Celestial Services which the World doth do. It is a Glorious Mirror wherin you may see the verity of all Religion: Enjoy the Remainders of Paradice and Talk with the Dietie. 5 Apply yourself Vigorously to the Enjoyment of it. For in it you shall see the face of God: and by Enjoying it, be wholy Converted to Him.

18

You shall be Glorified, you shall liv in Communion with Him, you shall ascend into the Throne of the Highest Heavens; you shall be Satisfied, you shall be made Greater then the Heavens, you shall be Like Him, when you enjoy the World as He doth; 5 you shall converse with His Wisdom Goodness and Power abov all Worlds, and therfore shall Know Him. To know whom is a Sublime thing: for it is Life Eternal.

19

They that Quarrel at the maner of GODs revealing Himself, are troubled, becaus He is Invisible. yet is it Expedient that He should be so: for whatsoever is Visible is a Body: whatsoever is a Body excludeth other Things out of the place where it self is. If GOD 5 therfore being infinit, were Visible He would make it Impossible for any thing to have a Being Besides. Bulk as such, in it self is Dead. Whatsoever is Visible is so in like maner. that which inspireth Bulk with Motion Life and Sence is Invisible; and in it self distinct from the Bulk which it inspireth. Were GOD therfore pure Bulk, He could neither move nor Will nor desire any thing, but being invisible, He leaveth Room for, and Effecteth all Things. He filleth nothing with a Bodily presence but includeth all. He is Pure Life, Knowledg, and Desire, from which all things flow: Pure Wisdom Goodnes and Lov to which all Things 15 return.

20

Hence we may know The Reason why GOD appeareth not in a visible maner, is, becaus indeed He is invisible. they who are angry with with the Diety for not shewing Himself to their Bodily Eys are not displeased with that maner of Revelation, but that He is such a God as He is. By pretending to be visible He 5 would but Delude the World which as Plato observeth [is contrary to the nature of the Dietie]. But tho He is invisible, yet say they, He may assume a Body, and make Himself visible therin. We ask therfore what kind of Body they desire. for if He should take upon Him self a visible Body, that Body must represent som of 10 His Perfections. What Perfections then would they hav that Body to Express? If His Infinity, that Body then must be infinit. Upon which the same Absurdity would follow as before. for being infinit it would exclude all Being beside out of Place. If His Eternity; that cannot by a Body be represented. Neither is any 15 sence able to judge of Infinity or Eternity. for if He should re-present Himself by an infinit Wall; sight being too short might apprehend it self Defectiv, and be assured that it could not apprehend the Ends of that Wall; but whether it had Ends, which it self was not able to discern, it could not be satisfied. Would you 20 therfore hav it to Express some other of His Perfections; as Parti-cularly that of His Beauty? Beauty being a thing consisting of Variety, that Body could not be one simple Being, but must be sweetly temperd of a Manifold and delightfull Mixture of figures and Colors: be som such Thing as Ezekiel saw in his 25 Vision. for uniform Beauty the Sun is the most Delightfull: yet is not the Sun the most Delightfull Thing that is Possible. A Body more Beautifull then it may be made. Suppose therfore the most Beautifull that is Possible were created. What would follow? Being a silent and Quiet Object of the Ey, it would be 30 no more noted, then if it had not a Being. The most Beautifull Object being always present, grows common and despised. Even as a Picture is at first admired, but at length no more regarded then the bare Wall. Since therfore the most Beautifull thing that is Possible, being always continued, would grow into contempt; 35

how do we know, but the World is that Body, which the Diety hath assumed to manifest His Beauty and by which He maketh Himself as visible, as it is Possible He should?

21

When Amasis the King of Egypt sent to the Wise Men of Greece, to Know, Quid Pulcherrimum? upon due and Mature Consideration, they answered, The WORLD. The World certainly being so Beautiful that nothing visible is capable of more.
5 Were we to see it only once, that first Appearance would amaze us. But being daily seen, we observ it not. ancient Philosophers hav thought GOD to be the *Soul of the World.* Since therfore this visible World is the Body of GOD, not his Natural Body, but which He hath assumed; let us see how Glorious His Wisdom is,
10 in Manifesting Himself therby. It hath not only represented His infinity and Eternity which we thought impossible to be represented by a Body, but His Beauty also, His Wisdom, Goodness, Power, Life and Glory, His Righteousness, Lov, and Blessedness: all which as out of a plentifull Treasurie, may be taken and collected
15 out of this World.

First His Infinity; for the Dimensions of the World are unsearchable. An infinit Wall is a poor thing to Expresse his Infinity. a Narrow Endless Length is nothing: might be, and if it were, were unprofitable. but the World is round, and endlessly un-
20 searchable every Way. What Astronomer, what Mathematician, what Philosopher did ever comprehend the Measures of the World? The very Earth alone being round and Globous, is illimited. It hath neither Walls nor Precipices, nor Bounds, nor Borders. A man may lose himself in the midst of Nations and
25 Kingdoms. And yet it is but a Centre compared to the Univers. The Distance of the Sun, the Altitude of the Stars, the Wideness of the Heavens on evry side passeth the Reach of Sight, and Search of the Understanding. And whether it be infinit or no, we cannot tell. The Eternity of GOD is so apparent in it, that the
30 Wisest of Philosophers thought the World Eternal. We com into it and leav it as if it had neither beginning nor Ending.

Concerning its Beauty I need say nothing. No man can turn unto it, but must be ravished with its Appearance. only thus much, Since these things are so Beautifull, how much more Beautifull is the Author of them? Which was the Note and Observation of 35 the Wise Man in the Book of   But the Beauty of GOD is Invisible   it is all Wisdom, Goodness, Life and Lov, Power, Glory, Blessedness &c. How therfore shall these be Expressed in a Material World? His Wisdom is expressed in manifesting His Infinity in such a commodious maner. He hath made a Penetrable 40 Body in which we may stand, to wit the Air, and see the Heavens and the Regions of the Earth, at Wonderfull Distances. His Goodness is manifest in making that Beauty so Delightfull, and its Varieties so Profitable. The Air to breath in, the Sea for Moisture, the Earth for fertility, the Heavens for Influences, the Sun for 45 Productions, the Stars and Trees wherwith it is Adorned for in[—]numerable Uses. Again His Goodness is seen, in the End to which He guideth all this Profitableness, in making it serviceable to supply our Wants and Delight our Sences: to Enflame us with His Lov, and make us Amiable before Him, and Delighters in 50 His Blessedness. GOD having not only shewed us His Simple Infinity in an Endless Wall, but in such an Illustrious maner, by an infinit variety, that He hath drowned our Understanding in a Multitude of Wonders: Transported us with Delights, and En[—]riched us with innumerable Diversities of Joys and Pleasures. 55 The very Greatness of our felicity convinceth us, that there is a GOD.

22

His Power is evident by Upholding it all. But how shall His Life appear in that which is Dead? Life is the Root of Activity and Motion. Did I see a Man sitting in a Chair, as long as he was quiet, I could not tell but His Body was inanimat: but if He stirred, if He moved his Lips, or stretched forth his Arms, if he 5 breathd or twinkled with his Eys: I could easily tell He had a Soul within Him. Motion being a far greater Evidence of Life, then all Lineaments whatsoever. Colors and features may be in a

H

dead picture, but Motion is always attended with life. What shall
10 I think therfore when the Winds Blow, the Seas roar, the Waters
flow, the Vapours ascend, the Clouds flie, the Drops of rain fall,
the Stars march forth in Armies, the Sun runneth Swiftly round
about the World? Can all these things move so without a Life,
or Spring of Motion? But the Wheels in Watches mov, and so
15 doth the Hand that pointeth out the figures. This being a Motion
of Dead things. Therfore hath GOD created Living ones: that
by Lively Motions, and Sensible Desires, we might be sensible of
a Diety. They Breath, they see, they feel, they Grow, they flourish,
they know, they lov. O what a World of Evidences. We are lost in
20 Abysses, we now are absorpt in Wonders, and Swallowed up of
Demonstrations. Beasts Fowls and Fishes teaching and evidencing
the Glory of their Creator. But these by an Endless Generation
might succeed each other from Everlasting. Let us therfore survey
their Order, and see by that whether we cannot Discern their
25 Governer. The Sun and Moon and Stars shine, and by shining
minister influences to Herbs and flowers. these Grow and feed the
Cattle: the seas also and springs minister unto them, as they do
unto fowls and fishes. All which are subservient unto Man a
more Noble creature, endued with understanding to Admire His
30 Creator Who being King and Lord of this World, is able to
Prize all in a Reflexiv maner, and render Praises for all with Joy,
living Blessedly in the fruition of them. None can Question the
Being of a Dietie, but one that is ignorant of Mans Excellencies,
and the Glory of his Dominion over all the Creatures.

23

Abov all, Man Discovereth the Glory of GOD: who being
Himself Immortal, is the Divinest Creature. He hath a Dominion
over all the rest and GOD over Him. By Him, the Fountain of
all these Things is the End of them: for He can return to their
5 Author deserved Praises. Sences cannot resemble that which
they cannot apprehend; nor express that which they cannot
resemble, but in a shady maner. But Man is made in the Image of
GOD, and therfore is a Mirror and Representativ of Him. And

therfore in Himself He may see GOD, which is His Glory and Felicitie. His Thoughts and Desires can run out to Everlasting. 10 His Lov can extend to all Objects, His Understanding is an end⁄less Light, and can infinitly be present in all Places, ånd see and Examine all Beings, survey the reasons, surmount the Greatness, exceed the Strength, contemplat the Beauty, Enjoy the Benefit, and reign over all it sees and Enjoys like the EternalGODhead. 15 Here is an Invisible Power, an Indivisible Omnipresence, a Spiritual Supremacy, an Inward, Hidden, unknown Being Greater then all. a Sublime and Soveraign Creature meet to live in Communion with GOD in the fruition of them.

24

That you are a Man should fill you with Joys, and make you to overflow with Praises. The Priviledge of your Nature being in⁄finitly infinit. And that the World servs you in this fathomless maner, Exhibiting the Dietie, and ministering to your Blessedness, ought daily to Transport you with a Blessed Vision, into Ravish⁄ 5 ments and Extasies. What Knowledg could you have had of God by an unprofitable Wall tho endless and infinit? For tho as Things now are, nothing can be, but it exhibits a Dietie; as the Apostle saith, By Things that are seen the Invisible things of GOD are manifested, even His power and Godhead. becaus 10 evry thing is a Demonstration of His Goodness and Power; by its Existence and the End to which it is guided: yet an Endles Wall could never manifest His Being, were it present with you alone: for it would deny that Infinity by its unprofitableness, which it sheweth by its Endlessness. The true exemplar of GODs infinity 15 is that of your Understanding, which is a lively Patern and Idea of it. It excludeth Nothing, and containeth all Things. Being a Power that Permitteth all Objects to be, and is able to Enjoy them. Here is a Profitable Endlessness of infinit valu, becaus without it in finit Joys and Blessings would be lost, which by it are Enjoyed. 20 How Great doth God appear, in Wisely preparing such an Understanding to Enjoy his Creatures; such an Endles Invisible and Mysterious Receiver? And how Blessed and Divine are you,

to whom GOD hath not only simply appeared, but whom He
25 hath exalted as an Immortal King among all His Creatures?

25

You are able to see His Righteousness and Blessedness and
Glory, which are invisible. Yea, which is infinitly more, to resemble and attain them, to Express them in your self, Enjoying
them and the Similitud of them. No Beast can see what Righteous-
5 ness is. Nor is any Bruit capable of Imitating it. You are: being
admitted into the fellowship and Order of Angels. Which have
neither Eys nor Ears, and yet see and understand things, which
are infinitly Higher then the Sphere of sences. You are able to
Discern, that in all these Things He is Lov to you; and that Lov
10 is a fountain of infinit Benefits. That being Lov to you He hath
don the Best of all Possible Things and made you the End of all
Things. for Lov is a fountain of infinit Benefits, and doth all that
is Possible for its Beloved Object. It endlessly desireth to Delight
it self, and its Delight is to Magnify its Beloved. You are able to
15 see the Righteousness of Lov in this. For in doing the Best of all
Possible Things it is Right Wise to it self and to all other Beings.
Right wise to it self in Glorifying it self in the Best of Maners, and
to all other Things in making them most Excellent. Right Wise to
it self in preparing for it self the Best of Treasures, and to its Object
20 in like maner, in making its Beloved the most Blessed. Right Wise
unto it self, in satisfying it self in its infinit Desire of becoming
Delightfull to its Object, in preparing for it self infinit Pleasures,
and in making for it self the most Delightfull Object that can
Possibly be made. Right Wise unto you, in making you that
25 Object: and providing all the Treasures of it self for you, and
making it self infinitly Joyous and Delightfull to you. Nothing is
so Righteous, or Right-wise as Lov. For by Making it self Glorious
it becometh infinit: and by loving its Object infinitly it enableth
it self to Delight infinitly in its Objects Happiness: and Wisely
30 prepareth infinit Treasures Right wisely therby at once enriching
it self and its Object. So that you are able evidently to Discern
that GOD is Lov, and therin to contemplat all His Perfections.

26

You are able therin to see the infinit Glory of your High Estate. For if GOD is Lov, and Lov be so Restles a Principle in Exalting its Object: and so Secure that it always promoteth and Glorifieth and Exalteth it self therby, where will there be any Bounds in your Exaltation? How Dreadfull, how Amiable how Blessed, 5 how Great, how unsearchable, how incomprehensible must you be in your true real inward Happiness? The Object of Lov is infinitly Exalted. Lov is infinitly Delightfull to its Object, GOD by all His Works manifesteth Himself to be Lov, and you being the End of them, are evidently its Object. Go where you will, 10 here alone shall you find your Happiness. Contemplat therfore the Works of GOD, for they serv you not only in manifesting Him, but in making you to know yourself and your Blessedness.

27

As Lov is Righteous in Glorifying it self and making its Object Blessed: so is it in all its Dealings and Dispensations towards it. Having made it Amiable it cannot but lov it. Which it is Righteous in doing, for to lov what is Lovly is a Righteous Thing. To make it infinitly Amiable is a Righteous Thing to infinit Lov: and to 5 lov it infinitly being infinitly Amiable. For therby infinit Lov doth right to it self and its Measure: yea to it self and its Object. To tender what is Amiable is a Righteous Thing: to Hurt it is Evil. Lov therfore is infinitly Righteous in being infinitly tender of its Objects Welfare: and in hating infinitly the Sin of Hurting it. It is 10 Righteous in commanding others to promote it, and in punishing those that injure or offend it. And thus have you a Gate, in the Prospect even of this World, wherby you may see into GODs Kingdom. For by His Works you see that God is Lov, and by His Lov see the Nature of all Righteousness opened and un- 15 folded: with the Ground and foundations of Rewards and Punishments.

28

But GOD being infinit, is infinitly Righteous. His Lov therfore is Righteous to it self and all its Works as well as its Object. To it self in requiring that be infinitly Esteemed, of which it is infinitly Desirous. The Contemners of it therfore it infinitly
5 Punisheth. To its Works not only in making them the Best that may be, but in requiring an Exact and due esteem, from the Enjoyers of them. Is not Lov Jealous of the Honor of its Gifts? Doth not a Contempt of its Presents, redound upon it self? The World therfore serveth you abundantly in teaching you your
10 Duty. They daily cry in a Living maner, with a silent, and yet most loud voice. We are all His Gifts: We are Tokens and Presents of His Lov. You must therfore Esteem us according to the Beauty and Worth that is in us, and the Lov from whence we came. Which to do, is certainly the most Blessed Thing in all
15 Worlds, as not to do it is most Wicked and most Miserable.

29

Lov further manifests it self in joyning Righteousness and Blessedness together. For wherin can Lov appear more then in making our Duty most Blessed. Which here is don by Making Obedience the fruition of ones Blessedness. GOD cannot therfore but be
5 infinitly provoked, when we break His Laws. Not only becaus Lov is Jealous and Cruel as the Grave, but becaus also our Duty being so Amiable, which it imposeth on us with infinit Obligations, they are all Despised. His Lov it self, our most Beautifull Duty and all its Obligations. So that His Wrath must be very
10 Heavy, and his Indignation infinit.

30

Yet Lov can forbear, and Lov can forgiv. Tho it can never be reconciled to an unlovly Object. And hence it is, that tho you hav so little considered the Works of God, and Prized his Lov, yet you are permitted to live: and live at ease, and enjoy your Pleasure.

But Lov can never be reconciled to an Unlovely Object, and you
are infinitly unlovly by Despising GOD, and His Lov so long.
Yea one Act only of Despite done to the smallest Creature made
you infinitly deformed. What shall becom of you therfore since
GOD cannot be reconciled to an Ugly Object? Verily you are
in Danger of Perishing Eternaly. He cannot indeed be reconciled
to an ugly Object as it is Ugly but as it is capable of being
otherwise He may. He can never therfore be reconciled to your
sin, becaus sin it self is uncapable of being Altered: but He may
be reconciled to your Person, becaus that may be restored: and,
which is an infinit Wonder, to Greater Beauty and Splendor
then before.

31

By how much the greater His Lov was, by so much the Greater
may his Sorrow be at the Loss of His Object: and by so much the
Greater His Desire also of its Restauration. His Lov therfore
being infinit, may do infinit Things for an Object infinitly
valued. Being infinit in Wisdom it is able also to Devise a Way
Inscrutable to us, wherby to Sever the Sin from the Sinner: and
to satisfy its Righteousness in Punishing the Transgression, yet
satisfy it self in saving the Transgressor: And to purge away the
Dross and incorporated filth and Leprosy of sin: restoring the
Soul to its Primitiv Beauty Health and Glory. But then it doth
this at an infinit Expense wherin also it is more Delighted. And
especialy Magnified, for it giveth another equaly Dear unto it self
to suffer in its steed. And thus we com again by the Works of
God to our Lord JESUS CHRIST.

32

Whoever suffereth innocently and justly in anothers steed, must
becom a Surety by His voluntary Act. And this an Angel or a
Cherubim might hav done. He might also perhaps hav suffered
an infinit Punishment in the Removal of that Lov of GOD which
he infinitly prized: and perhaps also He might hav payed an

Obedience which He owed not. For the Angels are bound to lov God with all their Might, and Men as themselvs, while they are innocent: and to liv by loving them in their Blessedness and Glory; yet they are not bound by vertu of this Law to die for men
10 being Wicked and Deformed, and therfore in undertaking this might hav undertaken more then was their Duty: and perhaps Loving God infinitly, (had they seen his Lov to man) they would. Yea perhaps also they might hav sufferd in our Nature; and been able to hav sustained infinit Wrath; which are all the
15 Conditions usualy reckoned up and numberd by Divines, as requisit in a Mediator and Redeemer of others. for they might hav been Hypostaticaly united to our Nature and tho they were Creatures: yet almighty Power can sustain a Creature under as Great a Punishment as Almighty Power can inflict. Almighty
20 Power upholding it being like the nether Milstone, and almighty Power Punishing like the Upper Milstone, between which two it is infinitly tormented. We must therfore search Higher: into the Causes of our Saviors Prelation above them.

33

one Great Caus why no Angel was admitted to this office, was becaus it was an Honor infinitly too Great and Sublime for them. GOD accounting none but His own Son worthy of that Dignity. Wherfore it is written, No man taketh this Honor to Himself,
5 but He that is called of God, as was Aaron. Neither did Jesus (tho He were the Son of GOD) make Himself an High Priest, but He that said unto Him Thou art a Priest for ever after the order of Melchisedec. Nor yet was it forced or imposed upon Him, but He voluntarily undertook it. for which caus God hath highly
10 exalted him and given Him a name which is abov every Name in Heaven and Earth becaus being in the Form of God, he thought it not Robbery to be Equal with God, yet took upon him the form of a Servant and being found in the fashion of a Man would humble Himself to the Death of the Cross for our sakes.
15 Where we learn several strange and Admirable Things. first How High an Honor it is to suffer for God in this World. secondly

In what an infinit Dignity Man is exalted for whom God counted none Worthy to suffer but His own son. And Thirdly the Equity of Gods Proceeding in Chastising another for our sins: (against the Socinians who being Blind in this Mysterie, are the Enemies of our Saviors Diety in this World.) For had He imposed this task upon one that was unwilling it had been Injustice. Had he imposed it upon one that was unable to perform it it had been folly: had he imposed it upon any one to his Harm, Cruelty: But laying it upon one that was Willing and Able, to his Highest Benefit, it was Righteousnes Wisdom and Glory. All Mercy Goodnes and Lov on evry side.

34

How vile are they, and Blind and Ignorant, that will not see evry one to be the Heir of the World, for whose sake all this was done:! He that spared not his own Son but gav Him up for us all, how shall He not with Him also freely giv us all Things? Is not He an Object of infinit Lov for whom our savior Died? Shall not all Things in Heaven and Earth serv Him in Splendor and Glory, for whom the Son of God came down, to Minister in Agonies and Sufferings? O here Contemplat the Glory of Man, and his High Exaltation in the Throne of GOD. Here consider how you are Beloved, and be Transported with Excess of Joy at this Wonderfull Mystery. leave the Trash and vanities of the World, to live here in communion with the Blessed Trinity. imitate S. Paul, who counted all Things but Dross and Dung, for the Excellency of the Knowledg of GOD in Christ. And thus the Works of GOD serv you in teaching you the Knowledg of our Lord and Savior.

35

Another reason for which our Redemption was denied to Angels and reserved only to be wrought by our Savior, is the Dignity of Man. *for the Redemption of their Soul is Precious, and ceaseth for ever.* None of them can by any Means redeem Him, nor giv to GOD

5 a ransom for him. Having Sinned he must be Clothed in the Righteousness óf GOD or perish for ever. All the Angels and Cherubims in Heaven, tho their Righteousness should be imputed to Him could not justify Him. No Created Righteousness is able to Cover Him. The Exceeding Glory of His Primitiv
10 Estate being so great, that it made His Sin infinitly infinit.

36

Yet further another reason why this Office was delegated to none of them, was this: He that Died for us must by His own Merits save us. [It was not Convenient that the Righteousness of the Judg Himself should be accepted for ours: but the Righteousness
5 of another, who on our Behalf should appear before our Judge. for which caus it was necessary that another, and not the Judge, should be Righteous in our steed. And that in suffering, as well as doing. Now no Angel could be Righteous in suffering. becaus tho by Almighty Power sustaining he might be upheld to suffer
10 infinit Punishments, yet by His own Strength He could not suffer infinit Punishments, at least not so, as to be Virtuous and Meritorious in suffering them, for us. For to suffer Virtuously and Meritoriously is so to suffer as to lov the Inflicter in the Midst of Sufferings. Which no Angel under Infinit Torments by His own
15 Strength was able to do, being Hated of GOD.] Being therfore our Savior was to Merit for us, by His own Actions, it was necessary that He should be such an one, who, by His own Power could sustain infinit Punishments, and offer them up to GOD on our behalf with infinit Lov as a Voluntary Obedience. Which only
20 Christ was able to do out of the Treasurie of His own Fulness. For the Divine Essence in Him could overcom infinit Punishments, and infinitly lov the inflicter of them: without any Repining, Despondency, or Hatred, returned for the same. Where it is Curious to observ, how fully our Savior satisfied for us. We
25 Hated GOD when He loved us: our Savior not only Loved GOD, while GOD loved Him; but loved Him also with infinit Lov, even while He expressed Hatred against Him.

37

Finaly another reason, was the Dignity of our Saviors Person. Who being infinitly more Excellent then all Angels, was in His Condescentions infinitly more Acceptable. Which Excellency both of His Person and Condescention is not a little Magnified by His Eternity. By His Sufferings He brought in Eternal Righteous- 5 nes. That He should stoop down for our sakes was infinitly Meritorious. And since the Will before GOD is the Highest Deed: Accepting this from all Eternity, it is as if from all Eternity He had suffered for us. His Lov to GOD and Man, in this Act, was infinit and Eternal. And therfore is it said, That He through 10 the Eternal Spirit, offered up Himself a Sacrifice to GOD for us. His Eternal Spirit from Everlasting offered up it self, when He said, Lo, I com: in the volum of the Book is it written of me: to do thy will O GOD: And He offered up Himself through the Eternal Spirit in Time when He was slain upon the Cross. Now 15 no Creature can offer up it self Eternaly, becaus it was not from Everlasting. Nor can any thing Work Eternal Righteousness for us, but GOD alone.

38

How then should we be saved? Since Eternal Righteousnes must be paid for our Temporal Iniquity, Since one must suffer by his own strength on our Behalf, and out of his own Fulness defray our Debt of infinit charity, and that in the midst of suffer- ings; which no Angel nor Seraphim is able: since He must Pay an 5 Obedience which He did not owe: both in Loving men when themselvs were Hatefull, and in Loving God when He was Hated of Him: since none but GOD could do this, and it was inconvenient for GOD to do it: whither shall we flie for Refuge? Verily we are in a great Strait: but in the midst of these Exigences 10 Lov prepareth for it self an Offering. One Mighty to Save con- cerning whom it is Written, *This Day hav I begotten Thee.*

39

GOD by Loving Begot His Son. For GOD is Lov. And by
loving He begot His Lov. He is of Him self, and by Loving He
is what He is *Infinit Lov*. GOD is not a Mixt and Compounded
Being, so that His Lov is one thing and Himself another: but the
5 most Pure and Simple of all Beings, All Act, and Pure Lov in
the Abstract. Being Lov therfore it self, by Loving He begot
Lov. Had He not loved He had not been what He now is, The
GOD of Lov. The most Righteous of all Beings, in being infinitly Righteous to Him self, and all. But by Loving He is
10 infinitly Righteous to Himself, and all. For He is of Himself,
Infinitly Blessed and Most Glorious; And all His Creatures are
of Him, in whom they are infinitly Delighted and Blessed and
Glorious.

40

In all Lov there is a Lov begetting, a Lov begotten, and a Lov
Proceeding. Which tho they are one in Essence, subsist Nevertheless in Three Several Maners. For Lov is, Benevolent Affection to
another. Which is of it self, and by it self relateth to its Object. It
5 floweth from it self, and resteth in its Object. Lov proceedeth of
Necessity from it self. for unless it be of it self it is not Lov. Constraint is Destructiv and Opposit to its Nature. The Lov from
which it floweth, is the Fountain of Love. the Lov which
streameth from it is the communication of Lov, or Lov com-
10 municated. and the Lov which resteth in the Object is the Lov
which Streameth to it. So that in all Lov the Trinity is Clear. By
secret Passages without Stirring it proceedeth to its Object, and is
as Powerfully present as if it did not Proceed at all. The Lov that
lieth in the Bosom of the Lover, being the Lov that is perceived
15 in the Spirit of the Beloved: that is, the same in Substance, tho
in the Maner of Substance, or Subsistence, different. Lov in the
Bosom is the Parent of Lov, Lov in the Stream is the Effect of
Lov, Lov seen, or Dwelling in the Object proceedeth from both.
Yet are all three one and the self same Lov: tho three loves

41

Lov in the Fountain, and Lov in the Stream are both the same. And therfore are they both Equal in Time and Glory. For Lov communicateth it self: And therfore Lov in the fountain is the very Lov communicated to its Object. Lov in the fountain is Lov in the Stream, and Lov in the Stream Equaly Glorious with lov in 5 the Fountain. Tho it Streameth to its Object it abideth in the Lover, and is the Lov of the Lover.

42

Where Lov is the Lover, Lov streaming from the Lover, is the Lover; the Lover streaming from Himself: and Existing in another Person.

43

This Person is the Son of GOD: Who as He is the Wisdom of the Father, so is He the Lov of the Father. For the Lov of the Father is the Wisdom of the Father. And this Person did God by loving us beget, that He might be the Means of all our Glory.

44

This Person differs in Nothing from the Father but only in this that He is Begotten of Him. He is Eternal with the Father, as Glorious and as Intelligent. He is of the same Mind in evry Thing in all Worlds, Loveth the same Objects in as infinit a Measure. Is the Means by which the Father Loveth, Acteth, Createth 5 Redeemeth Governeth and Perfecteth all Things. And the Means also by which we see and Lov the Father: our Strength and our Eternity. He is the Mediator between GOD and His Creatures. God therfore being willing to redeem us by His own Blood (Act 20.) by Him redeemed us, and in His Person died for us. 10

45

How Wonderfull is it, that GOD by being Lov should prepare a
Redeemer to Die for us? But how much more Wonderfull, that by
this means Himself should be: and be GOD by being LOV! By
this means also He refineth our Nature, and enableth us to Purge
5 out the Poyson and the filthy Plague of Sin. for Lov is so Amiable
and Desirable to the Soul that it cannot be resisted. Lov is the
Spirit of GOD. In Himself it is the Father, or els the Son, for
the Father is in the Son, and the Son is in the father: In us it is
the H. Ghost. The Lov of GOD being seen, being GOD in us.
10 Purifying, Illuminating, Strengthening and Comforting the Soul
of the Seer. For GOD by shewing communicateth Himself to
Men and Angels. And when He Dwelleth in the Soul, Dwelleth
in the Sight. And when He Dwelleth in the Sight Atchieving all
that lov can do for such a Soul. And thus the World serveth you
15 as it is a Mirror wherin you Contemplat the Blessed Trinity. for
it Plainly sheweth that GOD is Lov, and in His being Lov you
see the Unity of the Blessed Trinity, and a Glorious Trinity in the
Blessed Unitie.

46

In all Lov there is some Producer, som Means, and som End:
all these being Internal in the Thing it self. Lov Loving is the
Producer, and that is the father; Lov produced is the Means, and
that is the Son: for Lov is the Means by which a Lover loveth.
5 The End of these Means is Lov: for it is Lov, by loving: and that
is the H. Ghost. The End and the Producer being both the same,
by the Means attained. for by Loving Lov attaineth it self and
Being. The Producer is attained by Loving, and is the End of
Himself. That Lov is the End of it self, and that GOD loveth
10 that He might be lov, is as evident to him that considers spiritual
Things, as the Sun. Becaus it is impossible there should be a
Higher End, or a Better proposed. What can be more Desirable
then the most Delightfull Operation; what more Eligible, then the
most Glorious Being; what further can be proposed then the most

Blessed and Perfect Life. Since GOD therfore chuseth the most 15
Perfect Life, what can be more Perfect, then that Life and that
Being which is at once the fountain, and the End of all Things?
There being in it the Perpetual Joy of Giving and Receiving infinit
Treasures. To be the Fountain of Joys and Blessings is Delightfull.
And by being Lov GOD is the fountain of all Worlds. To receiv 20
all and to be the End of all is Equaly Delightfull, and by Being
Lov GOD receiveth, and is the End of all. For all the Benefits
that are don unto all, by Loving all, Himself receiveth. What
Good could heaven and Earth do Him, were it not for His Lov
to the children of Men? By being what He is, which is Lov unto 25
all, He Enjoyeth all.

47

What Life can be more Pleasant, then that which is Delighted in
it self, and in all Objects; in which also all Objects infinitly
Delight? What Life can be more Pleasant, then that which is
Blessed in all and Glorious before all? Now this Life is the Life of
Lov. For this End therfore did He desire to Lov, that He might 5
be LOV. Infinitly Delightfull to all Objects, infinitly Delighted
in all, and infinitly Pleased in Himself, for being infinitly Delight‐
full to all, and Delighted in all. All this He attaineth by Lov.
For Lov is the Most Delightfull of all Employments: all the
Objects of Lov are Delightfull to it, and Lov is Delightfull to all 10
its Objects. Well then may Lov be the End of Loving, which is
so Compleat. It being a Thing so Delightfull, that GOD infinitly
rejoyceth in Him self for being Lov. And thus you see how GOD
is the End of Himself. He doth what He doth, that He may be
what He is: Wise and Glorious and Bountifull and Blessed in 15
being Perfect Lov.

48

Lov is so Divine and Perfect a Thing, that it is Worthy to be the
very End and Being of the Dietie. It is His Goodness, and it is
His Glory. We therfore so Vastly Delight in Lov, becaus all these

Excellencies and all other, Whatsoever lie within it. By Loving a
5 Soul does Propagat and beget it self. By Loving it does Dilate
and Magnify it self. By Loving it does Enlarge and Delight it self.
By Loving also it Delighteth others, as by Loving it doth Honor
and Enrich it self. But abov all by Loving it does attain it self.
Lov also being the End of Souls, Which are never Perfect, till they
10 are in Act, what they are in Power. They were made to lov and
are Dark and Vain and Comfortless till they do it. Till they lov
they are Idle, or misemployed. Till they lov they are Desolat; without their Objects: and Narrow and Little and Dishonorable: but
when they Shine by Lov upon all Objects, they are accompanied
15 with them and Enlightened by them. Till we becom therfore all
Act as GOD is, we can never rest, nor ever be satisfied.

49

Lov is so Noble, that it Enjoyeth others Enjoyments. Delighteth in
giving all unto its Object, and in seeing all Given to its Object.
So that Whosoever loveth all Mankind, He Enjoyeth all the Goodness of GOD to the whole WORLD: and Endeavoreth the
5 Benefit of Kingdoms and Ages. With all Whom He is present
by Lov, which is the best maner of Presence that is Possible.

50

GOD is present by Lov alone. By Lov alone He is Great and
Glorious. By Lov alone He liveth and feeleth in other Persons.
By Lov alone He enjoyeth all the Creatures, by Lov alone He is
Pleasing to Him self. By Lov alone He is Rich and Blessed. O
5 why dost not Thou by Lov alone seek to Atchiev all these! By Lov
alone attain another Self. By Lov alone live in others. By Lov attain
thy Glory. The Soul is shriveld up and Buried in a Grave that
does not Lov. But that which does love Wisely and Truly is the
Joy and End of all the World, the King of Heaven and the Friend
10 of GOD, the shining Light and Temple of Eternity: The Brother
of Christ Jesus, and One Spirit with the Holy Ghost.

51

Lov is a far more Glorious Being then flesh and Bones. If thou wilt it is Endless and infinitly more sweet then thy Body can be to Thee and others. Thy Body is confined, and is a Dull Lump of Heavy Clay, by which thou art retarded, rather then doest move: It was given thee to be a Lantern only to the Candle of Lov that shineth in thy soul. by it Thou dost see and feel and eat and drink: but the End of all is, that Thou mightest be as GOD is: a Joy and Blessing by being Lov. Thy Lov is illimited. Thy Lov can Extend to all Objects. Thy Lov can see GOD and Accompany His Lov throughout all Eternity. Thy Lov is infinitly Profitable to thy self and others. to thy self for therby mayst thou receiv infinit Good things: to others, for therby thou art prone to do infinit Good to all. Thy Body can receiv but few pleasures. Thy lov can feed upon all: Take into it self all Worlds, and all Eternities above all Worlds and all the Joys of God before and after. Thy flesh and Bones can do but little Good: nor that little unles as by Lov it is inspired and directed. A Poor Carcase thy Body is; But Lov is Delightfull and Profitable to thousands. O liv therfore by the more Noble Part. Be like Him who Baptizeth with fire. feel thy Spirit, Awaken thy Soul, be an Enlarged Seraphim. an infinit GOOD, or like unto Him.

52

The true WAY we may go unto His Throne, and can never Exceed, nor be too High. All Hyperbolies are but little Pigmies, and Diminutiv Expressions, in Comparison of the Truth. All that Adam could propose to Himself or hope for was laid up in Store for Him, in a Better Way then he could Ask or think: but in seeking for it a fals way He lost all: what He had in Hope, and what He had in Fruition. To be as GODs, we are Prompted to Desire by the Instinct of Nature. And that we shall be by Loving all as He doth. But by loving Him? what, O What shall we be? By loving Him according to the greatness of His Lov unto us, according to His Amiableness, as we ought, and according to the Obligations that lie upon us; we shall be no Man can devise

what. We shall lov Him infinitly more then our selvs, and therfore liv infinitly more in Him then in our selvs: and be infinitly more
15 Delighted with His Eternal Blessedness then our own. We shall infinitly more delight him then our selvs. All Worlds all Angels all Men All Kingdoms all Creatures will be more ours in Him then in our selvs: so will His Essence and Eternall GODHEAD. Oh Lov what hast Thou don!

53

And He will so lov us, when all this Beauty of Lov is within us, that tho we by our Lov to Him seem more Blessed in His Blessed⁄ness then He, He is infinitly more Blessed then we even in our Blessedness. We being so united to each other, that Nothing can
5 Divide us for evermore.

54

Lov is infinitly Delightfull to its Object, and the more Violent the more glorious. It is infinitly High, Nothing can hurt it. And infinitly Great in all Extremes: of Beauty and Excellency. Excess is its true Moderation: Activity its Rest: and burning Fervency its
5 only Refreshment. Nothing is more Glorious yet nothing more Humble: Nothing more Precious, yet nothing more Cheap: Nothing more familiar, yet nothing so inaccessible: Nothing more Nice, yet Nothing more Laborious: Nothing more Liberal, yet Nothing more Covetous: It doth all things for its Objects sake,
10 yet it is the most self Ended thing in the Whole World. for of all things in Nature it can least endure to be Displeased. Since ther⁄fore it containeth so many Miracles It may well contain this one more, that it maketh evry one Greatest, and among Lovers evry one is Supreme and Soveraign.

55

GOD by Lov wholy Ministereth to others, and yet Wholy ministereth to Himself. Lov having this Wonder in it also, that among innumerable Millions, it maketh evry one the sole and single End of all Things: It attaineth all Unattainables: and Atchieveth Impossibles. that is seeming Impossibles to our In- 5 experience, and Real Impossibles to any other Means or En- deavors. for indeed it maketh evry one more then the End of all Things: and infinitly more then the Sole Supreme and Soveraign of all. for it maketh Him so first in Himself: and then in all. For while All Things in Heaven and Earth fall out after my Desire, 10 I am the End and Soveraign of all: which conspiring always to Crown my Friends with Glory and Happiness: And Pleasing all in the same maner whom I lov as my self: I am in evry one of them the End of all things again: being as much concerned in their Happiness as my own. 15

56

By Loving a Soul does Propagat and beget it self. becaus before it loved it lived only in it self: after it loved, and while it loveth it liveth in its Object. Nay it did not so much as live in it self, before it loved. for as the sun would be unseen, did it not Scatter, and spread abroad its Beams; by which alone it becometh Glorious: 5 so the Soul without Extending, and living in its Object, is Dead within it self. an Idle Chaos of Blind and confused Powers. for which when it loveth, it gaineth Three Subsistences in it self by the Act of Loving. A Glorious Spirit that Abideth within: a Glorious Spirit that floweth in the Stream. A glorious Spirit that 10 resideth in the Object. Insomuch that now it can Enjoy a Sweet Communion with it self: in contemplating what it is in it self, and to its Object.

57

Lov is so vastly Delightfull in the Lover, becaus it is the Com- munication of His Goodness. for the Natural End of Goodness is to be Enjoyed: it Desireth to be anothers Happiness. Which Good- ness of GOD is so deeply implanted in our Natures, that we never Enjoy our selvs but when we are the Joy of others: of all our Desires 5 the Strongest is to be Good to others. We Delight in Receiving, more in Giving. We lov to be Rich: but then it is, that we therby

might be more Greatly Delightfull. thus we see the Seeds of
Eternity Sparkling in our Natures.

58

Lov is so vastly Delightfull to Him that is Beloved, becaus it is
the fountain of all Affections Services and Endeavors; a Spring of
Honor and Liberality, and a secure Pledge of future Benefits. It
is the sole Title by which we reign in anothers Bosom, and the
5 only Throne by which we are exalted. The Body and Soul of
Him that loves is His that is Beloved. What then can Lov deny?
All Greatness Power and Dominion befalleth Him that is Beloved, in the Soul that loveth Him. So that while all the Glorious
Creatures in all Worlds Lov you, you Reign in all Souls, are the
10 Image of GOD, and exalted like GOD in every Bosom.

59

Tho no Riches follow, yet we are all naturaly Delighted with Lov:
both for what we receiv, and for what we give. when we are
Beloved we receiv the Quintessence and Glory of anothers Soul,
the End of Heaven and Earth, the cream and flower of all Per-
5 fections. The Tribute of GOD almighty, Peace and Welfare
Pleasure and Honor, Help and Safety, all in readiness. And som
thing infinitly more which we are not able to Express. when we
are beloved we attain the End of Riches in an immediat maner;
and having the End need not regard the Means. For the End of
10 Riches is that we may be Beloved. we receiv Power to see our
selvs Amiable in anothers Soul, and to Delight and Pleas another
Person. For it is impossible to Delight a Luke Warm Person, or
an Alienated Affection with giving Crowns and Scepters, so as
we may a Person that violently loves us with our very presence and
15 Affections.

60

By this we may Discern what Strange Power GOD hath given
to us by loving us infinitly. [Who more Prizeth our Naked Lov

then Temples full of Gold: Whose Naked Lov is more Delight⁄
full to us then all Worlds: And Whose Greatest Gifts and
Treasures are Living Souls and Friends, and Lovers. Who as He 5
hath Manifested His Lov by giving us His Son, hath Manifested
it also by giving us all His Sons and Servants. Commanding
them to lov us with that Precious Lov wherwith they do them
selvs. but most] He giveth us a Power more to pleas him, then if
we were able to Creat Worlds and present them unto Him.   10

61

How Happy we are that we may liv in all, as well as one; and
how All sufficient Lov is, we may see by this: The more we liv in
all the more we liv in one. For while He seeth us to live in all, we
are a more Great and Glorious Object unto Him; the more we
are Beloved of all, the more we are Admired by Him; The more 5
we are the Joy of all, the more Blessed we are to Him. The more
Blessed we are to Him the Greater is our Blessedness. We are all
Naturaly Ambitious of being Magnified in others, and of seeming
Great in others. Which Inclination was implanted in us that our
Happiness might be Enlarged by the Multitud of Spectators.   10

62

Lov is the true Means by which the World is Enjoyed. Our Lov
to others, and Others Lov to us. We ought therfore abov all
Things to get acquainted with the Nature of Lov. for Lov is the
Root and Foundation of Nature: Lov is the Soul of Life and
Crown of Rewards. If we cannot be satisfied in the Nature of 5
Lov we can never be satisfied at all. The very End for which
GOD made the World was that He might Manifest His Lov.
Unless therfore we can be satisfied with his Lov so manifested we
can never be satisfied. There are many Glorious Excellencies in
the Material World, but without Lov they are all Abortiv. We 10
might spend Ages in Contemplating the Nature of the Sun, and
entertain our selvs many yeers with the Beauty of the stars and
Services of the Sea: but the Soul of Man is above all these, it com⁄

prehendeth all Ages in a Moment; and unless it perceiv somthing
15 more Excellent, is very Desolat. All Worlds being but a Silent
Wilderness, without som living Thing, more Sweet and Blessed
after which it Aspireth. Lov in the fountain, and Lov in the End
is the Glory of the World, and the Soul of Joy. Which it infinitly
preferreth abov all Worlds, and delighteth in, and loveth to Con-
20 templat, more then all Visible Beings that are Possible. So that
you must be sure to see Causes, wherfore infinitly to be Delighted
with the Lov of GOD, if ever you would be Happy.

63

See Causes also wherfore to be Delighted in your Lov to Men,
and Lov of Men to you. For the World serves you to this End,
that you might lov them and be Beloved of them. And unless you
are pleased with the End for which the World serves you, you can
5 never be pleased with the Means leading to that End. Abov all
things therfore Contemplat the Glory of Loving Men, and of
being Beloved of them. For this End our Savior Died, and for
this End He came into the World, that you might be restored from
Hatred, which is the Greatest Misery. From the Hatred of GOD
10 and Men which was due for Sin, and from the Misery of Hating
GOD and Men; for to Hate and be Hated is the Greatest Misery.
The Necessity of Hating GOD and Men being the Greatest
Bondage, that Hell can impose.

64

When you lov men, the World Quickly becometh yours: and
your self becom a Greater Treasure then the World is. For all their
Persons are your Treasures, and all the Things in Heaven and
Earth that serv them, are yours. For those are the Riches of Lov,
5 which minister to its Object.

65

You are as Prone to lov, as the Sun is to shine. It being the most
Delightfull and Natural Employment of the Soul of Man: with-

out which you are Dark and Miserable, Consider therfore the
Extent of Lov, its Vigor and Excellency. For certainly He that
Delights not in Lov makes vain the Univers, and is of Necessity 5
to Himself the Greatest Burden. The Whole World ministers to
you as the Theatre of your Lov. It sustains you and all Objects
that you may continu to lov them. Without which it were Better
for you to hav no Being. Life without Objects is Sensible Emptiness. Objects without Lov are the Delusion of Life. The Objects 10
of Lov are its Greatest Treasures: and without Lov it is impossible
they should be Treasures. For the Objects which we lov are the
Pleasing Objects, and Delightfull Things. And whatsoever is not
pleasing and delightfull to us can be no Treasure. Nay it is Distastefull, and Worse then Nothing, since we had rather it should 15
hav no Being.

66

That Violence wherwith som times a man doteth upon one
Creature, is but a little spark of that lov, even towards all, which
lurketh in His nature. We are made to lov: both to satisfy the
Necessity of our Activ Nature, and to answer the Beauties in
evry Creature. By Lov our souls are married and sodderd to the 5
creatures: and it is our Duty like GOD to be united to them all.
We must lov them infinitly but in God, and for God: and God
in them: namely all His Excellencies Manifested in them. When
we dote upon the Perfections and Beauties of som one Creature:
we do not lov that too much, but other things too little. Never was 10
any thing in this World loved too much, but many Things hav
been loved in a fals Way: and all in too short a Measure.

67

Suppose a River or a Drop of Water, an Apple or a Sand, an Ear
of Corn, or an Herb: GOD knoweth infinit Excellencies in it
more then we: He seeth how it relateth to Angels and Men; How
it proceedeth from the most perfect Lover to the most Perfectly
Beloved; how it representeth all His Attributs; How it conduceth 5
in its place, by the best of Means to the Best of Ends: And for this

Caus it cannot be Beloved too much. GOD the Author and GOD the End is to be Beloved in it: Angels and Men are to be Beloved in it: And it is highly to be Esteemed for all their Sakes.
10 O what a Treasure is evry Sand when truly understood! Who can lov any Thing that God made too much? His infinit Goodness and Wisdom and Power and Glory are in it. What a World would this be, were evry thing Beloved as it ought to be!

68

Suppose a Curious and fair Woman. Som have seen the Beauties of Heaven, in such a Person. It is a vain Thing to say they loved too much. I dare say there are 10000 Beauties in that Creature which they hav not seen. They loved it not too much but upon
5 fals causes. Nor so much upon fals ones, as only upon som little ones. They lov a Creature for Sparkling Eys and Curled Hair, Lillie Brests and Ruddy Cheeks; which they should love more-over for being GODs Image, Queen of the Univers, Beloved by Angels, Redeemed by Jesus Christ, an Heires of Heaven, and
10 Temple of the H. Ghost: a Mine and fountain of all Vertues, a Treasurie of Graces, and a Child of GOD. But these Excellencies are unknown. They lov her perhaps, but do not lov God more: nor Men as much: nor Heaven and Earth at all. And so being Defectiv to other Things, perish by a seeming Excesse to that.
15 We should be all Life and Mettle and Vigor and Lov to evry Thing. And that would Poys us. I dare Confidently say, that evry Person in the Whole World ought to be Beloved as much as this: And she if there be any caus of Difference more then she is. But GOD being Beloved infinitly more, will be infinitly more our
20 Joy, and our Heart will be more with Him. So that no Man can be in Danger by loving others too much, that loveth GOD as He ought.

69

The Sun and Stars Pleas me in Ministering to you. They Pleas me in ministering to a thousand others as well as you. And you pleas me becaus you can live and lov in the Image of GOD: not

in a Blind and Bruitish maner, as Beasts do; by a meer Appetite
and rude Propensitie, but with a Regulated well orderd Lov s
Upon Clear Causes, and with a Rational Affection, guided to
Divine and Celestial Ends. Which is to lov with a Divine and
Holy Lov, Glorious and Blessed. We are all Prone to Love, but
the Art lies in Managing our Love: to make it truly Amiable and
Proportionable. To lov for GODs sake, and to this End, that we 10
may be Wel Pleasing unto Him: to lov with a Design to imitate
Him, and to satisfy the Principles of Intelligent Nature and to
becom Honorable: is to lov in a Blessed and Holy maner.

70

In one Soul we may be entertained and taken up with innumerable Beauties. But in the Soul of Man there are innumerable
Infinities. One Soul in the Immensity of its Intelligence, is Greater
and more Excellent then the whole World The Ocean is but
the Drop of a Bucket to it, the Heavens but a Centre, the Sun s
Obscurity, and all Ages but as one Day. It being by its Understanding a Temple of Eternity, and GODs Omnipresence. between which and the whole World there is no Proportion. Its
Lov is a Dominion Greater then that which Adam had in
Paradice: And yet the fruition of it is but Solitary. We need Spec- 10
tators; and other Diversities of Friends and Lovers, in whose Souls
we might likewise Dwell, and with whose Beauties we might be
Crowned and entertained. In all whom we can dwell exactly: and
be present with them fully. Lest therfore the other Depths and
Faculties of our Souls, should be Desolat and Idle, they also are 15
Created to entertain us. And as in many Mirrors we are so many
other selvs, so are we Spritualy Multiplied when we meet our
selvs more Sweetly, and liv again in other Persons.

71

Creatures are Multiplied, that our Treasures may be Multiplied
their Places enlarged, that the Territories of our Joyes might be
Enlarged. With all which our Souls may be present in immediat

maner. For Since the Sun which is a poor little Dead Thing, can
at once shine upon many Kingdoms, and be wholy present, not
only in many Cities and Realms upon Earth, but in all the Stars
in the firmament of Heaven: surely the Soul which is a far more
perfect Sun, nearer unto GOD in Excellency and Nature, can do
far more. But that which of all Wonders is the most Deep is, that
a Soul, wheras one would think it could Measure but one soul,
which is as large as it: can exceed that, and Measure all Souls,
wholy and fully. This is an infinit Wonder indeed. for Admit
that the Powers of one Soul were fathomles and infinit: are not the
Powers so also of another? One would think therfore, that one
Soul should be lost in another: And that two Souls should be
exactly Adequate. yet my Soul can examine and search all the
Chambers and Endles Operations of another: being prepared to
see innumerable Millions.

72

Here is a Glorious Creature! But that which maketh the Wonder
infinitly infinit, is this. That one Soul which is the Object of
mine, can see all Souls, and all the Secret Chambers, and endless
Perfections, in evry Soul: Yea and All Souls with all their Objects
in evry Soul. Yet mine can Accompany all these in one Soul: and
without Deficiency exceed that Soul, and accompany all these in
evry other Soul. Which shews the Work of GOD to be deep and
Infinit.

73

Here upon Earth perhaps where our Estate is imperfect this is
Impossible: but in Heaven where the Soul is all Act it is necessary.
For the Soul is there all that it can be: Here it is to rejoyce in what
it may be. Till therfore the Mystes of Error and Clouds of Ignorance
that confine this Sun be removed: it must be present in all Kingdoms and Ages virtualy, as the Sun is by Night. If not by Clear
Sight and Lov, at least by its Desire. Which are its Influences and
its Beams. Working in a latent and obscure maner on Earth,
abov in a Strong and Clear.

74

The World serveth you therfore, in maintaining all People in all Kingdoms. which are your Fathers Treasures, and your as yet Invisible Joys, that their Multitudes at last may come to Heaven, and make those Innumerable Thousands, whose Hosts and Employments will be your Joy. Whose Order Beauty Melody and Glory will be your Eternall Delights. And of whom you hav many a Sweet Description in the Revelation. These are they of whom it is said: After this I beheld, and lo a great Multitude which no man could number of all Nations and Kindred and People and Tongues stood before the Throne and before the Lamb, clothed with White Robes and Palms in their Hands, and they cried with a loud voice, saying Salvation to our GOD which sitteth upon the Throne and to the Lamb: of which it is said, They fell down before the Lamb, having evry one of them Harps and Golden Vials full of Odors which are the Prayers of the Saints, and they sung a new song, saying Thou art Worthy to take the Book and to open the Seals therof: for Thou wast slain, and hast redeemed us to God by thy Blood, out of evry Kindred and Tongue and People and Nation: And hast made us unto our GOD Kings and Priests. of whom it is said, I saw a Sea of Glass, and they that had gotten the Victory over the Beast standing on it, and they Sing the Song of Moses the Servant of God, and the Song of the Lamb, saying *Great and Marvellous are thy works Lord GOD Almighty; Just and True are thy Ways Thou King of Saints. Who shall not fear Thee O Lord and Glorify thy Name. for Thou only art Holy: for all Nations shall com and Worship before Thee, becaus thy Judgements are made Manifest.*

75

That all the Powers of your Soul shall be turned into Act in the Kingdom of Heaven is manifest by what S. John writeth, in the Isle Patmos. And I beheld and I heard the Voice of many Angels round about the Throne: and the Beasts and the Elders, and the Number of them was ten thousand times ten thousand, and

Thousands of Thousands: saying, With a loud Voice, *Worthy is the Lamb that was slain, to receiv Power and Riches and Wisdom, and Strength and Honor and Glory and Blessing. And evry Creature which is in Heaven and on earth, and under the Earth, and such as are in the Sea,*
10 *And all that are in them, heard I saying, Blessing and Honor, and Glory and Power, be unto Him that sitteth upon the Throne and unto the Lamb for ever and ever.*

76

These Things shall never be seen with your Bodily Eys. but in a more perfect maner. You shall be present with them in your Understanding. You shall be In them to the very centre and they in you. As Light is in a Piece of Chrystal, so shall you be with
5 every Part and Excellency of them. An Act of the Understanding is the presence of the Soul, which being no Body but a Living Act, is a Pure Spirit, and Mysteriously fathomless in its true Dimensions. By an Act of the Understanding therfore be present now with all the Creatures among which you live: and hear them
10 in their Beings and Operations Praising GOD in an Heavenly Maner. Som of them Vocaly, others in their Ministery, all of them Naturaly and Continualy. We infinitly wrong our selvs by Laziness and Confinement. All Creatures in all Nations and Tongues and People Prais God infinitly; and the more, for being your Sole
15 and Perfect Treasures. You are never what you ought till you go out of yourself and walk among them.

77

Were all your Riches here in som little place: all other Places would be Empty. It is necessary therfore for your Contentment, and true Satisfaction, that your Riches be Dispersed evry where. Whether is more Delightfull; to have som few privat Riches in
5 one, and all other Places void, or to hav all places evry where filled with our Proper Treasures? Certainly to hav Treasures in all Places. for by that means we are entertained evry where with Pleasures, are evry where at home Honered and delighted, evry where Enlarged, and in our own Possessions. But to hav a few

Riches in som narrow Bounds, tho we should suppose a King- 10
dom full, would be to hav our Delights Limited, and Infinit
Spaces Dark and Empty, wherin we might wander without
Satisfaction. So that God must of necessity to satisfy His Lov
give us infinit Treasures. And we of Necessity seek for our Riches
in all Places.   15

78

The Heavens and the Earth serv you, not only in shewing unto
you your fathers Glory, as all Things without you are your Riches
and Enjoyments. But as within you also, they Magnify, and
Beautify and Illuminat your Soul. For as the Sun Beams Illuminat
the Air and All Objects, yet are them selvs also Illuminated by 5
them, so fareth it with the Powers of your Soul. The Rays of the
Sun carry Light in them as they Pass through the Air, but go on
in vain till they meet an Object: and there they are Expresst. They
Illuminat a Mirror, and are Illuminated by it. For a looking glass
without them would be in the Dark, and they without the Glass 10
unperceived. There they revive and overtake them selvs, and
represent the Effigies from whence they came; both of the Sun
and Heavens and Trees and Mountains, if the Glass be seated
conveniently to receiv them. Which were it not that the Glass were
present there one would have thought even the Ideas of them 15
absent from the Place. Even so your Soul in its Rays and Powers
is unknown: and no man would believ it present evry where,
were there no Objects there to be Discerned. Your Thoughts and
Inclinations pass on and are unperceived. But by their Objects
are discerned to be present: being illuminated by them. for they 20
are Present with them and Activ about them. They recover and
feel them selvs, and by those Objects live in Employment. Being
turned into the figure and Idea of them. For as Light varieth upon
all objects whither it cometh, and returneth with the Form and
figure of them: so is the Soul Transformed into the Being of its 25
Object. Like light from the Sun, its first Effigies is simple Life,
the Pure resemblance of its Primitive fountain but on the Object
which it meeteth it is quickly changed, and by Understanding
becometh All Things.

79

Objectiv Treasures are always Delightfull: and tho we travail Endlessly, to see them all our own is infinitly Pleasant: and the further we go the more Delightfull. If they are all ours wholy and soly, and yet nevertheless evry ones too, it is the most Delightfull
5 Accident that is Imaginable. for therby two Contrary Humors are at once Delighted, and two Inclinations, that are both in our Natures, yet seem Contradictory are at once Satisfied. The one is the Avaricious Humor and Lov of Propriety: Wherby we refer all unto our selvs and naturaly desire to hav all alone in our Private
10 Possession, and to be the alone and single End of all Things. This we perceiv our selvs becaus all universaly and evry where is ours. The other is the Communicativ Humor that is in us, wherby we desire to hav Companions in our Enjoyments to tell our Joys, and to spread abroad our Delights, and to be our selvs The Joy and
15 Delight of other Persons. For Thousands Enjoy all as well as wee: and are the end of all: And God communicateth all to them as well as us. And yet to us alone, becaus He communicateth them to us, and maketh them our Rich and Glorious Com- panions: to whom we may tell our Joys and be Blessed again.
20 How much ought we to Prais GOD, for satisfying two such Insatiable Humors that are contrary to each other. One would think it Impossible that both should be pleased, and yet His Divine Wisdom hath made them Helpfull and Perfectiv to each other.

80

Infinit Lov cannot be Expressed in finit Room: but must hav infinit Places wherin to utter and shew it self. It must therfore fill all Eternity and the Omnipresence of God with Joys and Treasures for my Fruition. And yet it must be Exprest in a finit Room: by
5 making me able in a Centre to Enjoy them. It must be infinitly exprest in the smallest Moment by making me able in evry Moment to see them all. It is both ways infinit, for my Soul is an Infinit Sphere in a Centre. By this may you know that you are infinitly Beloved: GOD hath made your Spirit a Centre in

Eternity Comprehending all: and filled all about you in an End⸍ 10
less maner with infinit Riches: Which shine before you and sur⸍
round you with Divine and Heavenly Enjoyments.

81

Few will believ the Soul to be infinit: yet Infinit is the first Thing
which is naturaly Known. Bounds and Limits are Discerned only
in a Secondary maner. Suppose a Man were Born Deaf and
Blind. By the very feeling of His Soul He apprehends infinit
about Him, infinit Space, infinit Darkness. He thinks not of 5
Wall and Limits till He feels them and is stopt by them. That
things are finit therfore we learn by our Sences. but Infinity we
know and feel by our Souls: and feel it so Naturaly, as if it were
the very Essence and Being of the Soul. The truth of it is, It is
individualy in the Soul: for GOD is there, and more near to us 10
then we are to our selvs. So that we cannot feel our Souls, but we
must feel Him, in that first of Properties infinit Space. And this
we know so Naturaly, that it is the only Primo et Necessario
Cognitum in Rerum naturâ. Of all Things the only first and
most Necessarily Known. for we can unsuppose Heaven and 15
Earth, and Annihilat the World in our Imagination. but the
Place where they stood will remain behind, and we cannot un⸍
suppose or Annihilat that do what we can. Which without us is
the Chamber of our Infinit Treasures, and within us the Reposi⸍
torie, and Recipient of them. 20

82

What shall we render unto God for this infinit Space in our
Understandings! Since in Giving us this He hath laid the founda⸍
tion of infinit Blessedness, manifested infinit Lov, and made us in
Capacity infinit Creatures. In this He hath glorified and Gratified
infinit Goodnes; Exerted infinit Power: and made Himself therby 5
infinitly Delightfull. and infinitly Great, in being Lord and Up⸍
holder of such infinit Creatures. for Being wholy evry where, His

omnipresence was wholy in evry Centre: and He could do no
more, then that would bear: Communicat Himself wholy in evry
10 Centre. His Nature and Essence being the foundation of His
Power, and of our Happiness: of His Glory and our Greatness
of His Goodness and our Satisfaction. For we could never believ
that He loved us infinitly unless He Exerted all His Power. for
κατὰ Δύναμίν. is one of the Principal Properties of Lov: as wel as
15 ἐκείνου ἔνεκα. To the utmost of its Power, as well as for His Sake.

83

He therfore hath not made us infinit Treasures only in Extent:
and Souls infinit to see and Enjoy them: which is to measure and
run Parallel with them: but in Depth also they are evry where
infinit being infinit in Excellency. And the Soul is a Miraculous
5 Abyss of infinit Abysses, an Undrainable Ocean, an inexhausted
fountain of Endles Oceans, when it will exert it self to fill and
fathom them. for if it were otherwise, Man is a Creature of such
Noble Principles and Severe Expectations, that could he perceiv
the least Defect to be in the Diety, it would infinitly Displeas
10 Him. The smallest Distaste, Spreading like a Cloud from a Hand
over all the Heavens. Neither will any pretence serv the turn to
cover our Cowardice: which we call Modesty, in not Daring to
say or expect this of the Dietie. Unless we expect this with infinit
Ardency, we are a Lazy Kind of Creatures Good for Nothing.
15 Tis Mans Holiness and Glory to Desire Absolut Perfection in
GOD, with a Jealousy and Care infinitly Cruel: for when we so
desire it, that without this We should be infinitly Displeased, and
altogether lost and Desperat for ever: finding GOD to hav exceeded all our Desires: it becometh the foundation of infinit Lov.
20 In the fruition of the fruits of which, we are to liv in Communion
with Him for evermore.

Space perfects its stature
Objects its lineaments
84
Affections its Colors
Actions its Graces

Your Soul being naturaly very Dark, and Deformed and Empty
when Extended through infinit but empty Space: the World servs
you in Beautifying and filling it with Amiable Ideas; for the
Perfecting of its Stature in the Ey of GOD. for the thorow Understanding of which you must know, That GOD is a Being whose   5
Power from all Eternity was prevented with Act. And that He is
One infinit Act of KNOWLEDG and *Wisdom*, which is infinitly Beautified with many Consequences of Lov &c. Being one
Act of Eternal Knowledge. He Knows all which He is Able to
Know. All Objects in all Worlds being seen in His Understand- 10
ing. His Greatness is the presence of His Soul with all Objects in
infinit Spaces: and His Brightness the Light of Eternal Wisdom.
His Essence also is the Sight of Things. For He is all Ey and all
Ear. Being therfore Perfect, and the Mirror of all Perfection, He
hath Commanded us to be perfect as He is Perfect: And we are 15
to Grow up into Him till we are filled with the Fulness of His
GODhead. We are to be Conformed to the Image of His Glory:
till we becom the Resemblance of His Great Exemplar. Which
we then are, when our Power is Converted into Act, and covered
with it we being an Act of KNOWLEDG and Wisdom as He 20
is. When our Souls are Present with all Objects, and Beautified
with the Ideas and figures of them all. For then shall we be *Mentes*
as He is *Mens*. We being of the same Mind, with him who is an
infinit Eternal mind. As both Plato and Cato with the Apostle
term Him.
                                                              25

    Si Deus est Animus sit Pura Mente Colendus.
    If GOD as verses say a Spirit be
    We must in Spirit like the Dietie
    Becom. We must the Image of His Mind
    And Union with it in our Spirit find.
                                                              30

Heaven and Earth, Angels and Men, GOD and All Things
must be contained in our Souls, that we may becom Glorious
Personages, and like unto Him in all our Actions.

K

85

You know that Lov receivs a Grandure of Valu and Esteem from the Greatness of the Person, from whom it doth proceed. The Lov of a King is naturaly more Delightfull then the Lov of a Beggar. The Lov of God more Excellent then the Lov of a King.
5 The Lov of a Beautifull Person is more Pleasing then that of one Deformed. The Love of a Wise Man is far more Precious then the love of a fool. when you are so Great a Creature as to fill Ages and Kingdoms with the Beauty of your Soul, and to reign over them like the Wisdom of the father filling Eternity with Light and
10 Glory, your Lov shall be Acceptable and Sweet and Precious. The World therfore serveth you, not only in furnishing you with Riches, and Making you Beautifull, and Great and Wise, when it is Rightly used: but in Doing that which doth infinitly concern you, in making your Lov precious. For abov all Things in all
15 Worlds you naturaly desire most Violently that your Lov should be Prized: and the reason is, becaus that being the Best Thing you can do or giv, all is Worthless that you can do besides: and you have no more Power left to be Good, or to Pleas, or to do any Thing, when once your Lov is despised.

86

Since therfore Lov does all it is able, to make it self accepted. both in increasing its own vehemence, and in Adorning the Person of that Lover; as well as in offering up the most chois and Perfect Gifts. With what care ought [you] to Express your Lov in
5 Beautifying your self with this Wisdom, and in making your Person Acceptable? Especialy since your Person is the Greatest Gift, your Lov can offer up to GOD Almighty. Clothe your self with Light as with a Garment, when you com before Him: Put on the Greatness of Heaven and Earth, Adorn your self with the
10 Excellencies of GOD Himself. When you prepare your self to Speak to Him, be all the KNOWLEDG and Light you are able, as Great as Clear and as Perfect as is Possible. So at length shall you appear before GOD in Sion: and as GOD convers with GOD for evermore.

87

GOD hath made it Easy to convert our Soul into a Thought con⁄
taining Heaven and Earth, not that it should be Contemptible
becaus it is Easy: but don, becaus it is Divine. Which Thought is
as easily Abolished, that by a Perpetual Influx of Life it may be
maintained. If He would but suspend his Power, no doubt but 5
Heaven and Earth would strait be abolished which He upholds
in him self as easily and as continualy, as we do the Idea of them
in our own Mind. Since therfore All Things depending so Con⁄
tinualy upon His Care and Lov, the Perpetual Influx of His
Almighty Power is infinitly Precious and His Life exercised 10
incessantly in the Manifestation of Eternal Lov, in that evry
Moment throughout all Generations He continueth without fail⁄
ing to uphold all Things for us. We likewise ought to Shew our
infinit Lov by Upholding Heaven and Earth, Time and Eternity,
GOD and all Things in our Souls, without Wavering or Inter⁄ 15
mission: by the perpetual Influxe of our Life. To which we are
by the Goodnes of All Things infinitly Obliged. Once to ceas is
to draw upon our selvs infinit Darkness, after we hav begun to be
so Illuminated: for it shews a forgetfulnes and Defect in Lov: and
it is an infinit Wonder that we are afterward restored.   20

89

Being that we are here upon Earth Turmoiled with Cares and
often Shaken with Winds and by Disturbances distracted: It is
the infinit Mercy of GOD, that we are permitted to Breath and
be Diverted. For all the Things in Heaven and Earth attend upon
us, while we ought to Answer and Observ them, by upholding 5
their Beauty within: But we are spared and GOD winketh at our
Defect, all the World attending us while we are about some little
Trifling Business. But in the Estate of Glory the least Intermission
would be an Eternal Apostasie. But there by reason of our infinit
Union with GOD ⋅it is Impossible.   10

90

We could easily shew that the Idea of Heaven and Earth in the Soul of Man, is more Precious with GOD then the Things them selvs, and more Excellent in nature. Which becaus it will surprize you a little, I will. What would Heaven and Earth be Worth,
5 were there no Spectator, no Enjoyer? As much therfore as the End is better then the Means, the Thought of the World wherby it is Enjoyed is Better then the World. So is the Idea of it in the Soul of Man, better then the World in the Esteem of GOD: It being the End of the World, without which Heaven and Earth would
10 be in vain. It is better to you, becaus by it you receiv the World, and it is the Tribut you pay. It more immediatly Beautifies and Perfects your Nature. How Deformed would you be should all the World stand about you and you be Idle? Were you able to Creat other Worlds, GOD had rather you should think on this. for
15 therby you are united to Him. The Sun in your Ey, is as much to you as the Sun in the Heavens. for by this, the other is Enjoyed. It would shine on all Rivers Trees and Beasts, in vain to you, could you not think upon it. The Sun in your Understanding illuminates your Soul, the Sun in the Heavens inlightens the Hemisphere.
20 The World within you is an offering returned. Which is infinitly more Acceptable to GOD Almighty, since it came from him, that it might return unto Him. Wherin the Mysterie is Great. For GOD hath made you able to Creat Worlds in your own mind, which are more Precious unto Him then those which He Created:
25 And to Give and offer up the World unto Him, which is very Delightfull in flowing from Him, but much more in Returning to Him. Besides all which in its own Nature also a Thought of the World, or the World in a Thought is more Excellent then the World, becaus it is Spiritual and Nearer unto GOD. The Material
30 World is Dead and feeleth Nothing. But this Spiritual World tho it be Invisible hath all Dimensions, and is a Divine and Living Being, the Voluntary Act of an Obedient Soul.

91

Once more, that I might Close up this Point with an infinit
Wonder; As among Divines it is said, That evry Moments Pre-
servation is a New Creation: and therfore Blessings continued
must not be Despised, but be more and more esteemed: becaus
evry Moments Preservation is another Obligation: even so in the 5
Continual Series of Thoughts wherby we continue to uphold
the Frame of Heaven and Earth in the Soul towards God, evry
Thought is another World to the Diety as Acceptable as the first.
Yea the Continuance puts an infinit Worth and Lustre on them.
For to be Desultory and Inconstant is the Part of a fickle and care- 10
less Soul: and make the Imagination of it Worthless and Despised.
But to continu Serious in Upholding these Thoughts for GODs
sake, is the Part of a Faithfull and Loving Soul: which as it
therby continues Great and Honorable with GOD, so is it therby
Divine and Holy: and evry Act of it of infinit Importance: and 15
the Continuance of its Life Transcendently Esteemed. So that tho
you can build or demolish such Worlds as often as you pleas;
yet it infinitly concerneth you faithfully to continue them: and
Wisely to Repair them. for tho to make them suddainly be to a
Wise Man very easy: yet to uphold them always is very Difficult, 20
a Work of unspeakable Diligence, and an Argument of infinit
Lov.

92

As it becometh you to retain a Glorious sence of the World, becaus
the Earth and the Heavens and the Heaven of Heavens are the
Magnificent and Glorious Territories of GODs Kingdom, so are
you to remember always the unsearchable Extent and illimited
Greatness of your own Soul; the Length and Bredth and Depth 5
and Height of your own Understanding. Becaus it is the Hous of
GOD, a Living Temple, and a Glorious Throne of the Blessed
Trinity, far more Magnificent and Great then the Heavens: yea a
Person that in Union and Communion with GOD, is to see
Eternity, to fill His Omnipresence, to Possess his Greatness, to 10
Admire his Lov, to receiv his Gifts, to Enjoy the World, and to

live in His Image. Let all your Actions proceed from a sence of this Greatness, let all your Affections extend to this Endles Wide-ness, let all your Prayers be animated by this Spirit and let all your
15 Praises arise and ascend from this fountain. For you are never your true self, till you live by your Soul more then by your Body, and you never live by your Soul, till you feel its incomparable Excellency, and rest satisfied and Delighted in the Unsearchable Greatness of its Comprehension.

93

The World does serv you, not only as it is the Place and Receptacle of all your Joys, but as it is a Great Obligation laid upon all Man-kind, and upon evry Person in all Ages to lov you as Himself: as it also Magnifieth all your Companions, and sheweth your heavenly
5 Fathers Glory. Yea as it Exalteth you in the Eys of the Illuminat, and maketh you to be Honored and Reverenced by the Holy. For there is not a Man in the Whole World that Knows GOD, or Him self, but he must Honor you: not only as an Angel or a Cherubim, but as one Redeemed by the Blood of Christ, Be-
10 loved by all Angels Cherubims and Men, an Heir of the World, and as much Greater then the Universe, as He that possesseth the Hous is Greater then the Hous. O what a Holy and Blessed Life would men Lead, what Joys and Treasures would they be to each other, in what a Sphere of Excellency would evry Man mov, how
15 Sublime and Glorious would their Estate be, how full of Peace and Quiet would the world be, yea of Joy and Honor, Order and Beauty, did Men perceiv this of them selvs, and had they this Esteem for one another!

94

As the World servs you by shewing the Greatness of GODs Lov to you, so doth it serv you as fuel to foment and increas your Praises. Mens Lips are closed, becaus their Eys are Blinded: Their Tongues are Dumb, becaus their Ears are Deaf: and there is no
5 Life in their Mouths, becaus Death is in their Hearts. But did

they all see their Creators Glory, which appeareth chiefly in the Greatness of His Bounty; did they all know the Blessedness of their Estate, O what a Place full of Joys, what an Amiable Region and Territory of Praises would the World becom; yea, what a Sphere of Light and Glory! As no man can Breath out more Air then he draweth in: so no man can offer up more Praises, then he receiveth Benefits, to return in Praises. For Praises are Transformed and returning Benefits. And therfore doth GOD so Greatly desire the Knowledg of Him, becaus GOD when He is Known is all Lov: and the Praises which He desires, are the Reflexion of His Beams: which will not return till they are Apprehended. The World therfore is not only the Temple of these Praises, and the Altar wheron they are offered, but the fuel also that Enkindles them, and the very Matter that composeth them. Which so much the more servs you, becaus it enkindles a Desire in you, that GOD should be praised, and moves you to take Delight in all that Prais Him. So that as it incites yours, it gives you an Interest in others Praises: And is a Valley of Vision, wherin you see the Blessed Sight, of all Mens Praises Ascending, and of all Gods Blessings coming down upon them.

95

The World serves you, as it teaches you more abundantly to Prize the Lov of Jesus Christ. For since the Inheritance is so Great to which you are restored, and no less then the Whole World is the Benefit of your Saviors Lov, how much are you to Admire that Person, that redeemed you from the Lowest Hell to the fruition of it? Your forfeiture was unmeasurable and your Sin infinit, your Despair insupportable, and your Danger Eternal: How Happy are you therfore, that you hav so Great a Lord, whose Lov rescued you from the Extremest Misery? Had you seen Adam turned into Hell, and going out of this fair Mansion which the Lord had given him, into Everlasting Torments, or Eternal Darkness: you would hav thought the World a Glorious Place, which was Created for him, and the Light of Eden would hav appeared in Greater Lustre then it did before: and his Lov by whom He was

15 recovered the Greatest Jewel. It is a Heavenly thing to understand
His Lov, and to see it well. Had Adam had no Esteem for the
Place to which he was restored, he had not valued the Benefit of
His Restitution. But now looking upon it with those Eys wher/
with Noble Men look upon their Territories and Palaces, when
20 they are going to Die, His Mercy who died for Him, that He after
his Condemnation might return again into his Dear Enjoyments,
maketh Him by whom they were purchased the Best and Greatest
of all Enjoyments. Darius when he had Conquerd Babylon, by
the Art of Zopyrus, who cut off His Nose and Ears and Lips,
25 that making the Babylonians to confide in him, he might deliver
up the City into the Kings hands; Admiring the fidelity and
Lov of Zopyrus protested, that He had rather hav one Zopyrus
whole, then ten Babylons. Even so We were our Spirits Divine
and Noble and Genuin, should by the Greatness of the Benefit be
30 Excited abov our selvs, and to exceed the Gift, in the Lov of our
Savior. Being afterwards Asked upon the Sight of a Pomgranat
slit in the Midst, What Thing he would above all other desire,
might he hav as many of them as there were Seeds in that
Pomgranat, answered, *Tot Zopyrorum:* As Many Zopyruses. One
35 Savior is worth innumerable Worlds.

96

The World is a Pomgranat indeed, which GOD hath put into
mans Heart, as Solomon observeth in the Ecclesiastes, becaus it
containeth the Seeds of Grace and the Seeds of Glory. All Virtues
lie in the World, as Seeds in a Pomgranate: I mean in the fruition
5 of it. out of which when it is sown in Mans Heart they Naturaly
arise. The fidelity of Zopyrus and the Lov of Darius are included
ih it. For when we Consider, how Great a Lord gave us so Great
a Dominion: we shall think it abominable to be Treacherous and
Unfaithfull in the Midst of his Dominions. When we consider we
10 cannot chuse but Sin, if we sin at all, being surrounded with His
Gifts. And that the land we tread on is of his Munificence: how
can we erre against Him who gav it to us? Can we forsake Him,
whose Gifts we cannot leav? The Whole World is Better then

Babylon: and at Greater Expence then Zopyrus Lips was it purchased for us.   15

97

This visible World is Wonderfully to be Delighted in and Highly
to be Esteemed, becaus it is the Theatre of GODs Righteous
Kingdom. Who as Himself was Righteous becaus He made it
freely, so He made it that We might freely be Righteous too. For
in the Kingdom of Glory it is impossible to fall. No man can sin 5
that clearly seeth the Beauty of Gods face: Becaus no Man can
sin against his own Happiness. that is, none can when he sees it
Clearly willingly and Wittingly forsake it. Tempter, Temptation,
Loss and Danger being all seen: but here we see His Face in a
Glasse, and more Dimly behold our Happiness as in a Mirror: 10
by faith therfore we are to live, and to sharpen our Ey that we may
see his Glory, We are to be Studious and Intent in our Desires
and Endeavors. For we may sin, or we may be Holy. Holiness
therfore and Righteousness naturaly flow out of our fruition of
the World: For who can vilify and debase Himself by any Sin, 15
while he Actualy considers he is the Heir of it? It exalts a Man to
a Sublime and Honorable life: it lifts him abov Lusts and Makes
Him Angelical.

98

It makes Him sensible of the Reality of Happiness: it feeds Him
with Contentment, and fils Him with Gratitude. it delivers him
from the Lov of Mony which is the Root of all Evil. it causes him
to reign over the Pervers Customs and Opinions that are in the
World: it opens his Eys, and makes him to see Mens Blindness 5
and Errors. it sateth His Covetousness, feedeth his Curiosity and
pleaseth his Ambition. it makes him too Great for Preferments
and Allurements. it causeth him to delight in Retirement: and to
be in lov with Prayer and Communion with GOD. it lifteth
him up abov mens Scandals and Censures. it maketh him Zealous 10
of the Salvation of all. it filleth him with Courage on the Behalf
of GOD. it makes him to rejoyce in a present visible immovable

Treasure to which the rest of the World is Blind, and strengthens his faith and Hope of Invisible. yea it makes Him Wise, and many 15 invisible Joys doth He see in this. Glory and Dominion are invisible Joys. And so is that Great Interest a Man hath to all Kingdoms and Ages. Which a true Possessor of the World is more sensible off, then of his Houses and Lands. It makes him Meek in Pardoning all injuries, becaus He is abov the Reach of his 20 Enemies: and infinitly Secure in the midst of His Fruitions. How Great a Thing is the Enjoyment of the World, how highly to be esteemed and how zealously to be thirsted after, that eminently containeth all these! Verily it is a Thing so Divine and Heavenly, that it makes vices and virtues almost visible to our very Eys.

99

Varro citeth 288 Opinions of Philosophers concerning Happiness: they were so Blind in the Knowledg of it, and so different in their Apprehension. All which Opinions fall in here, as all Rivers fall into the Sea, and Agree together. Som Placed Happi- 5 ness in Riches, and som in Honor, som in Pleasure, and som in the Contempt of all Riches Honor and Pleasure; som in Wisdom, and som in firm Stability of Mind, som in Empire, and som in Lov. Som in bare and Naked Contentment, som in Contemplation, and som in Action: som in Rest, and som in Sufferings, and 10 som in Victory and Triumph. All which occur here. For here is Victory and Triumph over our Lusts, that we might live the Life of Clear Reason, in the fruition of all Riches Honors and Pleasures which are by Wisdom to be seen, and by Lov to be Enjoyed in the Highest Empire, with Great Contentation, in Solitud alone, 15 in Communion with all, by Action and Contemplation, attaining it by Sufferings, and resting in the Possession, with Perfect Victory and Triumph over the World and evil Men, or Sin Death and Hell, Maugre all the Oppositions of Men and Divels. Neither Angels nor Principalities nor Power, nor Height nor 20 Depth, nor Things present nor Things to com, being able to seperat us, from the Lov of God which is in Christ Jesus our Lord.

100

Felicity is a Thing coveted of all. The Whole World is taken with the Beauty of it: and he is no Man, but a Stock or Stone that does not desire it. Nevertheless Great Offence hath been don by the Philosophers and Scandal given, through their Blindness, many of them in making Felicity to consist in Negativs. They tell us it doth not consist in Riches, it doth not consist in Honors, it doth not consist in Pleasures. Wherin then saith a Miserable Man, doth it consist. Why, in Contentment, in Self sufficiency, in Vertues, in the Right Government of our Passions, &c. Were it not better to shew the Amiableness of Virtues and the Benefit of the Right Government of our Passions, the Objects of Contentment, and the Grounds of Self sufficiency by the truest Means? Which these never do. Ought they not to Distinguish between true and fals Riches as our Savior doth; between Real and fained Honors? between Clear and Pure Pleasures, and those which are Muddy and unwholsom? The Honor that cometh from abov, the True Treasures, those Rivers of Pleasure that flow at his right hand for evermore are by all to be sought and by all to be desired. For it is the Affront of Nature, a making vain the Powers, and a Baffling the Expectations of the Soul, to deny it all Objects, and a Confining it to the Grave, and a Condemning of it to Death to tie it to the inward unnatural mistaken Self sufficiency and Contentment they talk of. By the true Government of our Passions, we disentangle them from Impediments, and fit and guid them to their proper Objects. The Amiableness of Virtue consisteth in this, that by it all happiness is either attained or Enjoyed. Contentment and Rest ariseth from a full Perception of infinit Treasures. So that whosoever will Profit in the Mystery of Felicity, must see the Objects of His Happiness, and the Maner how they are to be Enjoyed, and discern also the Powers of His Soul by which He is to enjoy them, and perhaps the Rules that shall Guid Him in the Way of Enjoyment. All which you have here GOD, THE WORLD, YOUR SELF. *All Things* in Time and Eternity being the Objects of your Felicity GOD the Giver, and you the Receiver.

THE THIRD CENTURY

1

Will you see the Infancy of this sublime and celestial Greatness?
Those Pure and Virgin Apprehensions I had from the Womb,
and that Divine Light wherewith I was born, are the Best unto
this Day, wherin I can see the Universe. By the Gift of GOD
5 they attended me into the World, and by his Special favor I
remember them till now. Verily they seem the Greatest Gifts His
Wisdom could bestow. for without them all other Gifts had been
Dead and Vain They are unattainable by Book, and therfore I
will teach them by Experience. Pray for them earnestly: for they
10 will make you Angelical, and wholy Celestial. Certainly Adam
in Paradice had not more sweet and Curious Apprehensions of
the World, then I when I was a child.

2

All appeared New, and Strange at the first, inexpressibly rare, and
Delightfull, and Beautifull. I was a little Stranger which at my
Enterance into the World was Saluted and Surrounded with
innumerable Joys. My Knowledg was Divine. I knew by Intuition
5 those things which since my Apostasie, I Collected again, by the
Highest Reason. My very Ignorance was Advantageous. I seemed
as one Brought into the Estate of Innocence. All Things were
Spotles and Pure and Glorious: yea, and infinitly mine, and Joyfull and Precious. I Knew not that there were any Sins, or Com-
10 plaints, or Laws. I Dreamed not of Poverties Contentions or
Vices. All Tears and Quarrels, were hidden from mine Eys.
Evry Thing was at Rest, Free, and Immortal. I Knew Nothing
of Sickness or Death, or Exaction, in the Absence of these I was
Entertained like an Angel with the Works of GOD in their
15 Splendor and Glory; I saw all in the Peace of Eden; Heaven and

Earth did sing my Creators Praises and could not make more Melody to Adam, then to me. All Time was Eternity, and a Perpetual Sabbath. Is it not Strange, that an Infant should be Heir of the World, and see those Mysteries which the Books of the Learned never unfold?   20

3

The Corn was Orient and Immortal Wheat, which never should be reaped, nor was ever sown. I thought it had stood from everlasting to everlasting. The Dust and Stones of the Street were as Precious as GOLD. The Gates were at first the End of the World, The Green Trees when I saw them first through one of the Gates 5 Transported and Ravished me; their Sweetnes and unusual Beauty made my Heart to leap, and almost mad with Extasie, they were such strange and Wonderfull Thing: The Men! O what Venerable and Reverend Creatures did the Aged seem! Immortal Cherubims! And yong Men Glittering and Sparkling Angels 10 and Maids strange Seraphick Pieces of Life and Beauty! Boys and Girles Tumbling in the Street, and Playing, were moving Jewels. I knew not that they were Born or should Die. But all things abided Eternaly as they were in their Proper Places. Eternity was Manifest in the Light of the Day, and som thing infinit Behind 15 evry thing appeared: which talked with my Expectation and moved my Desire. The Citie seemed to stand in Eden, or to be Built in Heaven. The Streets were mine, the Temple was mine, the People were mine, their Clothes and Gold and Silver was mine, as much as their Sparkling Eys Fair Skins and ruddy faces. 20 The Skies were mine, and so were the Sun and Moon and Stars, and all the World was mine, and I the only Spectator and Enjoyer of it. I knew no Churlish Proprieties, nor Bounds nor Divisions: but all Proprieties and Divisions were mine: all Treasures and the Possessors of them. So that with much adoe I was corrupted; and 25 made to learn the Dirty Devices of this World. Which now I unlearn, and becom as it were a little Child again, that I may enter into the Kingdom of GOD.

4

Upon those Pure and Virgin Apprehensions which I had in my Infancy, I made this Poem.

1

That Childish Thoughts such Joys Inspire,
Doth make my Wonder, and His Glory higher;
   His Bounty, and my Wealth more Great:
It shews His Kingdom, and His Work Compleat.
   In which there is not any Thing,
Not meet to be the Joy of Cherubim.

2

He in our Childhood with us Walks,
And with our Thoughts Mysteriously He talks;
   He often Visiteth our Minds,
But cold Acceptance in us ever finds.
   We send Him often grievd away,
Who els would shew us all His Kingdoms Joy.

3

O Lord I Wonder at Thy Lov,
Which did my Infancy so Early mov:
   But more at that which did forbear
And mov so long, though sleighted many a yeer:
   But most of all, at last that Thou
Thy self shouldst me convert, I scarce Know how.

4

Thy Gracious Motions oft in vain
Assaulted me: My Heart did hard remain
   Long time! I sent my God away
Grievd much, that He could not giv me His Joy.
   I careless was, nor did regard
The End for which He all those Thoughts prepard.

5

But now, with New and Open Eys,   25
I see beneath, as if I were abov the Skies:
     And as I backward look again
See all His Thoughts and mine most Clear and Plain.
     He did approach, He me did Woe.
I Wonder that my GOD this thing would doe.   30

6

From Nothing taken first I was;
What Wondrous things His Glory brought to pass!
     Now in the World I Him behold,
And Me, Inveloped in Precious Gold;
     In deep Abysses of Delights,   35
In present Hidden Glorious Benefits.

7

Those Thoughts His Goodness long before
Prepard as Precious and Celestial Store:
     With Curious Art in me inlaid,
That Childhood might it self alone be said   40
     My Tutor Teacher Guid to be,
Instructed then even by the Dietie.

5

Our Saviors Meaning, when He said, He must be Born again and
becom a little Child that will enter into the Kingdom of Heaven:
is Deeper far then is generaly believed. It is not only in a Careless
Reliance upon Divine Providence, that we are to becom Little
Children, or in the feebleness and shortness of our Anger and 5
Simplicity of our Passions: but in the Peace and Purity of all our
Soul. Which Purity also is a Deeper Thing then is commonly
apprehended. for we must disrobe our selvs of all fals Colors, and
unclothe our Souls of evil Habits; all our Thoughts must be
Infant-like and Clear: the Powers of our Soul free from the Leven 10
of this World, and disentangled from mens conceits and customs.

Grit in the Ey or the yellow Jandice will not let a Man see those
Objects truly that are before it. And therfore it is requisit that
we should be as very Strangers to the Thoughts Customs and
15 Opinions of men in this World as if we were but little Children.
So those Things would appear to us only which do to Children
when they are first Born. Ambitions, Trades, Luxuries, inordinat
Affections, Casual and Accidental Riches invented since the fall
would be gone, and only those Things appear, which did to
20 Adam in Paradice, in the same Light, and in the same Colors.
GOD in His Works, Glory in the Light, Lov in our Parents,
Men, our selvs, and the Face of Heaven. Evry Man naturaly seeing
those Things, to the Enjoyment of which He is Naturaly Born.

6

Evry one provideth Objects, but few prepare Senses wherby, and
Light wherin to see them. Since therfore we are Born to be a
Burning and Shining Light, and whatever men learn of others,
they see in the Light of others Souls: I will in the Light of my
5 Soul shew you the Univers. Perhaps it is Celestial, and will teach
you how Beneficial we may be to each other. I am sure it is a
Sweet and Curious Light to me: which had I wanted: I would
hav given all the Gold and Silver in all Worlds to hav Purchased.
But it was the Gift of GOD and could not be bought with Mony.
10 And by what Steps and Degrees I proceeded to that Enjoyment
of all Eternity which now I possess I will likewise shew you. A
Clear, and familiar Light it may prove unto you.

7

The first Light which shined in my Infancy in its Primitive and
Innocent Clarity was totaly ecclypsed: insomuch that I was fain
to learn all again. If you ask me how it was ecclypsed? Truly by
the Customs and maners of Men, which like Contrary Winds
5 blew it out: by an innumerable company of other Objects, rude
vulgar and Worthless Things that like so many loads of Earth and
Dung did over whelm and Bury it: by the Impetuous Torrent of
Wrong Desires in all others whom I saw or knew that carried me

away and alienated me from it: by a Whole Sea of other Matters
and Concernments that Covered and Drowned it: finaly by the 10
Evil Influence of a Bad Education that did not foster and cherish
it. All Mens thoughts and Words were about other Matters; They
all prized New Things which I did not dream of. I was a stranger
and unacquainted with them; I was little and reverenced their
Authority; I was weak, and easily guided by their Example: 15
Ambitious also, and Desirous to approve my self unto them. And
finding no one Syllable in any mans Mouth of those Things, by
Degrees they vanishd, My Thoughts, (as indeed what is more
fleeting then a Thought) were blotted out. And at last all the
Celestial Great and Stable Treasures to which I was born, as 20
wholy forgotten, as if they had never been.

8

Had any man spoken of it, it had been the most easy Thing in the
World, to hav taught me, and to hav made me believ, that Heaven
and Earth was GODs Hous, and that He gav it me. That the
Sun was mine and that Men were mine, and that Cities and
Kingdoms were mine also: that Earth was better then Gold, and 5
that Water was, every Drop of it, a Precious Jewel. And that
these were Great and Living Treasures: and that all Riches whatsoever els was Dross in Comparison. From whence I clearly find
how Docible our Nature is in natural Things, were it rightly
entreated. And that our Misery proceedeth ten thousand times 10
more from the outward Bondage of Opinion and Custom, then
from any inward corruption or Depravation of Nature: And that
it is not our Parents Loyns, so much as our Parents lives, that
Enthrals and Blinds us. Yet is all our Corruption Derived from
Adam: inasmuch as all the Evil Examples and inclinations of the 15
World arise from His Sin. But I speak it in the presence of GOD
and of our Lord Jesus Christ, in my Pure Primitive Virgin Light,
while my Apprehensions were natural, and unmixed, I can not
remember, but that I was ten thousand times more prone to Good
and Excellent Things, then evil. But I was quickly tainted and 20
fell by others.

9

It was a Difficult matter to persuade me that the Tinsild Ware
upon a Hobby hors was a fine thing. They did impose upon me,
and Obtrude their Gifts that made me believ a Ribban or a
Feather Curious. I could not see where the Curiousness or fine-
5 ness: And to Teach me that A Purs of Gold was of any valu
seemed impossible, the Art by which it becomes so, and the
reasons for which it is accounted so were so Deep and Hidden to
my Inexperience. So that Nature is still nearest to Natural Things.
and farthest off from preternatural, and to esteem that the Reproach
10 of Nature, is an Error in them only who are unacquainted with it.
Natural Things are Glorious, and to know them Glorious: But
to call things preternatural Natural, Monstrous. Yet all they do it,
who esteem Gold Silver Houses Lands Clothes &c. the Riches
of Nature, which are indeed the Riches of Invention. Nature
15 Knows no such Riches. but Art and Error makes them. Not the
God of Nature, but Sin only was the Parent of them. The Riches
of Nature are our Souls and Bodies, with all their Faculties
Sences and Endowments. And it had been the Easiest thing in the
whole World, that all felicity consisted in the Enjoyment of all
20 the World, that it was prepared for me before I was born, and
that Nothing was more Divine and Beautifull.

10

Thoughts are the most Present things to Thoughts, and of the
most Powerfull Influence. My Soul was only Apt and Disposed
to Great Things; But Souls to Souls are like Apples to Apples,
one being rotten rots another. When I began to speak and goe.
5 Nothing began to be present to me, but what was present in
their Thoughts. Nor was any thing present to me any other
way, then it was so to them. The Glass of Imagination was the
only Mirror, wherin any thing was represented or appeared to me.
All Things were Absent which they talkt not of. So I began
10 among my Play fellows to prize a Drum, a fine Coat, a Peny, a
Gilded Book &c. who before never Dreamd of any such Wealth.

Goodly Objects to drown all the Knowledg of Heaven and
Earth: As for the Heavens and the Sun and Stars they disappeared,
and were no more unto me than the bare Walls. So that the
Strange Riches of Mans Invention quite overcame the Riches of 15
Nature. Being learned more laboriously and in the second Place.

11

By this let Nurses, and those Parents that desire Holy Children
learn to make them Possessors of Heaven and Earth betimes. to
remove silly Objects from before them, to Magnify nothing but
what is Great indeed, and to talk of God to them and of His
Works and Ways before they can either Speak or go. For Nothing 5
is so Easy as to teach the Truth becaus the Nature of the Thing
confirms the Doctrine. As when we say The Sun is Glorious, A
Man is a Beautifull Creature, Soveraign over Beasts and Fowls
and Fishes, The Stars Minister unto us, The World was made
for you, &c. But to say This Hous is yours, and these Lands are 10
another Mans and this Bauble is a Jewel and this Gugaw a fine
Thing, this Rattle makes Musick &c. is deadly Barbarous and
uncouth to a little Child; and makes him suspect all you say,
becaus the Nature of the Thing contradicts your Words. Yet
doth that Blot out all Noble and Divine Ideas, Dissettle his 15
foundation, render him uncertain in all Things, and Divide him
from GOD. To teach him those Objects are little vanities, and
that tho GOD made them, by the Ministery of Man, yet Better
and more Glorious Things are more to be Esteemed, is Natural
and Easy.   20

12

By this you may see who are the Rude and Barbarous Indians
For verily there is no Salvage Nation under the Cope of Heaven,
that is more absurdly Barbarous than the Christian World. They
that go Naked and Drink Water and liv upon Roots are like
Adam, or Angels in Comparison of us. But they indeed that 5
call Beads and Glass Buttons Jewels, and Dress them selvs with

feather, and buy pieces of Brass and broken hafts of Knives of our
Merchants are som what like us. But We Pass them in Barbarous
Opinions, and Monstrous Apprehensions: which we Nick Name
10 Civility, and the Mode, amongst us. I am sure those Barbarous
People that go naked, com nearer to Adam God, and Angels in
the Simplicity of their Wealth, tho not in Knowledg.

13

You would not think how these Barbarous Inventions spoyle your
Knowledg. They put Grubs and Worms in Mens Heads: that are
Enemies to all Pure and True Apprehensions, and eat out all their
Happines. They make it impossible for them, in whom they
5 reign, to believ there is any Excellency in the Works of GOD, or
to taste any Sweetness in the Nobility of Nature, or to Prize any
Common, tho never so Great a Blessing. They alienat men from
the Life of GOD, and at last make them to live without GOD
in the World. To liv the Life of GOD is to live to all the Works
10 of GOD, and to enjoy them in His Image. from which they are
wholy Diverted that follow fashions. Their fancies are corrupted
with other Gingles.

14

Being Swallowed up therfore in the Miserable Gulph of idle talk
and worthless vanities, thenceforth I lived among Shadows,
like a Prodigal Son feeding upon Husks with Swine. A Comfortless Wilderness full of Thorns and Troubles the World was,
5 or wors: a Waste Place covered with Idleness and Play, and
Shops and Markets and Taverns. As for Churches they were
things I did not understand. And Scholes were a Burden: so that
there was nothing in the World worth the having, or Enjoying,
but my Game and Sport, which also was a Dream and being
10 passed wholy forgotten. So that I had utterly forgotten all Goodness Bounty Comfort and Glory: which things are the very Brightness of the Glory of GOD: for lack of which therfore He was
unknown.

15

Yet somtimes in the midst of these Dreams, I should com a litle to my self. so far as to feel I wanted som thing, secretly to Expostu⁄late with GOD for not giving me Riches, to long after an un⁄known Happiness, to griev that the World was so empty, and to be dissatisfied with my present State becaus it was vain and for⁄ 5 lorn. I had heard of Angels, and much admired that here upon earth nothing should be but Dirt and Streets and Gutters. for as for the Pleasures that were in Great Mens Houses I had not seen them: and it was my real Happiness they were unknown. for becaus Nothing Deluded me, I was the more Inquisitive.   10

16

Once I remember (I think I was about 4 yeer old, when) I thus reasoned with my self. sitting in a little Obscure Room in my Fathers poor House. If there be a God, certainly He must be infinit in Goodness. And that I was prompted to, by a real Whispering Instinct of Nature. And if He be infinit in Goodness, 5 and a Perfect Being in Wisdom and Love, certainly He must do most Glorious Things: and giv us infinit Riches; how comes it to pass therfore that I am so poor? of so Scanty and Narrow a fortune, enjoying few and Obscure Comforts? I thought I could not believ Him a GOD to me, unless all His Power were Em⁄ 10 ployd to Glorify me. I knew not then my Soul, or Body: nor did I think of the Heavens and the Earth, the Rivers and the Stars, the Sun or the Seas: all those were lost, and Absent from me. But when I found them made out of Nothing for me, then I had a GOD indeed, whom I could Prais, and rejoyce in.   15

17

Som times I should be alone, and without Employment, when suddainly my Soul would return to it self, and forgetting all Things in the whole World which mine Eys had seen, would be carried away to the Ends of the Earth: and my Thoughts would be deeply

5 Engaged with Enquiries, How the Earth did End? Whether Walls
did Bound it, or Suddain Precipices. or Whether the Heavens by
Degrees did com to touch it; so that the face of the Earth and
Heaven were so neer, that a Man with Difficulty could Creep
under? Whatever I could imagin was inconvenient, and my
10 Reason being Posed was Quickly Wearied. What also upheld
the Earth (becaus it was Heavy) and kept it from falling; Whether
Pillars, or Dark Waters? And if any of these, What then upheld
those, and what again those, of which I saw there would be no
End? Little did I think that the Earth was Round, and the World
15 so full of Beauty, Light, and Wisdom. When I saw that, I knew
by the Perfection of the Work there was a GOD, and was satisfied, and Rejoyced. People underneath and feilds and flowers with
another Sun and another Day Pleased me mightily: but more
when I knew it was the same Sun that served them by night, that
20 served us by Day.

18

Som times I should Soar abov the Stars and Enquire how the
Heavens Ended, and what was beyond them? concerning which
by no means could I receiv satisfaction. som times my Thoughts
would carry me to the Creation, for I had heard now, that the
5 World which at first I thought was Eternal, had a Beginning:
how therfore that Beginning was, and Why it was; Why it was
no sooner, and what was before; I mightily desired to Know. By
all which I easily perceiv that my Soul was made to live in Communion with GOD, in all Places of his Dominion, and to be
10 satisfied with the Highest Reason in all Things. After which it so
Eagerly aspired, that I thought all the Gold and Silver in the
World but Dirt, in comparison of satisfaction in any of these.
Som times I Wondered Why Men were made no Bigger? I would
have had a Man as Big as a Giant, a Giant as big as a Castle, and
15 a Castle as big as the Heavens. Which yet would not serv: for
there was infinit Space beyond the Heavens, and all was Defectiv
and but little in Comparison: And for him to be made infinit, I
thought it would be to no Purpose, and it would be inconvenient.

Why also there was not a Better Sun, and better Stars, a Better
Sea and Better Creatures I much admired. Which thoughts pro- 20
duced that Poem upon Moderation, which afterwards was written.
Som part of the verses are these

19

In Making Bodies Lov could not Express
It self, or Art; unless it made them less.
O what a Monster had in Man been seen,
Had every Thumb or Toe a Mountain been!
What Worlds must He devour when he did eat? 5
What Oceans Drink! yet could not all His Meat,
Or Stature, make Him like an Angel Shine;
Or make His Soul in Glory more Divine.
A Soul it is that makes us truly Great,
Whose little Bodies make us more Compleat. 10
An Understanding that is Infinit,
An Endles Wide and Everlasting sight,
That can Enjoy all Things and nought exclude,
Is the most Sacred Greatnes may be viewd.
Twas inconvenient that His Bulk should be 15
An Endless Hill; He nothing then could see.
No figure hav, no Motion, Beauty, Place,
No Color, feature, Member, Light, or Grace.
A Body like a Mountain is but Cumber.
An Endless Body is but idle Lumber. 20
It Spoils Convers, and Time it self devours,
While Meat in vain, in feeding idle Powers.
Excessiv Bulk being most injurious found,
To those Conveniences which Men have Crownd.
His Wisdom did His Power here repress, 25
GOD made Man Greater while He made Him less.

20

The Excellencies of the Sun I found to be of another kind then
that Splendor after which I sought, even in unknown and invisible
Services; And that GOD by Moderation Wisely Bounding His
Almighty power, had to my Eternal Amazement and Wonder,
5 made all Bodies far Greater then if they were infinit: there not
being a Sand nor Mote in the Air that is not more Excellent then
if it were infinit. How Rich and Admirable then is the Kingdom
of GOD; where the Smallest is Greater then an infinit Treasure!
Is not this Incredible? Certainly to the Placits and Doctrines of
10 the Scholes: Till we all Consider, That infinit Worth shut up in
the Limits of a Material Being, is the only way to a Real Infinity.
GOD made Nothing infinit in Bulk, but evry thing there where
it ought to be. Which, becaus Moderation is a Vertu observing
the Golden Mean, in som other parts of the former Poem, is thus
15 Expressed.

21

His Power Bounded, Greater is in Might,
Then if let loos, twere wholy infinit.
He could hav made an Endless Sea by this.
But then it had not been a Sea of Bliss.
5 Did Waters from the Centre to the Skies
Ascend, twould drown whatever els we Prize
The Ocean bounded in a finit Shore,
Is better far becaus it is no more.
No Use nor Glory would in that be seen,
10 His Power made it Endless in Esteem.
Had not the Sun been bounded in its Sphere,
Did all the World in one fair flame appear
And were that flame a real Infinit
Twould yeeld no Profit Splendor nor Delight.
15 Its Corps confind, and Beams extended be
Effects of Wisdom in the Dietie.
One Star made infinit would all Exclude.
An Earth made infinit could nere be Viewd.

But one being fashioned for the others sake,
He bounding all, did all most usefull make: 20
And which is best, in Profit and Delight
Tho not in Bulk, they all are infinit.

22

These Liquid Clear Satisfactions, were the Emanations of the
Highest Reason, but not atchieved till a long time afterwards In
the mean time I was som times tho seldom visited and inspired
with New and more vigorous Desires after that Bliss which Nature
Whispered and Suggested to me. Evry New Thing Quickened 5
my Curiosity and raised my Expectation. I remember once, the
first time I came into a Magnificent or Noble Dining Room, and
was left there alone, I rejoyced to see the Gold and State and
Carved Imagery. but when all was Dead, and there was no
Motion, I was weary of it, and departed Dissatisfied. But after- 10
wards, when I saw it full of Lords and Ladies and Musick and
Dancing, the Place which once seemed not to differ from a
Solitary Den, had now Entertainment and nothing of Tedious-
ness but pleasure in it. By which I perceived (upon a Reflexion
made long after) That Men and Women are when well under- 15
stood a Principal Part of our True felicity. By this I found also
that nothing that stood still, could by doing so be a Part of
Happiness: and that Affection, tho it were invisible, was the best
of Motions. But the August and Glorious Exercise of Virtue,
was more Solemn and Divine which yet I saw not. And that all 20
Men and Angels should appear in Heaven.

23

Another time, in a Lowering and sad Evening, being alone in the
field, when all things were dead and quiet, a certain Want and
Horror fell upon me, beyond imagination. The unprofitableness
and Silence of the Place dissatisfied me, its Wideness terrified me,
from the utmost Ends of the Earth fears surrounded me. How did 5
I know but Dangers might suddainly arise from the East, and

invade me from the unknown Regions beyond the Seas? I was a
Weak and little child, and had forgotten there was a man alive in
the Earth. Yet som thing also of Hope and Expectation comforted
10 me from every Border. This taught me that I was concerned in all
the World: and that in the remotest Borders the Causes of Peace
delight me, and the Beauties of the Earth when seen were made to
entertain me: that I was made to hold a Communion with the
Secrets of Divine Providence in all the World: that a Remem⸝
15 brance of all the Joys I had from my Birth ought always to be with
me: that the Presence of Cities Temples and Kingdoms ought to
Sustain me, and that to be alone in the World was to be Desolate
and Miserable. The Comfort of Houses and friends, and the clear
Assurance of Treasures evry where, Gods Care and Lov, His
20 Goodnes Wisdom, and Power, His presence and Watchfulness
in all the Ends of the Earth, were my Strength and Assurance for
ever: and that these things being Absent to my Ey, were my Joys
and consolations: as present to my Understanding as the Wideness
and Emptiness of the Universe which I saw before me.

24

When I heard of any New Kingdom beyond the seas, the Light
and Glory of it pleased me immediatly, enterd into me, it rose up
within me and I was Enlarged Wonderfully. I entered into it, I
saw its Commodities, Rarities, Springs, Meadows Riches, In⸝
5 habitan[t]s, and became Possessor of that New Room, as if it had
been prepared for me, so much was I Magnified and Delighted in
it. When the Bible was read my Spirit was present in other Ages.
I saw the Light and Splendor of them: the Land of Canaan, the
Israelites entering into it, the ancient Glory of the Amorites, their
10 Peace and Riches, their Cities Houses Vines and Fig trees, the
long Prosperity of their Kings, their Milk and Honie, their
slaughter and Destruction, with the Joys and Triumphs of GODs
People all which Entered into me, and GOD among them. I saw
all and felt all in such a lively maner, as if there had been no other
15 Way to those Places, but in Spirit only. This shewd me the Liveli⸝
ness of interior presence, and that all Ages were for most Glorious

Ends, Accessible to my Understanding, yea with it, yea within it.
for without changing Place in my self I could behold and Enjoy
all those. Any thing when it was proposed, tho it was 10000 Ages
agoe, being always before me.   20

25

When I heard any News I received it with Greediness and Delight,
becaus my Expectation was awakend with som Hope that My
Happiness and the Thing I wanted was concealed in it. Glad
Tidings you know from a far Country brings us our Salvation:
And I was not deceived. In Jury was Jesus Killed, and from 5
Jerusalem the Gospel came. Which when I once knew I was very
Confident that evry Kingdom contained like Wonders and Causes
of Joy, tho that was the fountain of them. As it was the First fruits
so was it the Pledg of what I shall receiv in other Countries.
Thus also when any curious Cabinet, or secret in Chymistrie, 10
Geometry or Physick was offered to me, I diligently looked in it,
but when I saw it to the Bottom and not my Happiness I despised
it. These Imaginations and this Thirst of News occasioned these
Refléxions.

26

On News

I

News from a forrein Country came,
As if my Treasure and my Wealth lay there:
So much it did my Heart Enflame!
Twas wont to call my Soul into mine Ear.
Which thither went to Meet   5
The Approaching Sweet:
And on the Threshhold stood,
To entertain the Unknown Good.
It Hoverd there,
As if twould leav mine Ear.   10

And was so Eager to Embrace
The Joyfull Tidings as they came,
Twould almost leav its Dwelling Place,
To Entertain the Same.

2

15 As if the Tidings were the Things,
My very Joys themselvs, my forrein Treasure,
Or els did bear them on their Wings;
With so much Joy they came, with so much Pleasure.
My Soul stood at the Gate
20 To recreat
It self with Bliss: And to
Be pleasd with Speed. A fuller View
It fain would take
Yet Journeys back would make
25 Unto my Heart: as if twould fain
Go out to meet, yet stay within
To fit a place, to Entertain,
And bring the Tidings in.

3

What Sacred Instinct did inspire
30 My Soul in Childhood with a Hope so Strong?
What Secret Force movd my Desire,
To Expect my Joys beyond the Seas, so Yong?
Felicity I knew
Was out of View:
35 And being here alone,
I saw that Happiness was gone,
From Me! for this,
I Thirsted Absent Bliss,
And thought that sure beyond the Seas,
40 Or els in som thing near at hand
I knew not yet, (since nought did pleas
I knew.) my Bliss did stand.

4

But little did the Infant Dream
That all the Treasures of the World were by:
And that Himself was so the Cream   45
And Crown of all, which round about did lie.
           Yet thus it was. The Gem,
                The Diadem,
                The Ring Enclosing all
           That Stood upon this Earthy Ball;   50
                The Heavenly Ey,
                Much Wider then the Skie,
           Wher in they all included were
           The Glorious Soul that was the King
           Made to possess them, did appear   55
                A Small and little thing!

27

Among other things, there befel me a most infinit Desire of a Book
from Heaven. for observing all things to be rude and superfluous
here upon Earth I thought the Ways of felicity to be known only
among the Holy Angels: and that unless I could receiv informa⁄
tion from them, I could never be Happy. This Thirst hung upon 5
me a long time; Till at last I perceived that the God of Angels
had taken Care of me, and prevented my Desires. For He had
sent the Book I wanted before I was Born: and prepared it for me,
and also commended, and sent it unto me, in a far better maner
then I was able to imagine. Had som Angel brought it to me, 10
which was the best way wherin I could then desire it, it would
hav been a peculiar favor, and I should hav thought myself
therin Honored abov all Mankind. It would hav been the Soul
of this world, the Light of my Soul, the Spring of Life, and a
fountain of Happiness. You cannot think what Riches and De⁄ 15
lights I promised myself therin. It would hav been a Mine of
Rarities, Curiosities and Wonders, to hav entertained the Powers
of my Soul, to hav directed me in the Way of Life, and to hav
fed me with Pleasures unknown to the whole World.

28

Had som Angel brought it miraculously from Heaven, and left
it at my foot, it had been a Present meet for Seraphims. Yet had
it been a Dream in comparison of the Glorious Way wherin
GOD prepared it. I must hav spent time in studying it, and with
5 great Diligence, hav read it daily to drink in the Precepts and
Instructions it contained. It had in a narrow Obscure maner com
unto me, and all the World had been Ignorant of felicity but I.
Wheras now there are thousands in the World, of whom I being
a Poor Child was Ignorant, that in Temples, Universities and
10 Secret Closets enjoy felicity. whom I saw not in Shops, or Scholes
or Trades; whom I found not in Streets, or at feasts, or Taverns:
and therfore thought not to be in the World: Who Enjoy Communion with God, and hav fellowship with the Angels evry
Day. And these I discerned to be a Great Help unto me.

29

This put me upon two things: upon Enquiring into the Matter
contained in the Bible, and into the Maner wherin it came unto
me. In the matter I found all the Glad Tidings my Soul longed
after, in its Desire of News. in the maner, that the Wisdom of
5 GOD was infinitly Greater then mine and that He had appeared
in His Wisdom exceeding my Desires. Abov all things I desired
som Great Lord or Mighty King, that having Power in his hand,
to give me all Kingdoms Riches and Honors, was willing to do
it. And by that Book I found that there was an eternal GOD,
10 who loved me infinitly, that I was his Son, that I was to overcom
Death, and to liv for ever, that He Created the World for me, that
I was to Reign in His Throne and to inherit all Things. Who
would hav believed this had not that Book told me? It told me
also that I was to liv in Communion with Him, in the Image of
15 His Life and Glory, that I was to Enjoy all His Treasures and
Pleasures, in a more perfect maner then I could Devise, and that
all the truly Amiable and Glorious Persons in the World were to
be my friends and Companions.

30

Upon this I had enough. I desired no more the Honors and
Pleasures of this World, but gav my self to the Illimited and Clear
fruition of that: and to this Day see nothing wanting to my Felicity
but mine own Perfection. All other Things are well; I only, and
the Sons of Men about me are Disorderd. Nevertheless could I 5
be what I ought, their very Disorders would be my Enjoyments.
for all things shall work together for Good to them that lov GOD.
And if the Disorders then certainly the Troubles, and if the
Troubles, much more the Vanities of Men would be mine. Not
only their Enjoyments, but their very Errors and Distractions 10
increasing my Felicity. So that being Heir of the Whole World
alone, I was to walk in it, as in a Strange Marvellous and Amiable
Possession, and alone to render Praises unto God for its Enjoyment.

31

This taught me that those Fashions and Tinsild vanities, which
you and I despised ere while, fetching a litle Cours about, became
ours. And that the Wisdom of God in them also was very Con-
spicuous. For it becometh His Goodness to make all Things
Treasures: and His Power is able to bring Light out of Darkness, 5
and Good out of Evil. Nor would His Lov endure, but that I also
should hav a Wisdom, wherby I could draw Order out of Confusion. So that it is my Admiration and Joy, that while so many
thousand wander in Darkness, I am in the Light, and that while
so many Dote upon fals Treasures and Pierce themselvs thorow 10
with many Sorrows, I liv in Peace, and Enjoy the Delights of
God and Heaven.

32

In respect of the Matter, I was very sure that Angels and Cherubims could not bring unto me better Tidings then were in the
Scriptures contained: could I but believ them to be true. but I
was Dissatisfied about the Maner, and that was the Ground of

5 my Unbelief. For I could not think that GOD being LOV would neglect His Son, and therfore surely I was not His Son, nor He Lov: becaus He had not Ascertaind me more carefully, that the Bible was His Book from Heaven. Yet I was encouraged to hope well, becaus the Matter was so Excellent, abov my Ex-
10 pectation. And when I searched into it, I found the Way infinitly better then if all the Angels in Heaven had brought it to me.

33

Had the Angels brought it to me alone, these Several Incon-veniences had attended the Vision. 1. It had been but one Sud-dain Act wherin it was sent me: wheras Now GOD hath been all Ages in preparing it. 2. It had been don by inferior Ministers,
5 wheras now it is don by GOD Himself. 3. Being Satan is able to Transform Him self into an Angel of Light, I had been still Dubious, till having recours to the Excellency of the Matter, by it I was informed and Satisfied. 4. Being Corrupted, that one Miracle would hav been but like a Single Spark upon green
10 Wood, it would hav gon out immediatly: wheras I needed 10000 Miracles to Seal it, yea and to awaken me to the Meditation of the Matter that was revealed to me. 5. Had it been revealed no other Way, all the World had been Dark and Empty round about me: Wheras now it is my Joy and my Delight and Treasure,
15 being full of Knowledg, Light, and Glory. 6. Had it been re-vealed at no other Time, God had now only been Good unto me, wheras He hath Manifested His Lov in all Ages, and been Carefully and most Wisely Revealing it from the Beginning of the World. 7. Had He revealed it to no other Person, I had been
20 Weak in faith being Solitary, and sitting alone like a Sparrow upon the Hous top, who now hav the Concurrent and joynt affections of Kingdoms and Ages. Yea notwithstanding the Dis-advantage of this Weakness, I must hav gon abroad, and Pub-lished this faith to others, both in lov to God, and Lov to Men.
25 for I must hav don my Duty, or the Book would hav don me no Good, and Lov to God and Men must hav been my Duty. for without that I could never be Happy. Yea finaly had not the

Book been revealed before neither had GOD been Glorious, nor
I Blessed, for He had been Negligent of other Persons, His Good-
ness had been Defectiv to all Ages, Whom now I Know to be 30
GOD by the Universality of His Lov unto Mankind: and the
Perfection of His wisdom to evry Person.

34

To talk now of the Necessity of bearing all Calamities and Per-
secutions in preaching, is little: to consider the Reproaches, Mockings and Derisions I must have endured of all the World, while
they scoffed at me, for pretending to be the only man, that had a
Book from Heaven; is Nothing; nor is it much to Mention the 5
Impossibility of Convincing others, all the World having been
full of Darkness, and God always Silent before. All Ages had
been void of Treasure had not the Bible been revealed till the
other Day, wherin now I can Expatiat with Perfect Liberty, and
evry where See the Lov of GOD to all Mankind Lov to me alone. 10
All the World being adorned with Miracles Prophets Patriarchs
Apostles, Martyrs, Revelations from Heaven, Lively Examples
Holy Souls, Divine Affairs, for my Enjoyment. The Glory of
God and the Light of Heaven appearing evrywhere, as much as it
would hav don in that seeming Instant, had the Book I desired 15
com unto me any other Way.

35

You will not believ what a World of Joy this one Satisfaction and
Pleasure brought me. Thenceforth I thought the Light of Heaven
was in this World: I saw it Possible, and very Probable, that I
was infinitly Beloved of Almighty God, the Delights of Paradice
were round about me, Heaven and Earth were open to me, all 5
Riches were little Things, this one Pleasure being so Great that it
exceeded all the Joys of Eden. So Great a Thing it was to me, to
be satisfied in the Maner of Gods Revealing Himself unto Mankind. Many other Enquiries I had concerning the Maner of His
Revealing Himself, in all which I am infinitly satisfied. 10

M

36

Having been at the University, and received there the Taste and Tincture of another Education, I saw that there were Things in this World of which I never Dreamed, Glorious Secrets, and Glorious Persons past Imagination. There I saw that Logick,
5 Ethicks, Physicks, Metaphysicks, Geometry, Astronomy, Poesie, Medicine, Grammer, Musick, Rhetorick, all kind of Arts Trades and Mechanicismes that Adorned the World pertained to felicity At least there I saw those Things, which afterwards I knew to pertain unto it: And was Delighted in it. There I saw into the Nature of
10 the Sea, the Heavens, the Sun, the Moon and Stars, the Elements, Minerals and Vegetables All which appeared like the Kings Daughter, All Glorious within, and those Things which my Nurses and Parents should hav talkt of, there were taught unto Me.

37

Nevertheless som things were Defectiv too. There was never a Tutor that did professely Teach Felicity: tho that be the Mistress of all other Sciences. Nor did any of us Study these things but as *Aliena*, which we ought to hav Studied as our own Enjoyments.
5 We Studied to inform our Knowledg, but Knew not for what End we so Studied. And for lack of aiming at a Certain End, we Erred in the Maner. How beit there we received all those Seeds of Knowledg that were afterwards improved; and our Souls were Awakened to a Discerning of their faculties, and Exercise of their
10 Powers.

38

The Maner is in evry thing of greatest Concernment. Whatever Good thing we do, neither can we pleas God, unless we do it *Well*: nor can He pleas us, whatever Good He does, unless He do it *well*. Should He giv us the most Perfect Things in Heaven and
5 Earth to make us Happy, and not giv them to us in the Best of all Possible Maners, He would but Displeas us, and it were Impos⟋

sible for Him to make us Happy. It is not Sufficient therfore for us
to Study, the most excellent Things unless we do it in the most
Excellent of Maners. And what that is it is impossible to find till
we are Guided therunto by the Most Excellent End. with a Desire 10
of which I flagrantly Burned.

39

The Best of all Possible Ends is the Glory of GOD, but Happiness was that I thirsted after. And yet I did not erre. for the Glory
of God is to make us Happy. Which can never be don but by
giving us most Excellent Natures and Satisfying those Natures:
by Creating all Treasures of infinit Valu, and giving them to us in 5
an infinit maner, to wit both in the Best that to Omnipotence was
possible. This led me to Enquire, Whither all things were Excellent and of Perfect Valu, and whither they were mine in Propriety?

40

It is the Glory of God to giv all Things to us in the Best of all
possible maners. To Study Things therfore under the Double
Notion of Interest and Treasure, is to study all Things in the Best
of all possible Maners. Becaus in Studying so we Enquire after
GODs Glory and our own Happiness. And indeed enter into the 5
Way that leadeth to all Contentments Joys and Satisfactions, to
all Praises Triumphs and Thanksgivings, to All Virtues Beauties
Adorations and Graces, to all Dominion Exaltation Wisdom
and Glory, to all Holiness, Union and Communion with GOD,
to all Patience and Courage and Blessedness, which it is impos- 10
sible to meet any other Way. So that to Study Object for Ostentation, vain Knowledg or Curiosity is fruitless Impertinence. tho
GOD Himself, and Angels, be the Object. But to Study that
which will Oblige us to lov Him, and Feed us with Nobility and
Goodness toward Men, that is Blessed. And so is it to Study that, 15
which will lead us to the Temple of Wisdom, and Seat us in the
Throne of Glory.

41

Many Men Study the same Things, which hav not the Taste of, nor Delight in them. And their Palates vary according to the Ends, at which they Aim. He that Studies Politie Men and Maners, meerly that He may know how to behav Himself and get Honor 5 in this World has not that Delight in his Studies, as He that Con-templats these things that He might see the Ways of God among them: and Walk in Communion with Him. The Attainments of the one are narrow, the other Grows a Celestial King of all Kingdoms. Kings Minister unto Him, Temples are His Own, 10 Thrones are his Peculiar Treasure. Governments Officers Magis-trates and Courts of Judicature are His Delights in a way in-effable, and a maner Inconceivable to the others Imagination. He that Knows the Secrets of Nature with Albertus Magnus, or the Motions of the Heavens with Galilao, or the Cosmography of 15 the Moon with Hevelius, or the Body of Man with Galen, or the Nature of Diseases with Hippocrates, or the Harmonies in Melody with Orpheus, or of Poesie with Homer, or of Grammer with Lilly, or of whatever els with the greatest Artist; He is nothing. if he Knows them meerly for Talk or idle Speculation, or Transeunt 20 and External Use. But He that Knows them for Valu, and Knows them His own: shall Profit infinitly. And therfore of all Kind of Learnings, Humanity and Divinity are the most Excellent.

42

By Humanity we search into the Powers and Faculties of the Soul, enquire into the Excellencies of Humane Nature, consider its Wants, Survey its Inclinations Propensities and Desires. Ponder its Principles Proposals and Ends, Examine the Causes and fitness 5 of all, the Worth of all, the Excellency of all. Wherby we com to know what Man is in this World, What his Soveraign End and Happiness, and what is the Best Means by which He may attain it. And by this we com to see what Wisdom is: Which namely is a Knowledg Exercised in finding out the Way to Perfect Happi-10 ness, by discerning Mans real Wan[t]s and Soveraign desires.

We com more over to Know Gods Goodness, in seeing into the Causes, wherfore He implanted such faculties and Inclinations in us, and the Objects, and Ends prepared for them. This leadeth us to Divinity. For God gav Man an Endless Intellect to see All Things, and a Proneness to covet them, becaus they are His 15 Treasures; and an infinit Variety of Apprehensions and Affec-tions, that he might hav an Allsufficiency in Him self to Enjoy them: A Curiositie Profound and Unsatiable to stir him up to look into them: An Ambition Great and Everlasting to Carry him to the Highest Honors Thrones and Dignities. An Emulation wher-20 by he might be animated and Quickned by all Examples, a Tendernes and Compassion wherby He may be united to all Persons; A Sympathy and Lov to Vertu, a Tenderness of His Credit in evry Soul, that He might Delight to be Honored in all Persons: an Ey to behold Eternity and the Omnipresence of 25 GOD, that He might see Eternity and Dwell within it: A Power of Admiring Loving and Prizing, that seeing the Goodness and Beauty of God, He might be United to it for evermore.

43

In Divinity we are entertained with all Objects from Everlasting to Everlasting: becaus with Him whose Outgoings from Ever-lasting: being to Contemplat GOD, and to Walk with Him in all His Ways: And therfore to be Entertained with all Objects, as He is the Fountain, Governor, and End of them. We are to 5 Contemplat GOD in the Unity of His Essence, in the Trinity of Persons, in His Manifold Attributes, in all His Works, Internal and External, in his Counsels and Decrees, in the Work of Creation, and in His Works of Providence. And Man, as he is a Creature of GOD, capable of Celestial Blessedness, and a Sub-10 ject in His Kingdom: in his fourfold Estate of Innocency, Misery, Grace and Glory. In the Estate of Innocency we are to Contem-plate the Nature and Maner of His Happiness, the Laws under which He was governed, the Joys of Paradice, and the Immaculat Powers of His Immortal Soul. In the Estate of Misery we hav his 15 Fall the Nature of Sin Original and Actual, His Manifold

Punishments Calamity Sickness Death &c. In the Estate of
Grace; the Tenor of the New Covenant, the maner of its Exhibi‑
tion under the various Dispensations of the Old and New Testa‑
20 ment, the Mediator of the Covenant, the Conditions of it Faith
and Repentance, the Sacraments or Seals of it, the Scriptures
Ministers and Sabbaths, the Nature and Government of the
Church, its Histories and Successions from the Beginning to the
End of the World. &c. In the State of Glory; the Nature of
25 Seperat Souls, their Advantages Excellencies and Privileges, the
Resurrection of the Body, the Day of Judgment and Life Ever‑
lasting. Wherin further we are to see and understand the Com‑
munion of Saints, Heavenly Joys, and our Society with Angels.
To all which I was naturaly Born to the fruition of all which I
30 was by Grace redeemed, and in the Enjoyment of all which I am
to liv Eternaly.

44

Natural Philosophy teaches us the Causes and Effects of all Bodies
simply and in them selvs. But if you extend it a little further, to
that indeed which its Name imports, signifying the Lov of Nature,
it leads us into a Diligent inquisition into all Natures, their
5 Qualities, Affections, Relations, Causes and Ends, so far forth
as by Nature and Reason they may be Known. And this Noble
Science, as such is most Sublime and Perfect, it includes all
Humanity and Divinity together GOD, Angels, Men, Affec‑
tions, Habits, Actions, Virtues; Evry Thing as it is a Solid intire
10 Object singly proposed, being a subject of it, as well as Material
and visible Things But taking it as it is usualy Bounded in its
Terms, it treateth only of Corporeal Things, as Heaven, Earth
Air Water, Fire, the Sun and Stars, Trees Herbs, flowers, In‑
fluences, Winds, Fowles Beasts Fishes Minerals, and Precious
15 Stones; with all other Beings of that Kind. And as thus it is taken
it is Nobly Subservient to the Highest Ends: for it Openeth the
Riches of Gods Kingdom and the Natures of His Territories
Works and Creatures in a Wonderfull Maner, Clearing and pre‑
paring the Ey of the Enjoyer.

45

Ethicks teach us the Mysteries of Moralitie, and the Nature of Affections Virtues and Maners, as by them we may be Guided to our Highest Happiness. The former for Speculation, this for Practice. The former furnisheth us with Riches, this with Honors and Delights, the former feasteth us, and this instructeth us. For by this we are taught to liv Honorably among men, and to make our selvs Noble and Usefull among them. It teacheth us how to Manage our Passions, to Exercise Virtues, and to form our Maners, so as to liv Happily in this World. And all these put together Discover the Materials of Religion to be so Great, that it Plainly manifesteth the Revelation of GOD to be Deep and Infinit. For it is impossible for Language, Miracles, or Apparitions to teach us the Infallibility of GODs Word or to shew us the Certainty of true Religion, without a Clear Sight into Truth it self that is into the Truth of Things. Which will them selvs when truly seen, by the very Beauty and Glory of them, best Discover, and Prov Religion.

46

When I came into the Country, and being seated among silent Trees, had all my Time in mine own Hands, I resolved to Spend it all, whatever it cost me, in Search of Happiness, and to Satiat that burning Thirst which Nature had Enkindled, in me from my Youth. In which I was so resolut, that I chose rather to liv upon 10 pounds a yeer, and to go in Lether Clothes, and feed upon Bread and Water, so that I might hav all my time clearly to my self: then to keep many thousands per Annums in an Estate of Life where my Time would be Devoured in Care and Labor. And GOD was so pleased to accept of that Desire, that from that time to this I hav had all things plentifully provided for me, without any Care at all, my very Study of Felicity making me more to Prosper, then all the Care in the Whole World. So that through His Blessing I liv a free and a Kingly Life, as if the World were turned again into Eden, or much more, as it is at this Day.

47

1

A life of Sabbaths here beneath!
Continual Jubilees and Joys!
The Days of Heaven, while we breath
On Earth! Where Sin all Bliss Destroys.
This is a Triumph of Delights!
That doth exceed all Appetites.
No Joy can be Compard to this,
It is a Life of Perfect Bliss.

2

Of perfect Bliss! How can it be?
To Conquer Satan, and to Reign
In such a Vale of Miserie,
Where Vipers, Stings and Tears remain;
Is to be Crownd with Victorie.
To be Content, Divine and free,
Even here beneath is Great Delight
And next the Beatifick Sight.

3

But inward lusts do oft assail,
Temptations Work us much Annoy.
Weel therfore Weep, and to prevail
Shall be a more Celestial Joy.
To hav no other Enemie,
But one; and to that one to Die:
To fight with that and Conquer it,
Is better then in Peace to sit.

4

Tis Better for a little time:
For he that all His Lusts doth quell,
Shall find this Life to be His Prime,
And Vanquish Sin and Conquer Hell.

The Next shall be His Double Joy:
And that which here seemd to Destroy, 30
Shall in the Other Life appear
A Root of Bliss; a Pearl each Tear.

48

Thus you see I can make Merry with Calamities, and while I
griev at Sins, and War against them, abhorring the World, and
my self more: Descend into the Abysses of Humilitie, and there
Admire a New Offspring and Torrent of Joys, GODs Mercies.
Which accepteth of our fidelity in Bloody Battails, tho every 5
Wound defile and Poyson; and when we slip or fall, turneth our
true Penitent Tears into Solid Pearl, that shall abide with Him
for evermore. But Oh let us take heed that we never Willingly
commit a Sin against so Gracious a Redeemer, and so Great a
Father. 10

49

Sin!
O only fatal Woe,
That makst me Sad and Mourning go!
That all my Joys dost Spoil,
His Kingdom and my Soul Defile! 5
I never can Agree
With Thee!

2

Thou!
Only Thou! O Thou alone,
(And my Obdurat Heart of Stone,) 10
The Poyson and the Foes
Of my Enjoyments and Repose,
The only Bitter Ill:
Dost Kill!

3

15
Oh!
I cannot meet with Thee,
Nor once approach thy Memory,
But all my Joys are Dead,
And all my Sacred Treasures fled;
20
As if I now did Dwell
In Hell.

4

Lord!
O hear how short I Breath!
See how I Tremble here beneath!
25
A Sin! Its Ugly face
More Terror, then its Dwelling Place,
Contains, (O Dreadfull Sin!)
Within!

50

The Recovery

Sin! wilt Thou vanquish me!
And shall I yeeld the victory?
Shall all my Joys be Spoild,
And Pleasures soild
5
By Thee!
Shall I remain
As one thats Slain
And never more lift up the Head?
Is not my Savior Dead!
10
His Blood, thy Bane; my Balsam, Bliss, Joy, Wine;
Shall Thee Destroy; Heal, Feed, make me Divine.

51

I cannot meet with Sin, but it Kils me, and tis only by Jesus Christ that I can Kill it, and Escape. Would you blame me to be con⁄ founded, when I have offended my Eternal Father, who gav me all the Things in Heaven and Earth? One Sin is a Dreadfull Stumbling Block in the Way to Heaven. It breeds a long Paren⁄ 5 thesis in the fruition of our Joys. Do you not see my Friend, how it Disorders and Disturbs my Proceeding? There is no Calamity but Sin alone.

52

When I came into the Country, and saw that I had all time in my own hands, having devoted it wholy to the study of Felicitie, I knew not where to begin or End; nor what Objects to chuse, upon which most Profitably I might fix my Contemplation. I saw my self like som Traveller, that had Destined his Life to 5 journeys, and was resolved to spend his Days in visiting Strange Places: who might wander in vain, unless his Undertakings were guided by som certain Rule; and that innumerable Millions of Objects were presented before me, unto any of which I might take my journey. fain I would hav visited them all, but that was impos⁄ 10 sible. What then should I do? Even imitat a Traveller, who becaus He cannot visit all Coasts, Wildernesses, Sandy Deserts, Seas, Hills, Springs and Mountains, chuseth the most Populous and flourishing Cities, where he might see the fairest Prospects, Wonders, and Rarities, and be entertained with greatest Courtesie: 15 and where indeed he might most Benefit himself with Knowledg Profit and Delight: leaving the rest, even the naked and Empty Places unseen. For which caus I made it my Prayer to GOD Almighty, that He, whose Eys are open upon all Things, would guid me to the fairest and Divinest. 20

53

And what Rule do you think I walked by? Truly a Strange one, but the Best in the Whole World. I was Guided by an Implicit Faith in Gods Goodness: and therfore led to the Study of the

most Obvious and Common Things. For thus I thought within
5 my self: GOD being, as we generaly believ, infinit in Goodness,
it is most Consonant and Agreeable with His nature, that the
Best Things should be most Common. for nothing is more
Naturall to infinit Goodness, then to make the Best Things most
frequent; and only Things Worthless, Scarce. Then I began to
10 Enquire what Things were most Common: Air, Light, Heaven
and Earth, Water, the Sun, Trees, Men and Women, Cities
Temples &c. These I found Common and Obvious to all: Rubies
Pearls Diamonds Gold and Silver, these I found scarce, and to
the most Denied. Then began I to consider and compare the value
15 of them, which I measured by their Serviceableness, and by the
Excellencies which would be found in them, should they be taken
away. And in Conclusion I saw clearly, that there was a Real
Valuableness in all the Common things; in the Scarce, a feigned.

54

Besides these Common things I hav named, there were others as
Common, but Invisible. The Laws of God, the Soul of Man,
Jesus Christ and His Passion on the Crosse, with the Ways of
GOD in all Ages. And these by the General Credit they had
5 Obtained in the World confirmed me more. For the Ways of
God were transeunt Things, they were past and gon; our Saviors
Sufferings were in one particular Obscure Place, the Laws of
God were no Object of the Ey, but only found in the Minds of
Men; these therfore which were so Secret in their own Nature, and
10 made common only by the Esteem Men had of them, must of
Necessity include unspeakable Worth for which they were celebrated, of all, and so generaly remembered. As yet I did not see
the Wisdom and Depths of Knowledg, the Clear Principles, and
Certain Evidences wherby the Wise and Holy, the Ancients and
15 the Learned that were abroad in the World knew these Things,
but was led to them only by the fame which they had vulgarly
received. Howbeit I believed that there were unspeakable Mysteries
contained in them, and tho they were Generaly talkt of their valu
was unknown. These therfore I resolved to Study, and no other.

But to my unspeakable Wonder, they brought me to all the Things 20
in Heaven and in Earth, in Time and Eternity, Possible and Impossible, Great and Little, Common and Scarce, and Discovered
them all to be infinit Treasures.

55

That any thing may be found to be an infinit Treasure, its Place
must be found in Eternity, and in Gods Esteem. For as there is a
Time, so there is a Place for all Things. Evry thing in its Place is
Admirable Deep and Glorious: out of its Place like a Wandering
Bird, is Desolat and Good for Nothing. How therfore it relateth 5
to God and all Creatures must be seen before it can be Enjoyed.
And this I found by many Instances. The Sun is Good, only as
it relateth to the Stars, to the Seas, to your Ey, to the feilds, &c.
As it relateth to the Stars it raiseth their Influences; as to the Seas
it melteth them and maketh the Waters flow; as to your Ey, it 10
bringeth in the Beauty of the World; as to the feilds; it clotheth
them with Fruits and flowers: Did it not relate to others it would
not be Good. Divest it of these Operations, and Divide it from
these Objects it is Useless and Good for nothing. And therfore
Worthless, because Worthles and Useless go together. A Piece of 15
Gold cannot be Valued, unless we Know how it relates to Clothes,
to Wine, to Victuals, to the Esteem of Men, and to the Owner.
Som little Piece in a Kingly Monument severd from the rest hath
no Beauty at all. It enjoys its valu in its Place, by the Ornament it
gives to, and receivs from all the Parts. By this I discerned, that 20
even a little Knowledg could not be had in the Mysterie of Felicity,
without a great deal. And that that was the reason why so many
were ignorant of its nature, and why so few did attain it. for by
the Labor required to much Knowledg they were discouraged,
and for lack of much did not see any Glorious motives to allure 25
them.

56

Therfore of Necessity they must at first believ that Felicity is a
Glorious tho an unknown Thing. And certainly it was the

infinit Wisdom of God, that did implant by Instinct so strong a
Desire of felicity in the Soul, that we might be excited to labor
5 after it, tho we know it not, the very force wherwith we covet it
supplying the place of Understanding. That there is a Felicity we
all know by the Desires after, that there is a most Glorious felicity
we know by the Strength and vehemence of those Desires: And
that nothing but Felicity is worthy of our Labor, becaus all other
10 things are the Means only which conduce unto it. I was very much
animated by the Desires of Philosophers, which I saw in Heathen
Books aspiring after it. But the misery is *It was unknown*. An altar
was erected to it like that in Athens with this inscription TO
THE UNKNOWN GOD.

57

Two things in Perfect Felicity I saw to be requisite: and that
Felicity must be perfect, or not Felicity. The first was the Perfection
of its Objects, in Nature Serviceableness Number and Excellency.
The second was the Perfection of the Maner wherin they are
5 Enjoyed, for Sweetness Measure and Duration. And unless in
these I could be satisfied I should never be contented. Especialy
about the later. for the Maner is always more Excellent the Thing.
And it far more concerneth us that the Maner wherin we enjoy be
compleat and Perfect: then that the Matter which we Enjoy be
10 compleat and Perfect. For the Maner as we contemplat its Excellency is it self a great Part of the Matter of our Enjoyment.

58

In Discovering the Matter or Objects to be Enjoyed, I was greatly
aided by remembering that we were made in Gods Image. For
thereupon it must of Necessity follow that GODs Treasures be
our Treasures, and His Joys our Joys. So that by enquiring what
5 were GODs, I found the Objects of our felicity Gods Treasures
being ours. for we were made in his Image that we might liv in
His similitud. And herin I was mightily confirmed by the Apostles
Blaming the Gentiles, and charging it upon them as a very great

Fault that they were alienated from the life of God, for herby I
perceived that we were to liv the Life of God: when we lived the 10
tru life of Nature according to Knowledg: and that by Blindness
and Corruption we had Strayed from it. Now GODs Treasures
are his own Perfections, and all His Creatures.

59

The Image of God implanted in us, guided me to the maner
wherin we were to Enjoy. for since we were made in the similitud
of God, we were made to Enjoy after his Similitude. Now to Enjoy
the Treasures of God in the Similitud of God, is the most perfect
Blessedness God could Devise. For the Treasures of GOD are the 5
most Perfect Treasures and the Maner of God is the most perfect
Maner. To Enjoy therfore the Treasures of God after the similitud
of God is to Enjoy the most perfect Treasures in the most Perfect
Maner. Upon which I was infinitly satisfied in God, and knew
there was a Dietie, becaus I was satisfied. For Exerting Himself 10
wholy in atchieving thus an infinit felicity He was infinitly Delightfull Great and Glorious, and my Desires so August and Insatiable
that nothing less then a Deity could satisfy them.

60

This Spectacle once seen, will never be forgotten. It is a Great
Part of the Beatifick Vision. A Sight of Happiness is Happiness.
It transforms the Soul and makes it Heavenly, it powerfully calls
us to Communion with God, and weans us from the Customs of
this World It puts a Lustre upon GOD and all his Creatures and 5
makes us to see them in a Divine and Eternal Light. I no sooner
discerned this but I was (as Plato saith, In summâ Rationis Arce
Quies habitat) seated in a Throne of Repose and Perfect Rest.
All Things were well in their Proper Places, I alone was out of
frame and had need to be Mended. for all things were Gods 10
Treasures in their Proper places, and I was to be restored to Gods
Image. Wherupon you will not believ how I was withdrawn

from all Endeavors of altering and Mending Outward Things.
They lay so well methoughts, they could not be Mended: but I
15 must be Mended to Enjoy them.

61

The Image of God is the most Perfect Creature. Since there cannot
be two GODs the utmost Endeavor of Almighty Power is the
Image of GOD. It is no Blasphemy to say that GOD cannot
make a GOD: the Greatest Thing that He can make is His
5 Image: A most Perfect Creature, to enjoy the most perfect Treasures, in the most perfect Maner. A Creature endued with the
most Divine and perfect Powers, for Measure Kind Number
Duration Excellency is the most Perfect Creature: Able to see
all Eternity with all its Objects, and as a Mirror to Contain all
10 it seeth: Able to Lov all it contains, and as a Sun to shine upon
its loves. Able by Shining to communicat it self in Beams of
Affection, and to Illustrat all it Illuminats with Beauty and Glory:
Able to be Wise Holy Glorious Blessed in it self as God is, being
adorned inwardly with the same kind of Beauty, and outwardly
15 Superior to all Creatures.

62

Upon this I began to believ that all other Creatures were such that
GOD was Himself, in their Creation. that is *Almighty Power
wholy exerted:* And that evry Creature is indeed as it seemed in
my infancy: not as it is commonly apprehended. Evry Thing
5 being Sublimely Rich and Great and Glorious. Evry Spire of
Grass is the Work of His Hand: And I in a World where evry
Thing is mine, and far better then the Greater sort of Children
esteem Diamonds and Pearls. Gold and Silver being the very
Refuse of Nature, and the Worst Things in Gods Kingdom.
10 Howbeit truly Good in their Proper Places.

63

To be satisfied in God is the Highest Difficulty in the whole World And yet most easy to be don. To make it possible that we should be satisfied in GOD was an Atchievment of infinit Weight, before it was attempted, and the most difficult Thing in all Worlds before it was Attchieved. For we naturaly expect infinit Things of God: and can be satisfied only with the Highest Reason. So that the Best of all Possible Things must be wrought in God, or els we shall remain Dissatisfied. But it is most Easy at present, becaus GOD is. For GOD is not a Being compounded of Body and Soul, or Substance and Accident, or Power and Act but is All Act, Pure Act, a Simple Being. Whose Essence is to be, Whose Being is to be Perfect, so that He is most Perfect towards all and in all. He is most Perfect for all and by all. He is in Nothing imperfect becaus His Being is to be Perfect. It is Impossible for Him to be GOD, and Imperfect: And therfore do we so Ardently and infinitly desire His Absolut Perfection.

64

Neither is it Possible to be otherwise. All his Power being turned into Act, it is all Exerted: infinitly, and wholy. Neither is there any Power in Him Which He is not Able, and Willing to use: or which He cannot Wisely Guid to most Excellent Ends. So that we may expect most Angelical and Heavenly Rarities in all the Creatures. Were there any Power in GOD unimployed He would be Compounded of Power and Act. Being therfore GOD is all Act, He is a GOD in this, that Himself is Power Exerted. An infinit Act becaus infinit Power infinitly Exerted. an Eternal Act becaus infinit Power Eternaly Exerted. Wherin consisteth the Generation of His son, the Perfection of His Lov, and the Immutability of GOD. For God by Exerting Himself begot His Son, and doing wholy, for the sake of His Creatures is perfect Lov: and doing it wholy from all Eternity, is an Eternal Act and therfore Unchangable.

65

With this we are Delighted becaus it is absolutly impossible that
any Power Dwelling with Lov should continu Idle. Since
GOD therfore was infinitly and Eternaly Communicativ, all
Things were Contained in Him from all Eternitie. As Nazianzen
5 in his 38th Oration admirably Expresseth it, in these Words, *Becaus*
it was by no means sufficient for GOODNESS to move only in the
Contemplation of it self: but it became what was GOOD to be Diffused
and Propagated, that more might be affected with the Benefit (for this was
the part of the Highest Goodness:) first He thought upon Angelical and
10 *Celestial Vertues, and that Thought was the Work, which he wrought*
by the WORD, and fulfilled by the Spirit. Atque ita Secundi Splen-
dores Procreati Sunt primi Splendoris Administri. And so were there
Second Splendors Created, and made to Minister to the first
Splendor, so that all Motions Successions Creatures and Opera-
15 tions with their Beginnings and Ends were in Him from Everlasting. To whom Nothing can be Added, becaus from all Eternity
He was, whatsoever to all Eternity He can be. All Things being
now to be seen and Contemplated in His Bosom: and Advanced
therfore into a Diviner Light, being infinitly Older and more
20 Precious then we were aware. Time itself being in GOD Eternaly.

66

Little did I imagine that, while I was thinking these Things, I
was Conversing with GOD. I was so Ignorant that I did not
think any Man in the World had had such thoughts before. seeing
them therfore so Amiable, I Wonderd not a little, that nothing
5 was Spoken of them in former Ages. but as I read the Bible I was
here and there Surprized with such Thoughts and found by
Degrees that these Things had been written of before, not only in
the Scriptures but in many of the fathers and that this was the Way
of Communion with God in all Saints, as I saw Clearly in the
10 Person of David. Me thoughts a New Light Darted in into all his
Psalmes, and finaly spread abroad over the whole Bible. So that
things which for their Obscurity I thought not in being were there

contained: Things which for their Greatness were incredible, were made Evident and Things Obscure, Plain. GOD by this means bringing me into the very Heart of His Kingdom. 15

67

There I saw Moses blessing the Lord for the Precious Things of Heaven, for the Dew and for the Deep that coucheth beneath: and for the Precious fruits brought forth by the Sun, and for the Precious things put forth by the Moon: and for the chief things of the ancient Mountains and for the Precious things of the lasting 5 Hills: and for the Precious things of the Earth, and fulness therof. There I saw Jacob, with Awfull Apprehensions Admiring the Glory of the World, when awaking out of His Dream he said, How dreadfull is this Place? This is none other then the Hous of GOD, and the Gate of Heaven. There I saw GOD leading forth 10 Abraham, and shewing him the Stars of Heaven; and all the Countries round about him, and saying All these will I give Thee, and thy Seed after thee. There I saw Adam in Paradice, sur-rounded with the Beauty of Heaven and Earth, void of all Earthly Comforts to wit such as were devised, Gorgeous Apparel, Palaces, 15 Gold and Silver, Coaches, Musical Instruments &c, And enter-tained only with Celestial Joys. The sun and moon and stars, Beasts and fowles and fishes, Trees and fruits and flowers, with the other Naked and simple Delights of Nature. By which I evidently saw, that the Way to becom Rich and Blessed, was not 20 by heaping Accidental and Devised Riches to make ourselvs great in the vulgar maner, but to approach more near, and to see more Clearly with the Ey of our understanding, the Beauties and Glories of the whole world: and to hav communion with the Diety in the Riches of GOD and Nature. 25

68

I saw moreover that it did not so much concern us what Objects were before us, as with what Eys we beheld them; with what Affections we esteemed them, and what Apprehensions we had

about them. All men see the same Objects, but do not equaly
5 understand them. Intelligence is the Tongue that discerns and
Tastes them, Knowledg is the Light of Heaven. Lov is the Wis⁄
dom and Glory of GOD. Life Extended to all Objects, is the
Sence that enjoys them. So that Knowledg Life and Lov, are the
very means of all Enjoyment. which abov all Things we must seek
10 for and Labor after. All Objects are in God Eternal: which we
by perfecting our faculties are made to Enjoy. Which then are
turned into Act when they are exercised about their Objects. but
without them are Desolat and Idle; or Discontented and forlorn.
Wherby I perceived the Meaning of that Definition wherin Aris⁄
15 totle Describeth Felicity. when he saith Felicity is the Perfect Exer⁄
cise of Perfect Virtu in a Perfect Life. for Life is perfect when
it is perfectly Extended to all Objects, and perfectly sees them and
perfectly loves them: which is don by a perfect Exercise of Virtu
about them.

69

In Salem dwelt a Glorious King,
Raisd from a Shepherds lowly State,
That did his Praises like an Angel sing
Who did the World create.
5   By many great and Bloody Wars,
He was Advanced unto Thrones:
But more Delighted in the Stars,
Then in the Splendor of His Precious Stones.
Nor Gold nor Silver did his Ey regard:
10   The Works of GOD were his Sublime Reward.

2

A Warlike Champion he had been
And Many feats of Chivalrie
Had don: in Kingly Courts his Ey had seen
A Vast Variety

Of Earthly Joys: Yet he despis'd   15
Those fading Honors, and fals pleasures
Which are by Mortals so much Prizd;
And Placed his Happiness in other Treasures
No State of Life which in this World we find
Could yeeld contentment to his greater Mind.   20

3

His fingars touchd his Trembling Lyre,
And evry Quavering String did yeeld,
    A Sound that filled all the Jewish Quire
        And Ecchoed in the Field.
No Pleasure was so Great to Him   25
    As in a Silent Night to see
The Moon and Stars: A Cherubim
Abov them even here He seemd to be.
Enflamd with Lov it was his great Desire,
To Sing Contemplat Ponder and Admire.   30

4

He was a Prophet, and foresaw
Things extant in the World to com:
He was a Judg, and ruled by a Law
    That then the Hony Comb
Was Sweeter far: He was a Sage,   35
    And all His People could Advise;
    An Oracle, whose evry Page
Containd in vers the Greatest Mysteries
But most He then Enjoyd Himself, when he
Did as a Poet prais the Dietie.   40

5

A Shepherd, Soldier, and Divine,
A Judge, a Courtier, and a King,
Priest, Angel, Prophet, Oracle did shine
    At once; when He did sing.

45 Philosopher and Poet too
Did in his Melodie appear;
All these in Him did pleas the View
Of Those that did his Heavenly musick hear
And evry Drop that from his flowing Quill
50 Came down, did all the World with Nectar fill.

6

He had a Deep and perfect Sence
Of all the Glories and the Pleasures
That in Gods Works are hid, the Excellence
Of such Transcendent Treasures
55 Made him on Earth an Heavenly King,
And fild his Solitudes with Joy;
He never did more Sweetly Sing
Then when alone, tho that doth Mirth destroy.
Sence did his Soul with Heavenly Life inspire
60 And made him seem in Gods Celestial Quire.

7

Rich Sacred Deep and Precious Things
Did here on Earth the Man surround
With all the Glory of the King of Kings
He was most strangely Crownd.
65 His Clear Soul and Open Sight
Among the Sons of GOD did see
Things filling Angels with Delight
His Ear did hear their Heavenly Melodie
And when He was alone He all became,
70 That Bliss implied, or did increas His Fame.

8

All Arts He then did Exercise
And as His GOD He did Adore
By Secret Ravishments abov the Skies
He carried was, before

He died. His Soul did see and feel   75
What others know not; and became
While He before his GOD did kneel
A Constant Heavenly Pure Seraphick Flame.
Oh that I might unto His Throne Aspire;
And all His Joys abov the Stars Admire!   80

70

When I saw those Objects celebrated in His Psalmes which
GOD and Nature had proposed to me, and which I thought
chance only presented to my view: you cannot imagine how unspeakably I was delighted, to see so Glorious a Person, so Great
a Prince, so Divine a Sage, that was a Man after Gods own Heart 5
by the testimony of God Himself, rejoycing in the same things,
meditating on the same and Praising GOD for the same. For by
this I perceived we were led by one Spirit: and that following the
clew of Nature into this Labyrinth I was brought into the midst
of Celestial Joys: and that to be retired from Earthly Cares and 10
fears and Distractions that we might in sweet and heavenly Peace
contemplat all the Works of GOD, was to live in Heaven and
the only way to becom what David was a Man after Gods own
Heart. There we might be enflamed with those Causes for which
we ought to lov Him: there we might see those Viands which 15
feed the Soul with Angels food: there we might Bath in those
Streams of Pleasure that flow at His Right Hand for evermore.

71

That Hymn of David in the eighth Psalm, was supposed to be
made by night, wherin he celebrateth the Works of God; becaus
he mentioneth the Moon and Stars, but not the Sun in his meditation. When I consider the Heavens which Thou hast made, the
Moon and Stars which are the Works of thy fingars, What is 5
Man that Thou art Mindfull of him, or the Son of man that Thou
visitest him? Thou hast made him a little lower then the Angels,
and hast crowned him with Glory and Honor. Thou hast given

him Dominion over the Works of thy Hands, Thou hast put all
10 things in Subjection under his feet: All Sheep and Oxen, yea
and the Beasts of the field: the fowls of the Air and the fishes of the
Sea, and whatsoever passeth through the Paths of the Sea. This
Glory and Honor wherwith Man is Crowned ought to affect evry
Person, that is Gratefull, with celestial Joy: and so much the rather
15 becaus it is evry mans proper and sole Inheritance.

72

His Joyfull Meditation in the nineteenth Psalm directeth evry
Man to consider the Glory of Heaven and Earth. The Heavens
declare the Glory of God, and the firmament sheweth His Handy-
work. Day unto Day uttereth Speech, and Night unto Night
5 sheweth Knowledg. There is no Speech nor Language where
their voice is not heard. Their Line is gon throughout all the
Earth, and their voice to the End of the World. In them hath He
set a Tabernacle for the Sun, which is as a Bridegroom coming
out of his chamber, and rejoyceth as a Strong Man to run his
10 Race. His going forth is from the End of the heaven, and his Cir-
cuit to the Ends of it, and nothing is hid from the heat therof.
From thence he proceedeth to the Laws of God, as Things more
Excellent in their Nature then His Works. The Law of the Lord
is perfect converting the Soul; the Testimony of the Lord is sure
15 making Wise the Simple. The Statutes of the Lord are right
rejoycing the Heart, the Commandment of the Lord is Pure En-
lightening the Eys. The fear of the Lord is clean Enduring for
ever, the Judgments of the Lord are true and righteous altogether.
More to be desired are they then Gold, yea then much fine Gold;
20 Sweeter also then honey and the Honeycomb. Wherby he plainly
sheweth that Divine and Kingly Delights are in the Laws and
Works of God to be taken, by all those that would be Angelical
and Celestial Creatures. For that in the Kingdom of Heaven evry
one being disentangled from Particular Relations and Private
25 Riches, as if he were newly taken out of Nothing to the fruition of
all Eternity, was in these alone to solace himself as his peculiar
Treasures.

73

Ye that fear the Lord Prais Him; All ye Seed of Jacob Glorify Him and fear Him all ye Seed of Israel. For He hath not despised nor abhorred the Affliction of the Afflicted, neither hath He hid His face from him, but when he cried unto Him, He heard. My Prais shall be of Thee in the great Congregation; I will pay my 5 vows before them that fear Him. The Meek shall Eat and be satis⁄ fied. They shall Prais the Lord that seek Him; your Heart shall liv for ever. All the Ends of the World shall remember and turn unto the Lord, all the Kindreds of the Nations shall Worship before Thee. For the Kingdom is the Lords, and He is the Gover⁄ 10 nor among the Nations. All they that be fat upon Earth shall Eat and Worship: all they that go down to the Dust shall bow before Him, and none can Keep alive his own Soul. A seed shall serv Him, it shall be counted to the Lord for a Generation. They shall com and declare His Righteousness to a people that shall be born, 15 that He hath don this. Here he sheweth that it was his desire and Delight to hav all Nations Praising God: and that the Condescen⁄ tion of the Almighty in Stooping down to the Poor and Needy was the Joy of his Soul. He prophesieth also of the Conversion of the Gentiles to the Knowledg of Jesus Christ, which to see was 20 to him an Exceeding Pleasure.

74

The Earth is the Lords and the fullness therof, the round World and they that dwell therin. He observeth here that GOD by a comprehensiv Possession and by Way of Eminence, enjoyeth the whole World; All Mankind and all the Earth, with all that is therin, being His peculiar Treasures. Since therfore we are made 5 in the Image of God, to liv in his Similitud, as they are His, they must be our Treasures. We being Wise and Righteous over all as He is. Becaus they regard not the Works of the Lord, nor the Operation of His hands, therfore shall He destroy them and not build them up. 10

75

By the Word of the Lord were the Heavens made, and all the
Host of them by the Breath of His Mouth. He gathereth the Waters
of the Sea together, He laieth up the Depth in Storehouses. Let all
the Earth fear the Lord, let all the Inhabitants of the World stand
5 in Awe of Him. For He spake, and it was don, He commanded
and it stood fast. He frequently meditateth upon the Works of
God, and affirmeth the Contemplation of them to beget His fear
in our Hearts. for that He being great in Strength, not one faileth.

76

All my Bones shall say, Lord who is like unto Thee, who de-
liverest the Poor from him that is too strong for him; yea the Poor
and the Needy from him that Spoileth him! Thy Mercy O Lord
is abov the Heavens and Thy Faithfulness reacheth to the clouds.
5 Thy Righteousness is like the great Mountains, thy Judgments
are a great Deep: O Lord thou preservest Man and Beast. How
Excellent is Thy Loving Kindness O God! therfore the Children
of Men put their Trust under the Shadow of thy Wings. They
shall be abundantly satisfied with the fatness of thy Hous; and
10 Thou shalt make them Drink of the River of thy Pleasures. For
with Thee is the fountain of Life. In thy Light we shall see Light.
The Judgments of God, and his Loving Kindness, His Mercy
and faithfulness, are the fatness of his Hous, and his Righteousness being seen in the Light of Glory is the Torrent of Pleasure at
15 His right hand for evermore.

77

Hearken O Daughter and consider, and incline thine Ear; forget
also thine own People and thy fathers hous. so shall the King
greatly desire thy Beauty for He is thy Lord and Worship thou
Him. ¶ The Kings Daughter is all Glorious within, her clothing
5 is of wrought Gold. She shall be brought unto the King in
Raiment of Needle Work, the virgins her companions that follow

her, shall be brought unto Thee. With Gladness and rejoycing shall they be brought they shall enter into the Kings Palace. In, steed of thy fathers shall be thy children whom thou mayest make Princes in all the Earth. The Psalmist here singeth an Epithala, 10 mium upon the Marriage between Christ and His Church: whom he persuadeth to forsake her countrey and her fathers hous together with all the customs and vanities of this World: and to Dedicat her self wholy to our Saviors Service. since she is in exchange to enter into His Palace and becom a Bride to so 15 Glorious a Person. The Bridegroom and the Bride, the Palace (which is all the World) with all that is therin, being Davids Joy and his true Possession. Nay evry child of this Bride, is if a Male a Prince over all the Earth; if a Female Bride to the King of Heaven. And evry Soul that is a Spous of Jesus Christ, esteemeth 20 all the Saints her own Children and her own Bowels.

78

There is a River the streams wherof shall make Glad the City of God; the holy Place of the Tabernacle of the most High. He praiseth the Means of Grace, which in the Midst of this World are Great Consolations. and in all Distresses refresh our Souls. Com behold the Works of the Lord, what Desolations he hath 5 made in the Earth. He exhorteth us to Contemplat Gods Works, which are so perfect, that when His Secret and just Judgments are seen, the very destruction of Nations, and laying waste of Cities, shall be sweet and Delightfull.

79

O clap your Hands all ye people shout unto God with the voice of Triumph. For the Lord most High is Terrible, He is a Great King over all the Earth. He shall chuse our Inheritance for us, the Excellency of Jacob whom He loved. Beautifull for Situation, the Joy of the whole Earth is Mount Sion. on the Sides of the North 5 the City of the Great King. God is known in her Palaces for a

Refuge. Walk about Sion and go round about her, tell the Towers therof: Mark ye well her Bulwarks, Consider her Palaces, that ye may tell it to the Generation following. For this God is our God 10 for ever and ever. He will be our Guid even unto Death.

80

As in the former Psalms, he proposeth true and Celestial Joys, so in this following he discovereth the vanity of fals imaginations. They that trust in their Wealth, and boast them selvs in the Multitude of their Riches, None of them can by any Means redeem his 5 Brother, or giv unto God a Ransom for him. for the Redemption of their Soul is precious and it ceaseth forever. For he seeth that wise men die, likewise the fool and the Bruitish Person perish, and leav their Wealth to others. Their inward thought is, that their houses shall continu for ever, and their Dwelling Places to all 10 Generations: They call their Lands after their own Names. This their Way is their folly, yet their Posterity approve their Sayings. Like sheep they are laid in the Grave, Death shall feed sweetly on them, and the Upright shall hav Dominion over them in the Morning: and their Beauty shall consume in the Grave from their 15 Dwelling. Man that is in Honor and understandeth not, is like the Beast that Perisheth.

81

Hear O my People and I will speak; O Israel and I will testify against thee. I am GOD even thy GOD. I will not reprov thee for thy Sacrifices or thy Burnt offerings to hav been continualy before me. I will take no Bullock out of thy Hous, nor He goats 5 out of thy folds. For evry Beast of the Forest is mine, and the Cattle upon a thousand Hills. I know all the Fowls of the Mountains, and the Wilde Beasts of the field are mine. If I were Hungry I would not tell thee: for the World is mine, and the fulness therof. Will I eat the flesh of Buls or Drink the Blood of Goats? Offer 10 unto God Thanksgiving and pay thy Vows to the Most High. And call upon me in the Day of Trouble; I will Deliver Thee, and Thou shalt Glorify me. When I was a little child, I thought that evry one that lifted up his Eys to behold the sun, did me in looking on it Wonderfull service. And certainly being moved therby to Prais my Creator, it was in it self a service Wonderfully 15 Delightfull. For since GOD so much esteemeth Praises, that He preferreth them abov thousands of Rams and tens of thousands of Rivers of oyl: if I lov Him with that enflamed Ardor and Zeal I ought: His Praises must needs be Delightfull to me abov all Ser- vices and Riches whatsoever. That which hinders us from seeing 20 the Glory and Discerning the Sweetness of Praises; hinders us also from Knowing the maner how we are concerned in them. but God knoweth infinit reasons, for which he preferreth them. If I should tell you what they are you would be Apt to Despise them. Divine and Heavenly Mysteries being thirsted after till, they are 25 known, but by corrupted Nature undervalued Howbeit since Grace correcteth the Perversness of Nature, and tasteth in a better maner, it shall not be long, till somwhere we Disclose them.

82

Are not Praises the very End for which the World was created? Do they not consist as it were of Knowledg, Complacency, and Thanksgiving? Are they not Better then all the fowls and Beasts and fishes in the World? What are the Cattel upon a thousand Hils but Carcaises, without Creatures that can rejoyce in GOD, 5 and enjoy them? It is evident that Praises are infinitly more excel- lent then all the creatures becaus they proceed from Men and Angels. for as streams do they derive an Excellency from their Fountains, and are the last Tribut that can possibly be paid to the Creator. Praises are the Breathings of interior Lov, the Marks and 10 Symptoms of an Happy Life, Overflowing Gratitud, returning Benefits, an Oblation of the Soul, and the Heart ascending upon the Wings of Divine Affection to the Throne of GOD. GOD is a Spirit and cannot feed on Carcases: but He can be Delighted with Thanksgivings, and is infinitly pleased with the 15 Emanations of our Joy, becaus His Works are Esteemed, and Himself is Admired. What can be more Acceptable to Lov then that it should be Prized and Magnified. Becaus therfore God is Lov and his Measure infinit: He infinitly desires to be Admired and Beloved: and so our Praises enter into the very secret of His Eternal Bosom, and mingle with Him who Dwelleth in that Light which is inaccessible. What Strengths are there even in flattery to Pleas a great Affection? Are not your Bowels moved, and your Affections melted with Delight and Pleasure, when your Soul is Precious in the Ey of those you lov? when your Affection is Pleased; your Lov prized, and they satisfied? To Prize Lov is the Highest service in the Whole World that can be don unto it. But there are a thousand Causes moving GOD to Esteeme our Praises, more then we can well apprehend. However let these enflame you, and mov you to prais Him Night and Day for ever.

83

Of our Savior it is said, Sacrifice and Offering Thou wouldst not but a Body hast Thou prepared me, all Sacrifices being but Types and figures of Himself, and Himself infinitly more Excellent then they all. Of a Broken Heart also it is said, Thou desirest not Sacrifice els I would giv it. Thou Delightest not in Burnt Offering The Sacrifices of God are a broken Spirit, a broken and a contrite Heart O GOD Thou wilt not Despise. One Deep and Serious Groan is more Acceptable to God, then the Creation of a World. In Spiritual things we find the Greatest Excellency. As Praises becaus they are the Pledges of our Mutual Affection, so Groans becaus they are the Pledges of a Due Contrition are the Greatest Sacrifices. Both proceed from Lov. And in both we manifest and Exercise our friendship. In contrition we show our Penitence for having offended, and by that are fitted to rehears his Praises. All the Desire wherwith He longs after a Returning Sinner, makes Him to esteem a Broken heart. What can more melt and dissolv a Lover then the Tears of an offending and returning friend? Here also is the saying verified. The Falling out of Lovers is the Beginning of Lov: the renewing, the repairing and the Strengthen-ing of it.

84

An Enlarged Soul that seeth all the World Praising God, or Penitent by bewailing their Offences and converting to Him, hath his Ey fixed upon the Joy of Angels. It needeth nothing but the Sence of GOD to inherit all Things. We must borrow and derive it from Him by seeing His and Aspiring after it. Do but clothe 5 your self with Divine Resentments and the World shall be to you the valley of vision, and all the Nations and Kingdoms of the World shall appear in Splendor and celestial Glory.

85

The Righteous shall rejoyce when he seeth the vengeance, he shall Wash his feet in the Blood of the Wicked. But I will sing of thy Power, yea I will sing aloud of thy Mercy in the Morning. for Thou hast been my Defence in the Day of my Trouble. The Deliverances of your former Life are Objects of your Felicity, and 5 so is the Vengeance of the Wicked. with both which in all Times and Places you are ever to be present in your Memory and under, standing. for lack of Considering its Objects the Soul is Desolat.

86

My Soul thirsteth for Thee, my flesh longeth for Thee in a dry and thirsty Land where no Water is. To see thy Power and thy Glory so as I hav seen Thee in the Sanctuary. Becaus thy Loving Kind, ness is better then Life my Lips shall prais Thee. Thus will I Bless Thee while I live I will lift up my hands in thy Name. My soul 5 shall be satisfied as with Marrow and fatness, and my Mouth shall Prais Thee with joyfull Lips O Thou that hearest Prayer unto Thee shall all flesh com. Blessed is the Man whom Thou chusest and causest to approach unto Thee, that He may dwell in thy Courts. We shall be satisfied with the Goodnes of thy Hous even 10 of thy H. Temple. See how in the 65th Psal He introduceth the Meditation of Gods visible Works sweetly into the Tabernacle and maketh them to be the fatness of his hous even of his H. Temple.

God is seen when his Lov is manifested. God is enjoyed when his
15 Lov is prized. When we see the Glory of his Wisdom and Goodness and his Power exerted, then we see His Glory. And these
we cannot see till we see their Works. When therfore we see His
Works, in them as in a Mirror we see His Glory.

87

Make a Joyfull Nois unto God all ye Lands, sing forth the
Honor of his Name, make his Prais Glorious. Say unto God,
How terrible art Thou in thy Works? through the greatness of
thy Power shall thine Enemies submit them selvs unto Thee. All
5 the Earth shall Worship Thee and sing unto Thee, they shall sing
to thy Name. Com and see the Works of God He is Terrible in
His doing towards the Children of Men. The prospect of all
Nations Praising Him, is far sweeter then the Prospect of the feilds
or silent Heavens serving them. tho you see the Skies adorned with
10 Stars, and the feilds covered with corn and flocks of sheep and
Cattel. When the Ey of your Understanding shineth upon them,
they are yours in Him, and all your Joys.

88

God is my King of Old working Salvation in the midst of the
Earth. He divided the sea by His Strength. He brake the Heads
of Leviathan in Pieces. His Heart is always abroad in the midst of
the Earth: seeing and rejoycing in His Wonders there. His Soul is
5 busied in the Ancient Works of God for his People Israel. The
Day is thine, the Night also is thine, Thou hast prepared the
Light and the Sun. Thou hast set all the Borders of the Earth
Thou hast made Summer and Winter. He proposeth more Objects of our felicity. in which we ought to meet the Goodness of
10 God, that we might rejoyce before Him. The Day and Night,
the Light and the Sun are Gods Treasures, and ours also.

89

In the 78th Psalm he commandeth all Ages to record the Ancient Ways of God, and recommendeth them to our Meditation, shew, ing the Ordinance of God, that Fathers should teach their children, and they another Generation. Which certainly since they are not to be seen in the visible World, but only in the Memory and Minds of Men. The Memory and Mind are a strange Region of celestial Light, and a Wonderfull place as well as a large and sublime one in which they may be seen. What is contained in the Souls of Men being as visible to us as the very Heavens.

90

In the 84th Psalm He longeth earnestly after the Tabernacles of God, and preferreth a Day in his Courts abov a thousand. Becaus there as Deborah speaketh in her song, was the Place of Drawing Waters that is of repentance: and of rehearsing the Righteous Acts of the Lord. Which it is more Blessed to do then to inherit the Palaces of Wicked Men.

91

Among the Gods there is none like unto Thee. Neither are there any Works like unto thy Works. All Nations whom Thou hast made shall com and worship before Thee, O Lord, and shall glorify thy Name. For Thou art Great, and doest Wondrous things Thou art GOD alone. This is a Glorious Meditation, wherein the Psalmist gives himself Liberty to Examine the Excel, lency of Gods Works, and finding them infinitly Great and abov all that can be besides, rejoyceth, and admireth the Goodnes of God, and resteth satisfied with Complacency in them. That they were all his He Knew well, being the Gifts of God made unto him. and that He was to hav communion with God in the Enjoy, ment of them. But their Excellency was a thing unsearchable, and their Incomparableness abov all Imagination, which he found by much Study to his infinit Delectation.

92

In his other Psalms he proceedeth to Speak of the Works of God over and over again: somtimes stirring up all Creatures to Prais God for the very Delight he took in their Admirable Perfection somtimes shewing Gods Goodness and Mercy by them, and som-
5 times rejoycing Himself and Triumphing in them. By all this teaching us what we ought to do, that we might becom Divine and Heavenly. In the 103 psal. he openeth the Nature of Gods present Mercies, both towards himself in particular and towards all in general, turning Emergencies in this World into Celestial
10 Joys. In the 104. psal he insisteth wholy upon the Beauty of Gods Works in the Creation, making all things in Heaven and Earth and in the Heaven of Heavens, in the Wilderness and the Sea his Private and personal Delights. In the 105 and 106 Psalmes he celebrateth the Ways of God in former Ages with as much
15 vehemency Zeal and Pleasure as if they were New Things, and as if He were present with them seeing their Beauty and Tasting their Delight that very moment. In the 107 Psalm he Contemplates the Ways of God in the Dispensations of his Providence, over Travellers sick men sea men &c shewing that the way to be much
20 in Heaven, is to be much employd here upon Earth in the Medita-
tion of Divine and Celestial Things. for such are these tho they seem Terrestrial. All which he concludeth thus, Whoso consider-
eth these things, even he shall understand the Loving Kindness of the Lord. In the 119th Psalm, like an Enamord Person, and a Man
25 ravished in Spirit with Joy and pleasure he treateth upon Divine Laws, and over and over again maketh Mention of their Beauty and Perfection. By all which we may see what inward life we ought to lead with God in the Temple And that to be much in the Meditation of Gods Works and Ways and Laws, to see their
30 Excellency, to Taste their Sweetnes to behold their Glory, to Admire and Rejoyce and Overflow with Praises is to live in Heaven. But unlesse we hav a Communion with David in a Rational Knowledg of their Nature and Excellency We can never understand the Grounds of his Complacency or the Depth
35 of his Resentments.

93

In our outward Life towards Men the Psalmist also is an Ad/
mirable Precedent. In Weeping for those that forget Gods Law,
in publishing his Praises in the Congregation of the Righteous in
speaking of his Testimonies without Cowardice or shame even
before Princes, in delighting in the Saints, in Keeping Promises 5
tho made to his Hurt, in tendering the Life of his Enemies and
Clothing Himself with Sack/cloth when they were sick, in shew/
ing Mercy to the Poor, in enduring the Songs and Mockings of
the Drunkards, in taking care to Glorify the Author of all Bounty
with a Splendid Temple and Musical Instruments in this World, 10
in Putting his Trust and Confidence in God among all his
Enemies, evermore promoting his honor and Glory, Instructing
others in the Excellency of His Ways, and endeavouring to Estab/
lish his Worship in Israel. Thus ought we to the Best of our Power
to express our Gratitud and friendship to so Great a Benefactor in 15
all the Effects of Lov and fidelity. Doing His pleasure with all our
Might, and promoting his Honor with all our Power.

94

There are Psalmes more Clear wherin he Expresseth the Joy He
taketh in Gods Works and the Glory of them. wherin he teacheth
us at Divers times and in Divers manners to ponder on them.
Among which the 145 psal (and so onward to the last) are very
Eminent. In which he openeth the Nature of Gods Kingdom, 5
and so vigorously and vehemently Exciteth all Creatures to Praise
Him, and all Men to do it with all kind of Musical Instruments
by all Expressions, in all Nations for all Things as if 10000 vents
were not sufficient to eas his fulness, as if all the World were but
one Celestial Temple in which He was Delighted, as if all Nations 10
were present before him and he saw God face to face in this Earthly
Tabernacle, as if his Soul like an infinit Ocean were full of joys,
and all these but Springs and Chanels overflowing. So Purely so
Joyfully so Powerfully he walked with God, all Creatures, as they
brought a Confluence of Joys unto him, being Pypes to eas him. 15

95

His Soul recovered its Pristine Liberty and saw thorow the Mud
Walls of flesh and Blood. Being alive, he was in the Spirit all his
Days, while his Body therfore was inclosed in this World his Soul
was in the Temple of Eternity and clearly beholds the infinit Life
5 and Omnipresence of God. having Conversation with Invisible
Spiritual and Immaterial Things which were its companions it
self being Invisible Spiritual and Immaterial. Kingdoms and Ages
did surround him, as clearly as the Hills and Mountains: and
therfore the Kingdom of God was ever round about Him. evry
10 thing was one way or other his soveraign Delight and Transcendent
Pleasure, as in Heaven evry thing will be evry ones Peculiar
Treasure.

96

He saw these Things only in the Light of faith, and yet rejoyced
as if he had seen them in the Light of Heaven, which argued the
Strength and Glory of his faith And wheras he so rejoyced in all
the Nations of the Earth for Praising God, he saw them doing it
5 in the Light of Prophesie, not of History. Much more therfore
should we rejoyce, who see these Prophesies fulfilled, since the
fulfilling of them is so Blessed Divine and Glorious, that the very
Praevision of their Accomplishment Transported and Ravished
this Glorious Person. but we wither, and for lack of sence shrivell
10 up into Nothing who should be filled with the Delights of Ages.

97

By this we understand what it is to be the Sons of God and what
it is to live in Communion with him, what it is to be Advanced
to his Throne, and to reign in his Kingdom with all those other
Glorious and Marvellous Expressions that are applied to Men in
5 the H. Scriptures. To be the Sons of God is not only to Enjoy
the Privileges and the freedom of His Hous, and to bear the
Relation of Children to so Great a father, but it is to be like him
and to share with Him in all His Glory and in all his Treasures.

To be like Him in Spirit and Understanding, to be Exalted above
all Creatures as the End of them, to be present as He is by Sight 10
and Lov, without Limit and without bound with all his Works,
to be Holy towards all and Wise toward all as He is. Prizing all
his Goodness in all with infinit Ardor, that as Glorious and
Eternal Kings being Pleased in all we might reign over all for
ever more. 15

98

This Greatness both of God towards us, and of our selvs towards
him we ought always as much as Possible to retain in our understanding. And when we cannot effectualy Keep it alive in our
Sences, to cherish the Memory of it in the centre of our Hearts, and
do all things in the Power of it. for the Angels when they com to 5
us, so fulfill their outward Ministery, that within they nevertheless
maintain the Beatifick Vision: Ministering before the Throne of
God, and among the Sons of Men at the same time. The reason
wherof S. Greg. saith is this, Tho the Spirit of an Angel be
limited and Circumscribed in it self, yet the Supreme Spirit, 10
which is GOD, is uncircumscribed. He is evry where and wholy
evry where: which makes their Knowledg to be Dilated evry
where. for being wholy evry where They are immediatly present
with his Omnipresence in evry place and wholy. It filleth them
for ever. 15

99

This Sence that God is so Great in Goodnes, and we so Great in
Glory, as to be His Sons, and so Rich as to live in Communion
with Him; And so individualy united to Him, that He is in us,
and we in Him; will make us do all our Duties not only with
incomparable Joy, but Courage also. It will fill us with Zeal and 5
fidelity, and make us to overflow with Praises. for which one
cause alone the Knowledg of it ought infinitly to be Esteemed.
for to be Ignorant of this, is to sit in Darkness, and to be a Child
of Darkness: it maketh us to be without God in the World, exceeding Weak Timerous and feeble, Comfortless and Barren, 10
Dead and Unfruitfull, Lukewarm, Indifferent Dumb, unfaith-

full. To which I may adde that it makes us uncertain. for so
Glorious is the Face of God and True Religion, that it is impossible to see it, but in Transcendent Splendor. Nor can we Know
15 that God is, till we see Him infinit in Goodness. Nothing therfore
will make us certain of His Being but His Glory.

100

To Enjoy Communion with God is to abide with Him in the
fruition of His Divine and Eternal Glory, in all His Attributes
in all his Thoughts in all His Creatures; In His Eternity, Infinity,
Almighty Power, Soveraignty &c. In all those Works which from
5 all Eternity He wrought in Himself; as the Generation of His Son,
the Proceeding of the H. Ghost, the Eternal Union and Communion of the Blessed Trinity, the Councels of His Bosom, the
Attainment of the End of all His Endeavors wherin we shall see
our selvs exalted and Beloved from all Eternity. We are to enjoy
10 Communion with Him in the Creation of the World In the
Government of Angels, in the Redemption of Mankind, in the
Dispensations of His Providence in the Incarnation of his Son, in
His Passion Resurrection and Ascension, in His shedding abroad
the H.G. in his Government of the Church in His Judgment of
15 the World, in the Punishment of his Enemies, in the Rewarding
of his friends, in Eternal Glory. All these therfore Particularly
ought to be near us, and to be esteemed by us as our Riches;
being those Delectable Things that Adorn the Hous of GOD
which is Eternity; and those Living fountains, from whence we
20 suck forth the streams of Joy, that everlastingly overflow to
refresh our Souls.

THE FOURTH CENTURIE

I

Having spoken so much concerning his Enterance and Progress in Felicity, I will in this Centurie speak of the Principles with which your friend endued Himself to enjoy it! for besides Con-templativ, there is an Activ Happiness; which consisteth in Blessed Operations. And as som things fit a man for Contemplation, so there are others fitting him for Action: which as they are infinitly necessary to Practical Happiness, so are they likewise infinitly con-duciv to Contemplativ it self.

2

He thought it a Vain Thing to see Glorious Principles lie Buried in Books, unless he did remove them into his Understanding; and a vain thing to remov them unless he did revive them, and rais them up by continual exercise. Let this therfore be the first Prin-ciple of your soul. That to have no Principles, or to liv beside them, is equaly Miserable. And that Philosophers are not those that speak, but Do great Things.

3

He thought that to be a Philosopher a Christian and a Divine, was to be one of the most Illustrious Creatures in the World; and that no man was a Man in Act, but only in Capacity, that was not one of these; or rather all. for either of these Three include the other two. A Divine includes a Philosopher and a Christian, a Christian includes a Divine and a Philosopher, a Philosopher includes a Christian and a Divine. Since no man therfore can be a Man, unless he be a Philosopher, nor a true Philosopher unless he be a Christian, nor a Perfect Christian unless he be a Divine; evry man ought to spend his time, in studying diligently Divine Philosophy.

4

This last Principle needs a little Explication. Not only becaus Philosophy is condemned for vain, but becaus it is Superfluous among inferior Christians, and impossible as som think unto them. We must distinguish therfore of Philosophy, and of Chris-
5 tians also. Som Philosophy, as St Paul saith is vain, but then it is vain Philosophy. But there is also a Divine Philosophy, of which no Books in the World are more full then His own. That we are naturaly the Sons of GOD, (I speak of Primitiv and upright Nature,) that the Son of GOD is the first Beginning of evry
10 Creature, that we are to be Changed from Glory to Glory into the same Image, that we are Spiritual Kings, that Christ is the Express Image of His Fathers Person, that by Him all Things are made, whether they are Visible or Invisible, is the Highest Philosophy in the World, and so is it also to treat as he does of the Nature of
15 Virtues and Divine Laws. Yet no Man I suppose will account these Superfluous, or vain. for in the right Knowledg of these Eternal Life consisteth. And till we see into the Beauty and Blessedness of Gods Laws, the Glory of His Works, the Excel-lency of our Souls &c. we are but Children of Darkness, at least
20 but Ignorant and imperfect: neither able to rejoyce in God, as we ought, nor to liv in Communion with Him. Rather we should remember that Jesus Christ is the Wisdom of the father, and that since our Life is hid with Christ, in GOD; we should spend our Days in Studying Wisdom, that we might be like unto Him:
25 that the Treasures of Heaven are the Treasures of Wisdom, and that they are hid in him As it is written, In Him are hid all the Treasures of Wisdom and Knowledg.

5

In distinguishing of Christians, we ought to Consider that Chris-tians are of two sorts, Perfect or imperfect, Intelligent and Mature; or Weak and Inexperienced: (I will not say Ignorant, for an Ignorant Christian is a Contradiction in Nature. I say not that
5 an Imperfect Christian is the most Glorious Creature in the whole

World, nor that it is necessary for him, if he loves to be Imperfect, to be a Divine Philosopher. But he that is Perfect is a Divine Philosopher, and the most Glorious Creature in the whole World. Is not a Philosopher a Lover of Wisdom? That is the Significa⁄ tion of the very Word. And sure it is the Essence of a Christian 10 or very near it to be a Lover of Wisdom. Can a Christian be so degenerat, as to be a Lover of Imperfection? Does not your very Nature abhor Imperfection? Tis true a Christian so far as he is Defectiv and imperfect may be Ignorant. yet still He is a Lover of Wisdom, and a Studier of it. he may be defectiv, but so far as he 15 is defectiv he is no Christian. for a Christian is not a Christian in his Blemishes, but his Excellencies. Nor is a Man indeed a Man in his Ignorances, but his Wisdom. Blemishes may mar a Man, and spoil a Christian, but they cannot make him. Defects may be in Him and cleav unto him, but they are to be shaken off and 20 repented. Evry man therfore according to his Degree, so far forth as He is a Christian, is a Philosopher.

6

Furthermore doth not S. Paul command us *in understanding to be Men?* That implies that with little Understanding we are but children, and without understanding are not Men. but insigni⁄ ficant Shels, and meer Apparitions. Doth he not Earnestly Pray, that their Hearts may be Comforted, being Knit together in Lov, 5 unto all the Riches of the full Assurance of Understanding to the Acknowledgment of the Mystery of God, and of the Father and of Christ? This Plainly shews, that tho a Weak Christian may believ great things by an implicit faith, yet it is very desirable, his faith should be turned into Assurance, and that cannot be, but 10 by the Riches of Knowledg and Understanding. for He may beleiv that GOD is and that Jesus Christ is his Savior, and that His Soul is immortal, and that there are Joys in Heaven, and that the Scriptures are Gods Word, and that GOD loves him &c. so far as to yeeld Obedience in som measure, but he can never com 15 to a full Assurance of all this, but by seeing the Riches of the full Assurance i.e. those things which are called the Riches of the full

Assurance; becaus being Known they giv us Assurance of the Truth of all Things. The glory of GODs Laws, the True Dignity
20 of His own Soul, the Excellency of GODs Ways, the Magnificent Goodness of His Works, and the Real Blessedness of the State of Grace. All which a Man is so Clearly to see, that He is not more sensible of the Reality of the Sun Beams. How els should he liv in Communion with GOD; to wit, in the Enjoyment of them?
25 for a full Assurance of the Reality of his Joys, is infinitly necessary to the Possession of them.

7

This Digression steals me a little further. Is it not the shame and reproach of Nature, that men should spend so much time in studying Trades, and be so ready skild in the Nature of clothes, of Grounds, of Gold and Silver, &c. and think it much to spend
5 a little time, in the study of God, Themselvs, and Happiness? What hav men to do in this World, but to make them selvs Happy? Shall it ever be praised, and despised? Verily Happiness being the Soveraign and Supreme of our Concerns, should hav the most peculiar portion of our Time: and other things what she
10 can spare. It more concernes me to be Divine, then to hav a Purs of Gold. And therfore as Solomon said, We must dig for her as for Gold and silver; and that is the way to understand the fear of the Lord, and to find the Knowledg of God. It is a strange thing that Men will be such Enemies to them selvs: Wisdom is the
15 Principal Thing yet all neglect her. wherfore Get Wisdom, and with all thy Getting get understanding. Exalt her and she shall promote thee, she shall bring thee to Honor when thou dost embrace her. She shall giv to thy Head an Ornament of Grace, a Crown of Glory shall she deliver to Thee. Had you certain
20 Tidings of a Mine of Gold, would the care of your Ordinary Affairs detain you, could you hav it for the Digging? Nothing more ruins the world, then a Conceit, that a little Knowledg is sufficient. Which is a mere lazy Dream, to cover our Sloth or Enmity against GOD. Can you go to a Mine of Gold, and not
25 to Wisdom; (to dig for it;) without being guilty, either of a Base

Despondency and Distrust of Wisdom, that she will not bring you to such Glorious Treasures as is promised; or els of a vile and Lazy Humor that makes you despise them, becaus of that little, but long labor, you apprehend between? Nothing keeps men out of the Temple of Honor, but that the Temple of Vertue stands 30 between. But this was His Principle that loved Happiness, and is your friend. I came into this World only that I might be Happy. And whatsoever it cost me, I will be Happy. A Happiness there is, and it is my desire to enjoy it.

8

Philosophers are not only those that Contemplat happiness, but Practise Virtue. He is a Philosopher that subdues his vices, Lives by Reason, Orders his Desires, Rules his Passions, and submits not to his sences, nor is guided by the Customs of this World. He despiseth those Riches which Men esteem, he despiseth those 5 Honors which men esteem, he forsaketh those Pleasures which Men Esteem. And having proposed to him self a Superior End, then is commonly discerned, bears all Discouragements, breaks thorow all Difficulties and lives unto it: That having seen the Secrets, and the Secret Beauties of the Highest reason, orders his 10 Conversation, and lives by Rule: tho in this Age, it be held never so strange that He should do so. Only He is Divine becaus he does this upon Noble Principles, Becaus GOD is, becaus Heaven is, becaus Jesus Christ hath Redeemd him, and becaus he Lovs Him: not only becaus vertue is Amiable, and felicity Delightfull; 15 but for that also.

9

Once more we will distinguish of Christians. There are Christians, that place and desire all their Happiness in another Life, and there is another sort of Christians that desire Happiness in this. The one can defer their Enjoyment of Wisdom till the World to com: And dispence with the Increas and Perfection of Know- 5 ledg for a little time: the other are instant and impatient of Delay;

and would fain see that Happiness here, which they shall enjoy
herafter. Not the vain Happiness of this World, falsly called
Happiness, truly vain: but the real Joy and Glory of the Blessed:
10 which Consisteth in the Enjoyment of the Whole World in
Communion with God, not this only, but the Invisible and
Eternal: which they earnestly covet to Enjoy immediatly: for
which reason they daily Pray Thy Kingdom come; and travail
towards it by learning Wisdom as fast as they can. Whether the
15 first sort be Christians indeed, look you to that. They hav much
to say for themselvs. Yet certainly they that put of felicity with long
delays, are to be much suspected. for it is against the Nature of
Lov and desire to defer. Nor can any reason be given, why they
should desire it at last, and not now. If they say Becaus God hath
20 Commanded them, that is fals: for He offereth it now, Now they
are commanded to have their Conversation in Heaven, now they
may be full of Joy and full of Glory. Ye are not streightned in me,
but in your own Bowels. Those Christians that can defer their
felicity may be contented with their Ignorance.

10

He that will not Exchange his Riches now will not forsake them
herafter. He must, but will hardly be persuaded to do it willingly.
He will leav them, but not forsake them. for which caus two
Dishonors cleav unto him; and if at Death, eternaly. first, he
5 coms of the Stage unwillingly, which is very unhandsom: and
secondly He prefers his Riches abov his Happiness. Riches are
but servants to Happiness, when they are Impediments they
ceas to be Riches. As long as they are Conduciv to Felicity they
are desirable; but when they are incompitable Abominable. for
10 what End are Riches endeavored, Why do we desire them but
that we may be more Happy? When we see the Persuit of them
destructiv to Felicity, to desire them is of all things in Nature the
most absurd and the most foolish. I ever thought that Nothing
was desirable for it self but Happiness, and that whatever els we
15 desire, it is of valu only in relation, and Order to it.

11

That Maxim also which your Friend used, is of very Great and Divine Concernment: *I will first spend a great deal of time in seeking Happiness, and then a Great deal more in Enjoying it.* For if Happiness be worthy to be Sought, it is worthy to be Enjoyed. As no folly in the world is more vile then that pretended by Alchymists, 5 of Having the Philosophers Stone, and being contented without using it: so is no Deceit more Odious, then that of Spending many Days in Studying, and none in Enjoying, Happiness. that Base pretence is an Argument of Falshood and meer forgery in them: that after so much toil in getting it they refuse to use it: 10 Their pretence is that they are so abundantly satisfied in having it, they care not for the use of it. So the Neglect of any Man that finds it, shews that indeed he hath lost of Happiness. That which he hath found is Counterfeit Ware, if he neglect to use it: Tis only becaus he cannot: Tru Happiness being to precious, to ly by 15 Despised. Shall I forsake all Riches and Pleasures for Happiness, and persue it many Days and Moneths and yeers; and then neglect and Bury it when I hav it? I will now spend Days and Nights in Possessing it. as I did before in seeking it. It is better being Happy, then Asleep. 20

12

Happiness was not made to be Boasted, but enjoyed. tho others count me miserable, I will not believ them; if I know and feel my self to be Happy; nor fear them. I was not born to approv my self to them: but GOD. A Man may enjoy very Great Delights, without telling them. 5

> Tacitus si pasci potuisset Corvus, haberet
> Plus Dapis; et rixæ minus, invidiæque.

> Could but the Crow in lonely Silence Eat,
> She then would hav less Envy, and more Meat.

Heaven is a Place where our Happiness shall be seen of all. We 10 shall there enjoy the Happiness of being seen in Happiness, with-

out the Danger of Ostentation: But here Men are Blind and Cor⁄
rupted, and cannot see: if they could, we are corrupted, and in
danger of abusing it. I knew a Man that was mightily derided
¹⁵ in his persuit of Happiness, till he was understood, and then
Admired. but he lost all by his Miscarriage.

13

One great Discouragement to Felicity, or rather to great Souls in
the Persuit of Felicity, is the Solitariness of the Way that leadeth
to her Temple. A man that studies Happiness must sit alone like
a Sparrow upon the Hous Top, and like a Pelican in the Wilder⁄
⁵ ness. And the reason is becaus all men Prais Happiness and
despise it. very few shall a Man find in the way of Wisdom: And
few indeed that having given up their Names to Wisdom and
felicity, that will persevere in seeking it. Either He must go on
alone, or go back for company People are tickled with the Name
¹⁰ of it, and som are persuaded to Enterprize a little, but quickly
draw back when they see the trouble yea cool of them selvs with⁄
out any Trouble. Those Mysteries which while men are Ignorant
of, they would giv all the Gold in the World for, I hav seen when
Known to be despised. Not as if the Nature of Happiness were
¹⁵ such that it did need a vail: but the Nature of Man is such, that
it is Odious and ingratefull. For those things which are most
Glorious when most Naked, are by Men when most Nakedly
reveald most Despised. So that GOD is fain for His very Names
sake, lest His Beauties should be scorned to conceal her Beauties:
²⁰ and for the sake of Men, which naturaly are more prone to prie
into secret and forbidden things then into Open and common.
Felicity is amiable under a Vail, but most Amiable when most
Naked. It hath its times, and seasons for both. There is som Pleasure
in breaking the Shell: and many Delights in our Addresses,
²⁵ previous to the Sweets in the Possession of her. It is som Part of
Felicity that we must seek her.

14

In order to this, he furnished him self with this Maxime. *It is a Good Thing to be Happy alone.* It is better to be Happy in Company, but Good to be Happy alone. Men owe me the Advantage of their Society, but if they deny me that just Debt, I will not be unjust to my self, and side with them in bereaving me. I will not ₅ be discouraged, least I be Miserable for Company. More Company increases Happiness, but does not leighten or Diminish Misery.

15

In Order to Interior or Contemplativ Happiness, it is a Good Principle: that Apprehensions within are better then their Objects. Morneys Simile of the Saw is admirable. If a man would cut with a saw, he must not apprehend it to be a Knife, but a Thing with Teeth; otherwise he cannot use it. He that mistakes his Knife to ₅ be an Auger, or his Hand to be his Meat, confounds him self by misapplications. These Mistakes are Ocular. but far more Absurd ones are unseen. To mistake the World, or the Nature of ones soul, is a more Dangerous Error. He that Thinks the Heavens and the Earth not his, can hardly use them: he that thinks the ₁₀ Sons of Men impertinent to his Joy and Happiness can scarcely lov them. But he that Knows them to be Instruments and what they are will delight in them, and is able to use them. Whatever we misapprehend we cannot use. Nor well enjoy, what we cannot use. Nor can a thing be our Happines, we cannot enjoy. Nothing ₁₅ therfore can be our Happiness, but that alone which we rightly apprehend. To apprehend God our Enemie destroys our Happiness. Inward Apprehensions are the very light of Blessednes, and the Cement of Souls and their Objects.

16

Of what vast Importance right Principles are, we may see by this, *Things Prized are Enjoyed.* All Things are ours; All Things serv us and Minister to us, could we find the way: Nay they are ours,

and serv us so perfectly, that they are best enjoyed in their proper
5 places: even from the Sun to a Sand, from a Cherubim to a
Worm. I will not except Gold and Silver and Crowns and
Precious Stones, nor any Delights or secret Treasures in Closets
and Palaces. For if otherwise GOD would not be perfect in
Bounty. But suppose the World were all yours if this Principle
10 be rooted in you, to Prize nothing that is yours, it blots out all at
one Dash, and bereavs you of a whole World in a Moment.

17

Tho God be yours, and all the Joys and Inhabitants in Heaven,
if you be resolvd to prize nothing Great and Excellent, nothing
Sublime and Eternal; you lay waste your Possessions; and make
vain your Enjoyment of all permanent and Glorious Things. So
5 that you must be sure to inure yourself frequently to these Principles and to impresse them deeply; *I will Prize all I hav: And
nothing shall with me be less esteemed, becaus it is Excellent. A Daily
Joy shall be more my Joy, becaus it is continual. A Common Joy is more
my Delight becaus it is Common. For all Mankind are my Friends And
10 evry Thing is Enriched in serving them.* A little Grit in the Ey destroy-
eth the sight of the very Heavens: and a little Malice or Envy a
World of Joys. One wry Principle in the Mind is of infinit Consequence. *I Will ever Prize what I hav, and so much the more becaus
I hav it.* To Prize a thing when it is gon breedeth Torment and
15 Repining: to Prize it while we hav it Joy and Thanksgiving.

18

All these relate to Enjoyment, but those Principles that relate to
Communication are more Excellent. These are Principles of
Retirement and Solitude; but the Principles that aid us in Conversation are far better: and help us, tho not so immediatly to
5 Enjoyment in a far more Blessed and Diviner maner. For it is more
blessed to giv then to receiv: and we are more happy in Communication then Enjoyment, but only that Communication is
Enjoyment; as indeed what we giv we best receiv. for the Joy of

Communicating and the Joy of receiving maketh perfect Happi' ness. And therfore are the Sons of Men our Greatest Treasures, 10 becaus they can giv and receiv: Treasures perhaps infinit as well as Affections. But this I am sure they are our Treasures. And therfore is Conversation so Delightfull becaus they are the Greatest.

19

The World is best enjoyed and most immediatly while we con' vers Wisely and Blessedly with Men. I am sure it were desirable that they could giv and receiv infinit Treasures. And perhaps they can. for whomsoever I lov as my self, to him I giv my self and all my Happiness. which I think is infinit: and I receiv Him and all 5 His Happiness. Yea in him I receiv GOD, for GOD delighteth me for being his Blessedness. So that a Man Obligeth me infinitly that maketh Himself Happy; and by making Himself Happy giveth me Himself and all His Happiness. Besides this he loveth me infinitly, as GOD doth; and he dare do no less for Gods sake. 10 Nay he loveth God for loving Me, and Delighteth in Him for being Good unto me. So that I am Magnified in his Affections, represented in his Understanding Tenderly Beloved Caressed and Honored: and this maketh Society Delightfull. But here upon Earth it is subject to Changes. And therfore this Principle is 15 always to be firm, as the foundation of Bliss, GOD only is my Soveraign Happiness and Friend in the World. Conversation is full of Dangers, and Friendships are Mortal among the Sons of Men. But Communion with GOD is infinitly Secure, and He my Happiness. 20

20

He from whom I received these things, always thought, that to be Happy in the midst of a Generation of Vipers was becom his Duty. for men and he are faln into Sin. Were all men Wise and Innocent, it were easy to be Happy. for no man would injure and molest another. But he that would be Happy now must be Happy 5 among Ingratefull and Injurious Persons. That Knowledg which would make a man Happy among just and Holy persons, is unusefull now: and those Principles only Profitable that will make a Man Happy, not only in Peace, but Blood. On every side we are environed with Enemies, surrounded with Reproaches en-compassed with Wrongs, beseiged with offences, receiving evil for Good, being disturbed by fools, and invaded with Malice. This is the true Estate of this World. Which lying in Wickedness, as our savior Witnesseth, yeeldeth no better fruits, then the bitter Clusters of folly and Perversness: the Grapes of Sodom, and the Seeds of Gomorrah. Blind Wretches that Wound themselvs, offend me. I need therfore the Oyl of Pitty and the Balm of Lov to remedie and heal them. Did they see the Beauty of Holiness or the face of Happiness, they would not do so. To think the World therfore a General Bedlam, or Place of Madmen, and one self a Physician, is the most necessary Point of present Wisdom: an important Imagination, and the Way to Happiness.

21

He thought within himself that this World was far better then Paradice had men Eys to see its Glory, and their Advantages. for the very Miseries and sins and offences that are in it, are the Materials of his Joy and Triumph and Glory. So that He is to learn a Diviner Art that wil now be Happy: and that is like a Royal Chymist to reign among Poysons to turn Scorpions into fishes, Weeds into flowers Bruises into Ornaments, Poysons into Cordials. And he that cannot this Art, of Extracting Good out of evil, is to be accounted Nothing. Hertofore, to Enjoy Beauties, and be Gratefull for Benefits was all the Art that was required to Felicity, but now a Man must like a GOD, bring Light out of Darkness, and Order out of Confusion. Which we are taught to do by His Wisdom, that Ruleth in the midst of Storms and Tempests.

22

He generaly held, that Whosoever would enjoy the Happiness of Paradice must put on the Charity of Paradice. And that Nothing was his Felicity but his Duty. He called his Hous the Hous of

Paradice: not only becaus it was the Place wherin he enjoyed the whole World, but becaus it was evry ones hous in the whole world. for observing the Methods, and studying the Nature of Charity in Paradice, he found that all men would be Brothers and Sisters throughout the whole World. and evermore love one another as their own selvs, tho they had never seen each other before. from whence it would proceed that evry man approaching him, would be as welcom as an Angel, and the coming of a Stranger as Delightfull as the Sun, all things in his Hous being as much the forreiners as they were his own. Especially if he could infuse any Knowledg or Grace into Him.

23

To establish him self thorowly in this Principle, he made much of another. For he saw that in Paradice a great help to this kind of Life, was the Cheapness of commodities, and the natural fertility of the then innocent and Blessed Ground. By which means it came to pass that evry man had enough for him self, and all. But that now the Earth being cursed and Barren, there was danger of want, a necessity of Toyl and labor and Care, and Maintenance of Servants. Therfore he concluded, That the Charity of Men ought to supply the Earths Sterility. who could never want, were they all of a Mind, and Liberal to each other. But since this also faileth, and mens hearts are Cursed and Barren as the Ground, What is wanting in them God will supply. And that to live upon Gods Provisions is the most Glorious Dependance in the whole world. And so he made the Lov of God his true foundation, and builded not his Hopes on the charity of men, but fled unto God as his last Refuge. Which he thought it very safe and blessed to do, becaus the Trial of his faith was more Glorious, and the Lov of God supplied the Defect of Charity in men: and he that had commanded had faithfully promised and was able to perform.

24

He thought the Stars as fair now, as they were in Eden, the sun as
Bright, the Sea as Pure: and nothing pesterd the World with
Miseries, and destroyed its order Peace and Beautie but sins and
vices. Rapine, covetousness envy Oppression Luxury Ambition
5 Pride &c. filled the World with Briars and Thorns, Desolations
Wars Complaints and Contentions. And that this made Enormi-
ties to be vices. But Universal Charity did it breath among Men,
would blow all these away, as the Wind doth Chaff and Stubble:
and that then the Heavens would be as serene and fair, and the
10 Lands as rich as ever they were. And that as all things were
improved by the Work of Redemption, Trades and Occupations
that were left behind, would be pleasant Ornaments and Innocent
Recreations. for whence have we all our Cities Palaces and
Temples, whence all our Thrones and Magnificent Splendors,
15 but from Trades and Occupations.

25

But Order and Charity in the midst of these, is like a Bright Star
in an obscure Night, like a summers day in the Depth of Winter,
like a sun shining among the clouds, like a Giant among his
Enemies, that receiveth Strength from their Numbers, like a King
5 sitting in the Midst of an Army. By how much the more scarce it
is, by so much the more Glorious. by how much the more
Assaulted by so much the more invincible, by how much the
more lonely, by so much the more pittied of God and Heaven.
And surely He, who being Perfect Lov, designed the felicity of
10 the world with so much Care, in the Beginning, will now be
more tender of a Soul that is like Him in its Deordination.

26

He thought that men were more to be Beloved now then before.
And which is a strange Paradox, the Worse they are the more
they were to be beloved. The Worse they are the more they were

to be Pittied and Tendered and Desired, becaus they had more need, and were more Miserable. tho the Better they are, they are more to be Delighted in. But his true Meaning in that saying was this, Comparing them with what they were before they were faln, they are more to be Beloved. They are now Worse yet more to be Beloved. For Jesus Christ hath been Crucified for them. God loved them more, and he gave his Son to die for them, and for me also. which are Strong Obligations, leading us to Greater Charity. So that Mens unworthiness and our vertu are alike increased.

27

He conceived it his Duty and much Delighted in the Obligation; That he was to treat evry Man in the whole World as the Representativ of Mankind, And that he was to meet in him, and to Pay unto Him all the Lov of God Angels and Men.

28

He thought that he was to treat evry man in the Person of Christ. That is both as if Himself were Christ in the Greatnes of his Lov, and also as if the Man were Christ he was to use him. having respect to all others. for the Lov of Christ is to Dwell within Him, and evry Man is the Object of it. God and he are to becom one Spirit, that is one in Will, and one in desire. Christ must liv within him. He must be filled with the H. Ghost which is the God of Lov, He must be of the same Mind with Christ Jesus, and led by His Spirit. for on the other side he was well acquainted with this Mystery, That evry man being the Object of our Saviors Lov, was to be treated as our Savior. Who hath said, Inasmuch as ye hav don it to the least of these my Brethren ye hav don it unto me. And thus he is to liv upon Earth among Sinners.

29

He had another saying, He lives most like an Angel that lives upon least Himself, and doth most Good to others. For the Angels neither eat nor Drink, and yet do Good to the whole World.

Now a Man is an Incarnat Angel. And He that lives in the midst
5 of Riches as a poor man Himself, Enjoying God and Paradice,
or Christendom which is Better, conversing with the Poor, and
seeing the valu of their Souls through their Bodies, and Prizing
all things cleerly with a due esteem, is arrived here to the Estate of
Immortality. He cares little for the Delicacies either of food or
10 Raiment himself: and Delighteth in others. God Angels and
Men are his Treasures. He seeth through all the Mists and Vails of
Invention, and possesseth here beneath the true Riches. And he
that doth this always is a rare Phœnix: But he confessed that he
had often caus to bewail his Infirmities.

30

I speak not His Practices but His Principles. I should too much
Prais your friend did I speak his Practices, but it is no shame for
any man to declare his Principles, tho they are the most Glorious
in the world. Rather they are to be Shamed that have no Glorious
5 Principles: or that are ashamed of them. This he desired me to tell
you becaus of Modesty. But with all, that indeed his Practices are
so short of these Glorious Principles, that to relate them would
be to his Shame; and that therfore you would never look upon
him but as clothed in the Righteousness of Jesus Christ. Never
10 theless I hav heard him often say, That he never allowd himself
in Swerving from any of these. And that he repented deeply of
evry Miscarriage: and moreover firmly resolved as much as was
possible never to erre or wander from them again.

31

I heard him often say that Holiness and Happiness were the same
and he coated a mighty Place of Scripture, All her ways are
pleasantness and her Paths are Peace. But he delighted in giving
the Reason of Scripture, and therfore said, That Holiness and
5 Wisdom in Effect were one. for no man could be Wise that Knew
Excellent Things, without doing them. Now to do them is Holi

ness, and to do them Wisdom. No man therfore can be further Miserable then he swerveth from the Ways of Holiness and Wis-dom.

32

If he might hav had but one Request of GOD Almighty it should hav been abov all other, that he might be a Blessing to Mankind. That was his Daily Prayer abov all his Petitions. He wisely knew that it included all Petitions. for He that is a Blessing to Mankind must be Blessed, that he may be so, and must inherit all their 5 Affections and in that their Treasures. He could not Help it. But he so desired to lov them, and to be a Joy unto them, that he protested often, that He could never Enjoy Himself, but as He was enjoyed of others, and that above all Delights in all Worlds, he desired to be a Joy and Blessing to others. Tho for this he was 10 not to be commended, for he did but Right to God and Nature, who had implanted in all that Inclination.

33

The desire of Riches was removed from Himself pretty Early. He often Protested, If he had a Palace of Gold and a Paradice of Delights, besides that he enjoyed, he could not understand a farthing worth of Benefit that he should receiv therby, unless in giving it away. but for others he somtimes could desire Riches. 5 till at last perceiving that Root of Covetousness in Him, and that it would grow as long as it was Shrouded under that Mould: He rooted it quite up with this Principle. *Somtimes it may so Happen, that to contemn the World in the Whole Lump, was as Acceptable to GOD, as first to get it with solicitud and care, and then to retail it out in* 10 *Particular Charities.*

Phocion

34

After this he could say with Luther, that Covetousness could never fasten the least hold upon Him. And concerning his friends even to the very Desire of seeing them rich, he could say as Phocion

the Poor Athenian did of his children. Either they will be like, me
or not, if they are like me they will not need Riches, if they are not
they will be but needless and Hurtfull Superfluities.

35

He desired no other Riches for his friends, but those which cannot
be Abused: to wit the True Treasures, God and Heaven and
Earth and Angels and Men, &c. with the Riches of Wisdom and
Grace to enjoy them. And it was his Principle That all the
Treasures in the whole World would not make a Miser Happy.
A Miser is not only a Covetous Man but a fool. Any Needy Man,
that wanteth the World, is Miserable. He wanteth God and all
Things.

36

He thought also that no Poverty could befall him that enjoyd
Paradice. for when all the Things are gone which Men can giv,
A Man is still as Rich as Adam was in Eden: who was Naked
there. A Naked man is the Richest Creature in all Worlds: and
can never be Happy; till he sees the Riches of his Nakedness. He
is very Poor in Knowledg that thinks Adam poor in Eden. See
here how one Principle helps another. All our Disadvantages
contracted by the fall are made up and recompensed by the Lov
of God.

37

Tis not Change of Place, but Glorious Principles well Practiced
that establish Heaven in the Life and Soul. An Angel will be
Happy any where; and a Divel Miserable. Becaus the Principles
of the one are always Good, of the other Bad. from the Centre to
the utmost Bounds of the Everlasting Hills, all is Heaven before
God, and full of Treasure. And he that walks like God in the
midst of them, Blessed.

38

lov God Angels and Men, Triumph in Gods Works, delight in
Gods Laws, Take Pleasure in Gods Ways in all Ages, Correct
Sins, bring good out of evil, subdue your Lusts order your sences,
Conquer the Customs and Opinions of men, and render Good
for evil, you are in Heaven evry where. Abov the Stars earthly 5
Things will be celestial Joys, and here beneath will things delight
you that are above the Heavens. All Things being infinitly Beauti⁄
full in their Places: and wholy yours in all their Places. Your
Riches will be as infinit in value and Excellency, as they are in
Beauty and Glory, and that is, as they are in Extent.   10

39

Thus He was Possessor of the whole World, and held it his
Treasure, not only as the Gift of GOD, but as the Theatre of
Virtues. Esteeming it principaly his, becaus it upheld and minis⁄
tered to Many objects of his Lov and Goodness. Towards whom,
before whom, among whom he might do the work of fidelity and 5
wisdom, exercise his Courage and Prudence, shew his Tem⁄
perance and Bring forth the fruits of faith and Repentance. For all
those are the Objects of our Joy that are the Objects of our Care,
They are our true Treasures about whom we are wisely Employed.

40

He had one Maxime of notable concernment, and that was, That
GOD having reservd all other Things in his own Disposal, had
left his Heart to Him. Those things that were in GODs Care he
would commit to GOD, those things that were committed to his,
he would take care about. He said therfore, that he had but one 5
thing to do and that was to order and keep his Heart which alone
being well guided, would order all other things Blessedly and
Successfully. The Things about him were innumerable and out
of his Power, but they were in Gods Power. And if he pleased
God in that which was committed to Him, God would be sure 10

to pleas Him in things without committed unto God. for He was faithfull that had promised, in all that belonged unto him God was perfect, all the Danger being, lest we should be imper′ fect in ours, and unfaithfull in those Things that pertain unto us.

41

Having these Principles nothing was more easy then to enjoy the world. which being enjoyed, he had nothing more to do, then to spend his Life in Praises and Thanksgivings. All his Care being to be sensible of Gods Mercies, and to behave himself as the
5 Friend of God in the Univers. If any thing were amiss, he still would have recours to his own heart, and found nothing but that out of frame. by restoring which al things were rectified, and made Delightfull. As much as that had swerved from the Rule of Justice Equity and Right, so far was he miserable, and no more. so that by
10 Experience he found the Words of the Wise Man True, and worthy of all Acceptation; *In all thy Keeping, Keep thy Heart, for out of it are the Issues of Life and Death.*

42

One thing he saw, which is not commonly discerned; and that is, that God made Man a free Agent for his own Advantage; and left him in the hand of his own Counsel, that he might be the more Glorious. It is hard to conceiv how much this tended to his Satis′
5 faction. for all the things in Heaven and Earth being so Beautifull, and made as it were on purpose for his own Enjoyment, he infinitly admired Gods Wisdom. in that it salved his and all Mens Exigencies, in which it fully answerd his Desires. for his Desire was that all Men should be happy as well as he. And he admired
10 his Goodness, which had enjoyned no other Duty, than what pertained to the more convenient fruition of the World which he had given: and at the Marvellous Excellency of his Lov, in com′ mitting that Duty to the Sons of Men, to be performed freely. For therby he adventured such a Power into the Hands of his Creatures,
15 which Angels and Cherubims wonder at, and which when it is

understood all Eternity will admire the Bounty of Giving. For he therby committed to their hands a Power to do that which he infinitly hated. which nothing certainly could mov him to Entrust them with, but some infinit Benefit which might be attained therby. What that was if you desire to Know, it was the Excel- 20 lency Dignity and Exaltation of his Creature.

43

O Adorable and Eternal GOD! hast thou made me a free Agent! And enabled me if I pleas to offend Thee infinitly! What other End couldst Thou intend by this, but that I might pleas Thee infinitly! That having the Power of Pleasing or displeasing I might be the friend of God! Of all Exaltations in all Worlds this 5 is the Greatest. To make a World for me was much, to command Angels and Men to lov me was much, to prepare Eternall Joys for me was more. But to giv me a Power to displeas thee, or to set a Sin before Thy face, which Thou infinitly hatest, to profane Eternity, or to defile thy Works, is more stupendious then all these. 10 What other couldst thou intend by it, but that I might infinitly please Thee? And having the Power of Pleasing or Displeasing, might pleas thee and my self infinitly, in being Pleasing! Hereby Thou hast prepared a new fountain and Torrent of Joys, Greater then all that went before, seated us in the Throne of God, made 15 us thy Companions, endued us with a Power most Dreadfull to ourselvs, that we might liv in sublime and Incomprehensible Blessednes for evermore. For the Satisfaction of our Goodness, is the most Soveraign Delight of which we are capable. And that by our own Actions we should be wel pleasing to Thee, is the 20 Greatest Felicity Nature can contain. O Thou who art infinitly Delightfull to the Sons of Men, make me, and the Sons of Men, infinitly Delightfull unto Thee. Replenish our Actions with Amiableness and Beauty, that they may be answerable to thine, and like unto Thine in sweetness and value. That as Thou in all 25 thy Works art pleasing to us, we in all our Works may be so to Thee; our own Actions as they are pleasing to Thee being an Offspring of Pleasures sweeter then all.

44

This he thought a Principle at the Bottom of Nature, That what⁄
soever satisfied the Goodness of Nature, was the Greatest Treasure.
Certainly men therfore Erre becaus they Know not this Principle.
for all Inclinations and Desires in the Soul flow from, and tend
5 to the Satisfaction of Goodness. Tis strange that an Excess of
Goodness should be the fountain of all Evil. An Ambition to
pleas, a Desire to Gratifie, a great Desire to Delight others being
the Greatest snare in the world. Hence is it that all Hypocrisies
and Honors arise, I mean Esteem of Honors. Hence all Imitations
10 of human customs, hence all compliances and submissions to the
Vanities and Errors of this World. For Men being mistaken in
the Nature of Felicity, and we by a strong inclination prone to
pleas them, follow a Multitud to do evil. We naturaly desire to
approve our selvs to them, and abov all other things covet to be
15 Excellent, to be Greatly Beloved, to be Esteemed, and Magnified,
and therfore endeavor what they endeavor, Prize what they prize,
Magnifie what they desire, desire what they Magnify: ever doing
that which will render us accepted to them; and coveting that
which they admire and Prais: that so we might be delightfull.
20 And the more there are that delight in us the more Great and
Happy we account our selvs.

45

This Principle of Nature, when you remov the Rust it hath con⁄
tracted by Corruption, is Pure Gold; and the most Orient Jewel
that shines in Man. Few consider it either in it self, or in the Design
of the Implanter. No man doubts but it is Blessed to receiv. To
5 be made a Glorious Creature, and to hav Worlds given to one is
Excellent. But to be a Glorious Creature and to Giv, is a Blessed⁄
ness unknown. It is a Kind of Paradox in our Savior, and not (as
we read of) revealed upon earth, but to S. Paul from heaven, *It
is more Blessed to Giv then to receiv*. It is a Blessedness too high to be
10 understood. To Giv is the Happiness of GOD; to Receiv, of
Man. But O the Mystery of His Loving Kindness, even that also
hath He imparted to us. Will you that I ascend higher? In giving

us him self, in giving us the World, in giving us our Souls and Bodies he hath don much, but all this had been Nothing, unless he had given us a Power to hav given him our selvs. in which is 15 contained the Greatest Pleasure and Honor that is. We lov our selvs earnestly, and therfore rejoyce to have Palaces and Kingdoms. but when we have these, yea Heaven and Earth, unless we can be Delightfull and Joyous to others they will be of no value. One soul to whom we may be pleasing is of Greater Worth then all 20 Dead Things. Som unsearchable Good lieth in this, without which the other is but a vile and desolate Estate. So that to hav all Worlds, with a certain sence that they are infinitly Beautiful and Rich and Glorious is miserable vanity, and leavs us forlorn, if all things are Dead, or if our selvs are not Divine and Illustrious 25 Creatures.

46

O the Superlative Bounty of GOD! Where all Power seemeth to ceas, he proceedeth in Goodness: and is wholy infinit Unsearchable and Endless. He seemeth to hav made as many things depend upon Mans Liberty, as his own. When all that could be wrought by the Use of His own Liberty were attained, by Mans Liberty 5 he attained more. This is Incredible, but Experience will make it Plain. By his own Liberty he could but Creat Worlds and giv himself to creatures Make Images and endow them with faculties, or seat them in Glory. But to see them Obedient, or to enjoy the Pleasure of their Amity and Praises, to make them Fountains of 10 Actions like his own, (without which indeed they could not be Glorious:) or to enjoy the Beauty of their free Imitation, this could by no means be, without the Liberty of his Creatures intervening. Nor indeed could the World be Glorious, or they Blessed without this Attainment. For can the World be Glorious unless it be 15 Usefull? And to what Use could the World serv Him, if it served not those, that in this were supremely Glorious that they could Obey and Admire and Lov and Prais, and Imitat their Creator? Would it not be wholy useless without such Creatures? In Creating Liberty therfore and giving it to his Creatures he Glorified All 20 Things: Himself, his Works, and the Subjects of His Kingdom.

47

You may feel in your self how Conduciv this is to your Highest
Happiness. For that you should be Exalted to the fruition of
Worlds, and in the midst of innumerable most Glorious Creatures
be vile and Ingratfull, Injurious and Dishonorable, Hatefull and
5 evill, is the Greatest Misery and Dissatisfaction imaginable. But
to be the Joy and Delight of innumerable Thousands, to be ad⁄
mired as the Similitud of God, to be Amiable and Honorable,
to be an Illustrious and Beautifull Creature, to be a Blessing. O
the Good we perceiv in this! O the Suavity! O the Contentation!
10 O the infinit and unspeakable Pleasure! Then indeed we Reign
and Triumph when we are Delighted in. Then are we Blessed
when we are a Blessing. When all the World is at Peace with us
and takes Pleasure in us, when our Actions are Delightfull, and
our Persons lovly when our Spirits Amiable, and our Affections
15 inestimable, then are we Exalted to the Throne of Glory. for things
when they are usefull are most Glorious, and it is impossible for
you or me to be usefull but as we are Delightfull to GOD and
his Attendants. And that the Head of the World, or the End for
which all Worlds were made should be useles, as it is impropor⁄
20 tiond to the Glory of the Means, and Methods of his Exaltation,
so is it the Reproach of his Nature and the utter undoing of all his
Glory. It is improportionable to the Beauty of his Ways who
made the World, and to the Expectation of his Creatures.

48

By this you may see, that the Works or Actions flowing from your
own Liberty are of Greater Concernment to you then all that
could possibly happen besides. And that it is more to your Happi⁄
ness what you are, then what you enjoy. Should God giv him
5 self and all Worlds to you, and you refuse them, it would be to no
purpose. should he lov you and magnify you, should he giv his
Son to Dy for you and command all Angels and Men to lov you,
should he Exalt you in his Throne, and giv you Dominion over
all his Works and you neglect them it would be to no purpose.

Should he make you in his Image, and employ all his Wisdom 10
and Power to fill Eternity with Treasures, and you despise them
it would be in vain. In all these Things you hav to do; and ther/
fore your Actions are great and Magnificent, being of infinit
Importance in all Eys. While all Creatures stand in Expectation
what will be the result of your Liberty. Your Exterior Works are 15
little in Comparison of these. And God infinitly desires you
should demean your self Wisely in these Affairs: that is Rightly.
Esteeming and receiving what he gives, with Veneration and Joy
and infinit Thanksgiving. Many other Works there are, but this
is the Great Work of all Works to be performed. Consider 20
Whether more depends upon Gods Lov to you, or your Lov to
Him. From His Lov all the Things in Heaven and Earth flow
unto you; but if you lov neither Him nor them, you bereav your
self of all, and make them infinitly evil and Hurtfull to you and
your self abominable. So that upon your Lov naturaly depends 25
your own Excellency and the Enjoyment of His. It is by your Lov
that you enjoy all His Delights, and are Delightfull to Him.

49

It is very observable by what small Principles infusing them in the
Beginning GOD attaineth infinit Ends. By infusing the Principle
of Self lov he hath made a Creature Capable of Enjoying all
Worlds: to whom, did he not lov him self, nothing could be given.
By infusing Gratefull Principles, and inclinations to Thanks/ 5
giving He hath made that Creature Capable of more then all
Worlds, yea of more then Enjoying the Dietie in a Simple Way:
tho we should suppose it to be infinit. For to Enjoy God as the
fountain of infinit Treasures, and as the Giver of all, is infinit
Pleasure: But He by his Wisdom infusing Gratefull Principles, 10
hath made us upon the very Account of Self Lov to lov him
more then our selvs. And us, who without self Lov could not be
pleased at all, even as we lov our selvs he hath so infinitly pleased,
that we are able to rejoyce in him and to lov him more then our
selvs. And by loving him more then our selvs, in very Gratitud 15
and Honor, to take more Pleasure in his Felicity then in our own,

By which way we best Enjoy Him. To see his Wisdom Goodness and Power Employed in Creating all Worlds for our Enjoyment, and infinitly Magnified in Beautifying them for us, and Governing them for us; satisfies our self lov; but withall it so obligeth us, that
20 in Lov to Him, which it createth in us, it maketh us more to Delight in those Attributs as they are his, then as they are our own. And the truth is, without this we could not fully Delight in them. for the most Excellent and Glorious Effect of all had been un-atchieved. But now there is an infinit Union between Him and
25 us, He being infinitly Delightfull to us and we to Him. For he infinitly Delighteth to see Creatures Act upon such Illustrious and Eternal Principles, in a maner so Divine Heroick, and most truly Blessed. and we delight in seeing Him giving us the Power.

50

That I am to receiv all the Things in Heaven and Earth is a Prin-ciple not to be Sleighted. That in receiving I am to behav my self in a Divine and Illustrious Maner, is equaly Glorious. That GOD and all Eternity are mine is surely Considerable: That I
5 am His, is more. How ought I to Adorn my self, who am made for his Enjoyment? If Mans heart be a Rock of Stone, these things ought to be Engraven in it with a pen of a Diamond: and evry letter to be filled up with Gold that it might Eternaly Shine in Him and before him: Wherever we are living, whatever we are doing
10 these things ought always to be felt within him. Abov all Trades, abov all Occupations this is most Sublime. this is the Greatest of all Affairs. Whatever els we do, it is only in order to this End that we may live Conveniently to Enjoy the World, and GOD within it; which is the Soveraign Employment including and crowning
15 all. the celestial Life of a Glorious Creature, without which all other Estates are Servile and Impertinent.

51

Man being to liv in the Image of GOD, and thus of Necessity to becom productiv of Glorious Actions, was made Good, that he

might rejoyce in the fruits, which himself did yeeld. That Goodness which by Error and Corruption becomes a Snare, being in
the clear and pure Estate of Innocency, the fountain and the
chanell of all His Joys.

52

Thus you see how GOD has perfectly pleased me: It ought also
to be my care perfectly to pleas Him. He has given me freedom,
and adventured the Power of Sinning into my Hands: it ought to
be a Principle engraven in me, to use it Nobly. to be Illustrious
and Faithfull, To please him in the Use of it, to consult his
Honor, and having all the Creatures in all Worlds by His Gift
Ministering unto Me, to behav my self as a faithfull Friend to so
Great a Majesty, so Bountifull a Lord, so Divine a Benefactor.
Nothing is so Easy as to yeeld ones Assent to Glorious Principles,
nothing so Clear in upright Nature, nothing so Obscure to find
in Perverted, nothing so Difficult to Practice at all. In the Rubbish
of Depraved Nature they are lost, tho when they are found by any
one, and shewn, like Jewels they shine by their Nativ Splendor.

53

If you ask, what is becom of us since the Fall? becaus all these
things now lately named seem to pertain to the Estate of Innocency;
Truly Now we hav superadded Treasures: Jesus Christ. And are
restored to the Exercise of the same Principles, upon higher
Obligations: I will not say with More Advantage. Tho perhaps
Obligations them selvs are to us Advantage. For what enabled
Adam to lov God? Was it not that God loved him? What con-
strained him to be avers from God? Was it not that God was
avers from Him? When he was faln he thought GOD would
hate him, and be his Enemy Eternaly. And this was the Miserable
Bondage that Enslaved him. But when he was restored; O the
infinit and Eternal Change! His very lov to Himself made him
to prize His Eternal Lov. I mean his Redeemers. Do we not all
lov our selvs? Self lov maketh us to lov those that lov us, and to

15 hate all those that hate us. So that Obligations themselvs are to us Advantage. How we com to lose those Advantages I will not stand here to relate. In a Clear Light it is certain no Man can Perish. For GOD is more Delightfull then He was in Eden. Then he was as Delightfull as was possible but he had not that 20 occasion, as by Sin was offered, to superad many more Delights then before. Being more Delightfull and more Amiable, He is more Desirable and may now be more Easily yea Strongly Beloved. for the Amiableness of the Object Enables us to lov it.

54

It was your friends Delight to Meditat the Principles of Upright Nature: and to see how things stood in Paradice before they were Muddied and Blended and Confounded. for now they are lost and buried in Ruines. Nothing appearing but fragments, that are 5 worthless shreds and Parcels of them. To see the Intire Piece ravisheth the Angels. It was his Desire to recover them and to Exhibit them again to the Eys of Men. Abov all things he desired to see those Principles which a Stranger in this World would covet to behold upon his first appearance. And that is what Prin- 10 ciples those were, by which the Inhabitants of this World, are to liv Blessedly and to Enjoy the same. He found them very Easy, and infinitly Noble: very Noble, and productiv of unspeakable Good, were they well persued.We hav named them, and they are such as these, A Man should Know the Blessings he enjoyeth. 15 A Man should prize the Blessings which he Knoweth. A Man should be Thankfull for the Benefits which he prizeth. A Man should rejoyce in that for which He is Thankfull. These are easy things, and so are those also which are drowned in a Deluge of Errors and Customs, That Blessings the more they are, are the 20 sweeter; the longer they continue the more to be Esteemed; the more they serv, if Lovers and Friends, the more Delightfull, yet these are the hard lessons, in a pervers and Retrograde World to be practiced: and almost the only Lessons necessary to its Enjoy- ment.

55

He was a Strict and Severe Applier of all Things to Himself.
And would first hav his Self Lov satisfied, and then his Lov of all
others. It is true that Self Lov is Dishonorable, but then it is when
it is alone. And Self endedness is Mercinary, but then it is when it
endeth in oneself. It is more Glorious to lov others, and more 5
desirable, but by Natural Means to be attained. That Pool must
first be filled, that shall be made to overflow. He was ten yeers
studying before he could satisfy his Self Lov. And now finds
nothing more easy then to lov others better than oneself. And that
to love Mankind so is the comprehensiv Method to all felicity. 10
For it makes a Man Delightfull to GOD and Men, to Himself
and Spectators, and God and Men Delightfull to Him, and
all creatures infinitly in them. But as not to lov oneself at all
is Bruitish: or rather Absurd and Stonish: (for Beasts do lov
themselvs) so hath GOD by rational Methods enabled us to lov 15
others better then our selvs, and therby made us the most Glorious
Creatures. Had we not loved our selvs at all we could never hav
been obliged to lov any thing. So that self Lov is the Basis of all
Lov. But when we do lov our selvs, and self Lov is satisfied
infinitly in all its Desires and possible Demands, then it is easily 20
led to regard the Benefactor more then it self, and for his sake
overflows abundantly to all others. So that God by satisfying my
self Lov, hath enabled, and engaged me to love others.

56

No man loves, but he loves another more then Himself. In mean Instances
this is apparent. If you com into an Orchard with a person you
lov, and there be but one ripe cherry you prefer it to the other. If
two lovers Delight in the same piece of Meat, either takes pleasure
in the other, and more esteems the Beloveds Satisfaction. What 5
ailes men, that they do not see it? In greater Cases this is Evident.
A mother runs upon a sword to save her Beloved. A Father
leaps into the fire to fetch out his Beloved. Lov brought Christ
from Heaven to Die for his Beloved. It is in the Nature of Lov to

10 Despise it self: and to think only of its Beloveds Welfare. Look to it, it is not right Lov, that is otherwise. Moses and S. Paul were no fools. God make me one of their Number. I am sure Nothing is more Acceptable to him, then to lov others so as to be willing to impart even ones own Soul for their Benefit and welfare.

57

Nevertheless it is infinitly rewarded: tho it seemeth Difficult. for by this Lov do we becom Heirs of all Mens Joys, and Coheirs with Christ. For, what is the reason of your own Joys, when you are Blessed with Benefits? Is it not self Lov? Did you lov others 5 as you lov your self, you would be as much affected with their Joys. Did you lov them more, more. for according to the Measure of your Lov to others will you be Happy in them. for according therto you will be Delightfull to them, and Delighted in your felicity. The more you lov men, the more Delightfull you will be 10 to God, and the more Delight you will take in God, and the more you will enjoy Him. So that the more like you are to Him in Goodness, the more abundantly you will enjoy his Goodness. By loving others you liv in others to receiv it.

58

Shall I not lov him infinitly for whom GOD made the World and gav his Son? Shall I not lov him infinitly who loveth me infinitly? Examin your self Well, and you will find it a difficult matter to lov God so as to Die for him, and not to lov your 5 Brother so as to die for Him in like maner. Shall I not lov Him infinitly whom God loveth infinitly, and commendeth to my Lov, as the Representativ of Himself, with such a Saying, What ye do to Him is don unto me? And if I lov him so can I forbear to Help him? Verily had I but one Crown in the World, being 10 in an open field, where both he and I were ready to perish, and twere necessary that one of us must hav it all, or be Destroyed, tho I knew not where to hav relief, he should hav it, and I would die with Comfort. I will not say, How small a comfort so small a

succor is did I keep it: but how Great a Joy, to be the occasion
of anothers Life! Lov Knows not how to be Timerous, becaus it
receives what it gives away. And is unavoidably the End of its
own Afflictions and anothers Happiness. Let him that pleases
Keep his mony I am more rich in this Noble Charity to all the
World, and more enjoy my self in it, then he can be in both the
Indies.   20

59

Is it unnatural to do what Jesus Christ hath don? He that would
not in the same Cases do the same things can never be saved. for
unless we are led by the Spirit of Christ we are none of His. Lov
in him that in the same Cases would do the same Things, will be
an Oracle allways inspiring and teaching him what to doe: how
far to adventure upon all occasions. And certainly he, Whose
Lov is like his Saviors, will be far greater then any that is now
alive, in Goodness and Lov to GOD and Men. This is a sure
Rule. Lov studies not to be scanty in its Measures, but how to
abound and overflow with Benefits. He that Pincheth and Studieth
to Spare is a pittifull Lover: unless it be for others sakes. Lov
studieth to be Pleasing Magnificent and Noble, and would in all
Things be Glorious and Divine unto its Object. Its whole Being
is to its Object, and its whole felicity in its Object. And it hath
no other thing to take care for. It doth Good to its own Soul while
it doth Good to another.

60

Here upon Earth, it is under many Disadvantages and Impediments that maim it in its Exercise. But in Heaven it is most
Glorious. And it is my Happiness that I can see it on both sides
the Vail or Skreen. There it appeareth in all its Advantages for
evry Soul being full, and fully satisfied, at Eas, in rest, and Wanting nothing, easily overflows and shines upon all. It is its perfect
Interest so to do, and nothing Hinders it. Self Love there being
swallowed up and made perfect in the Lov of others. But here it
is pinched and straitned by wants: here it is awakend and put in

10 mind of it self: here it is divided and Distracted between two. It
has a Body to provide for, necessities to reliev and a person to
supply. Therfore is it in this world the more Glorious, if in the
midst of these Disadvantages it exert it self in its Operations. In
the other World it swimmeth down the stream and acteth with its
15 interest. Here therfore is the Place of its Trial where its Operations
and its Interest are Divided. And If our Lord Jesus Christ as
som think, Knew the Glory to which he should ascend, by Dying
for others, and that all was safe which he undertook, becaus in
humbling Himself to the Death of the Cross he did not forsake
20 but attain his Glory: The like Fate shall follow us. only let us
expect it after Death as he did. And remember that this and the
other life are made of a Piece: but this is the time of Trial, that of
Rewards. The Greatest Disadvantages of Lov are its Highest
Advantages. in the Greatest Hazzards it atchieveth to it self the
25 Greatest Glory. It is seldom considered; but a Lov to others
Stronger then what we bear to our selvs, is the Mother of all the
Heroick Actions that hav made Histories pleasant and Beautified
the World.

61

Since Lov will thrust in it self as the Greatest of all Principles, let
us at last willingly allow it Room. I was once a Stranger to it, now
I am familiar with it as a Daily acquaintance. Tis the only Heir
and Benefactor of the World. It seems it will break in evry where,
5 as that without which the World could not be Enjoyed. Nay as
that without which it would not be Worthy to be Enjoyed. for
it was Beautified by Lov, and commandeth the Lov of a Donor
to us. Lov is a Phoenix that will revive in its own Ashes, inherit
Death, and smell sweetly in the Grave.

62

These two properties are in it. that it can attempt all, and suffer all.
And the more it suffers the more it is Delighted, and the more it
attempteth the more it is enriched. for it seems that all Lov is so

Mysterious, that there is somthing in it which needs Expression, and can never be understood by any Manifestation, (of it self, in it self:) but only by Mighty Doings and Sufferings. This moved GOD the Father to Creat the World and GOD, the Son to die for it. nor is this all. There are many other ways wherby it mani/ fests it self as well as these. there being still somthing infinit in it behind. In its Laws in its Tenderness, in its Provisions, in its Caresses, in its Joys as well as in its Hazzards, in its Honors as well as in its Cares nor does it ever ceas till it has poured out it self in all its Communications. In all which it ever rights and satisfies it self. For abov all Things in all Worlds it desires to be Magnified, and taketh pleasure in being Glorified before its Object. for which caus also it does all those Things, which magnify its object and increase its Happiness.

63

Whether Lov principaly intends its own Glory, or its Objects Happiness is a Great Question: and of the more importance, becaus the right ordering of our own Affections depends much upon the Solution of it. for on the one side, to be Self Ended is Mercenary, and Base and Slavish, and to do all things for ones own Glory, is servile, and vain Glory. On the other GOD doth all things for Himself, and seeketh his Glory as his last End, and is himself the End whom he seeks and attains in all His Ways. How shall we reconcile this Riddle? or untie this Knot? for som Men hav taken occasion herby seeing this in Lov, to affirm that there is no true Lov in the World. But it is all self Lov whatsoever a Man doth. Implying also that it was self lov in our Savior, that made Him to undertake for us. Wherupon we might justly Ques/ tion, whether it were more for his own Ends, or more for ours? As also whether it were for his own End that God created the World or more for ours? for Extraordinary much of our Duty and felicity hangeth upon this Point: and whatsoever sword untieth this Gordian Knot, will open a World of Benefit and Instruc/ tion to us.

64

GOD doth desire Glory as his Soveraign End, but True Glory. From whence it followeth that he doth soveraignly and supremely desire both his own Glory and Mans Happiness. Tho that be Miraculous, yet its very Plain. for True Glory is to lov another 5 for his own sake, and to prefer his Welfare and to seek His Happiness. Which God doth becaus it is true Glory. So that he seeks the Happiness of Angels and Men as his Last End, and in that his Glory: to wit His Tru Glory. fals and vain Glory is inconsistent with His Nature but True Glory is the very Essence of his 10 Being. Which is Lov unto His Beloved, Lov unto Himself, Lov unto His Creatures.

65

How can God be Lov unto Him self, without the Imputation of Self Lov? Did He lov Him self under any other Notion then as He is the Lover of his Beloved: there might be som Danger. But the reason why He loves Himself being becaus He is Lov: nothing 5 is more Glorious then his Self Lov. For he loves himself becaus he is infinit and Eternal Lov to others. Becaus he loves himself He cannot endure that His Lov should be Displeased. And loving others vehemently and infinitly, all the Lov he bears to himself is Tenderness towards them. All that wherin he pleaseth 10 Himself is Delightfull to them: He magnifieth Himself in Magnifying them. And in fine, His Lov unto Himself is his Lov unto them. And His Lov unto them is Lov unto Him self. They are individualy one. which it is very Amiable and Beautifull to Behold. Becaus therin the Simplicity of God doth evidently 15 appear. The more he loveth them the Greater he is and the more Glorious. The more he loveth them the more precious and Dear they are to Him. The more he loveth them the more Joys and Treasures He possesseth. The more He loveth them the more he Delighteth in their Felicity. The more he loveth them, the more 20 he delighteth in himself for being their felicity. The more he loveth them, the more he rejoyceth in all his Works for serving them: and in all his Kingdom for Delighting them. And being Lov to them the more he loveth Himself and the more jealous he is least himself should be Displeased, the more he loveth them and tendereth them and secureth their Welfare. And the more he desires his own Glory the more Good he doth for them, in the more Divine and genuine maner. You must lov after his similitude.

66

He from whom I derived these things delighted always that I should be acquainted with Principles, that would make me fit for all Ages. And truly in Lov there are enough of them. For since Nature never Created anything in vain, and Lov of all other is the most Glorious there is not any Relick or Parcel of that that shall be unused. It is not like Gold made to be Buried and Concealed in Darkness. But like the Sun to Communicat it self wholy in its Beams unto all. It is more Excellent and more Communicativ. It is hid in a Centre, and no where at all, if we respect its Body. But if you regard its Soul, it is an interminable Sphere, which as som say of the Sun, is infinities infinita, in the Extention of its Beams, being equaly vigorous in all Places, equaly near to all Objects, Equaly Acceptable to all Persons, and equaly abundant in all its Overflowings. Infinitly evry where. This of Naked and Divested Lov in its true Perfection. Its own Age is too little to Contain it, Its Greatness is Spiritual, like the Dieties. It filleth the World, and exceeds what it filleth. It is present with all Objects, and Tasts all Excellencies, and meeteth the Infinitness of GOD in evry Thing. So that in Length it is infinit as well as in Bredth, being equaly vigorous at the utmost Bound to which it can extend as here, and as wholy there as here and wholy evry where. Thence also it can see into further Spaces, Things present and Things to come Hight and Depth being open before it, and all things in Heaven Eternity and Time equaly near.

67

Were not lov the Darling of GOD, this would be a Rash and a bold Salley. But since it is His Image, and the Lov of GOD, I

may almost say the GOD of GOD, becaus His Beloved: all this Happeneth unto Lov. And this Lov is your tru Self when you
5 are in Act what you are in Power. the Great Dæmon of the World, the End of all Things. the Desire of Angels and of all Nations. A creature so Glorious, that having seen it, it puts an End to all Curiosity and Swallows up all Admiration. Holy, Wise, and Just towards all Things, Blessed in all Things, the
10 Bride of GOD, Glorious before all, His Offspring and first Born, and so like Him that being described, one would think it He. I should be afraid to say all this of it, but that I know Him, How He delighteth to hav it magnified. And how He hath magnified it infinitly before becaus it is his Bride and first Born. I will speak
15 only a little of its Violence and Vigor afar off. It can lov an Act of Virtu in the utmost Indies, and hate a Vice in the Highest Heavens It can see into Hell and Adore the Justice of GOD among the Damned, it can behold and Admire his Lov from Everlasting. It can be present with his infinit and Eternal Lov,
20 it can rejoyce in the Joys which it foreseeth. can Lov Adam in Eden, Moses in the Wilderness, Aaron in the Tabernacle, David before the Ark, S. Paul among the Nations, and Jesus either in the Manger or on the crosse All these it can lov with violence. And when it is restored from all that is Terrene and Sensual, to
25 its tru Spiritual Being, it can lov these and any of these as violently as any Person in the Living Age.

68

Shall it not lov violently what God loveth, what Jesus Christ loveth, what all Saints and Angels lov? Moses Glorified GOD in a Wonderfull Maner, he prophesied of Christ he Plagued the Egyptians, he Brought the Israelites out of the Land of Egypt,
5 he Guided them in the Wilderness he gav us the Law, He Loved the People more then his own life: yea then his own self and all the possible Glory that might have accrued to Him. Shall not He be Beloved? And what shall we think of Christ Himself? Shall not all our Lov be where his is? Shall it not wholy follow and
10 Attend Him? Yet shall it not forsake other Objects. but lov them

all in Him, and Him in them, and them the more becaus of Him, and Him the more becaus of them. for by Him it is redeemed to them. So that as God is omnipresent our Lov shall be at once with all: that is We: having these Strengths to Animat and Quicken our Affection. 15

69

To lov one Person with a Private Lov, is poor and miserable: to lov all is Glorious. To lov all Persons in all Ages, All Angels, all Worlds is Divine and Heavenly. To lov all Cities and all Kingdoms, all Kings and all Peasants, and evry Person in all Worlds with a natural intimat familiar Lov, as if Him alone, is Blessed. 5 This makes a Man Effectualy Blessed in all Worlds, a Delightfull Lord of all Things, a Glorious friend to all Persons, a concerned Person in all Transactions, and ever present with all Affairs. So that he must ever be filled with Company, ever in the midst of all Nations, ever joyfull, and ever Blessed. The Greatness of this 10 Mans Lov no Man can measure, it is stable like the Sun, it endureth for ever as the Moon, it is a faithfull Witness in Heaven. It is stronger and more Great than all Privat Affections. It representeth evry person in the Light of Eternity, and loveth him with the Lov of all Worlds. With a Lov conformable to Gods, Guided 15 to the same Ends and founded upon the same causes. Which however Lofty and Divine it is, is ready to humble it self into the Dust to serv the Person Beloved. And by how much the more Glorious and Sublime it is, is so much the more Sweet and Truly Delightfull. Majesty and Pleasure concurring together. 20

70

Now you may see what it is to be a Son of God more clearly. Lov in its Glory is the friend of the Most High. It was begotten of Him and is to sit in his Throne, and to reign in Communion with Him. It is to Pleas him, and to be pleased by Him, in all his Works Ways and Operations. It is ordained to hold an Eternal 5 Correspondence with Him in the Highest Heavens. It is here in

its Infancy, there in its Manhood and perfect Stature. He wills
and commands that it should be reverenced of all, and takes
Pleasure to see it Admired in its Excellencies. If Lov thus displayed
10 be so Glorious a Being, how much more Glorious and Great is
He that is Soveraign Lord of all Lords, and the Heavenly King
of all these? So many Monarchs under one Supreme, mightily set
forth the Glory of his Kingdom. If you ask by what Certainty, or
by what Rules we discover this? As by the Seed we conjecture
15 what Plant will arise, and know by the Acorn what Tree will
Grow forth, or by the Eagles Egge what Kind of Bird; so do we
by the Powers of the Soul upon Earth, Know what kind of Being,
Person, and Glory it will be in the Heavens. Its Blind and latent
Powers shall be turned into Act, its Inclinations shall be com-
20 pleted, and its Capacities filled, for by this Means is it made Perfect. A Spiritual King is an Eternal Spirit. Lov in the Abstract
is a Soul Exerted. Neither do you esteem yourself to be any other
then LOV alone. GOD is Lov. And you are never like Him,
till you are so: Lov unto all Objects in like maner.

71

To sit in the Throne of GOD is the most supreme Estate that
can befall a Creature. It is Promised in the Revelations. But few
understand what is promised there, and but few believ it.

72

To sit in the Throne of God is to inhabit Eternity. To Reign
there is to be pleased with all Things in Heaven and Earth from
Everlasting to everlasting, as if we had the Soveraign Disposal of
them. For He is to Dwell in us, and We in Him, becaus He
5 liveth in our Knowledg and we in His. His Will is to be in our
Will, and our Will is to be in His Will, so that both being joyned
and becoming one, We are pleased in all his Works as He is; and
herin the Image of God perfectly consisteth. No Artist maketh a
Throne too Wide for the Person. GOD is the Greatest and
10 Divinest Artist. Thrones proper and fit for the Persons, are always

prepared by the Wisest Kings. for little Bodies Bodily Thrones:
for Spirits invisible. GODs Throne is His Omnipresence, and
that is infinit. who Dwelleth in Himself, or in that Light which
is inaccessible. The Omnipresence therfore and the Eternity of
GOD are our Throne. wherin we are to reign for evermore. His 15
infinit and Eternal Lov are the Borders of it, which evry where
we are to meet, and evry where to see for evermore. In this Throne
our savior sitteth, who is the Alpha and Omega, the first and the
last, the Amen, and the faithfull Witness, who said, The Glory
which Thou hast given me, I hav given them, That they may be 20
one as we are one. In Him the fulness of the Godhead dwelleth
Bodily. If that bee too Great to be applied to Men, remember
what follows, His Church is the fullness of Him that filleth all
in all. The fulness of the Godhead Dwelleth in Him for our
sakes. And if yet it seemeth too Great to be Enjoyed: by the sur⁄ 25
passing Excellency of His Eternal Power, it is made more then
ours. for in Him we shall more Enjoy it, then if it were infinitly,
and wholy, all in our selvs.

73

If any thing yet remaineth that is Dreadfull, or Terrible or Doubt⁄
full, that seemeth to Startle us, there is more behind that will more
amaze us. for God is infinit in the Expression of his Lov, as we
shall all find to our Eternal Comfort. Objects are so far from
Diminishing, that they magnify the faculties of the Soul behold⁄ 5
ing them. A sand in your conception conformeth your soul, and
reduceth it to the Cize and Similitud of a sand. A Tree appre⁄
hended is a Tree in your Mind, the whole Hemisphere and the
Heavens magnifie your soul to the Wideness of the Heavens. All
the Spaces abov the Heavens enlarg it Wider to their own Dimen⁄ 10
sions. And what is without Limit maketh your Conception
illimited and Endless. The infinity of GOD is infinitly Profit⁄
able as well as Great: as Glorious as Incomprehensible: so far
from streightening that it magnifieth all Things. And must be
seen in you, or GOD will be Absent. Nothing less then infinit 15
is GOD, and as finit he cannot be Enjoyed.

74

But what is there more that will more Amaze us? Can any thing
be behind such Glorious Mysteries? Is GOD more Soveraign in
other Excellencies? Hath He shewed Himself Glorious in any
thing besides? Verily there is no End of all His Greatness, his
5 understanding is infinit, and His Ways innumerable. How
Precious, saith the Psalmist, are thy Thoughts to me O God,
when I would count them they are more then can be numbered.
There is no man that reckoneth them up in order unto Thee.
O my Lord I will endeavor it: and I will Glorify Thee for ever
10 more. The most Perfect Laws are agreeable only to the most
Perfect Creatures. Since therfore thy Laws are the most perfect of
all that are Possible, so are thy Creatures. And if infinit Power be
wholy exprest, O Lord what Creatures! what Creatures shall we
becom! What Divine, what Illustrious Beings! Souls worthy of
15 so Great a Lov, Blessed for ever. Made Worthy, tho not found
for Lov either findeth, or maketh an Object Worthy of it self. for
which caus Picus Mirandula admirably saith, in his Tract De
Dignitate Hominis, I hav read in the Monuments of Arabia, that
Abdala, the Saracen being Asked, Quid in hâc quasi mundanâ
20 Scenâ admirandum maxime Spectaretur? What in this World
was most Admirable?, Answerd, MAN. then whom he saw
nothing more to be Admired. Which Sentence of his is seconded
by that of Mercurius Trismegistus, Magnum, O Asclep., Mira-
culum, Homo. Man is a Great and Wonderfull Miracle. Ruminat-
25 ing upon the Reason of these Sayings, those things did not satisfy
me, which many hav spoken concerning the Excellency of Human
Nature. As that Man was Creaturarum Internuncius; Superis
familiaris, Inferiorum Rex; sensuum perspicaciâ, Rationis In-
dagine, Intelligentiæ Lumine, Naturæ Interpres. Stabilis Ævi et
30 fluxi Temporis Interstitium, et (qd Persæ dicunt) Mundi Copula
immo Hymenæus. A Messenger between the Creatures, Lord of
Inferior things, and familiar to those abov; by the Keeness of his
sences, the Peircing of his Reason, and the Light of Knowledg,
the Interpreter of Nature, A seeming Intervall between Time and
35 Eternity and the Inhabitant of both, the Golden link or Tie of

the World, yea the Hymenæus Marrying the Creator and his
Creatures together; made as David witnesseth a little lower then
the Angels. All these things are Great, but they are not the
Principal: that is, They are not those which rightly chalenge the
name and title of most Admirable. And so he goeth on, Admiring 40
and Exceeding all that had been spoken before concerning the
Excellency of Man. Why do we not rather Admire the Angels
and the Quires abov the Heavens? At length I seemed to understand, Why Man was the most Happy, and therfore the most
Worthy to be Admired of all the Creatures: and to Know that 45
Estate, which in the order of Things he doth enjoy, not only abov
the Beasts but abov the Stars, and that might be envied even of
the Supra Celestial Spirits, which he stileth, Ultra-Mundanis
Mentibus invidiosam.

75

The Supreme Architect and our Everlasting father, having made
the World, this most Glorious Hous, and Magnificent Temple of
his Divinity, by the Secret Laws of his Hidden Wisdom; He
adorned the Regions above the Heavens with most Glorious
Spirits, the Spheres he Enlivened with Eternal Souls, the Dreggy 5
Parts of the Inferior World he filled with all Kind of Herds of
Living Creatures. Sed Opere Consummato, but His Work
being Compleated, He desired som one, that might Weigh and
reason, lov the Beauty, and admire the Vastness of so Great a
Work. All things therfore being, (as Moses and Tymæus Wit- 10
ness) already finished, at last he thought of Creating Man. But
there was not in all the Platforms before conceived any Being after
whom He might form this New Offspring: Nor in all his
Treasures what He might giv this New Son by way of Inheritance:
nor yet a Place in all the Regions of the World, wherin this Con- 15
templator of the Univers might be seated. All Things were already
full, all things were already distributed into their various Orders
of Supreme Middle and Inferior. But it was not the Part of infinit
Power, to fail as Defectiv in the last Production; it was not the Part
of infinit Wisdom, for want of Counsel to fluctuat in so Necessary 20

an Affair. it was not the part of infinit Goodness, or Soveraign Lov, that He, who should be raised up to Prais the Divine Bounty in other Things, should condemn it in himself. statuit tandem Opt. Opifex, ut cui dari nihil proprium poterat Commune esset, 25 quod privatum singulis fuit. The Wisest and Best of Workmen appointed therfore, that he to whom nothing proper to himself could be added, should have som thing of all that was peculiar to evry thing. And therfore he took Man, the Image of all his Work, and placing him in the Middle of the World, spake thus unto 30 him

76

O Adam, we hav given Thee neither a certain seat, nor a Private face, nor a Peculiar office, that whatsoever seat or face or office thou dost desire, thou mayst Enjoy. All other things hav a Nature bounded within certain Laws, Thou only art loos from all, and 5 according to thy own Counsel in the hand of which I hav put Thee, mayst chuse and prescribe what Nature thou wilt to thy self. I hav placed Thee in the Middle of the World, that from thence thou mayst behold on every side more commodiously evry thing in the whole World. We hav made Thee neither heavenly 10 nor Earthly Neither Mortal nor Immortal, that being the Honored Former and Framer of thy self, thou mayst shape thy self into what Nature thy self pleaseth.

77

O Infinit Liberality of God the father! O Admirable and supreme felicity of Man! to whom it is given to hav what he desires and to be what he Wisheth. The Bruits when they are brought forth bring into the world with them what they are to 5 possess continualy. The Spirits that are abov were, either from the beginning or a little after, that which they are about to be to all Eternities. Nascenti Homini omnigena vitæ Germina indidit Pater, God infused the Seeds of evry Kind of Life into Man, Whatever seeds evry one chuseth those spring up with him, and 10 the fruits of those shall he bear and enjoy. If sensual Things are chosen by Him he shall becom a Beast, if Reasonable a Celestial Creature; if Intellectual an Angel and a Son of God; And if being content with the lot of no Creatures, he withdraws Himself into the Centre of His own Unitie, he shall be one Spirit with GOD, and Dwell abov all in the Solitary Darkness of his Eternal Father. 15

78

This Picus Mirandula spake in an Oration made before a most learned Assembly in a famous university. Any man may perceiv, that He permitteth his fancy to wander a little Wantonly after the maner of a Poet: but most deep and serious things are secretly hidden under his free and luxuriant Language. The Changeable 5 Power he Ascribeth to Man is not to be referred to his Body. for as he wisely saith, Neither doth the Bark make a Plant, but its stupid and nothing-perceiving nature: neither doth the Skin make a Beast, but his bruitish and sensual Nature, Neither doth Seperation from a Body make an Angel but his Spiritual Intelligence. So 10 neither doth his Rinde or Coat or Skin or Body make a Man; to be this or that, but the Interior Stupidness, or Sensuality, or Angelical Intelligence of his Soul, make him accordingly a Plant a Beast, or an Angel. The Deformity, or Excellency is within.

79

neither is it to be believed, that God filled all the World with Creatures before he thought of man: but by that little Fable he teacheth us the Excellency of Man. Man is the End, and therfore the Perfection of all the Creatures. but as Eusebius Pamphilus saith (in the Nicene Council) He was first in the Intention, tho 5 last in the Execution. All Angels were Spectators as well as He, all Angels were free Agents as well as He: as we see by their Trial, and the fall of Som; All Angels were seated in as convenient a Place as he. But this is true, that He was the End of all and the last of all. And the Comprehensiv Head and the Bond of all, and 10 in that more Excellent then all the Angels. As for whom the visible and Invisible Worlds were made, and to Whom all Creatures ministered: as one also, that contained more Species in his Nature then the Angels, which is not as som hav thought Derogatory, but perfectiv to His Being. It is true also that GOD hath prevented Him, and satisfied all Wishes, in giving Him such a Being as he now enjoyeth. And that for infinit Reasons it was best that He should be in a Changeable Estate, and hav power to chuse what himself listed. for he may so chuse as to becom One Spirit with GOD Almighty.

80

By chusing a Man may be turned and Converted into Lov. Which as it is an Universal Sun filling and shining in the Eternity of GOD, so is it infinitly more Glorious then the Sun is, not only shedding abroad more Amiable and Delightfull Beams, Illuminat' ing and Comforting all Objects: yea Glorifying them in the Supreme and Soveraign Maner, but is of all sensibles the most Quick and Tender; being able to feel like the longlegged Spider, at the utmost End of its Divaricated feet: and to be wholy present in every place where any Beam of it self extends. The Sweetness of its Healing Influences is Inexpressible. And of all Beings such a Being would I chuse to be for ever. One that might inherit all in the most Exquisit Maner, and be the Joy of all in the most Perfect Measure.

81

Nazianzen professed him self to be a Lover of right reason. and by it did undertake even to speak Oracles. Even so may we by Right Reason discover all the Mysteries of heaven. And what Our Author here observeth, is very considerable, that Man by retiring from all Externals and withdrawing into Him self, in the centre of his own Unity becometh most like unto GOD. What Mer' curius said in the Dialogue is most true, Man is of all other the Greatest Miracle. yea verily should all the Miracles that ever were don be drawn together, Man is a Miracle Greater then they.

And as much may be written of Him alone as of the whole World. 10
The Dividing of the sea, the commanding of the sun, the making
of the World is nothing to the single Creation of one soul. there
is so much Wisdom and Power expressed in its faculties and
Inclinations. Yet is this Greatest of all Miracles unknown becaus
Men are addicted only to Sensible and Visible Things. So Great 15
a World in the Explication of its Parts is easy: but here the Dimensions of Innumerable Worlds are shut up in a Centre. Where it
should lodg such innumerable Objects, as it doth by knowing
whence it should derive such infinit streams, as flow from it by
Loving, how it should be a Mirror of all Eternity, being made of 20
Nothing, how it should be a fountain or a sun of Eternity out of
which such abundant Rivers of Affection flow, it is impossible
to declare. but abov all, how having no Material or Bodily
Existence, its Substance tho invisible should be so Rich and
Precious. The Consideration of one Soul is sufficient to convince 25
all the Atheists in the whole World.

82

The Abundance of its Beams, the Reality of its Beams, the
freedom of its Beams, the Excellency and valu of its Beams are all
Transcendent. They shine upon all the Things in Heaven and
Earth and cover them all with Celestial Waters: Waters of Refreshment, Beams of Comfort. They flow freely from a Mind 5
desiring to be Obedient Pleasing and Good. The Soul com-
municates it self wholy by them: and is Richer in its Communications then all Odors and Spices whatsoever. It containeth in its
Nature the Influences of the stars by way of Eminence, the
Splendor of the Sun, the verdure of Trees, the valu of Gold, the 10
Lustre of precious stones the sence of Beasts and the Life of Angels:
the fatness of feasts, the Magnificence of Palaces, the Melody of
Musick, the Sweetness of Wine, the Beauty of the Excellent, the
Excellency of vertue and the Glory of cherubims. The Harmony
and the Joys of Heaven appear in Lov. for all these were made for 15
her, and all these are to be enjoyed in her.

83

Whether it be the Soul it self, or God in the Soul, that shines by Lov, or both it is difficult to tell: but certainly the Lov of the Soul is the sweetest Thing in the world. I have often admired what should make it so Excellent. If it be God that lovs it is the Shining
5 of his Essence, if it be the Soul it is His Image: If it be both, it is a double Benefit.

84

That GOD should lov in the Soul is most easy to believ, becaus it is most easy to conceiv. But it is a Greater Mystery that the Soul should lov in it self. If God loveth in the Soul it is the more precious, if the Soul Loveth it is the more Marvellous. If you ask
5 how a Soul that was made of Nothing can return so many flames of Lov? Where it should hav them or out of what Ocean it should communicat them, it is impossible to declare. (for it can return those flames upon all Eternity, and upon all the Creatures and Objects in it.) Unless we say, as a Mirror returneth the very self-
10 same Beams it receiveth from the Sun, so the Soul returneth those Beams of Lov that shine upon it from God. For as a Looking Glass is nothing in Comparison of the World, yet containeth all the World in it, and seems a real fountain of those Beams which flow from it so the Soul is Nothing in respect of God, yet all
15 Eternity is contained in it, and it is the real fountain of that Lov that proceedeth from it. They are the Sun Beams which the Glass returneth: yet they flow from the Glass and from the Sun within it. The Mirror is the Well-Spring of them, becaus they Shine from the Sun within the Mirror, Which is as deep within the Glass as
20 it is high within the Heavens. And this sheweth the Exceeding Richness and preciousness of Lov, It is the Lov of God shining upon, and Dwelling in the Soul. for the Beams that Shine upon it reflect upon others and shine from it.

85

That the Soul shineth of it self is equaly manifest. for it can lov with a lov distinct from GODs. It can lov irregularly. And no irregular Lov is the Lov of GOD. It can forbear to lov while God loveth. It can lov while GOD forbeareth. It can lov a Wicked Man, Wickedly, and in his Wickedness. This shews 5 plainly that it can lov regularly, with a Lov that is not meerly the Reflexion of Gods. for which caus it is not called a Mirror, but esteemed more, a real fountain. Cant. . . . My Lov is a Spring shut up a fountain sealed. That is, Shut up like a letter, and con᷍ cealed yet: but in the Kingdom of Heaven, her Contents and 10 Secrets shall be Known, and her Beauty read of all Men. Her own Waters whence she should receiv them it is most admirable. Con᷍ sidering the Reality and Beauty of them. But in this God hath magni᷍ fied his infinit Power, that He hath made them. Made them freely, made them her own, out of her self to flow from her: Creatures as 15 it were to which her self givs their Existence. For indeed she could not lov, were not her Beams of Lov, her own. Before she loves they are not, when she lovs they are. And so she givs them their Being. Being Good her self, becaus she can lov. Who els would be a Drie and Withered Stick, having neither Life, nor value. But now 20 she can Exalt a Creature abov all the Things in Heaven and Earth, in her self: Esteem it most Dear, Admire it, Honor it, Tender it, Desire it Delight in it, be united to it, prefer it, forsake all things for it, giv all things to it, Die for it. It can languish after it, when absent; take Pleasure in it, when present; rejoyce in its 25 happiness, liv only to it, study to please it, Delight in suffering for it, feed it with Pleasures Honors and Caresses, Do all things for its sake, Esteem Gold and Pearl but Dross in Comparison, lay Crowns and Scepters at its feet, Make it a Lord of Palaces, Delight in its own Beauties Riches and pleasures, as they feed only and 30 satisfy its Beloved; be ravished with it. it can desire infinitly that Good things should be added to it. And all this shall we enjoy in evry Soul in the Kingdom of Heaven. All there being like so many Suns Shining upon one. All this Goodness is so like Gods, that Nothing can be more. And yet that it is Distinct from his, is 35 manifest becaus it is the Return or Recompence of it. The only thing which for and abov all worlds he infinitly Desires.

86

Here upon Earth Souls lov what GOD hates, and hate what GOD loves. Did they keep their Ey Open always upon what He lovs, and see His Lov to them, and to all, they could not chuse but lov as He does. And were they Mirrors only that return his
5 Lov, one would think it impossible, while he shines upon them, to forbear to shine. but they are like the Ey, Mirrors with Lids, and the Lid of Ignorance or Inconsideration interposing, they are often times Ecclypsed, or shine only through som Cranies; so that here upon Earth having free Power to hold open or shut their Lids, to
10 send, or turn away their Beams; they may lov me, or forbear. The loss of their Lov is an Evil past Imagination. for it is a Removal of the End of Heaven and Earth, the Extinction of a Sun infinitly more Glorious then that in the Heavens. The Sun was made to serv this more Divine and Glorious Creature. The Lov of this
15 Creature is the End of Heaven and Earth, becaus the End for which Heaven and Earth were made for it. And in Recompence for all that God hath don for it it is to lov me. So that GOD hath Glorified me, by giving me a Communion with Himself in the End for which the World was made. And hath made that
20 Creature to lov me, and given me so Great a Certainty of its Lov and Title to it, that first it must ceas to lov it self, or to lov God before it bereav me. It must ceas to be Wise, and forfeit all its Interest in Heaven and Earth, before it can ceas to lov me. In doing it it ruines it self and apostatizeth from all its Happiness.

87

In the Estate of Innocency the Lov of Man, seemed nothing but the Beams of Lov reverted upon another. for he loved no Person but of whom he was beloved. All that he loved was Good, and nothing evil. His Lov seemed the Goodness of a Being expressed
5 in the Soul, or apprehended in the Lover, and returned upon it

self. But in the Estate of Misery, (or rather Grace;) a Soul lovs freely and purely of its own self, with Gods Lov, things that seem uncapable of Lov, Naught and evil. For as GOD shewed his Eternity and Omnipotency, in that he could Shine upon Nothing, and lov an Object when it was Nought or Evil; As he did Adam when he raisd him out of Nothing, and Mankind when He redeemd them from Evil: so now we can lov sinners, and them that Deserv nothing at our Hands. Which as it is a Diviner Lov, and more Glorious then the other, so were we redeemed to this Power, and it was purchased for us with a Greater Price.   15

88

It is a Generous and Heavenly Principle, that where a Benefit is fairly intended, we are equaly obliged for the Intention or Success. He is an Ungratefull Debtor, that measureth a Benefactor by the Success of His Kindness. A clear Soul and a generous Mind is as much obliged for the Intent of his freind, as the Prosperity of it: 5 And far more, if we seperat the Prosperity from the Intent. for the Goodness lies principaly in the Intention. Since therfore God intended me all the Joys in Heaven and Earth, I am as much Obliged for them as if I received them. Whatever intervening Accident bereaved me of them, He realy intended them. And in 10 that I contemplat the Riches of His Goodness. Whether Mens Wickedness in the present Age, or my own perversness, or the fall of Adam; he intended me all the Joys of Paradice, and all the Honors in the World, whatever hinders me. In the Glass of His Intention therfore I enjoy them all: And I do confess my Obliga- 15 tion. It is as Great as if nothing had intervened, and I had wholy received them. Seeing and Knowing Him to be infinitly Wise and Great and Glorious, I rejoyce that he loved me, and confide in his Lov. His Goodness is my Soveraign and Supreme Delight. That God is of such a Nature in himself is my infinit Treasure. 20 Being He is my Friend, and delighteth in my Honor, tho I rob my self of all my Happiness, he is justified. That He intended it, is His Grace and Glory. But it animates me, as well as comforts me, to see the Perfection of His Lov towards me. As Things

25 stood, He used Power enough before the Fall to make me Happy.
If he refuseth to use any more since the Fall: I am obliged. But
He hath used more. New Occasions begot New Abilities. He
redeemed me by His Son. If He refuseth to use any more I cannot
complain. If He refuseth to curb my perverseness unless I consent,
30 His Lov was infinitly shewed. He desireth that I should by
Prayers and Endeavors clothe my self with Grace. If in Default of
mine, he doth it Himself freely giving His H. Spirit to me; it is
an infinit Mercy, but infinitly new, and superadded. If he refuseth
to overrule the Rebellion of other men, and to bring me to Honor,
35 notwithstanding their Malice; or refuseth to make them lov me,
whether they will or no. I cannot repine. By other signes, he hath
plainly shewd, that He loveth me infinitly, which is enough for
me, and that He desireth my Obedience.

89

This Estate wherin I am placed is the Best for me: tho Encom-
passed with Difficulties. It is my Duty to think so, and I cannot
do otherwise. I cannot do otherwise, without reproaching my
Maker: that is, without suspecting, and in that offending His
5 Goodness and Wisdom. Riches are but Tarnish and Gilded
Vanities, Honors are but Aery and Empty Bubles, Affections
are but Winds, perhaps too Great. for such a ship as mine; of too
light a Ballast: Pleasures, yea all these, are but Witches that draw
and steal us away from GOD; Dangerous Allurements, inter-
10 posing Skreens, unseasonable Companions, Counterfeit Realities,
Honied poyson, Combersom Distractions. I hav found them so.
At least they lull us into Lethargies. And we need to be Quickened.
Som times they Puff us up with vain Glory and we need to be
humbled. Always they delude us if we place any Confidence in
15 them, and therfore it is as Good always to be without them. But
it is as Good also, were it not for our Weakness, somtimes to hav
them. Becaus a good use may be made of them. And therfore they
are not to be contemned when God doth offer them. But He is to
be Admired that maketh it Good on both sides, to hav them, and
20 to be without them. Riches are not to be Hated, nor Coveted,

But I am to Bless God in all Estates. Who hath given me the
World, my Soul, and Himself: and ever to be Great in the true
Treasures. Riches are Good, and therfore is it Good somtimes to
Want them: that we might shew our Obedience and Resignation
to God, even in being without those things that are Good, at 25
his Appointment: and that also we might cloth our selves with
Patience and Faith and Courage, which are Greater Ornaments
then Gold and Silver, and of Greater Price: And that shall stand
us in stead of all the Splendor of Alms Deeds. Assure your self,
till you prize one Vertu, abov a Trunk of Mony, you can never 30
be Happy. One Vertu before the face of God, is better then all the
Gold in the whole World.

90

Knowing the Greatness and Sweetness of Lov, I can never be
poor in any Estate. How Sweet a Thing is it as we go or ride or
eat or drink or convers abroad to remember, that one is the Heir
of the Whole World, and the Friend of GOD! That one has so
Great a Friend as God is: and that one is exalted infinitly by all 5
His Laws! That all the Riches and Honors in the World are ours
in the Divine Image to be Enjoyed. That a Man is tenderly
Belovd of God and always walking in his fathers Kingdom,
under his Wing, and as the Apple of his Ey! Verily that God
hath don so much for one in His Works and Laws, and Expresd
so much Lov in His Word and Ways, being as He is Divine and 10
Infinit, it should make a man to walk abov the stars, and seat
Him in the Bosom of Men and Angels. It should always fill Him
with Joy, and Triumph, and lift Him up abov Crowns and
Empires.

91

That a Man is Beloved of God, should melt him all into Esteem
and Holy Veneration. It should make Him so Couragious as an
Angel of God. It should make him Delight in Calamities and
Distresses for Gods sake. By giving me all things els, he hath made
even Afflictions them selvs my Treasures. The Sharpest Trials, 5

are the finest furbishing. The most Tempestious Weather is the
Best seed Time. A Christian is an Oak flourishing in Winter.
GOD hath so magnified and Glorified His Servant, and Exalted
him so highly in his Eternal Bosom, that no other Joy should be
10 able to mov us but that alone. All sorrows should appear but
Shadows, besides that of his Absence. And all the Greatness of
Riches and Estates swallowed up in the Light of his favor. Incredible Goodness lies in his Lov. And it should be Joy enough
to us to contemplat and possess it. He is Poor whom GOD hates.
15 Tis a tru Proverb. And besides that, we should so lov Him, that
the Joy alone of approving our selvs to Him, and making our
selvs Amiable and Beautifull before Him should be a continual
Feast, were we starving. A Beloved cannot feel Hunger in the
Presence of His Beloved. Where Martyrdom is pleasant, what can
20 be Distastefull. To fight, to famish, to Die for ones Beloved,
especialy with ones beloved, and in his Excellent Company,
unless it be for his trouble, is truly Delightfull. God is always
present, and always seeth us.

92

Knowing my self Beloved and so Glorified of God Almighty in
another World, I ought to Honor Him in this always, and to
Aspire to it. At Midnight will I rise to Giv Thanks unto Thee
becaus of thy Righteous Judgements. Seven times a Day will I
5 Prais Thee, for thy Glorious Mercy. Early in the Morning will I
Bless Thee, I will Triumph in thy Works, I will Delight in thy
Law Day and Night, At Evening will I prais Thee. I will ever
be speaking of thy Marvellous Acts, I will tell out of thy Greatness,
and talk of the Glorious Majesty of thy Excellent Kingdom; these
10 Things ought ever to breath in our souls. We ought to covet to
liv in Privat, and in privat ever to overflow in Praises. I will
Boast in Thee all the Day Long, and be Glad in the Lord. My
Exceeding Joy, my Life, my Glory, what shall I render to Thee,
for all His Benefits? I will sing and be Glad. Let all Nations sing
15 unto Him. for he covereth the Earth as it were with a sheild. My
Lips shall be fain when I sing unto Thee and my Soul O Lord

which Thou hast redeemed. God is unseen till He be so Known: and Davids Spirit an inscrutable Mysterie, till this Experienced.

93

Our Friendship with God ought to be so Pure and so Clear, that Nakedly and Simply for his Divine Lov, for his Glorious Works and Blessed Laws, the Wisdom of His Counsels, his Ancient Ways and Attributs towards us, we should ever in Publick endeavor to Honor Him. Always taking care to Glorify Him 5 before Men: to Speak of His Goodness to Sanctify His Name, and do those Things that will stir up others, and occasion others to Glorify Him. Doing this so Zealously, that we would not for- bear the least Act wherin we might serv Him for all Worlds. It ought to be a firm Principle rooted in us, that This Life is the 10 most precious Season in all Eternity, becaus all Eternity dependeth on it. Now we may do those Actions which herafter we shall never hav occasion to do. And now we are to do them in another maner, which in its place is the most Acceptable in all Worlds. namely by Faith and Hope, in which God infinitly Delighteth. 15 With Difficulty and Danger, which God infinitly commiserats, and Greatly esteems. So piecing this Life with the life of Heaven, and seeing it as one with all Eternity. a Part of it, a Life within it. Strangely and Stupendiously Blessed in its Place and Season.

94

Having once studied these Principles you are Eternaly to Practice them. You are to warm your self at these fires, and to hav recours to them evry Day. When you think not of these Things you are in the Dark. And if you would walk in the Light of them, you must frequently Meditat. These Principles are like Seed in the Ground, 5 they must continualy be visited with Heavenly Influences, or els your Life will be a Barren feild. Perhaps they might be cast into Better frame, and more Curiously Exprest; but if well Cultivated they will be as fruitfull, as if every Husk were a Golden Rinde. It is the Substance that is in them that is productive of Joy, and Good to all. 10

95

It is an Indelible Principle of Eternal Truth. That Practice and Exercise is the Life of all. Should God giv you Worlds, and Laws, and Treasures, and Worlds upon Worlds and Himself also in the Divinest Maner, If you will be lazy, and not Meditat, you lose
5 all. The Soul is made for Action, and cannot rest, till it be employd. Idlenes is its Rust. Unless it will up and Think and Taste and see, all is in vain. Worlds of Beauty and Treasure and Felicity may be round about it, and it self Desolat. If therfore you would be Happy, your Life must be as full of Operation, as God of
10 Treasure. Your Operation shall be Treasure to Him, as His Operation is Delightfull to you.

96

To be Acquainted with celestial Things is not only to know them, but by frequent Meditation to be familiar with them. The Effects of which are Admirable. for by this those things that at first seemed uncertain becom Evident, those things which seemed
5 Remote becom near, those things which appeared like shady clouds becom solid Realities; finaly those Things which seemed impertinent to us, and of little concernment, appear to be our own, according to the strictest Rules of Propriety and of infinit Moment.

97

General and Publick concernments seem at first unmanageable, by reason of their Greatness: but in the soul there is such a Secret Sufficiency, that it is able upon Trial, to manage all Objects with Equal Ease; things infinit in Greatness as well as the smallest sand.
5 But this Secret Strength is not found in it, but meerly upon Experience, nor discerned but by Exercise. The Eternity of God himself is manageable to the understanding, and may be used innumerable Ways for its Benefit, so may his Almighty Power and infinit Goodness: His Omnipresence and Immensity, the

Wideness of the world, and the multitude of Kingdoms. Which 10 argueth a Peculiar Excellency in the Soul; becaus it is a Creature that can never be Exceeded. for Bodily Strength by this is per- ceived to be finite, that Bulk is unweildy and by the Greatness of its Object may easyly be overcom: but the Soul through God that Strengtheneth her is able to do all Things. Nothing is too Great, 15 nothing too Heavy, nothing unweildy; it can rule and manage any thing with infinit Advantage.

98

Becaus the Strength of the Soul is Spiritual it is generaly despised. But if ever you would be Divine, you must admit this Principle: That Spiritual Things are the Greatest, and that Spiritual Strength is the most Excellent, Usefull and Delightfull. for which caus it is made as Easy, as it is Endless and Invincible. Infinity is but one 5 Object, Almighty Power is another Eternal Wisdom is another; which it can contemplat. from Infinity it can go to Power, from Power to Wisdom, from Wisdom to Goodnes from Goodness, to Glory, and so to Blessedness, and from these to any Object, or all, whatsoever, Contemplating them as freely as if it had never 10 seen an Object befor. If any one say, that tho it can proceed thus from one Object to another, Yet it cannot comprehend any one of them: All I shall answer is this, it can comprehend any one of them as much as a Creature can possibly do: and the Possibility of a Creature dependeth Purely upon the Power of GOD: for a 15 creature may be made able to do all that, which its Creator is able to make it to doe. So that if there be any Defect in his Power there must of necessity a Limit follow in the Power of his creature, which even God himself cannot make a Creature to Exceed. But this you will say, is an Argument only of what may be, not of what is. 20 tho considering GODs infinit Lov, it is sufficient to shew what is Possible; becaus his Lov will do all it can for the Glory of it self and its Object: yet further to discover what is, we may Adde this, that when a Soul hath contemplated the Infinity of GOD, and passeth from that to another Object, all that it is able to contemplat 25 on any other, it might have added to its first contemplation. So that its Liberty to Contemplat all shews its Illimitedness to any one. And truly I think it Pious to believ that God hath without a Metaphore infinitly Obliged us.

99

The reason why learned Men have not Exactly measured the faculties of the Soul, is becaus they Knew not to what their Endless Extent should serv. for till we Know the Universal Beauty of GODs Kingdom, and that all Objects in His Omnipresence are 5 the Treasures of the Soul; to enquire into the Sufficiency and Extent of its Power is impertinent. But when we know this, nothing is more Expedient then to consider whether a Soul be able to Enjoy them. Which if it be its Powers must extend as far as its Objects. for no Object without the Sphere of its Power, can 10 be enjoyed by it. It cannot be so much as perceived, much lesse Enjoyed. From whence it will proceed, that the Soul will to all Eternity be Silent about it. A Limitation of Praises, and a Parsi- mony in Love following therupon, to the Endangering of the Perfection of Gods Kingdom.

100

Upon the Infinit Extent of the Understanding and Affection of the Soul, strange and Wonderfull Things will follow. 1. A manifestation of GODs infinit Lov. 2. The Possession of infinit Treasures. 3. a Return of infinit Thanksgivings. 4. A Fulnes of 5 Joy which nothing can exceed. 5. an infinit Beauty and Greatness in the Soul. 6. An infinit Beauty in GODs Kingdom. 7. an Infinit Union between GOD and the soul, (as well in Extent, as fervor.) 8. An Exact fitness between the Powers of the Soul and its Objects. Neither being Desolat, becaus neither Exceedeth the 10 other. 9. An Infinit Glory in the Communion of Saints, Every one being a Treasure to all the Residue and Enjoying the Residue, and in the Residue all the Glory of all Worlds. 10. A Perfect Indwelling of the Soul in GOD, and GOD in the Soul. So that as the fulness of the GODHEAD dwelleth in our Savior, it shall dwell in us; and the Church shall be the fulness of Him that 15 filleth all in all: GOD being manifested therby to be a King infinitly Greater, becaus Reigning over infinit Subjects. To Whom be all Glory and Dominion, for ever and ever. Amen.

THE FIFTH CENTURIE

1

The objects of Felicitie, and the Way of enjoying them, are two
Material Themes; wherin to be instructed is infinitly desirable,
becaus as Necessary, as Profitable. Whether of the Two, the
Object, or the Way be more Glorious; it is difficult to determine.
5 God is the Object, and God is the Way of Enjoying. God in all
his Excellencies, Laws and Works, in all his Ways and Counsels
is the Soveraign Object of all Felicitie. Eternity and Time, Heaven
and Earth, Kingdoms and Ages, Angels and Men, are in him to
be enjoyed. In him, the fountain, in him the End; in him the
10 Light, the Life, the Way, in him the Glory and Crown of all.
Yet for Distinction sake, we will speak of several eminent Particulars. Beginning with his Attributes.

2

The Infinity of God is our Enjoyment, because it is the Region
and Extent of his Dominion. Barely as it comprehends infinit
Space, it is infinitly Delightfull; becaus it is the Room and the
Place of our Treasures, the Repositorie of our Joys, and the
5 Dwelling Place, yea the Seat and Throne, and Kingdom of our
Souls. But as it is the Light wherin we see, the Life that inspires
us, the Violence of his Love, and the Strength of our Enjoyments,
the Greatness and Perfection of evry Creature, the Amplitude
that enlargeth us, and the field wherin our Thoughts expaciate
10 without Limit or Restraint, the Ground and Foundation of all
our Satisfactions, the Operative Energie and Power of the Deitie,
the Measure of our Delights, and the Grandure of our Souls, it is
more our Treasure, and ought more abundantly to be delighted
in. It surroundeth us continualy on evry side, it filles us, and
15 inspires us. It is so Mysterious, that it is wholy within us, and even

then it wholy seems, and is without us. It is more inevitably and
constantly, more neerly and immediately our Dwelling Place,
then our Cities and Kingdoms and houses. Our Bodies them
selvs are not so much ours, or within us as that is. The Immensitie
of God is an Eternal Tabernacle. Why then we should not be 20
sensible of that as much as of our Dwellings, I cannot tell, unless
our Corruption and Sensuality destroy us. We ought always to
feel, admire, and walk in it. It is more clearly objected to the Ey
of the Soul, then our Castles and Palaces to the Ey of the Body.
Those Accidental Buildings may be thrown down, or we may be 25
taken from them, but this can never be removed, it abideth for
ever. It is impossible not to within it, nay to be so surrounded as
evermore to be in the centre and midst of it, wherever we can
possibly remov, is inevitably fatal to evry Being.

3

Creatures that are able to dart their Thoughts into all Spaces, can
brook no Limit or Restraint, they are infinitly endebted to this
illimited Extent, becaus were there no such Infinitie, there would
be no Room for their Imaginations; their Desires and Affections
would be coopd up, and their Souls imprisoned. We see the 5
Heavens with our Eys, and Know the World with our Sences.
But had we no Eys, nor Sences, we should see Infinitie like the
H. Angels. The Place wherin the World standeth, were it all
annihilated would still remain, the Endless Extent of which we
feel so realy and palpably, that we do not more certainly know the 10
Distinctions and figures, and Bounds and Distances of what we
see, then the Everlasting Expansion of what we feel and behold
within us. It is an Object infinitly Great and Ravishing: as full of
Treasures as full of Room, and as fraught with Joy as Capacitie.
To Blind men it seemeth dark, but is all Glorious within, as 15
infinit in Light and Beauty, as Extent and Treasure. Nothing is
in vain, much less Infinity. Evry Man is alone the Centre and
Circumference of it. It is all his own, and so Glorious, that it
is the Eternal and Incomprehensible Essence of the Deitie. A

20 Cabinet of infinit Value equal in Beauty Lustre and Perfection to all its Treasures. It is the Bosom of God, the Soul and Securitie of every Creature.

4

Were it not for this Infinitie, Gods Bountie would of Necessitie be limited. His Goodness would want a Receptacle for its Effu-sions. His Gifts would be confined into Narrow Room, and his Almighty Power for lack of a Theatre Magnificent enough, a 5 Storehouse large enough be Straitned. But Almighty Power in-cludes Infinitie in its own Existence. For becaus God is infinitly able to do all Things, there must of Necessity be an infinit Capacitie to answer that Power, becaus Nothing it self is an Obedient Subject to work upon: and the Eternal Privation of 10 infinit Perfections is to almighty Power a Being Capable of all. As sure as there is a Space infinit, there is a Power, a Bounty, a Goodness a Wisdom infinit, a Treasure, a Blessedness, a Glory.

5

Infinity of Space is like a Painters Table, prepared for the Ground and feild of those Colors that are to be laid theron. Look how great he intends the Picture, so Great doth he make the Table. It would be an Absurditie to leav it unfinished, or not to fill it. 5 To leav any part of it Naked and bare, and void of Beauty, would render the whole ungratefull to the Ey, and argue a Defect of Time or Materials, or Wit in the Limner. As the Table is infinit so are the Pictures. Gods Wisdom is the Art, his Goodness the Will, his Word the Penicill, his Beauty and Power the Colors, 10 his Pictures are all his Works and Creatures. infinitly more Real, and more Glorious, as well as more Great and Manifold then the Shadows of a Landscape. But the Life of all is, they are the Spectators own. He is in them as in his Territories, and in all these, views his own Possessions.

6

One would think that besides infinit Space there could be no
more Room for any Treasure. yet to shew that God is infinitly
infinit, there is Infinit Room besides, and perhaps a more Wonder⁄
full Region making this to be infinitly infinit. No man will believ
that besides the Space from the Centre of the Earth to the utmost
bounds of the Everlasting Hills, there should be any more. Beyond
those Bounds perhaps there may, but besides all that Space that
is illimited and present before us, and absolutly endles evry Way,
where can there be any Room for more? This is the Space that is
at this Moment only present before our Ey, the only Space that was, 10
or that will be, from Everlasting to Everlasting. This Moment
Exhibits infinit Space, but there is a Space also wherin all Moments
are infinitly Exhibited, and the Everlasting Duration of infinit
Space is another Region and Room of Joys. Wherin all Ages
appear together, all Occurrences stand up at once, and the 15
innumerable and Endless Myriads of yeers that were before the
Creation, and will be after the World is ended are Objected as
a Clear and Stable Object, whose several Parts extended out at
length, giv an inward Infinity to this Moment, and compose an
Eternitie that is seen by all Comprehensors and Enjoyers. 20

7

Eternity is a Mysterious Absence of Times and Ages: an Endless
Length of Ages always present, and for ever Perfect. For as there
is an immovable Space wherin all finit Spaces are enclosed, and
all Motions carried on, and performed: so is there an Immovable
Duration, that contains and measures all moving Durations. 5
Without which first the last could not be; no more then finit
Places, and Bodies moving without infinit Space. All Ages being
but successions correspondent to those Parts of that Eternitie wherin
they abide, and filling no more of it, then Ages can do. Whether
they are commensurat with it or no, is difficult to determine. But 10
the infinit immovable Duration is Eternitie, the Place and Dura⁄

tion of all Things even of Infinit Space it self: the Cause and End, the Author and Beautifier, the Life and Perfection of all.

8

Eternitie magnifies our Joys exceedingly. for wheras things in them selvs began, and quickly end. Before they came, were never in Being; do service but for few Moments; and after they are gone, Pass away and leav us for ever. Eternity retains the Moments of
5 their Beginning and Ending within it self: and from Everlasting to Everlasting those Things were in their Times and Places before God, and in all their Circumstances Eternaly will be, serving him in those Moments wherin they existed, to those Intents and Pur╯ poses for which they were Created. The Swiftest Thought is
10 present with him Eternaly: the Creation and the Day of Judge╯ ment, his first Consultation Choise and Determination, the Result and End of all just now in full Perfection, ever Beginning, ever Passing, ever Ending: with all the Intervalles of Space between things and Things. As if those Objects that arise many thousand
15 yeers one after the other were all together. We also were our selvs before God Eternaly: And hav the Joy of seeing our selvs Eternaly beloved, and Eternaly Blessed, and infinitly Enjoying all the Parts of our Blessedness, in all the Durations of Eternity appearing at once before our selvs, when perfectly Consummat in the King╯
20 dom of Light and Glory. The smallest Thing by the Influence of Eternity, is made infinit and Eternal. We pass thorow a standing Continent or Region of Ages, that are already before us, Glorious and perfect while we com to them. Like men in a ship we pass for╯ ward, the shores and Marks seeming to go backward, tho we move,
25 and they stand still. We are not with them in our Progressive Motion, but prevent the Swiftness of our Course, and are present with them in our Understandings. Like the Sun we dart our Rayes before us, and occupy those Spaces with Light and Contempla╯ tion, which we move towards, but possess not with our Bodies.
30 And seeing all Things in the Light of Divine Knowledg eternaly serving God, rejoyce unspeakably in that service, and enjoy it all.

9

His Omnipresence is an ample Territory or Field of Joys, a Transparent Temple of infinit Lustre, a Strong Tower of Defence, a Castle of Repose, a Bulwark of Security, a Palace of Delights, an Immediat Help, and a present Refuge in the needfull time of Trouble, a Broad and a vast Extent of fame and Glory. a Theatre 5 of infinit Excellency, an infinit Ocean by means wherof evry Action, Word and Thought, is immediatly diffused like a Drop of Wine in a Pail of Water, and evry where present evry where seen and Known, infinitly delighted in, as well as filling infinit Spaces. It is the Spirit that pervades all his Works, the Life and Soul of 10 the Univers, that in evry point of Space from the Centre to the Heavens, in evry Kingdom in the world in evry City in evry Wilderness in evry house, evry soul evry Creature, in all the Parts of his infinity and Eternitie sees our Persons loves our virtues, inspires us with it self, and crowns our Actions with Praise and 15 Glory. It makes our Honor infinit in Extent, our Glory immense, and our Happiness Eternal. The Rayes of our Light are by this Means darted from Everlasting to Everlasting. This Spiritual Region makes us infinitly present with God, Angels and Men in all Places from the utmost Bounds of the Everlasting hills, through- 20 out all the unwearied Durations of his Endless Infinitie, and gives us the sence and feeling of all the Delights and Praises we occasion, as well as of all the Beauties and Powers, and Pleasures and Glories which God enjoyeth or createth.

10

Our Bridegroom and our King being evry where, our Lover and Defender watchfully governing all Worlds, no Danger or Enemie can arise to hurt us, but is immediatly prevented and supprest, in all the Spaces beyond the utmost Borders of those unknown Habitations which he possesseth. Delights of inestimable valu are 5 there preparing. For evry thing is present by its own Existence. The Essence of God therfore being all Light and Knowledg,

Lov and Goodness, Care and Providence, felicity and Glory, a Pure and simple Act; it is present in its Operations, and by those
10 Acts which it eternaly exerteth, is wholly Busied in all Parts and places of his Dominion, perfecting and compleating our Bliss and Happiness.

II

NOTES ON THE CENTURIES

TRANSCRIPTION OF THE TEXT

TRAHERNE'S writing, though small and eye-wearying, is almost always well-formed and legible. I have hardly ever been defeated even by his interlinear additions, and very seldom by his deleted words. On the other hand, the inconsistencies of his spelling prevent any word from being taken for granted: one can never assume in a draft transcript that either 'lov' or 'love' is right. I am certain that in this edition no word is spelt in a way impossible for Traherne, and I hope that each word is spelt in each place as Traherne actually spelt it there. Exactness is attainable, in theory at least.

With capitalization exactness is not attainable. There is never any doubt about A, B, D, G, H, I, J, L, Q, R, T, Z: nor about F, though Traherne uses F more sparingly than any other capital. C, K, M, N, O, U, V, W, Y are capitals or not according to size: it is often impossible to be sure, and quite probable that Traherne was not sure either. E is specially difficult. The two forms of small e are sparingly used, the capital E is sometimes written so small that Traherne was probably not intending a capital. One has to guess and I may have capitalized too often. The same applies to P. S is also difficult. There is an undoubted capital, but there is also a rather large small s which is undoubtedly intended for a capital sometimes: again some guessing is inevitable. In any case, Traherne's capitalization is no more consistent than his spelling: there is less of it in added passages.

Traherne tends to a rather heavy punctuation, which is not always dependent on the logic of grammar. Care is sometimes necessary in reading, but, granted that, the punctuation does not produce obscurity.

The manuscript contains, though not consistently, the common abbreviations & = and, y = th, m̄ = mm, m^t = ment, and so on. I have usually expanded them, but have left S. or St. for Saint and, from II. 40 onwards, H. for Holy to preserve some of the flavour of the manuscript.

This edition is, of course, not one which any seventeenth-century publisher would have produced. Such a publisher would, in the main, have introduced his own spelling and punctuation. He would have produced a book more readable in some respects than an attempt to reproduce the author's manuscript *literatim* (except for abbreviations) and *punctuatim*. He would have done for his age exactly what Dobell did in 1908. I take this opportunity of saying that, though I have found some mistakes of transcription in Dobell, they are neither many nor serious. Dobell's modernized text can safely be recommended to the 'general reader'. Its existence has, of course, saved me much labour.

I have taken pains to record all deletions and changes in the text. Many are trivial, but the accumulated evidence that Traherne went through his manuscript tightening up his style is interesting. Some are important, e.g. in II. 84, lines 23–24, where, before finding that 'infinit Eternal mind' was an interpolation, I set out on a wild-goose chase through Plato, Cato, and 'the Apostle'.

The stylistic improvements often take the form of removing unnecessary short words. When Traherne did this at the beginning of a sentence, he more often than not failed to capitalize the word which now begins the sentence. With some hesitation I have left such words as Traherne left them. In any case he did sometimes start a sentence with a small letter.

It is not possible to be quite accurate or consistent in reproducing Traherne's emphasis. Even between 'GOD' and 'God' one sometimes has to make an unsatisfactory decision. Underlining is reproduced in the usual way by italics, but his underlining sometimes stops too soon. The device of spaced letters, which I reproduce as such in the *Poems*, is only rarely used in the *Centuries*, and it is not always easy to be sure about it. Where it is certain, I have used italics.

PRESENTATION QUATRAIN

The new blank notebook had been given to Traherne by the person for whom he wrote the *Centuries* (I. 1, line 4). Now he returns it to her that she may use the forty-nine blank leaves for her own writing. In spite of the '11' on 91^v, Traherne had decided that he had finished the work of instruction and could now send it off. It has been suggested that he was on his death-bed and knew he could write no more. There is no evidence for this suggestion, and the writing has no obvious signs of weakness. For a further argument against it see notes on *The Approach*.

line 1 *the friend* must be Susanna Hopton.
    my best friend, God.

line 2 originally began 'As the true Token'. The two latter words were deleted, and 'of' inserted above and between the first two. The change was obviously made in the process either of composition or, if this began as a fair copy, of transcription. It was, however, almost certainly not a fair copy, since higher on the page are two abortive beginnings of other presentation formulas, a capital 'I' to the left of the page and a little lower, in the middle, the word 'from'.

    In the top left-hand corner of the page, in Traherne's writing, is

        Remember the [? stones]
        and the [word deleted] [? Calvary]

THE FIRST CENTURY

This heading does not occur in the manuscript. Traherne did not start with the idea of 'Centuries'.

In order to give the reader a guiding thread, and to show that Traherne does not ramble though he may digress, I have attempted a summary for each *Century*. This has limited value only, for a single sentence or heading is in no way a substitute for the intellectual and emotional fervour of Traherne's paragraphs or for the wide spread of their recurrent themes.

Summary

I. 1 Traherne states his purpose.
2 He is going to tell her what she longs to know.
3 She is Heir of the World: he will explain this as it has never been explained before.
4 His method will be peaceful and loving.
5 He goes back to explain the passage from Ephesians quoted in I. 3. That is what human life is for.
6 He continues to explain his intention. Giving her the 'Whole World' will lead her to God's love and so to 'contemn the World'.
7 The paradox of both Contemning and Enjoying the World explained.
8 God's Love enjoyed by Meditation. Thinking well and ill.
9 The World easily seized by the mind but not easily retained there.
10 Thinking well is serving God.
11 I am going to give you enjoyment of the World in order that you may 'accomplish the End of your Creation' and so please God.
12 Development of the theme of 'Accomplishing the End for which you are Created', prizing all things 'according to their value'.
13 i.e. valuing them as God values them, and having 'his Mind'.
14 This right valuing of the World leads straight to enjoying it. Each individual, like Adam, can enjoy it solely and wholly and is the reason for its existence.
15 Development of this last idea—'I alone am the End of the World'.
16 This is self-evident in experience, 'if you know your self, or God, or the World'.
17 On knowing God.
18 On knowing the World.
19 On knowing yourself.
20 God's laws command enjoyment of his works.
21 Your senses give you enjoyment of the world. Use them, and, as in the parable of the talents, you will be given far more.
22 Expatiation on 'Insatiableness is Good' at the end of the preceding section.
23 The right and wrong way of Insatiableness.
24 Right enjoyment of the world satisfies desires and removes dissatisfactions.
25 Everything is to be enjoyed.

26 Enjoyment is spiritual and mental (it needs what we should now call Imagination). Example from acorns.

27 Example from wine.

28 You must wake every morning in Heaven.

29 You must contain and inherit the whole universe.

30 The thought of 29 developed.

31 Your enjoyment must be conscious and missionary.

32 The missionary thought leads to thought of the blindness and ingratitude of
the non-enjoyers.

33 The wrong aims of the non-enjoyers and their evil results.

34 The absurdity of these wrongheaded men, who seek the 'Riches of Darkness'
(33, line 1).

35 Contrast the 'Riches of the Light'.

36 The error of the non-enjoyers is most dangerous.

37 An explanation of the error may lie in the very wonderfulness of the world.

38 After the digression of 32-37 Traherne returns to explicit instruction how to
'Enjoy the World aright'. You must have the right qualities and principles.

39 To enjoy aright you must love as God loves.

40 On Wants, i.e. Enjoyment is a satisfying of a need. We have great needs.
Socrates was wrong.

41 Felicity equals Supplying of Wants.

42 God wants and has.

43 Infinite joy is produced by infinite wanting.

44 This is how God wants and enjoys.

45 So you must be conscious of your wants—life, God, Eternity. Then you will
enjoy.

46 Be conscious of your need of the Sun and Sea. Then you will prize them.

47 Prizing blessings is essential for enjoyment. It is to be in Heaven. Not to
prize them is to be in Hell.

48 This idea of Heaven and Hell is further dwelt upon.

49 Denizens of Hell.

50 Prizing what we have, we escape from Hell.

51 Wants bind God and us together. We were created to love God.

52 How Love joins man to God.

53 The necessity of willing as God wills. (N.B.—This is not a matter of resignation, but of actively willing Creation and Redemption.) Then you are 'in
all, and with all'.

54 Consequently you cannot be lonely. Eternity is your 'Habitation'.

55 'The Contemplation of Eternity maketh the Soul Immortal': in spirit we
can be in any time or place, especially at the Cross.

56–64 (and, more or less, the rest of the first *Century*) The Cross and Christ.

56 Contemplation of the Cross, which draws all to it.

57 Expatiation on how the Cross draws.

58 What the Cross is.

59 The uniqueness of the Cross.

60 Further intense contemplation of the Cross.

61 What we learn at the Cross.

62 A prayer to the Redeemer.

63 Traherne's yearning to be like Christ.

64 The love of Christ shown by his wounds, but also by the world he has made for man.

65 If I had been the first man, I should have realized the glory of the world.

66 Thanksgiving for the Body.

67 I am God's Image!

68 Why God created not one man but many.

69 Yet each is the end (i.e. purpose) of all things. 'I in all, and all in Me.'

70 God is each man's friend and sole object.

71 Therefore, since we must live by some laws, let us live by the laws of Nature, i.e. the laws of him who loves us.

72 Infinity of Love.

73 Expatiation on Love.

74 The divineness of the mutual love of all.

75 This intention temporarily frustrated by the Fall, my Fall. The Cross restores.

76 Gratitude for this restoration (first of four sections addressed to the Lord).

77 Greatness of the love shown by the Cross, for the love was of sinners.

78 Prayer for goodness.

79 Prayer for love.

80 A summing up of sections 56–79 and their lesson.

81 Love and help those for whom Jesus died.

82 Seek out kindred souls and attract them to you.

83 The delight and profit of them.

84 How to treat their failings.

85 Communion with the saints in adoration.

86 Addressed to Jesus, who communicates himself to all souls.

87 Prayer for union with Jesus.

88 Addressed to Jesus. Prayer for communion with him.

89 Addressed to Jesus (and so in the main till section 98 inclusive). The Cross.

90 The glory of the Incarnation.

91 Prayer for love of Jesus.

92 The Friendship of Christ.

93 The need for Christ.

94 Prayer to be filled with God.

95 Prayer for the Holy Spirit.

96 Prayer for Grace.

97 The Communion of Saints.

98 Prayer for the Spirit of Truth.

99 When the Spirit of God is present.

100 How Christ dwells in our hearts.

In this first *Century* the following twenty-five sections are clearly not addressed to the friend: 62-64, 66-70, 76-79, 86-98. Several others need not be. Much of the second half of the *Century*, therefore, consists of meditation or prayer, but it is a main part of the promised 'Profitable Wonders' (section 1).

1. line 1. *Empty ... Soul*: Dobell compares Earle, *Micro-cosmographie*, 1, *A Childe*, 'His Soule is yet a white paper unscribled with observations of the world, wherewith at length it becomes a blurr'd Note-booke.'
   line 5 *without Knowing them* is over an erasure.
   line 7 *Enriching Truths*: the letters of these words are spaced for emphasis. Traherne in the *Centuries* does this occasionally for emphasis or to indicate quotation. He also occasionally underlines. I use italics for both in the *Centuries*, but in the *Poems* in this edition examples of Traherne's spacing may be found reproduced, e.g. *The Salutation*, 34, 'World'.

2. line 7 *Loadstone*, a word in use since the sixteenth century.

3. lines 1-2 *I will open ... World*, Matthew 13³⁵.
   line 5 *Heir of the World*, Romans 4¹³. Cf. *Thanksgivings* almost *passim* and the poem *Haeres Mundi*. If Traherne had given this work a title, he might very well have called it 'The Heir of the World'.
   lines 5-6 *Is it not a very Enriching Veritie*, written above 'A Great Truth, a Great Mystery' deleted.
   lines 6-7 *the Fellowship ... GOD*, Ephesians 3⁹.
   line 8 *hath been*, followed by 'Manifest' deleted.
   line 9 *so been*, deleted and rewritten above.
      Explained, followed by 'and considered' deleted.
   line 11 *unfold it*, followed by 'to you' deleted.

4. line 2 *advance* is over an erasure.
      the Gentle, followed by 'and Easy' deleted.
   line 3 *intends*, preceded by a short erasure.
   line 5 *Methods*, for 'Ways' deleted.
   line 7 *is*, for 'shall be' deleted.
   line 15 *not*, for 'scarcely' deleted.

5. line 2 *Creation*, followed by 'of the World' deleted.
   line 3 *End*, followed by 'of it' deleted.
   lines 5-6 *The God ... Christ*, 1 Peter 5¹⁰.
      called, followed by full stop in the manuscript.
   line 7 *Methods*, preceded by 'Arts and' deleted.

6. line 2 *Shewing*, followed by 'and Giving' deleted.
   line 3 *Lov*, preceded by 'true' deleted.
   line 9 *Bestowing*, for 'Giving' deleted.
   lines 9-10 *your own Greatness*, for 'how great you are' deleted.

line 11 *and*, an insertion.

    Religion, followed by 'the Hope of Heaven' deleted: 'in' inserted between 'Religion' and 'the Hope of Heaven' is also deleted.

7. line 5 *Beautifull. Before* for 'Beautifull, and before' first written.

line 7 *Invented*, preceded by 'Trades, fals Wealth', deleted.

line 8 *Giv . . . all*: see *Imitation of Christ*, III. v, *Of the wonderful Effect of Divine Love*, 'Love gives all for all'.

8. *Meditation*: for the importance of systematic meditation in the seventeenth century see L. L. Martz, *The Poetry of Meditation*, 1954.

9. Cf. the poem *Ease*.

line 4 *For*, perhaps 'for'. It is written over an original 'For' in darker ink.

10. line 1 *Interior Court*: Traherne is presumably thinking of the inner court, or Court of the Israelites, in the Temple, as opposed to the outer Court of the Gentiles. Cf. Theophilus Gale's formidable work *The Court of the Gentiles*, of which the first part was published in 1669.

line 2 *to*, preceded by 'is' deleted.

line 4 *Holy*: Traherne wrote 'H.' which I have kept in some places (see note on transcription).

11. line 7 *GOD* written over 'Him'.

13. line 1 *Desire*, followed by 'this' deleted.

    Esteem, followed by 'it' deleted.

line 3 *Silver*, followed by 'for Worlds, for any thing' deleted.

    Decline, followed by 'it' deleted.

line 4 *most like Him*, followed by 'and then' deleted.

line 5 *our Minds are* (second occurrence), shortened from 'And our Minds are then'.

line 7 *hav . . . and*, inserted above a caret.

lines 8–9 *God . . . rightly*, for 'He so Prizeth them' deleted.

line 10 *to the Knowledg*: 'to' is above a caret and in darker ink.

14. line 1 *ours*, for 'seated' deleted.

    Places, followed by 'and are all ours as much as is possible, and serv us already as much as we can desire, then' deleted.

line 4 *Evry . . . Place*, inserted over a caret.

15. line 1 *and*, followed by 'in' deleted.

line 3 *the Supernumerary . . . his*, changed from 'and the Supernumerary Persons Enrichers of Mine'.

line 5 *Jewels*, followed by 'and Peculiar Treasures' deleted.

lines 9–10 *for . . . Advancement* for 'to please me' deleted.

line 10 *The Receiver*, preceded by 'only Exalted in being' deleted. An intermediate stage was the substitution of 'as' for 'in being'.

lines 11–12 *Deus . . . soli*: Traherne quotes this same passage in *Christian Ethicks*, pp. 100–1.

16. line 2 *manifest*, followed by 'it in themselvs' deleted.
    line 3 *testify*, for 'shew' deleted, which was a substitution for 'declare it' deleted.

17. line 1 GOD is written over 'God'.
    line 7 *Giving*, followed by 'to his Creatures' deleted.
    line 8 *Plutarch*: this is not an exact quotation but is the general sense of Plutarch's *De Superstitione*.
    line 13 *Lord*, followed by 'that is all Lov' deleted.
    With this section cf. *Christian Ethicks*, p. 222, 'Among other Objects of Felicity to be enjoyed, *the Ways of GOD* in all Ages are not the least considerable and Illustrious'.

18. line 2 *this*, substituted for 'it' deleted.

19. line 8 *Suppose*, preceded by 'The Omni' deleted. Cf. line 13.
    line 10 *both here and*, substituted for 'and beneath them in extent on the other side'.
    Antipodes, followed by 'millions of Millions more' deleted.
    line 11 *Space*, followed by 'into which you enter' deleted.
    line 12 *Travelling*, followed by 'round the World' deleted.
    lines 12–13 *you com . . . leave it*, originally 'he cometh unto it, he passeth it in an Instant, and leaveth it behind his back'.
    lines 16–18 *World . . . Day*: cf. Isaiah 40^{12} and Psalm 90^4.

20. line 3 *Whom . . . lov*, changed from 'For if you lov him'.
    lines 7–8 *you will ever desire . . . pleas Him*, inserted above a caret.
    line 12 *God*, originally followed only by 'and your Palace. And the Laws.'
    line 20 *to your great advantage*, inserted above a caret.
    line 21 *serv* for 'lov' deleted.
    lines 22–23 *The Enterance . . . Simple*, Psalm 119^{130}, the psalm about God's laws.
    line 24 *Enriched*, preceded by 'you are' deleted.

21. line 2 *Hemisphere*, i.e. of the sky, cf. I. 30, line 8.
    line 4 *Amiable*, lovable.
    Influences, the usual astrological word though not with an astrological meaning here.
    line 5 *Body*, i.e. the Air.
    Breath in, not in which to breathe, but to take into the lungs.
    line 6 *Spirits*, in the usual seventeenth-century sense, cf., for example, Donne, *The Ecstasy*, quoted in note to *Thanksgivings for the Body*, line 51.
    lines 6–7 'To' or 'to' is deleted before 'repair', 'revive', 'Cool', and 'fill'.
    line 10 *Souls*, followed by 'as Great' deleted.

lines 10–11 *Be faithfull . . . much*, based on Matthew 25²³ 'thou hast been faithful over a few things, I will make thee ruler over many things.'

line 11 *'if'*, preceded by 'But' deleted: therefore not 'If' (see note on transcription).

lines 13–14 *Prizing all. there*, shortened from 'Prizing all the Residue, for there'.

line 14 *present mercies*, changed from 'these'.

line 16 *Gaping*, followed by 'insatiably' deleted.

22. line 1 *Insatiable*, cf. Blake, *There is No Natural Religion*, 'More! More! is the cry of a mistaken soul; less than All cannot satisfy Man.'

lines 1–2 *hath . . . Prone*, shortened from 'hath met with an infinit Benefactor. That is so infinitly Prone.'

line 4 *covet*, followed by 'it' deleted.

lines 6–20 This is from Plutarch's Life of Pyrrhus.

line 17 *all*, followed by 'the World' deleted.

line 18 *return*, followed by 'home' deleted.

our selvs at, changed from 'Peace and'.

line 22 *two*, followed by 'do' deleted.

line 25 *it all*, followed by 'rest and' deleted.

line 30 *so*, preceded by 'For' deleted.

line 31 *Tennis-Balls*: Traherne would have seen tennis at Oxford. The covered court behind the houses in Oriel Street was 'probably of the 17th century' (*Royal Commission on Historical Monuments, City of Oxford*).

23. line 3 *Triumphant* is an addition.

line 8 *by it*, changed from 'freely', which reappears in the next line, where *freely, without any cost of ours* is an addition: the sentence originally ended with *Manners*.

line 11 *And*, followed by 'by' deleted.

line 12 *are*, followed by 'all' deleted.

line 14 *freely*, changed from 'for us'.

Glorious, changed from 'Accessible'.

lines 18–22 *into Parts . . . Goodness*: this passage originally ran 'into its Parts, and to examine asunder the Excellencies of the Sun Skies Seas &c. And if we find them so Excellent that Better Things could not Possibly be made If another made them, He satisfied us, and saved us the Labor.'

line 25 *grounded*, followed by 'and fathomless' deleted (presumably as incongruous).

line 26 *Conquests*, preceded by 'Superficial' deleted.

acquire, preceded by 'in any Wise' deleted.

24. line 2 *Suspicion*, preceded by 'all' deleted.

25. line 1 Cf. the openings of §§ 27, 28, 29, 30, 31, 38, 39.

line 2 *in it*, followed by 'even to any Sand lying in the Indies' deleted.

line 3 *Exchequer yours also*, originally 'Exchequer wholly yours'.

line 4 *take*, written over 'hav'.

line 5 *evry Thing*, followed by '(that is Infinit Goodness)'. Above a caret after 'Infinit' is an illegible addition of about four words ending with '&'. It is not clear whether this addition was meant to stand.

line 7 *Dust of the Streets*: for the nature mysticism of which almost anything can be the occasion see R. C. Zaehner, *Mysticism Sacred and Profane*, 1957.

line 8 *Infant Eys*, changed from 'Enjoying Ey'. The *Infant Eys* are, however, to be understood literally (cf. C III. 3): this is not the almost technical use as in the poem *An Infant-Ey*.

26. line 1 *Services*, harking back to 'Service' in 25, line 4.

line 5 *nor*, preceded by 'no' deleted.

27. line 1 *Sand*, cf. Blake, *Auguries of Innocence*, 'To see a World in a Grain of Sand'.

28. line 2 *see*, preceded by 'and' deleted.

and, substituted for 'till you' deleted.

line 3 *Air*, preceded by 'H' erased (for 'Heaven'?).

line 4 *Reverend*, followed by 'and Sacred' deleted.

were, followed by 'ever' deleted.

line 5 *Angels*, preceded by 'H.' (the usual abbreviation for 'Holy') deleted.

29. With this section cf. Blake, *Jerusalem*, 27, 'Man anciently contain'd in his mighty limbs all things in Heaven & Earth'.

line 4 *World*, followed by 'Becaus were no Man in it, it were wholly yours'.

line 5 *evry one Sole Heirs*: the idea is the same as Wordsworth's 'Joy in widest commonalty spread' (*The Recluse*, 773), or, as one might put it,

> So might all men themselves employ
> In shared but undiminished joy.

30. line 8 *Hemisphere*, as in 21, line 2.

lines 11–12 *the Palace of your Glory*: the last word was substituted for 'Pleasure' and the whole phrase for an original 'it'.

line 12 *made*, preceded by 'Newly' deleted.

31. line 6 *Damned*, deleted before 'Ingratitud' and reinserted before 'folly'.

lines 12–13 *God . . . Heaven*, Genesis 28[16, 17], as often in Traherne not a verbally exact quotation.

32. lines 10–11 *they walk . . . understand*, Psalm 82[5] where the two phrases are in reverse order. See 36, lines 4–5.

lines 14–15 *According . . . course*, an addition crammed into the space between §§ 32 and 33.

All . . . course, the conclusion of Psalm 82[5].

33. line 1 *those*, followed by 'Riches' deleted.

lines 2 *us*, followed by 'from Him and' deleted.

line 3 *Contention*, followed by 'and' deleted.

line 4 *Vanity*, substituted for an original 'Poverty'.

line 6 *the Corruption . . . mistake*, substituted for 'Mens having at the first swerved from God'.

line 7 *God*, over 'he' erased.

lines 8–10 *they . . . Treasures*, substituted for 'for the Riches they invented were scarce and Rare, Insufficient, Hard to be gotten, as well as useless'.

line 10 *Persue them*, substituted for 'Persued'.

line 12 *Mad, yet having*, shortened from 'Mad, being faln into Sin, and go a Whoring after their own Inventions: yet Doting Extremely upon them and having'.

line 15 *Knoweth*, followed by 'they are in the Rode to Hell'.

line 16 *For*, followed by 'upon this Occasion and'.

line 18 *and feeble*, an addition.

line 19 *fals*, an early addition.

lines 20–21 *Theft . . . contention*, an addition: originally '&' preceded *Drowning*.

line 24 *Devised*, cf. *Wonder* 49, 'Cursd and Devisd Proprieties'.

their, substituted for 'such'.

34. line 1 *one*, substituted for 'a Man'.

in, followed by 'Ribbans and' deleted.

line 3 *Piece of Gold*, cf. Blake, *Vision of the Last Judgment*, ad fin. 'When the Sun rises, do you not see a round disk of fire somewhat like a Guinea?' &c.

line 10 *a WORK*, preceded by 'yea' deleted, followed by 'of GOD' deleted.

Divine, followed by 'Most Glorious and Miraculous' deleted.

line 11 *Transparency*, followed by 'necessary and Serviceable Diaphaniety and Clearness' deleted.

35. lines 2–3 *his sons . . . therin*, an addition.

line 8 *The*, changed from 'These'.

line 11 *to*, preceded by 'and' deleted, and followed by 'and common Interest in' deleted.

line 12 *Treasures*, followed by 'and this Sence, that we are the chiefest to one another', deleted.

line 13 *in*, followed by 'and in serving' deleted.

lines 13–14 *Others Happiness*, expanded from 'other'.

line 15 *Him*, followed by 'intirely' deleted.

line 16 *and*, followed by 'he Delights' deleted.

36. lines 4–6 *and now . . . Cours*, Psalm 82⁵. Cf. § 32.

line 5 *they . . . Darkness*, an addition.

line 9 *Mystery*, substituted for 'Happiness'.

lines 9–10 *And a Mercy it is*, originally 'And that this Mercy should be Conceded to us'.

line 11 *Hell*, followed by 'is Joy unspeakable and full of Glory' deleted.

One is rather glad to see Traherne moderating his rapture at this point.

lines 11–12 *for . . . Persons*, an addition made when the sentence was changed as above.

37. line 3 *It*, substituted for 'And'.
    line 5 *They*, substituted for 'but'.
    line 6 *filled . . . Glory*, cf. *Te Deum*, 'Heaven and earth are filled with the Majesty of thy Glory'.
    line 8 *within it*, an addition.
    line 10 *like the Cherubims*, cf. Presentation Quatrain, 4.

38. line 4 *For*, substituted for 'How'.
    line 9 *making*, preceded by 'by' deleted.
    line 17 *Treasure*, followed by 'and Blessing unto others' deleted.
    it, followed by 'inconvenient, or' deleted.

39. line 3 *sweeter . . . Comb*, Psalm 19^{10}.
    lines 13–14 *while . . . Bosom*, an addition crammed into the space between this and the next section.

40. line 1 *Socrates*, followed by 'that Glorious Philosopher' deleted.
        The anecdote is an expansion of Diogenes Laertius, *Socrates*, Saepe cum eorum quae publice vendebantur multitudinem intueretur, secum ista volvebat, quam multis ipse non egeo. (Traherne may not have got it from Diogenes direct, but, if he did, he is pretty certain to have used the latin translation by Ambroise, e.g. as in the Leyden edition of 1596 from which I quote.)
        They are, originally, 'that They were'.
    line 8 *That*, followed by 'Gods needed nothing at all, and they' deleted in the course of composition or transcription, since the words, where they occur below, are part of Traherne's original text.
    lines 8–10 Expanded from Diogenes Laertius, *Socrates*, Eumque diis maxime propinquum, qui minimis egeat.

41. line 1 *Curious*, exquisite, cf. Marvell, *The Garden*, 37, 'curious Peach'.
    line 2 *not be*, written above 'be' deleted which is followed by 'Pictures' deleted: above the latter a short illegible word is deleted.
    line 10 *DIETIES*, substituted for 'GODs'. For this spelling (and pronunciation?) cf. Lovelace, *Amyntor's Grove*, 54.
    lines 12–13 *Eternity Wanted like a GOD*, shortened from 'Eternity therfore Wanted. Wanted what? Wanted like a GOD, Wanted infinitly.'
    line 16 *wanted*: I am not sure whether there is an unintentional switch here from 'wanted' (desired) to 'wanted' (lacked). This last sentence is an addition.

42. line 2 *Blessedness*, followed by 'Yea, and' deleted.
    line 3 *as Glorious as Infinit*, originally 'Glorious therfore, as well as Infinit'.
    line 4 *Satisfied*, followed by 'He is from Eternity full of Treasure, but' deleted.
    line 5 *of Want*, followed by 'to Enjoy His Treasure' deleted.

line 6 *Treasure*, substituted for 'Satisfactions'.
  Incridible, followed by 'and Mysterious' deleted.
line 8 *a Treasure*, shortened from 'an infinit Treasure'.

43. line 5 *yet*, preceded by 'And' deleted (hence *y*, not *Y*).
  lines 8–9 *sacred . . . Felicitie*, substituted, at the revision, for 'Heavenly Treasures'.

44. line 3 *are*, followed by 'in Him' deleted: 'in his Nature' (line 4) was substituted.
  line 8 *Lively*, followed by 'felt' deleted.
  line 14 *stable Immutable*, an addition.
    Perfectiv, preceded by 'Or rather they are' deleted when the above addition was made.
  line 19 *Wants*, followed by 'should those Treasures be removed' deleted.
    his Treasures were, substituted for 'they were'.
  line 20 *Wants*, followed by 'therfore' deleted.

45. line 1 *enough*, followed by 'for you' deleted.
  line 11 *Everlasting*, followed by 'with your Treasures' deleted.
  line 14 *Treasures*, followed by 'That your Wants may be Treasures' deleted.

46. For the Sun cf. C II. 7.

47. line 7 *gone*, followed by 'is to be in Hell, and' deleted.

48. line 2 *here*, followed by 'being seen' deleted.

49. line 11 *Miserable*, followed by 'He that is most foolish is most miserable' deleted.

50. line 4 *Disquiet . . . shew*, Psalm 39[6].

51. line 5 *Treasures*, preceded by 'infinit' deleted.

52. line 1 *another*, followed by 'and of Enjoying another' deleted.
  line 3 *is so*, an addition.
  line 4 *his*, an addition.
  line 6 *Afflicted . . . Afflictions*, Isaiah 63[9].
  lines 7–8 *Will not . . . Enjoyments*, an addition.
  line 13 *concerned*, preceded by 'most' deleted.
  lines 13–14 *in Him . . . Being*, Acts 17[28].
  line 14 *and mov . . . Being*, an addition.

53. line 5 *and . . . Perfection*, an addition.
    you, preceded by 'And' deleted.
  line 8 *truly*, substituted for 'infinitly'.
  line 10 *be*, followed by 'Glorious' deleted.
  line 11 *wherin . . . Son*, an addition.
  line 12 *as he is*, an addition.
  line 14 *and Wise and Glorious*, an addition.
  line 28 *in all Places of His Dominion*, Psalm 103[22].

lines 31–32 *what he willeth*, substituted for 'them'.

line 36 *GOD is yours*, substituted for 'Yours is GOD'.

54. line 5 *Ey*, followed by 'And he reigneth over them' deleted.

line 6 *Him*, followed by 'And Minister unto Him.' deleted.

Doctors, followed by 'the Libraries and the' deleted.

line 14 *entertain*, substituted for 'fill' (probably a slip).

55. line 4 *Presence*, substituted for 'Sight'.

line 8 *Bodies*, preceded by 'very' deleted.

line 11 *it*, substituted for me.

Noah in His Ark, cf. with this whole passage *Christian Ethicks*, p. 215, 'The Objects and Transactions which in former Ages occur to our Eys, (I mean the Spiritual Eys of the intelligible Soul, that are seated within) are by Faith received, and brought to the understanding.'

Cf. also Blake, *Vision of the Last Judgment*: 'If the Spectator could enter into these Images in his Imagination, approaching them on the Fiery Chariot of his Contemplative Thought, if he could Enter into Noah's Rainbow or into his bosom, or could make a Friend & Companion of one of these Images of wonder, which always intreats him to leave mortal things (as he must know), then would he arise from his Grave, then would he meet the Lord in the Air & then he would be happy.'

line 11 *swim*, followed by 'in it' deleted.

line 12 *Rod*, followed by 'at the Red Sea' deleted: 'the Sea' in line 13 was substituted for the deletion.

lines 23–24 *Heaven . . . Glory*, cf. *Te Deum*.

56. lines 9–10 *Where . . . together*, Matthew 24^{28}.

lines 12–13 *lifted up . . . unto me*, John 12^{32}.

line 14 *Jeremie . . . Dungeon*, Jeremiah 38$^{6-13}$.

line 15 *S. Peters Sheet*, Acts 10$^{10-16}$.

lines 18–19 *Cords of . . . Lov*, Hosea 11^4.

57. line 3 *Coronation*: Charles II's was on 23 April 1661. Cf. *The Person*, 6–9, *Fullnesse*, 32–35 and notes.

lines 15 *Commoditie*, expediency.

lines 17–18 *They . . . Peirced*, Revelation 1^7.

line 20 *Cross*, followed by 'upon Mount Calvery' deleted.

58. Cf. George Herbert, e.g. *Prayer*, for the catalogue.

59. lines 2–5 *an Ensign . . . Earth*, Isaiah 11$^{10, 12}$.

lines 5–6 If the soul is weighted with love, so that it falls towards the universe's centre, it will fall towards the Cross ('this Object', line 7) which is the universe's centre.

line 9 *and . . . it*, substituted for 'towards it'.

line 12 *Rock of Ages*: Traherne has deleted 'the' before 'Ages', but the phrase occurring here in manuscript, a century before Toplady's hymn was written, is noteworthy. Traherne's immediate source may be the A.V. marginal 'Heb. the rock of ages' to Isaiah 26⁴, 'in the Lord Jehovah is everlasting strength'.

line 16 *An Innocent Malefactor*, followed by 'and' deleted.

line 18 *Eternity*, preceded by 'all' deleted.

line 21 *truly*, an addition.

line 26 *that . . . Savior*, an addition.

60. line 2 *Joyfull*, line 3 *saints*, are additions.

line 3 *Publishing*, making known, cf., for example, Luke 8³⁹.

line 9 *Son of GOD as you are*, cf., for example, John 1¹² 'to them gave he power to become the sons of God', and possibly even Blake, as reported by Crabb Robinson, on Christ, 'He is the only God. . . . And so am I and so are you'.

line 10 *seemed*, followed by 'only' deleted.

line 11 *you hav*: since § 53 Traherne has not directly addressed her till this section.

61. line 1 *you*, direct address again.

line 4 *Contentation and Thanksgiving*, an addition.

line 10 *Here . . . all*, an addition.

62. line 4 *Thanksgiving*, substituted for 'Prais shall I return'.

line 21 *Abraham . . . Glad*, John 8⁵⁶.

was, preceded by 'seeing it' deleted.

line 22 *and this Day*, an addition.

line 24 *Transeunt*, see *My Spirit*, 66, *The Instruction*, 13 and notes.

Thou, preceded by 'And' deleted.

line 27 *Wise*, followed by 'as the Son of GOD' deleted.

63. lines 6–7 *Thy Goodness . . . saved*, an addition.

lines 10–11 *Let the same . . . Christ Jesus*, Philippians 2⁵.

lines 11–12 *For He . . . none of His*, Romans 8⁹.

line 12 *I Admire thy Lov*, an addition.

line 17 *this . . . Skull*: even though the ointments are suggested by those of Nicodemus and Joseph of Arimathea (John 19³⁸⁻⁴⁰) and the theme is still the Crucifixion, it is remarkable to find Traherne thus depreciating this world.

line 18 *then*, followed by 'thy Lov' deleted.

64. lines 4–5 *in which . . . Bodily*, Colossians 2⁹.

line 5 *Characters*, letters.

lines 10–11 *Who . . . Everlasting*: this marks the transition from the contemplation of the Cross (end of § 55 to middle of § 64) to gratitude for this life on earth.

line 13 *Heavens*, preceded by 'fair' deleted.

Earth, followed by 'Such a Sun! Such Glorious Stars, such Gliding Streams, such Reviving Air!' deleted.

line 15 *Dominion over them from the Beginning,* i.e. since Genesis 1²⁸.

line 18 *How . . . unto me,* an addition.

line 19 *for me,* followed by 'to Enjoy' deleted.

lines 21–23 *the Wisdom . . . redeem me,* an addition.

65. line 1 *steed,* followed by 'and first Created, when I rose out of my Dust' deleted.

line 2 *the . . . world,* an addition.

line 4 *in the sight of,* substituted for 'to hav seen so Glorious a World'.

lines 6–7 *and for me alone,* an addition over 'And' deleted.

line 8 *moon,* preceded by 'Sun and' deleted.

and stars, an addition. These changes were made for accuracy, the passage from 'When I consider' (line 7) to 'Glory and Honor' (line 12) coming from Psalm 8³⁻⁵.

line 16 *Curious,* cf. 41, line 1 and note.

lines 16–17 *It . . . as it was Glorious,* an addition.

66. line 1 *What,* followed by 'Creature' deleted.

line 4 *Possessor,* followed by 'Thou has Created' deleted.

Lims, cf. *The Salutation,* 1, 21.

line 5 *Gold,* followed by 'but that they Exceed it; My Flesh!' deleted. Consequently in line 6 *them* was substituted for 'it'.

lines 10–11 *and pitty my Dulnes, who,* substituted for 'that I'.

line 13 *Thou,* preceded by 'Becaus' deleted.

line 14 *aware,* followed by 'O my God!' deleted.

line 15 *I believ,* preceded by 'And' deleted.

line 18 *yea tho,* substituted for 'if'.

me, an addition substituted for 'unto Me' deleted after *Kings.*

67. line 5 *GOD,* followed by 'offered unto Thee' deleted.

offered inserted later instead of the deletion.

lines 12–13 *the Likeness . . . Similitude,* an addition.

lines 14–15 *was infinitly . . . He,* an addition.

line 16 *Lovly,* preceded by 'infinitly' deleted: *so,* substituted for 'Lov'.

line 17 *having,* preceded by 'And' deleted.

He saw, preceded by 'from all Eternity' (repeated) deleted.

line 18 *none,* followed by 'Imaginable or Possible' deleted.

line 20 *Unspeakable,* followed by 'His IMAGE' deleted.

line 21 *see,* followed by 'by this' deleted.

hath, followed by 'both' deleted.

line 23 *Lovely,* substituted for 'Amiable'.

God is, followed by 'Infinitly' deleted.

Amiable, substituted for 'is infinitly Lovly'.

line 29 *what,* preceded by 'O' deleted.

68. line 8 *One,* preceded by 'And' deleted: 'one' changed to 'One'.

line 10 *Treasures,* followed by 'and more then infinit' over a caret but deleted.

line 11 *Creat it,* followed by 'and Giv it self' deleted.

line 12 *being,* substituted for 'by how much the more' deleted.

    Inaccessible, followed by 'it is' deleted.

line 18 *be,* an addition.

line 19 *all,* an addition.

    Beloved, followed by 'Object. and to Delight it self in Enjoying its Object in the Midst of them' deleted. Above 'Delight' is 'Pleas'.

line 20 *been so Good,* followed by 'to Thee' deleted.

line 21 *now,* an addition, possibly intended here, possibly after 'been so Good' above.

line 22 *more good . . . [?],* an addition. I cannot read the last word, a short one.

lines 24–25 *yet wholy . . . all,* an addition.

lines 25 *it self,* followed by 'and its Power' deleted.

lines 26 *Beloved,* followed by 'Object' deleted.

line 27 *Creatures,* followed by 'for Thee' deleted.

line 28 *Since,* preceded by 'Why' deleted.

69. Cf. § 15.

    line 1 *don,* followed by 'for me' deleted.

    line 3 *Created,* followed by 'in thine Image' deleted.

    line 4 *self,* followed by 'and thy self' deleted.

    line 6 *Sublime,* preceded by 'High and Great and' deleted.

70. line 5 *He,* substituted for 'And'.

    lines 6–7 *the World. . . . Mansions,* an addition. I do not understand the full stop after 'World'.

    line 8 *for,* substituted for 'to Advance'.

    line 10 *telleth,* followed by 'all' deleted.

71. line 1 *Thou,* followed by 'thy self' deleted.

    line 2 *thy self be,* substituted for 'hav it'.

    line 4 *What,* followed by 'therfore' deleted.

    lines 5–6 *Surely . . . Blessedness:* as first written this sentence ran 'The Laws of Nature, since thy Nature and GODs are so Excellent, and the Laws of Blessedness.'

    line 8 *Thou,* preceded by 'And' deleted.

    lines 10–11 *Thee, and in,* an addition.

    line 13 *Arrow,* perhaps suggested by Psalm 91[5], 'the arrow that flieth by day'.

    lines 13–14 *in that . . . Safeguard,* an addition, probably suggested in part by Ecclesiastes 8[8], 'there is no discharge in that war'.

    Charm, perhaps suggested by Psalm 58[5], 'Which will not hearken to the voice of charmers, charming never so wisely'.

    lines 15 *Thing* (if I have read the word right), substituted for 'End'.

line 19 *Delighted*, preceded by 'to be' deleted.

line 20 *approached*, preceded by 'to be' deleted.

requires Lov, followed by 'and Delight in it' deleted.

72. line 1 *infinit*: with this pervading thought in the *Centuries*, cf. *Christian Ethicks*, ch. xxviii, 'Of Magnanimity', pp. 457-8, 'Infinite Hopes and infinite Desires, infinite Fears, and Despairs, and Sorrows, infinite Joys, and Delights, and Glories, infinite Adorations, Praises and Thanksgivings, infinite and eternal Objects are the only fit and proper Concerns for the Affections of a Great and *Magnanimous* Soul.'

ine 2 *Goodness*, followed by 'and infinitly Delightfull' deleted.

It . . . Diligent: as first written the phrase was 'first it infinitely Delighteth'.
Good, followed by 'it would Creat Millions of Worlds for its Object' deleted.

line 7 *Angels*, followed by 'Cherubims and Seraphims' deleted.

unsatiable, followed by 'first' deleted.

line 11 *It*, substituted for 'And this'.

that, possibly 'yet' (y^t).

line 12 *it*, followed by 'of Thee' deleted.

line 18 *Law of*, followed by 'Lov, or' deleted.

lines 19-21 *His Lov . . . unto all*, an addition.

73. lines 10-11 *Soveraign friend*, cf. Presentation Quatrain, 1.

line 11 *his*, followed by 'Friends' deleted.

74. line 1 *one*, followed by 'infinitly: and' deleted.

line 4 *wholy*, an addition.

line 5 *evry one*, substituted for 'all'.

lines 6-7 *as . . . infinitly Happy*, first written 'infinitly Happy as there are Happy Persons'.

line 9 *He is*, preceded by 'And' deleted.

line 10 *Comprehending* (second time), substituted for 'Comprehend both'.

line 11 *Oh how Happy*, originally 'Oh what a Happy! Glorious Blessed Person!'

75. line 1 *without*, an addition.

line 2 *Advantages*, preceded by 'Mysterious' deleted.

line 3 *was*, preceded by 'I' deleted.

line 6 *my*, followed by 'so very Divine and Glorious a' deleted.

line 7 *World*, followed by 'And Himself also, in Magnifying his Wisdom Goodness and Power in doing all these Wonderfull and Glorious Things for me' deleted.

But, substituted for 'And'.

line 8 *suffering*, followed by 'for me and' deleted.

76. line 6 *Hope*, followed by 'and Possession' deleted.

lines 8-9 *sweeter . . . Comb*, Psalm 19^10. Cf. § 39, line 3.

lines 9–10 *more precious . . . Silver*, Psalm 119[72].
line 17 *upon*, preceded by 'And making it new' deleted.
line 18 *As I have . . . another*, John 13[34]. Cf. § 96, line 4.

79. line 5 *confess*, followed by 'O Lord' deleted.

80. A large cross deletes the whole section after the changes mentioned below had been made.
line 1 *My Excellent friend*: Traherne now returns to conscious instruction.
line 5 *are*, followed by 'you see' deleted.
line 11 *100 Miles*, roughly the distance from London to Herefordshire. This supports the opinion that the *Centuries* were written when Traherne was with Bridgeman.
line 15 *Beloved*, followed by 'At least ever Pleased in that Thing wherin it is Beloved. Do you but' deleted.
lines 19–21 *the Treasure . . . mean time*, substituted for 'and my Treasures in all Worlds. In the mean time till we come to Heaven.'

81. lines 1–2 *My Goodness . . . Delight*, Psalm 16[2, 3]. This section opens with a quotation (not exact): it is not, like §§ 76–79, addressed to the Lord.
line 14 *yea more*, followed by 'then His feet' deleted.
line 15 *yea more*, followed by 'then his Ey' deleted.
line 23 *Embracing . . . Savior*, an addition.

82. line 1 *Companions*, followed by 'and Joys' deleted.
line 2 *they*, followed by 'are hidden and' deleted.
line 4 *Wicked*, followed by 'Multitude' deleted.
line 6 *Digd for*, followed by 'and infinitly Prized' deleted.
line 9 *becaus it is*, substituted for 'it being'.
line 17 *Spirit*, substituted for 'Souls'.

83. line 5 *Relations*, followed by 'and Friends' deleted.
whatsoever, followed by 'I mean Earthly friends' deleted.

85. line 12 *Resentments*, feelings, cf., for example, C III. 84, line 6.
line 15 *God*, followed by 'in all the World' deleted. The words were re-inserted after 'Himself'.

86. line 2 *Lov*, followed by 'and Presence' deleted.

87. line 2 *stars . . . World*, substituted for the one word 'Kingdoms'.
line 3 *Hemispheres*, of the heavens, I think, rather than of the earth.

88. lines 3–4 *shades, clouds*: not Traherne's usual idea of the body. Note what follows, and also § 90.
line 6 *remain*, substituted for 'be'.
lines 12–13 *Ground . . . Open*, Matthew 27[51, 52].
line 15 *vail rendeth*, Matthew 27[51].
line 20 *rent*, rend (see *OED*).

89. line 3 *Dismal*, substituted for 'Heavy'.

    line 7 *silent*, substituted for 'the'.

    line 11 *Contusions*, followed by 'what Marks and Prints' deleted.

    line 20 *Merry*, followed by 'in idle Company' deleted.

    line 22 *Cross*, substituted for 'Ground'.

    line 24 *a*, preceded by 'of' deleted in each of the three places.

    line 25 *World*, preceded by 'whole' deleted.

90. line 1 *a Pillar*, substituted for 'was', no doubt with reference to Exodus 13²¹, 'a pillar of a cloud, to lead them the way'. Traherne here modifies his statement in § 88 about shades and clouds.

    line 3 *colours* (note spelling), substituted for 'Maner'.

    line 11 *Himself*, followed by 'He' deleted.

91. line 6 *Anselm*: see *Cur Deus Homo*, i. 21 (Anselm's fourth short speech), Remove hanc necessitatem; et de solo hoc peccato considera, si possis illud facere pro teipso redimendo. *Boso*. Aperte video, quia non possum.

    lines 8–9 *Length . . . Love*, Ephesians 3¹⁸.

    line 9 *Thee be*, followed by 'Infinitly infinit!' deleted.

    line 12 *Candle*, Leviticus 24³, ⁴.

    line 13 *shine*, followed by 'continualy' deleted.

92. line 4 *fairer . . . Men*, Psalm 45².

    line 5 *Lov*, followed by 'unto me' deleted.

        dust, preceded by 'Obscure' deleted.

    line 6 *Friend*, followed by 'so near unto me' deleted.

    line 7 *according to the world*, substituted for 'if I respect my Fathers house, to a small number of Honors Relations Riches and Possessions' deleted.

    line 8 *in the way of heaven*, an addition made when the change above was made.

    line 9 *Heavenly*, preceded by '[?] of' deleted.

        Mysteries, followed by 'such a [?]' deleted.

    line 10 *in thy*, followed by 'invisible and yet [? eternal, ? external] and' deleted.

    line 12 *house*, an addition. There is a reference to Abraham, Genesis 12¹.

    line 14 *all thy Ways*, preceded by 'that' deleted and followed by 'should' deleted.

    line 15 *near*, followed by 'unto me' deleted.

    lines 18–19 *Interminable*, boundless.

    line 21 *immediatly*, followed by 'present and' deleted.

    line 22 *that Endless*, substituted for 'an Endless'.

    line 23 *further*, followed by 'from me' deleted.

    line 24 *all*, followed by 'these' deleted.

    line 26 *of Ages*, over a caret but not a later addition.

93. lines 4–5 *Having Eys . . . hear not*, Psalm 135¹⁶, ¹⁷.

    line 7 *Captain of my Salvation*, Hebrews 2¹⁰.

lines 9–10 *let them* . . . *Holy Hill*, Psalm 43³.
line 17 *of itself*, over a caret but not a later addition.

94. line 12 *I desire not to learn*, substituted for the one word 'not'.
lines 16–21 *of whom* . . . *GOD*, Ephesians 3¹⁵, ¹⁶ ¹⁸, ¹⁹.

95. lines 1–2 *O Thou* . . . *Men*, Psalm 68¹⁸.
line 10 *rooted* . . . *Lov*, Ephesians 3¹⁷.
line 16 *their Works*: the last two letters of 'their' are deleted, but this must be a
mistake.

96. line 4 *As* . . . *another*, John 13³⁴, cf. § 76, line 18.
line 14 *Paul prayed*, e.g. 1 Timothy 1².

97. line 8 *Lovers*, followed by 'of each other' deleted.
line 10 *End*, followed by 'of all Things' deleted.
line 18 *Dwell* . . . *in me*, John 6⁵⁶.

98. lines 1–3 *Wisely* . . . *Truth*, John 14¹⁶, ¹⁷.
lines 26–31 *Thou* . . . *forever*: this passage is an immediate addition. Traherne
finished at 'Strength for evermore' and just below wrote '99' to head the
next section, but then overwrote the figures.

99. lines 1–2 *We are* . . . *Him not*, 1 John 3¹.
lines 15–16 *Chosen* . . . *People*, 1 Peter 2⁹.

100. line 2 *which* . . . *understood*, an addition.
line 4 *eight maners of In-being*, see Aristotle, *Physics* IV. iii.
lines 28–31 *Sing* . . . *Saints*, Revelation 15³. Cf. II. 74, lines 22–24.

THE SECOND CENTURY

Summary

II. 1 Transcendent services rendered by the world.
     2 To enjoy it fully, suppose yourself alone in it.
     3 Consciousness of possessing the world is necessary to understanding sin, the
       Fall, and the Redeemer's love.
     4 Misery of the Fall.
     5 What we fell from must always be remembered.
     6 God gave me the world: so why should He not have given me His Son?
     7 What a gift the Sun is!
     8 Services done by the Sun.
     9 Blessedness of the alternation of day and night.
    10 The same thought developed.
    11 The finiteness of the Sun a good thing.
    12 Excellence of the creation as it is.
    13 All things serve you.

14 God's goodness in giving you the world.

15 The world serves you.

16 Some services done by the world seem outwardly significant but are inwardly the opposite: some are the other way round.

17 Sublimer services of the world,

18 leading to communion with God.

19 Why God is invisible.

20 The same argument continued with reference to God's Infinity and His Beauty.

21 God shows His Infinity and Beauty in the World.

22 Since God is alive, the world is a world of motion, activity, and service.

23 God displays Himself especially in man.

24 The 'exemplar of Gods Infinity is that of your Understanding'.

25 Only man can discern God's love and its righteousness.

26 So you discern your blessedness.

27 Traherne returns to the righteousness of God's love.

28 This infinite righteousness requires to be infinitely esteemed.

29 Otherwise it entails 'Indignation infinit'.

30 God cannot be reconciled to your sin, but can to your person.

31 This He does by the vicarious sufferings of Jesus Christ.

32 Why could not an Angel have suffered to redeem Man?

33 Chiefly because only Christ was worthy of the honour.

34 Value that redemptive love as it should be valued.

35 The 'Dignity of Man' also a reason why an Angel could not redeem.

36 Only Christ had the merits to redeem Man.

37 Finally the 'Dignity of our Saviors Person' was a reason.

38 The question of salvation asked again. The answer is in God's Son.

39 God's Son begotten by Love.

40 The nature of Love, a Trinity.

41 The nature of Love, continued.

42 The same, continued. Love is creative.

43 Creative Love begets the Son of God.

44 The Son is God, and, as Mediator, is the Redeemer.

45 The world a mirror of the Trinity of Love.

46 God's perfection due to Love.

47 The same, continued.

48 Love is 'the End of Souls' and the condition of Happiness.

49 The disinterestedness of Love.

50 Love is all-sufficient.

51 Superiority of Love to the Body.

52 Love the one way to God.

53 And God will love us.

54 Praise of Love.

55 Love exalts Lover and Beloved equally.

97 Consciousness of our inheritance exalts a man 'to a Sublime and Honorable life'.

98 And 'makes Him sensible of the Reality of Happiness'.

99 All definitions of Happiness are here united.

100 The insufficiency of philosophers' definitions of Happiness. The true mystery of Felicity.

The above sections may be roughly grouped as follows:

1–16 The world serves you.

17–30 It leads you to God, but you need the Atonement.

31–38 The Atonement.

39–72 The Atonement due to Love: nature of Love.

73–91 The Soul as Act.

92–100 The Soul's greatness and the greatness of its inheritance.

1. Traherne goes back to the main topic, last specially touched on in I. 65.

2. Cf. I. 65.
line 1 *in it*, followed by 'alone. For it is as much yours' deleted.
line 2 *Created*, followed by 'in it' deleted.
     And, followed by 'then' deleted.
line 3 *doth*, followed by 'unto you' deleted.
line 7 *bestows*, followed by 'is the World' deleted.
lines 8–9 *Blind . . . know*, originally 'Blind, and do not see; they know'.
line 9 *Liberal*, followed by 'and Bountifull. And' deleted.
line 10 *they proceed*, originally 'proceed in Error'.

3. line 3 *one*, preceded by 'And' deleted.
line 4 *us*, substituted for 'one'.

4. line 2 *Lov*, followed by 'Obligation and Blessedness' deleted.
line 10 *unavoidably*, followed by 'infinitly' deleted.
lines 13–15 *For . . . to us*, an addition.

5. lines 3–4 *Remember . . . Repent*, Revelation 2[5].

6. line 3 *in the*, followed by 'Sight of Delights, and in the midst of the' deleted.
line 9 *also*, followed by 'to Die' deleted.

7. line 9 *for you*, followed by '(for there is nobody else, to Enjoy it with you,)' deleted.
line 10 *Divine*, followed by 'and Glorious' deleted.
line 11 *Purs of Gold*, cf. I. 34, line 3 and note.

8. line 12 *Motion*, followed by 'about the World' deleted.
lines 13–14 *the Swiftness*, shortened from 'becaus by the infinit Swiftness'.
line 14 *Universe*, followed by 'it' deleted.

9. line 4 *cool*, substituted for 'close'.
     With Traherne on the Sun cf. Sir Thomas Browne, *Pseudodoxia*, VI. v, 'A Digression of the wisdom of God in the site and motion of the Sun'.

11. lines 5–6 These lines are from Traherne's poem on Moderation (see C III. 21, lines 7–8). The considerable verbal differences may indicate that the quotation here is from an earlier draft.

12. lines 5–6 *unspeakable*, substituted for 'infinit'.

13. line 4 *alone*, preceded by 'Were you' deleted. Hence, as not uncommonly, the sentence is left beginning without a capital letter.
    bound, preceded by 'infinitly' deleted.
    line 7 *Earth*, followed by 'and' deleted.
    line 8 *Stars!* preceded by 'the' deleted and followed by 'for you! Oh' deleted.
    line 9 *It*, substituted for 'And yet it'. Here a capital letter does begin the beheaded sentence.

14. lines 4–5 *Heavens . . . Throne*, Isaiah 66[1] (modified).
    line 8 *in you*, an addition.
    line 9 *Impressions*, preceded by 'Deep' deleted.
    remaining, followed by 'within you' deleted.
    lines 14–16 *My Lips . . . Temple*, Psalms 71[8] and 48[9].

15. line 2 *Build*, preceded by 'clothe you, and' deleted and followed by 'for you' deleted.
    line 3 *for you*, an addition, i.e. transferred from above.
    Govern, originally followed immediately by 'But these are inferior and Menial Services.'
    line 4 *for you*, followed by 'that God who hath infinitly obliged you to lov and Admire Him. Those' deleted.
    vertue, followed by 'and those' deleted.
    line 5 *Honor*, followed by 'you' deleted.
    line 7 *beside*, an addition.
    line 8 *Enjoy and*, an addition.
    in all, preceded by 'and' deleted and followed by 'alone to Prais Almighty GOD for all' deleted.
    being, an addition.

16. line 4 *corrupted*, an addition.
    lines 5–6 *Magnifica . . . penetrali*: I cannot find the reference, although the late word *frontispicio* should provide a clue.
    lines 7–8 *These . . . understood*, thoroughly Wordsworthian.

17. line 1 *Pleasures*, followed by 'and low services' deleted.
    line 2 *do*, followed by 'you' deleted.

18. line 7 *Sublime*, preceded by 'very' deleted.

19. line 2 *yet is it*, preceded by 'And' deleted, and followed by 'infinitly' deleted.
    line 3 *Body* (both places), substituted for 'Bulk'.

line 5 *He would*, followed by 'be a Visible Bulk filling all Spaces and'
deleted. For 'Bulk' cf. *As in a Clock*, 26, and C III. 19, line 15.

line 6 *in it*, preceded by 'and' deleted.

20. line 1 *Hence . . . know*, an addition.

line 2 *indeed*, an addition.

invisible, followed by 'By pretending therfore to be Visible, He would but
delude the World. Which as Plato learnedly Observeth, is contrary to the
nature of the Dietie. And it is Worthy the noting, that' deleted. Everything
up to 'And' included was first deleted and 'it' changed to 'It', but then the
rest was deleted.

lines 3–4 *shewing . . . Eys*, substituted for 'revealing Himself in a visible maner'.

lines 5–7 *By . . . Dietie*: from 'By' to 'observeth' is an addition written very
small in between the lines. The words I have put in square brackets must
have been omitted here inadvertently: I have supplied them from the deleted
passage above.

Plato: not an exact quotation but the sense of the concluding sections of
Republic II.

line 23 *Variety*, followed by 'no uniform thing, but a sweet and delightfull
Mixture of figures and Colors' deleted.

lines 24–25 *of . . . Colors*, an addition made not at the same time as the above
deletion but later.

line 26 *Vision*, preceded by 'transcendent' deleted. See Ezekiel 1$^{4-28}$, 'This
was the appearance of the likeness of the glory of the Lord'.

Delightfull, followed by 'Imaginable' deleted.

line 29 *created*, followed by 'to represent the Diety' deleted.

line 30 *Being*, followed by 'visible, and' deleted.

it would, preceded by 'at last' deleted.

line 31 *noted*, followed by 'being always before it' deleted.

a Being, substituted for 'been'.

line 32 *Object*, followed by 'imaginable' deleted.

grows, substituted for 'would be'.

line 35 *Possible*, preceded by 'absolutly'.

contempt, followed by 'and ceas to affect us' deleted.

21. line 1 *Amasis*: Plutarch, VII Sapientum Convivium, viii. Traherne's recollection was inaccurate. The answer to 'Quid pulcherrimum?' was 'Lux'.
It was to 'Quid maximum?' that the answer was 'Mundus'.

line 5 *would*, followed by 'surprize and' deleted.

line 6 *we*, followed by 'being conversant with it all our life long' deleted.

it not, followed by 'Wherunto to make it Perfect, we may further adde,
that' deleted.

ancient Philosophers, e.g. Plotinus. Cp. Pope, *Essay on Man*, i. 267, 8.

> All are but parts of one stupendous whole,
> Whose body Nature is, and God the Soul.

line 7 *World*, followed by 'If GOD then be the Soul of the World, the World is His Body' deleted.

line 30 *Philosophers*, followed by 'Aristotle by name' deleted.

World, followed by 'realy' deleted.

Eternal: the reference, not necessarily at first hand, is probably to *Metaphysics*, Λ vi, 'it is necessary that there should be an eternal unmovable substance' (trans. W. D. Ross).

line 31 *into it*, followed by 'when we are born, we' deleted, for which *and* was substituted.

leav it, followed by 'when we die, and can scarcely believ it hath' deleted, for which *as if it had neither* was substituted.

Ending, followed by 'It is so Great a Mirror of Gods Eternity' deleted.

line 36 Traherne left the blank. Dobell noted that the reference is to Wisdom of Solomon 13$^{1-5}$.

line 39 *His Wisdom*, preceded by 'Why first' deleted.

lines 42–43 *His . . . manifest*, substituted for 'Secondly'.

line 47 *Again*, an addition.

seen, followed by 'in it' deleted.

line 55 *us*, followed by 'to amazement' deleted.

22. line 8 *Lineaments*, followed by 'or features' deleted.

line 13 *World*, followed by 'yea in the Space of 24 Hours' deleted.

lines 14–16 Is this the measure of the difference between Traherne and Paley?

line 26 *Herbs*, substituted for 'fruits'.

line 31 *Reflexiv*, reflective.

23. line 1 *Discovereth*, shows.

lines 11–12 *endless*, substituted for 'infinit'.

24. lines 9–10 *By Things . . . Godhead*, Romans 1^{20}.

25. line 16 *Right Wise*, righteous. OED says the spelling 'righteous' appears in the first half of the sixteenth century.

28. line 12 *Lov*, followed by 'to you' deleted.

29. line 6 *Lov . . . Grave*, Song of Solomon 8^6, 'love is strong as death; jealousy is cruel as the grave'. Traherne's variation is remarkable.

line 8 *they are all*, substituted for 'it is'.

32. line 17 *Hypostatically*, in their substance, as Christ was. Hypostasis = substance.

line 22 *is*, followed by 'grounded to Pieces, and' deleted.

We: the W is over a B.

33. line 1 At the beginning 'Whether the Sufferings of an Angel could hav been Meritorious or no, I will not Dispute. but' was deleted, and consequently *no Angel* substituted for 'none of them' after 'why'.

line 3 *Dignity*, followed by 'So that it was an Honor and No injury to be called to it. And so Great an Honor: that it was an Ornament to God Himself, and an Honor even to the Second Person in the Trinity' deleted.

lines 4–5 *Wherfore . . . Aaron*, Hebrews 5⁴.

lines 7–8 *Thou . . . Melchisedec*, Hebrews 5⁶.

line 9 *it*, followed by 'when it was offered' deleted.

lines 9–14 *for which . . . sakes*, Philippians 2⁶⁻⁹.

line 15 Here, as in § 21, we have a second paragraph, a very rare occurrence.

line 19 *another*, substituted for 'his Son'.

line 24 *folly*, substituted for 'Cruelty', a change made *currente calamo* since 'Cruelty' later is not a substitution or addition.

line 26 *Benefit*: Traherne first wrote 'Glory', then added 'and Honor', then deleted the three words and substituted this.

34. lines 1–2 *evry one*, substituted for 'Men'.

line 2 *World*, preceded by 'Whole' deleted.

lines 3–4 *He that . . . all Things*, Romans 8³².

line 7 *to Minister*, originally 'and Ministered to Him'.

line 11 *Trash*, followed by 'of earthly Riches'.

vanities, preceded by 'the' deleted.

of the World, substituted for 'poor and Beggarly pleasures'.

line 12 *imitate* preceded by 'Here imitat be Encouraged to' deleted. Presumably 'imitat' was deleted first.

lines 13–14 *counted . . . Christ*, Philippians 3⁸.

35. lines 3–5 *for the . . . for him*, Psalm 49⁷, ⁸. In the Psalm man cannot redeem man: Traherne adapts it to his argument that an Angel could not redeem man.

36. lines 3–15 The square brackets are mine. The passage is deleted in the manuscript.

line 25 *us*, followed by 'at least despised Him: for which' deleted.

line 27 *Lov*, followed by 'admiring and adoring His Justice' deleted.

expressed, followed by 'infinit' deleted.

37. line 11 *offered up Himself*, Hebrews 7²⁷.

lines 13–14 *Lo . . . GOD*, Hebrews 10⁷.

38. line 11 *Offering*, followed by 'And the Lov wherwith we were Beloved from all Eternity provided for us a Deliverer' deleted.

line 12 *This Day . . . Thee*, Hebrews 5⁵.

39. §§ 39–72 are concerned with Love.

line 1 At the beginning 'It is a very Great Mystery, that' is deleted.

His Son, substituted for 'Himself' and followed by 'It is very Plain' deleted.

line 5 *Pure*, substituted for 'Naked'.

line 6 *Abstract,* originally preceded by 'Pure', then 'Very', then 'Naked', finally nothing.

40. line 1 At the beginning 'Being Lov He begot His Lov, for' is deleted and 'in' changed to 'In'.
    begetting, followed by 'and' deleted.
    line 2 *Proceeding,* followed by 'The Lov begetting is the Lov Begotten, and the Lov begotten is the Lov Proceeding.' deleted.
    line 3 *Lov is,* followed by 'a Will in Act, or a Willing Act of' deleted.
    line 4 *another. Which,* originally 'another Object. Which Act'.
    lines 8–10 *Fountain . . . Lov which resteth,* originally 'Fountain of the Lov which Streameth to the Object, and the Lov which resteth.'
    line 17 *Parent,* preceded by 'fountain or' deleted.
    lines 17–18 *the Effect of Lov,* substituted for 'Begotten by it'.
    line 19 *Yet . . . loves,* an addition with no stop at the end. At the same time 'both' in line 18 was written over something not now legible.
    A lovely section.

41. line 3 *self,* followed by 'by Being' deleted.
    therfore, over the same word deleted.
    line 4 *fountain,* followed by 'therfore' deleted.

42. Original form 'Where Lov is the Lover, the Lover being so Pure and Simple a Being that His All is Lov, Lov streaming from the Lover, is the Lover, Begotten by the Lover; the Lover streaming from Himself: and Existing therfore in another Person. This'.

44. line 10 *Act 20:* Traherne left a space to insert the verse number. See Acts 20[28] 'purchased with his own blood'.

46. line 2 *all,* shortened from 'and all within its Nature, all'.
    line 4 *Son,* followed by 'The Means by which it Loveth' deleted.
    line 5 *of,* substituted for 'which it attaineth by'.
    Means, followed by 'the Immediat End' deleted.

48. line 12 *Idle,* followed by 'and Dead, or Evil' deleted.

50. lines 6–7 *alone attain . . . thy Glory:* original form 'Thou attainest another Self. By Lov thou livest in another Person. By Lov thou alone attainest a Perfect and Glorious self.'

51. line 2 *Endless,* followed by 'infinit and Eternal' deleted.
    sweet, originally 'Delightfull and sweet', then 'sweet and Delightfull': all five words in the line, changes being made *currente calamo.*
    line 5 *It,* substituted for 'And'.
    Lantern, cf. *Nature,* 23–28.
    lines 5–6 *that shineth in thy soul,* an addition.
    by it, shortened from 'It is that by which'.
    and feel, inserted over a caret.

line 7 *mightest be as GOD is: a*: original form 'mightest Lov, and be Lov as GOD is: and be like GOD a'.

line 8 *illimited*, followed by 'and unconfined' deleted.

line 9 *Objects*, followed by 'in Heaven and Earth' deleted.

line 10 *Eternity*, followed by 'and Admire His Lov and be mingled with it in all Places of his Dominion' deleted. An earlier deletion is 'it' after 'Admire', which suggests that Traherne was here composing not copying.

lines 10–13 *Profitable . . . Good to all*: original form 'Profitable to thy self for therby mayst thou receiv infinit Good things: GOD and all His creatures'.

line 13 *pleasures*, followed by 'a little food and a little Drink' deleted.

line 14 *self*, followed by 'Enjoy and Delight in' deleted.

line 15 *all*, followed by 'Joys even' deleted.

line 18 *Profitable to thousands*, shortened from 'infinitly Profitable to thousands and Millions'.

line 20 *Enlarged*, liberated (I think, but cf. 61, line 10).

GOOD, changed (rather messily) from 'GOD', but the rest of the sentence left unchanged.

52. line 9 *'what, O'*, an addition.

lines 12–13 *we shall . . . what*, an addition.

lines 15–16 *then our own . . . our selvs*, an addition: the word I read as 'him' is a mere scrawl.

line 17 *Him*, followed by '10000 fold' deleted.

line 18 *so*, preceded by 'and' deleted.

53. line 2 *His*, followed by 'Glory and' deleted.

line 3 *then He*, followed by 'yet the Controversy is renewed: And' deleted.
even, inserted over a caret.

line 4 *other*, followed by '(by living in each other,)' deleted.

54–61. These sections were originally misnumbered 53–60. Traherne noticed it when he got to 62 and corrected them.

He did not notice later on that he jumped from 87 to 89.

54. line 3 *Excess*, followed by 'only' deleted.

line 8 *Nice*, fastidious.

55. line 4 *It*, substituted for 'And'.

line 12 *Happiness*, followed by 'they always do' deleted.

56. line 3 *Nay*, followed by 'verily' deleted.

line 4 *unseen*, followed by 'and buried in it self' deleted.

line 7 *an*, substituted for 'For one'.

lines 7–8 *for which when*, substituted for 'therefore which it is before'.

line 9 *Spirit*, followed by 'Delightfull to another, and pleasing to it self: in the Act of Lov' deleted.

lines 9–10 *a Glorious Spirit*, substituted for 'in the Act of Lov'.

line 10 *A glorious Spirit*, substituted for 'in the Act of love'.

57. line 2 *Goodness,* followed by 'unto others' deleted.
    line 3 *it,* shortened from 'and it violently'.
    line 4 *implanted,* followed by 'and Engraven' deleted.
    line 5 *of all,* preceded by 'And' deleted.
    line 6 *Receiving,* followed by 'but' deleted.
    line 7 *Rich,* followed by 'and to be made Amiable' deleted.
    line 8 *Delightfull,* followed by 'unto others. And' deleted.
    line 9 *Sparkling,* changed from 'to Sparkle'.

58. line 9 *Souls,* followed by 'and' deleted.
    line 10 *and,* an addition when previous 'and' was deleted.

59. line 2 *when,* preceded by 'For' deleted.
    line 6 *Pleasure, Help,* both preceded by 'and' deleted.
    line 7 *which . . . Express,* substituted for 'Deep and Pleasant then all Riches, yet'.
    line 10 *we receiv Power,* substituted for 'But we are more Pleased, because of the Power we receiv'.
    line 12 *Person* (first time), followed by 'by our presence and Affections' deleted.
    or, substituted for 'a Stranger'.
    line 13 *Scepters,* followed by 'and all Kind of Treasures' deleted.

60. lines 2–9 *Who more . . . but most:* the whole passage is deleted. The square brackets are mine as in II. 36.
    lines 9–10 *but most . . . Him,* an addition. The section originally ended with 'them selvs'.

61. line 7 *Him,* followed by 'and more Blessed we are in our selvs. and' deleted.
    Blessedness, substituted for 'Happiness'.
    line 9 *others,* followed by 'Bosoms' deleted.
    line 10 *Enlarged,* followed by 'and enlarged infinitly' deleted. An intermediate version was 'and that infinitly'.

62. line 3 *Lov,* followed by 'that we know, and rest satisfied with its Excellencies' deleted. An intermediate state was 'till we rest . . . Excellencies'.
    lines 8–9 *Unless . . . never be satisfied,* an addition.
    line 10 *World,* followed by 'in which we might be Delighted' deleted.
    Abortiv, followed by 'short little Things, Dead and Distastfull' deleted.

63. line 2 *and,* followed by 'in their' deleted.

65. lines 9–10 *Emptiness,* followed by 'and that is a Greater Misery then Death or Nothing' deleted.
    line 10 *Life,* followed by 'since they are insipid and tasteless vanity' deleted.

66. line 3 *His,* changed from 'its'.
    lov, followed by 'evry Creature infinitly' deleted.
    lines 4–5 *Beauties . . . Creature,* changed from 'beauties in it': this was followed

by 'It Proceedeth from infinit lov, it Endeth in infinit lov, and hath infinit invisible Beauties in it' now deleted.

line 12 *Measure*, followed by 'Because all other Things are Beloved too little, that one seems to be Beloved so much. But there are more Beauties in it then yet are seen, or can be Imagined. And GOD and Christ love it more, then we can pretend.' deleted.

67. line 1 *Sand*, cf. Blake, *Auguries of Innocence*, 1, 'To see a World in a Grain of Sand'.

68. line 1 *Curious*, exquisite, cf. C I. 41, line 1.
line 2 *Heaven*, followed by 'and the Riches of Eternity' deleted.
　　　Person, followed by 'with all the Pleasures, as they hav thought, of GOD and His Kingdom' deleted. With this deleted passage cf. *Rise noble soule*, 17–20.

69. line 4 *maner*, substituted for 'Inclination'.

70. line 14 *be present*, preceded by 'at once' deleted.
　　　fully, followed by 'and Wholy' deleted.
line 15 *Desolat*, preceded by 'Idle and' deleted.
line 16 *as*, followed by 'in our Bodies' deleted.
line 17 *so are we*, followed by 'in these' deleted.
　　　when, substituted for another word which may be 'seeing'.

71. line 1 *Multiplied*, followed by 'And Space' deleted.
line 2 *Joyes*, followed by 'and Treasuries' deleted.
lines 5 *Kingdoms, and*, followed by 'at such vast Distances' deleted.
　　　present, followed by 'by his Beams' deleted.
line 7 *Heaven*, followed by 'and wholy present with evry Star, yea and with evry Sand in evry Region' deleted.
line 8 *Sun*, followed by 'a more Glorious Creature' deleted.
line 9 *Deep*, followed by 'and Incredible' deleted.
line 10 *one soul*, followed by 'to wit' deleted.
line 14 *another*, followed by 'being wholy taken up and absorpt in it' deleted.
line 16 *Adequate*, followed by 'and Parallel to each other. And' deleted.
　　　yet, followed by 'indeed' deleted.
line 17 *Operations*, followed by 'and Powers' deleted.

72. line 1 *Creature!*, followed by 'indeed!' deleted.
line 2 *Soul*, followed by 'which I contemplat, and' deleted.
line 4 *Perfections*, followed by 'Operations, and Varieties' deleted.

73. line 2 Cf. III. 64 for what is meant by the Soul being all Act, i.e. having no power unemployed.

74. lines 8–13 *After this . . . Lamb*, Revelation 7[9, 10].
line 13 *of which*, i.e. of the Lamb, not of the Multitude, since in Revelation 5 it is the four beasts and four and twenty elders, not the great multitude, which adore the Lamb.

lines 14–20 *They fell . . . Priests*, Revelation 5^{8-10}.

lines 19–20 *And hast made . . . and Priests*, an addition made *currente calamo*.

lines 20–27 *I saw . . . Manifest*, Revelation 15^{2-4}.

In this section there is some rather uncertain spacing of the letters in the earlier quotations (lines 8–20). Traherne, if the section had been printed, would probably have liked three types, one for his own words, a second for the words of the author of Revelation, a third (the most outstanding) for the Song (lines 23–27).

75. lines 3–12 *And I beheld . . . ever and ever*, Revelation 5^{11-13}.

76. line 1 *shall*, substituted for 'can'.

line 3 *You shall be,* an addition.

them, followed by 'all' deleted.

line 4 *Light is*, followed by 'in the Sea, or' deleted.

line 11 *in*, substituted for 'of'.

lines 15–16 *You are . . . them*, an addition.

77. line 1 *som*, substituted for 'one'.

line 3 *be*, followed by 'Scattered and' deleted.

line 5 *one*, followed by 'place' deleted.

void, followed by 'and Empty' deleted.

line 8 *Pleasures*, followed by 'and Delights' deleted.

delighted, substituted for 'Pleased'.

line 9 *and*, an addition.

line 11 *Limited*, followed by 'and Enclosed' deleted.

line 14 *Treasures*, followed by 'in all Places' deleted.

seek, preceded by 'must' deleted.

line 15 *in all Places*, substituted for 'all abroad '(hence the deletion of 'in all Places' above).

78. line 24 *whither it cometh*, an addition.

line 27 *Pure*, preceded by 'Res' deleted.

79. line 5 *Accident*, happening.

line 8 *Propriety*, property, cf. *Wonder* 49, 57.

80. line 6 *in*, an immediate addition.

81. line 16 *World*, substituted for 'Stars'.

82. line 3 *in*, preceded by 'infi' deleted.

lines 3–4 *in Capacity*, potentially.

line 4 *glorified and*, an addition.

Gratified, followed by 'and Exerted' deleted.

line 5 *Exerted*, preceded by 'as well as' deleted.

line 7 *Being*, changed from 'being'.

line 8 *Centre*: C is written over S, cf. C III. 21, line 5, note.

lines 14–15 Κατὰ Δύναμίν . . . ἐκείνου ἕνεκα, translated in the rest of line 15, 'To the utmost . . . Sake'.

83. lines 6–7 *to fill and fathom them,* shortened from 'to fill them all, and to fathom them all'.

   line 10 *smallest,* followed by 'Tittle of' deleted.

   from, followed by 'the Bigness of' deleted: cf. 1 Kings 18⁴⁴.

   line 11 *pretence,* substituted for 'excuse'.

   line 14 *Ardency,* followed by 'and Zeal and Vehemency' deleted.

   Lazy, shortened from 'Worthless Lazy Indifferent'.

   line 16 GOD, followed by 'Almighty' deleted.

   line 18 *finding,* substituted for 'and beyond all our Expectation see'.

   line 19 *Lov,* followed by 'and Delight in Him'. A very short word inserted over a caret after 'Lov' is also deleted.

84. The four short lines written to the right of the numerals are a later addition. They are a summary of the contents of the section, 'its' meaning 'the soul's'.

   line 1 *Dark,* followed by 'and Narrow when Idle' deleted.

   line 2 *but empty,* an addition.

   lines 15–16 *filled . . . GODhead,* Ephesians 3¹⁹ 'filled with all the fullness of God'.

   line 20 *we being,* shortened from 'being all Act. And we are'.

   lines 23–24 *with him who is an infinit Eternal mind,* an addition. It is important to note this, since 'As . . . term Him' refers only to 'Mind' and not to the adjectives.

   line 24 *Plato,* perhaps generally rather than in a specific passage, or Traherne may be thinking of Neo-Platonism, cf. II. 21, lines 6, 7, and notes.

   Cato: the first of the *Disticha Catonis* is

   > Si deus est animus, nobis ut carmina dicunt,
   > hic tibi praecipue sit pura mente colendus.

   This collection, popularly attributed to the elder Cato but certainly much later, has also been attributed to an unknown Dionysius Cato. Caxton printed a translation. The definitive edition is by M. Boas, Amsterdam, 1952. Traherne telescopes two lines into one, but translates the omitted 'ut carmina dicunt'.

   The Apostle, probably St. John is meant: John 4²⁴. 'God is a Spirit' is exactly apposite to Traherne's translation below.

   line 32 *contained,* followed by 'and Represented' deleted.

85. line 4 *The Lov . . . King,* an addition.

   line 5 *that,* substituted for 'the Lov'.

   line 7 *the love,* substituted for 'that'.

   when, preceded by 'Much more' deleted.

   fill, followed by 'All' deleted.

   line 9 *filling,* followed by 'all' deleted.

   line 10 *shall,* transferred from before 'your Lov'.

   line 18 *giv,* followed by 'if it be Despised' deleted.

   line 20 *when . . . despised,* an addition made when the above deletion was made.

86. line 4 [*you*], omitted by Traherne who accidentally wrote 'to' twice.
lines 7–8 *Clothe . . . Garment*, Psalm 104² 'Who coverest thyself with light as with a garment'.
line 11 *Him*, followed by 'or to com before Him' deleted.
line 13 *you . . . Sion*, Psalm 84⁷ 'every one of them in Zion appeareth before God'.

87. line 1 *Easy*, preceded by 'infinitly' deleted. With this section cf. Blake on Imagination, e.g. in the prose introduction to *Jerusalem*, ch. iv.

89. There is no 88. Traherne misnumbered from 89 onwards, but did not correct as he did 54–61. This is an indication that in the main the *Centuries* are immediate composition, not a fair copy.
§ 89 follows naturally on § 87. There is nothing to suggest a hiatus.
line 8 *Estate of Glory*, cf. *Christian Ethicks*, ch. xxiv, 'Of Patience', p. 357, where Traherne lists the Four Estates of Innocence, Misery, Grace, and Glory.

90. line 14 *on this*, on this world, I think, not on your ability to create other worlds, yet cf. lines 23–24 where we have a most Blake-like thought.
line 17 *would*, substituted for 'might'.
line 19 *Soul*, followed by 'that the Hemisphere only' deleted.
Heavens, substituted for 'Hemisphere'.
lines 27–28 *Besides . . . Excellent*, i.e. furthermore the very nature of a thought of the world (or the world in a thought) is more excellent.

91. lines 2–3 *evry . . . Creation*: the idea goes back to Origen, and cf. Hagenback, *History of Doctrines* (tr. by C. W. Buch, 3rd edn., 1858), ii. 306: 'The preservation of the world was understood to be Creatio continua, perennis.' He goes on to quote Melanchthon in loc. *de creatione*.
lines 10–11 *careless*, substituted for 'Worthless'.
line 18 *concerneth*: above this, which is the middle word of a line in the manuscript, is '292' (*sic*) imperfectly erased. Traherne was going to stop at 'Esteemed' (line 16), but thought of more to write.
lines 19–20 Traherne first wrote 'be very easy to a Wise Man', then deleted the first three words and wrote them again after 'to a Wise Man', then he deleted 'be' and rewrote it before 'to a Wise Man'.
line 21 *a Work . . . Diligence*, a later addition.

92. lines 5–6 *Length . . . Height*, Ephesians 3¹⁸, as elsewhere.
line 7 *Living Temple*, 2 Corinthians 6¹⁶ 'ye are the temple of the living God'.
line 8 *far more*, preceded by 'yea a Person' deleted.
lines 13–14 *Wideness*, followed by 'and be enlarged by it' deleted.

93. line 6 *the Holy*, substituted for 'them'.

94. line 4 *Dumb*, substituted for 'Quiet': cf. *Dumnesse* and *Silence*.
line 23 *Valley of Vision*, Isaiah 22¹.

95. line 23 *Darius when*, originally 'When Darius'.
    he is deleted but is necessary.
  line 25 *in him*, followed by '[*illegible*] by the King' deleted.
  line 29 *Benefit*, substituted for 'Gift'.
  line 30 *abov*, followed by 'the Gift' deleted. The story of Zopyrus is told by Herodotus iii. 154–6, but Traherne evidently read it elsewhere with elaboration.

96. lines 1–2 *Pomgranat . . . Ecclesiastes*: the reference is not to Ecclesiastes and I have failed to find what Traherne had in mind. The pomegranate is mentioned three times in the Song of Solomon but not compared to the world.
  line 3 *Seeds*, followed by 'of all vir' deleted.
  line 11 *is*, followed by 'his' deleted: 'of his Munificence' was substituted in the line.

97. line 8 *forsake*, preceded by 'des' (desert) deleted.
  lines 9–10 *see . . . Mirror*, cf. 1 Corinthians 13^{12}.

98. line 3 *Lov . . . Evil*, 1 Timothy 6^{10}

99. line 1 *Varro*: Varro makes an ingenious calculation that there are 288 sects of philosophers: Propter has differentias potest etiam triplicari numerus iste Sectarum, et ad ducentas octoginta octo perduci, *De Philosophia* (*Opera Omnia*, Dordrecht, 1619, Fragmenta, p. 171).
  lines 19–22 *Neither . . . Lord*, Romans 8$^{38, 39}$.

100. line 32 *Enjoyment*, preceded by 'Attainment and' deleted.

THE THIRD CENTURY

Summary

III. 1 I was born with a divine light which I will try to convey to you.
  2 My first state of blissful Innocence.
  3 A gleam[1] was on everything and everybody.
  4 He quotes his poem *The Approach*.
  5 What to 'becom a little Child' means.
  6 The Light of the Soul.
  7 My original light was eclipsed by 'the Customs and maners of Men'.
  8 Yet I could so easily have been taught the truth.
  9 It was less easy to teach me what was false.
  10 But I learnt to value only the trivial.
  11 Importance of right teaching in very early years.

---

[1] In Wordsworth's terminology.

12 As it is, our values are falser than those of savages.

13 The silly toys we prize are enemies to real happiness.

14 This happened to me as a boy.

15 But sometimes I felt a want of something better.

16 I remember especially one such occasion.

17 My childish wonderings about the Earth were later satisfied by learning of its roundness and of the antipodes.

18 Childish wonderings about the universe.

19 Excerpt from Traherne's Poem upon Moderation.

20 God's wisdom shown by his moderation (presumably this section covers part of the ground of the lost poem).

21 Another excerpt from the same poem.

22 Return to the subject of §§ 15, 16. Occasional intimations of something better.

23 Another early recollection: a desolate feeling turned to comfort.

24 The liveliness of my imagination of other places and times.

25 So with news.

26 The poem *On News*.

27 My desire for 'a Book from Heaven'.

28 Such a book, if miraculously presented to me, would have had its disʹ advantages.

29 Discovery that this book existed, the Bible.

30 The Bible showed that all is well except for man's imperfection.

31 But God can give man wisdom.

32 Question of the source of the Bible.

33 Advantages of the Bible over a special revelation to me.

34 The same thought developed.

35 The joy brought by the Bible.

36 The enlightenment brought to me by the University.

37 Defects and merits of the University: we 'Knew not for what End we so Studied'.

38 Ignorance of the 'End' causes a defective 'Maner'.

39 The 'Glory of God' as 'End' harmonizes with Happiness.

40 The right way of study.

41 Value is what matters: therefore 'Humanity and Divinity are the most Excellent' studies.

42 What 'Humanity' is and does.

43 The content of 'Divinity'.

44 University studies continued: Natural Philosophy.

45 Ethics.

46 The beginning of my deliberate and conscious 'Search of Happiness' or 'Study of Felicity'.

47 Poem, 'A life of Sabbaths'.

48 The war against sin can lead to bliss.

49 Poem, 'Sin!'

50 Poem, *The Recovery*.

51 Sin is the only calamity.

52 The student of Felicity had to make a choice of objects of contemplation.

53 I chose the commonest objects.

54 And also what was 'Common, but Invisible', i.e. 'the Ways of GOD in all Ages'.

55 Understanding the value of things, one must understand their relation: this is essential for Felicity.

56 We must 'first believ that Felicity is a Glorious tho an unknown Thing'.

57 Felicity is not Felicity unless it is perfect in its objects and its manner.

58 The objects are the same as God's, we being in his image.

59 Similarly the manner.

60 This leads to an unforgettable experience: 'A Sight of Happiness is Happiness'.

61 'The Image of God is the most Perfect Creature'.

62 God is in all created things. So my infantile apprehension was justified.

63 Difficulty and easiness of being 'satisfied in GOD'.

64 God is all Act or 'Power Exerted': he has no Power unemployed.

65 Therefore everything is eternally contained in God.

66 These discoveries I found had been made before, especially in the Bible.

67 The Bible illustrates the value I put on common things.

68 What matters most is the manner in which we behold objects.

69 Poem, 'In Salem dwelt a Glorious King'. This poem on David introduces the group of sections in which Traherne illustrates his thesis from the Psalms.

70 My delight at finding my own thoughts in the Psalms.

71 Psalm 8—the Glory of Man.

72 Psalm 19—the Glory of Heaven and Earth.

73 Psalm 22—all people called on for praise.

74 Psalms 24, 28—all things are God's.

75 Psalm 33—David meditates on the Works of God.

76 Psalms 35, 36—from God is the 'Torrent of Pleasure'.

77 Psalm 45—an Epithalamium on the marriage of Christ and his Church.

78 Psalm 46—the means of Grace and the perfectness of God's works.

79 Psalms 47, 48—the 'true and Celestial Joys'.

80 Psalm 49—'the vanity of fals imaginations'.

81 Psalm 50—the need to praise and glorify God.

82 Development of the thought suggested by Psalm 50.

83 Psalm 51—'the Sacrifices of God'.

84 'It needeth nothing but the Sence of God to inherit all Things.'

85 Psalms 58, 59—Conscious consideration of its objects necessary for the soul.

86 Psalms 63, 65—God's glory seen in his Works.

87 Psalm 66—the prospect of all nations praising God.

88 Psalm 74—David 'proposeth more Objects of our felicity'.

89 Psalm 78—reflexion on God in history.

90 Psalm 84—How amiable are thy Tabernacles.

91 Psalm 86—The Excellency of God's Works.

92 Other Psalms, especially 103, 104, 105, 106, 107, and 119—various aspects of God's Works.

93 The Psalmist in 'our outward Life towards Men'.

94 Psalms 145-50—a crescendo of praise of God's Kingdom.

95 David's 'Soul recovered its Pristine Liberty'.

96 David lived 'in the Light of faith'.

97 'What it is to be the Sons of God'.

98 God's greatness towards us and ours towards God.

99 Results of realising this.

100 What communion with God is.

The above sections may be grouped as follows:

1. This *Century* is more clearly a fresh start from II than II is from I.

line 2 *Pure . . . Apprehensions*, repeated in § 4, line 1.

from the Womb, substituted for 'in my Infancy'.

line 3 *are the Best*, originally 'is the Best light'.

line 5 *attended*, substituted for 'followed'.

lines 8-9 *and therfore . . . Pray*, originally 'Study, Information or Art. Pray therfore.' The word 'or' is over a caret, and 'Art' is written a little oddly.

line 10 *make you Angelical*, cf. Presentation Quatrain, 4.

line 11 *sweet and*, over a caret but an immediate insertion.

line 12 *was*, followed by 'Born' deleted.

2. Cf. Blake, *Songs of Innocence*, and Traherne's poems, especially *The Salutation, Wonder, Eden, Innocence.*

lines 1-2 *at the first . . . Delightfull*, originally 'and Rare, and inexpressibly Delightfull'.

line 2 *Beautifull*, followed by 'unto me!' deleted when a full stop was put after 'Beautifull'.

line 3 *Enterance into*, converted from 'Entertainment in'.

line 4 *Apostasie*, followed by 'and Fall' deleted. Cf. *The Apostacy.***

line 5 *Collected again*, originally 'again Collected'. Cf. Wordsworth, *Ode*,
105–8:

> Mighty Prophet! Seer blest!
> On whom those truths do rest,
> Which we are toiling all our lives to find.

line 6 *Advantageous*, followed by 'to me' deleted.
line 8 *Pure*, followed by 'and Clear and Divine' deleted.
line 11 *Quarrels*, followed by 'and Labors' deleted.
line 13 *Exaction*, shortened from 'Rents, or Exactions, either for Tribute or
Bread. And'.
line 14 *their*, substituted for 'the'.
line 17 *then*, followed by 'they did' deleted.
line 19 *World*, preceded by 'whole' deleted.

3. line 1 *Orient*, radiant.
line 4 *Gates*, of the walled city of Hereford. There were five: see quotation in
Wade, p. 17.
line 6 *unusual*, an addition. The ravishment was, of course, not because the
child Traherne had never before seen green trees, but because of his first
sight of them framed in the gateway—a visionary sight which to Wordsworth
would have left a permanent memory of a 'spot of time'.
line 8 *The Men*, cf. Wordsworth on the mountain shepherds.
line 17 *The Citie*, cf. the poem *The City*.**
line 23 *Churlish Proprieties*, cf. *Wonder*, 49, 57.
line 27 *again*, an addition.

4. line 1 *Pure and Virgin Apprehensions*, repeated from § 1, line 2.
This poem, *The Approach*, is found in both D and F, the title being suggested
by line 29. See notes in vol. ii, p. 346.
The first word of Stanza 7 ('Those') is over erasure.

5. line 1 *Born again*, John 3³.
line 2 *little Child . . . Heaven*, Mark 10¹⁵.
lines 17–18 *inordinat Affections*, Colossians 3⁵.
line 20 *Adam*, cf. *Eden* 29 foll.
line 21 *Lov in*, followed by 'Men' deleted.

6. line 7 *Curious*, exquisite.

7. line 1 *shined in my Infancy*, cf. Vaughan, *The Retreate*, 1, 2:

> Happy those early dayes! when I
> Shin'd in my Angell-infancy

and indeed the whole poem. Presumably Traherne knew *Silex Scintillans*
(published 1655). One can almost understand Grosart's attribution of
Traherne's poems to Vaughan.

8. line 6 *evry Drop of it a*, substituted for 'a Living Clear and'.
line 10 *Misery*, substituted for 'Corruption'.
lines 11–12 *Custom . . . Nature*, cf. *Nature*, 1.
lines 12–21 Traherne almost abandons Article of Religion IX, 'as the Pelagians do vainly talk'.
line 18 *natural*, preceded by 'only' deleted.

9. line 1 *Tinsild*, cf. § 31, line 1.
lines 3–4 *Ribban or a Feather*, cf. *The Apostacy*,** 42–45.
line 9 *preternatural*, unnatural.
line 13 *Clothes*: the beginning of the word is over '&c'.

10. line 1 *Thoughts*, cf. the poems so entitled.
line 4 *goe*, walk. The 'first Light' (§ 7) belongs to a very early infancy.
line 6 *their Thoughts*, originally 'anothers Thoughts'.
line 7 *The Glass*, preceded by 'Me' (Men?) deleted.
line 13 *disappeared*, cf. Blake, *The Gates of Paradise*, 'My Eternal Man set in repose'.

13. lines 2–3 *Grubs . . . eat out*: note the strong metaphor.
lines 3–4 *and eat out all their Happines*, an addition.
lines 8–9 *without GOD in the World*, Ephesians 2¹².
line 12 *Gingles*, jingles, but odd here.

14. line 2 *Shadows*, preceded by 'Dreams and' deleted.
line 7 *Scholes*: there is no external evidence that Traherne was at Hereford Cathedral School or any other school. The plural suggests he was at more than one.

15. line 3 *not . . . Riches*, cf. *Poverty*.**
line 5 *be dissatisfied*, preceded by 'griev at' deleted.

16. Cf. *Poverty*** throughout, e.g. lines 43–41.
line 1 *4 yeer*: N.B.

18. line 9 *in all Places of his Dominion*, Psalm 103²² a favourite quotation of Traherne's.
lines 19–20 *a Better Sea*, preceded by 'and' deleted.

19. W thinks this poem early for metrical reasons. The argument is perhaps reinforced by the *naïveté* of the thought. The *naïveté*, however, is less apparent in the excerpt in § 21 from the same poem upon Moderation. There the whole problem of limitation is brought up.
At the beginning of this section 'O what a' (see line 3) is deleted.
line 8 *Or*, preceded by 'Tis Wis' deleted.
    Glory: the G is over a W (for Wisdom).
line 9 *truly*, preceded by 'more' deleted.
line 13 *Things*: all but T is a correction.

20. line 9 *Placits*, i.e. placita, a contemporary use easily confused with 'placets'.
    lines 10–11 *That infinit . . . Infinity*: a deeper thought and the key to Traherne's discovery of Felicity in this world.
    This section may cover the ground of parts of the lost poem not included in the excerpts in §§ 19 and 21.

21. The occurrence of this excerpt, with some variations, within the longer excerpt in *Christian Ethicks*, *As in a Clock* (q.v.), supplied the final proof of Traherne's authorship of the *Centuries* and poems. See Dobell's Introduction (reprinted W, p. xci).

His Power Bounded		*As in a Clock*	
lines 1–4	correspond to lines	9–12 (with variations)	
5–6	„	15–16	„
7–8	„	13–14	„
11–14	„	17–20 (with much variation)	
17–22	„	21–26	

    Since Traherne prepared *Christian Ethicks* for the press, though he did not see it through, the *Centuries* version must be the earlier. Traherne's habits of revision also make it practically certain that the *Centuries* version is not an exact transcript from his early poem: the excerpt has it own unity.
    line 5 *Centre*, preceded by S or Se deleted. W plausibly suggests 'Seas'.
    lines 7–8 Quoted with variations in C II. 11, lines 5–6, where see note.

22. line 4 *Bliss*, substituted for 'felicity'.
    line 6 *I remember*: this would seem to be a very early memory before the Puritan victory. Did Philip the innkeeper cater for some local entertainment and bring the small boy to see the hall both before and during the entertainment?
    lines 14–15 *Reflexion . . . after*: N.B.

23. line 1 *in a*, preceded by 'being alo' deleted.
    line 2 *when all things were*, originally 'all things being then'.
    line 3 *Horror*: although the word may be understood here merely in its modern sense, this shuddering which is combined with a sense of awe is peculiarly a lonely experience under a darkening sky, cf. Marvell, *Appleton House*, 671, 'such an horror calm and dumb'.
    line 7 *unknown*, preceded by 'utmost' deleted.
    line 11 *the World*, preceded by a redundant second 'all' which I have omitted. *World* is substituted for 'Earth'.
    line 14 *Divine Providence*: here Providence is not quite a mere synonym for God, a use of which the earliest example quoted in *OED* is dated 1602.

24. With this whole section cf. Blake, *Vision of the Last Judgement*, as quoted in the note on C I. 55, line 11, and also *Descriptive Catalogue*, Number II, where

Blake speaks of his imagination active on ancient art, 'Those wonderful originals seen in my visions'.

lines 2–3 *entered into . . . me and*, an addition.

line 7 *read*, followed by 'I was' deleted.

25. line 2 *My*: M is written over 'the' (y^e).

26. This poem and *The Recovery* (III. 50) are the only two poems in the *Century* there given a title.

For the F version see vol. ii, p. 88, 89.

line 3 *Enflame*, cf. *The Rapture*, 12.

line 14 *the Same*: for the circumlocution cf. *Dissatisfaction*,** 5 and note. This whole line is over erasure.

line 38 *Thirsted*, used transitively as late as 1718.

line 51 *The Heavenly*: all except y is over erasure.

line 52 Cf. *The Preparative*, 13. This looks like a reference to that rather than vice versa; if so, *On News* was written later than *The Preparative*.

27. With this section cf. *Dissatisfaction*,** 71 to end.

line 7 *prevented*, anticipated.

29. Cf. *The Bible*.**

30. line 7 *all things . . . GOD*, Romans 8²⁸.

line 9 *Vanities*, i.e. Comedy is a part of Felicity.

31. line 1 *Tinsild*, cf. § 9, line 1.

line 2 *fetching . . . about*: the digression, more or less on education, consisted of most of §§ 7–14.

line 3 *And*, over 'For' or the beginning of it.

lines 8–12 *So that . . . Heaven*: Traherne's felicity does not admit an intense grief at the divagations of others, though he will work hard to teach them the right way. Cf. § 33 ad fin. and especially *Mankind is sick*, stanzas 6–13.

32. line 7 *Ascertaind*, informed.

33. line 5 *Being*, since, a use found several times in Traherne, e.g. III, 64, line 7.

lines 5–6 *Satan . . . Light*, 2 Corinthians 11¹⁴.

lines 20–21 *alone . . . Hous top*, Ps. 102⁷.

36. line 7 *Mechanicismes*, not in *OED*.

line 8 *afterwards*: felicity belongs to a post-University period.

lines 11–12 *Kings . . . within*, Psalm 45¹³.

line 13 *Nurses and Parents*, cf. § 11, line 1.

should hav talkt, as opposed to the actual upbringing of §§ 7–14.

39. line 1 Dobell quotes Shorter Catechism 1645, 'What is the chief end of Man? To glorify God and enjoy Him for ever.'

40. line 2 *Double*, over erasure.
    line 4 *in*, over erasure.

41. line 13 *Albertus Magnus*, ⁇ 1206–80.
    line 14 *Galilao* (this and not 'Galilaeo' is, I think, Traherne's spelling),
    1564–1642.
    line 15 *Hevelius*, 1611–87, published *Selenographia* in 1647.
    Galen, second century A.D.
    line 16 *Hippocrates*, fifth to fourth century B.C.
    line 18 *Lilly*, ⁇ 1468–1522, grammarian.
    The range from Orpheus and Homer to Hevelius is noteworthy.

42. line 8 *Which*, over erasure.
    line 10 *Wan[t]s*, written 'Wans'.
    line 27 *seeing*, over erasure.

43. line 2 *Outgoings* needs 'are' after it.
    line 3 *being*, i.e. Divinity being.
    line 11 *fourfold Estate*, cf. the passage in *Christian Ethicks* referred to in the
    note on C II. 89, line 8.
    line 17 *Punishments*, followed by 'Death Sick' deleted.

44. line 16 *Ends* may be over the beginning of a different word.

45. line 12 *Apparitions*, substituted for 'Words'.

46. line 1 *came*, perhaps during a vacation, but more probably after graduation
    in 1656. See Introduction, pp. xxiii, xxxvi, xxxvii.
    line 2 *Trees*, followed by 'and Meads and Hills' deleted.
    lines 5–9 *I chose . . . Labor*: this need not imply that Traherne actually had an
    offer of such lucrative employment, but that he declined to embark on a
    lucrative career, e.g. by studying law.

47. §§ 47–51 contain a poetical digression started by the concluding lines of § 46.
    lines 10–11 *Reign . . . Miserie*, here and now, without waiting for the next
    world where 'we shall also reign with him' (2 Timothy 2¹²).
    line 22 *Die*, unto sin, cf., for example, Romans 6.¹⁰, ¹¹

48. line 2 *and . . . them*, over erasure.
    World, followed by 'becaus I Dwell with Vipers' deleted. Cf. C IV. 20,
    line 2.
    line 3 *Abysses*, followed by 'and Depths' deleted.

49. line 15 *Oh!*: h has perhaps been added in the manuscript to distinguish the
    mere interjection from the vocative.
    line 26 *Place*, Hell.

50. Between the title and the first line is ¶. In D this comes before titles, and its
    curious position here may indicate that the title is an afterthought. Traherne
    used the same title for a poem in D.

W (p. 296) writes of the poems in §§ 47, 49, 50 that 'these last three poems dealing with temptation and sin strike a note rarely heard in Traherne's later writings'. One cannot, however, assume that the poems were written for the *Centuries*. It is more likely that he had them by him: *On News* and *The Approach* are actually found elsewhere.

51. *line 2 Escape*, followed by 'When I came into the Country' imperfectly erased and also deleted. The phrase was postponed until the beginning of the next section.

55. lines 4–5 *out . . . Bird*, Proverbs 27[8].

56. line 4 *Soul, that,* followed by 'the very force' deleted.
lines 13–14 Acts 17[23].

58. line 9 *alienated . . . God*, Ephesians 4[18].

59. line 5 *For*, an immediate insertion over a caret.
line 10 *Exerting*, preceded by 'in' deleted.

60. Traherne's unequivocal statement of the power of the creative imagination.
line 2 *Vision*, followed by 'to see the Perfection of the Nature of Happiness' deleted.
lines 7–8 *In summa . . . habitat*, not a sentence from Plato's works.
line 13 *Things*, after this an interlinear addition of six or seven words is erased.

61. line 1 *Creature*, i.e. created thing.
line 3 *Blasphemy*, followed by 'but real Truth' deleted.
line 4 *the Greatest*, preceded by 'And that therfore' deleted.
line 8 *is the most Perfect Creature*, an addition.
lines 9–10 *all it seeth*, originally 'all within it self'.
contains, substituted for 'seeth'.
line 11 *loves*, substituted for 'Objects'.
line 12 *and Glory*, an addition.
line 13 *in it self*, an addition.
line 15 *Creatures*, preceded by 'the' deleted.

62. line 2 *Himself*, followed by 'a Dietie' deleted.
that is, followed by 'that He was' deleted.
line 8 *esteem*, followed by 'or Think' deleted.
Pearls, followed by 'or Rubies to be' deleted.

63. line 8 *shall remain*, substituted for 'are'.
line 11 *Pure Act*, cf. § 64 and also C II. 73, line 2.

64. line 4 *Ends*, followed by 'It is impossible for any Power to Dwell' deleted.

65. line 4 *Nazianzen* (329–89), St. Gregory.
lines 5–12 *Becaus . . . Administri*, the beginning of Section IX of Oratio XXXVIII. Traherne, as often, used the latin translation.

66. line 2 *I was so,* preceded by 'And God Knows' deleted.
    line 3 *thoughts,* followed by 'and Studies' deleted.
    seeing, preceded by 'And therfore' deleted.
    line 4 *therfore,* an addition.
    lines 4–5 *that . . . them,* changed from 'to see Nothing Spoken of such Things'.
    lines 7–8 *before, . . . fathers,* an addition.
    line 12 *Obscurity,* followed by 'before' deleted.
    line 15 *Heart,* followed by 'and Centre' deleted.

67. lines 1–6 *Moses . . . therof,* Deuteronomy 33$^{13-16}$.
    lines 9–10 *How dreadfull . . . Heaven,* Genesis 28^{17}.
    lines 11–13 *Abraham . . . after thee,* Genesis 13$^{14, 15}$ and 15^5.
    line 21 *Devised,* cf. *Wonder* 49.

68. lines 15–16 *Felicity . . . Perfect Life,* not an exact quotation but the sense of *Nicomachean Ethics,* i. 7–10. Cf. *Christian Ethicks,* p. 15, 'Felicity is rightly defined, to be *the Perfect fruition of a Perfect Soul, acting in perfect Life by Perfect Virtue*'.

69. This poem introduces that part of the *Century* in which Traherne illustrates his thesis from the Psalms.
    line 7 Cf. lines 25–27 and note.
    line 20 *to his greater,* changed from 'too or pleas'.
    line 23 *A Sound*: Traherne began the line with 'Sacred' but deleted it.
    lines 25–27 Though moon and stars are not actually mentioned in Psalm 19, 'Silent Night' indicates that Traherne has it in mind ('night unto night sheweth Knowledge. There is no speech nor language').
    line 28 *even here,* changed from 'all on Earth'.
    lines 34–35 Cf. Psalm 19^{10}.
    line 53 *the,* changed from 'their'.
    line 58 *tho that doth Mirth destroy,* changed from 'removd from all Annoy'.
    line 70 *did increas,* changed from 'Glorified'.

70. line 1 *Objects,* followed by 'which God' deleted. This change is consistent with either immediate composition or transcription.
    line 5 *a Man . . . Heart,* 1 Samuel 13^{14}.

71. lines 4–12 *When I consider . . . the Sea,* Psalm 8$^{3-8}$.
    As often, Traherne's quotation is not exact. It is A.V. rather than Prayer Book, but 'in subjection' is from the Prayer Book version.
    line 14 *Person,* preceded by 'Gratefull' deleted.

72. lines 2–11 *The Heavens . . . therof,* Psalm 19$^{1-6}$.
    line 8 *which,* followed by 'rejoyceth' deleted.
    lines 13–20 *The Law . . . Honeycomb,* Psalm 19$^{7-10}$ *verbatim*: perhaps at this point Traherne looked it up.

73. lines 1–16 *Ye that . . . don this*, Psalm 22²³⁻³¹, *verbatim* except for the omission of 'and' before 'all the Kindreds' (line 9) and 'shall' before 'declare His Righteousness' (line 15). It looks as if Traherne continued with his Bible open, and, incidentally, that this is composition, not fair copy.

line 10 *Thee*, written over 'Him'.

74. lines 1–2 *The Earth . . . therin*, Psalm 24¹: 'round' is not in A.V.; the Prayer Book has 'the Compass of the world'.

lines 8–10 *Becaus . . . them up*, Psalm 28⁵: 'therfore' is not in A.V.

75. lines 1–6 *By the Word . . . stood fast*, Psalm 33⁶⁻⁹ *verbatim*.

76. lines 1–3 *All my Bones . . . Spoileth him*, Psalm 35¹⁰.

lines 3–11 *Thy Mercy . . . see Light*, Psalm 36⁵⁻⁹, where A.V. has 'in the heavens', not 'abov the Heavens' (line 4).

77. lines 1–4 *Hearken . . . Him*, Psalm 45¹⁰, ¹¹.

lines 4–10 *The Kings Daughter . . . Earth*, Psalm 45¹³⁻¹⁶.

The paragraph sign ❡, with which in D Traherne indicates a new poem, is used here uniquely to indicate a new quotation.

78. lines 1–2 *There is . . . most High*, Psalm 46⁴.

lines 5–6 *Com behold . . . Earth*, Psalm 46⁸.

79. lines 1–3 *O clap . . . Earth*, Psalm 47¹, ².

line 1 *God*, substituted for 'the Lord', which was probably due to a faulty memory.

lines 3–4 *He shall chuse . . . He loved*, Psalm 47⁴.

lines 4–7 *Beautifull . . . Refuge*, Psalm 48², ³.

lines 7–10 *Walk about . . . Death*, Psalm 48¹²⁻¹⁴.

80. lines 3–6 *They that trust . . . forever*, Psalm 49⁶⁻⁸. For verses 7, 8 see also C II. 35, lines 3–5, and note.

lines 6–10 *For he seeth . . . Names*, Psalm 49¹⁰, ¹¹.

lines 10–15 *This their Way . . . Dwelling*, Psalm 49¹³, ¹⁴.

lines 15–16 *Man . . . Perisheth*, Psalm 49²⁰.

81. lines 1–12 *Hear . . . Glorify me*, Psalm 50⁷⁻¹⁵.

lines 19–20 *Services*, preceded by 'Riches and' deleted.

lines 23–24 *If I should tell . . . Despise them*: a little hard on Susanna Hopton?

82. line 23 *moved*, preceded by 'melted' deleted.

83. lines 1–2 *Sacrifice . . . prepared me*, Hebrews 10⁵, which is modified from Psalm 40⁶.

lines 4–7 *Thou desirest . . . Despise*. Psalm 51¹⁶, ¹⁷.

lines 18–20 *The Falling . . . of it*, a verbose translation of Terence's five words *Amantium irae amoris integratio est* (*Andria*, 555).

84. line 2 *converting*, turning (intransitive).

line 6 *Resentments*, emotions, as elsewhere, cf. C I. 85, line 12, III. 92, line 35.

line 7 *valley of vision*, Isaiah 22¹, cf. C II. 94, line 23.

85. lines 1–2 *The Righteous . . . Wicked*, Psalm 58^{10}.
lines 2–4 *But I will . . . Trouble*, Psalm 59^{16}.
line 6 *Vengeance of*, i.e. vengeance taken on.

86. *lines 1–7 My Soul . . . joyfull Lips*, Psalm 63$^{1-5}$.
lines 7–8 *O Thou . . . com*, Psalm 65^2.
lines 8–11 *Blessed . . . Temple*, Psalm 65^4.

87. lines 1–7 *Make . . . Men*, Psalm 66$^{1-5}$.

88. lines 1–3 *God . . . Pieces*, Psalm 74$^{12-14}$ (which changes).
lines 3–5 *His Heart . . . Israel*, an interlinear addition in very small writing
lines 5–8 *The Day . . . Winter*, Psalm 74$^{16,\ 17}$.
line 9 *felicity*, followed by 'before us' deleted.

89. line 4 *and they*, followed by 'reveal them to' deleted.
lines 7–8 *as well as a large and sublime one*, an addition.

90. line 1 *Tabernacles*, Psalm 84^1.
line 2 *Day . . . thousand*, Psalm 84^{10}.
lines 3–5 *Place . . . Lord*, Judges 5^{11}.
line 6 *Palaces of Wicked Men*, perhaps a reference to Luke 11^{21}.

91. lines 1–5 *Among . . . GOD alone*, Psalm 86$^{8-10}$.
line 10 *He knew*, preceded by 'own' and followed by 'very', both deleted.
line 12 *Excellency*, followed by 'and Perfection' deleted.
line 13 *which*, preceded by 'and' deleted.

92. line 13 *Private*, followed by 'Joys' deleted.
line 21 *tho they*, substituted for 'which'.
lines 23–24 *things . . . Lord*, Psalm 107^{43}.
line 29 *Ways*, written partly over 'Laws' deleted.
line 35 *Resentments*, cf. § 84, line 6.

93. In this section Traherne collects examples of David's 'outward Life towards Men' from the Psalms and elsewhere. Specific references to the Psalms include in line 7 'when they were sick, my clothing was sackcloth' (Psalm 35^{13}) and in lines 8–9 'I was the song of drunkards' (Psalm 69^{12}), but in line 6 the reference is probably to the two occasions on which David spared Saul's life (1 Samuel 24, 26) and in line 10 the reference to the Temple is to David's intention which was carried out by Solomon.

94. The handwriting now deteriorates until § 98.
line 1 *Clear*, followed by 'then these' deleted.
line 4 *last*, substituted for 'very'.
line 7 *Musical Instruments*, Psalm 150$^{3-5}$.
lines 12–13 *as if . . . overflowing*, an addition.
line 14 *God*, substituted for 'Him. And'.
line 15 *being Pypes*, substituted for 'so were they Pypes and Chanels'.

95. line 1 *Mud*, an addition.
     line 4 *the infinit*, substituted for 'His'.
     line 5 *of God*, an addition made when the above substitution was made.
     line 8 *as clearly*, preceded by 'and were' and followed by 'present', all deleted.
     lines 8–9 *and . . . Him*, an addition.
     line 9 *evry*, preceded by 'And' deleted.

96. line 2 *in*, substituted for 'by Intuition, which is'.
     line 5 *therfore*, an addition.
     line 7 *Blessed*, an addition.

97. line 5 *H* is what was first written: over it is something I cannot decipher.
98. The handwriting recovers, no doubt because of a new pen.
     line 1 *our selvs*, substituted for 'us'.
     line 9 *S. Greg*: Gregory the Great. The passage Traherne had in mind is in
     Dial. Lib. IV, c. 29, Moral ii, c. 3, but he makes quite a different point.
     line 14 *in evry place and wholy*, an addition.

99. line 9 *without God in the World*, Ephesians 2¹². [rendered as] Ephesians 2^{12}.
     World, followed by 'almost' deleted.
     line 14 *Splendor*, followed by 'and Soveraign Glory' deleted.
     line 15 *Goodness*, preceded by 'Eternal' deleted.

100. line 20 *streams*: the last letter is written above to get it in, 'streams' being the
     last word of a line. This is one of several indications that the pages were
     not cut for binding *after* Traherne had used them. *forth* is above the line.

THE FOURTH CENTURY

Summary

IV. 1 Object of Century IV: the Principles of Enjoying Felicity.
     2 Principle i: To have principles but not exercise them is as bad as to have
       none.
     3 Principle ii: Study 'Divine Philosophy', because to be a Philosopher, a
       Christian, and a Divine are mutually inclusive.
     4 What Divine Philosophy is.
     5 A Christian must be a Philosopher.
     6 A digression: the necessity of being men in understanding.
     7 A further digression on what is essential, leading up to Principle iii:
       'I came into this World only that I might be Happy'.
     8 Definition of a Philosopher.
     9 Two kinds of Christians.
    10 Folly of preferring riches to happiness.
    11 Principle iv: 'I will first spend a great deal of time in seeking Happiness,
       and then a Great deal more in Enjoying it'.

12 Happiness is independent of being reputed happy.

13 Discouragements to the pursuit of Felicity, especially solitariness.

14 Principle v: 'It is a Good Thing to be Happy alone'.

15 Principle vi: 'Apprehensions within are better then their Objects'.

16 'Things Prized are Enjoyed'.

17 Principle vii: 'I will Prize all I hav'.

18 He turns from Principles of Enjoyment to Principles of Communication.

19 Nevertheless, Principle viii: 'GOD only is my Soveraign Happiness and Friend in the World'.

20 One must realize that the world is a Bedlam needing a physician,

21 Who must aim at transforming the world.

22 Principle ix: 'Whosoever would Enjoy the Happiness of Paradice must put on the Charity of Paradice'.

23 Principle x: 'the Lov of God his true foundation'.

24 Need for universal charity to restore Eden.

25 Rarity of order and charity.

26 Principle xi: Men are more to be beloved than before the Fall.

27 Principle xii: Treat every man as representative of mankind.

28 Principle xiii: 'treat evry man in the Person of Christ'.

29 Principle xiv: 'He lives most like an Angel that lives upon least Himself, and doth most Good to others'.

30 Traherne acknowledges that his practice falls short of his principles.

31 Principle xv: Holiness and Happiness are the same.

32 His great desire to be a blessing to others.

33 Principle xvi: 'Somtimes it may so Happen, that to contemn the World in the Whole Lump, was as Acceptable to GOD, as first to get it with solicitud and care, and then to retail it out in Particular Charities'.

34 He entirely got rid of covetousness.

35 Principle xvii: 'That all the Treasures in the whole World would not make a Miser Happy'.

36 Principle xviii: 'no Poverty could befall him that enjoyd Paradice'.

37 Heaven is established by principles, not place.

38 How to be in Heaven.

39 Thus Traherne was 'Possessor of the whole World'.

40 Principle xix: 'he had but one thing to do . . . to order and keep his Heart'.

41 By keeping his heart and these principles he could enjoy the world.

42 Why God made man a free agent.

43 The same continued and developed.

44 Principle xx: 'That whatsoever satisfied the Goodness of Nature, was the Greatest Treasure'.

45 The blessedness of giving.

46 Man's liberty increases the gloriousness of the world,

47 and is conducive to our highest happiness.

48 What you are, your love, matters most.

49 God attains infinite ends by 'infusing' small principles, e.g. self-love, into us.

50 The 'celestial Life of a Glorious Creature' should be ours.

51 Man was made good.

52 Principle xxi: to use my freedom nobly.

53 Since the Fall we have 'superadded Treasures'.

54 The 'Principles of Upright Nature', i.e. of Paradise. A summary.

55 How self-love is a basis of love for others.

56 'No man loves, but he loves another more then Himself'.

57 Love of others leads to Felicity.

58 Love for another means readiness to die for him.

59 'Lov studies not to be scanty in its Measures'.

60 Comparison and contrast of Love on Earth and in Heaven.

61 Supremacy of Love.

62 Properties and manifestations of Love.

63 Problem of Love and self-love.

64 How God desires glory.

65 How Love and self-love are reconciled in God.

66 Infinity of Love.

67 'Violence and Vigor' of Love.

68 The same continued.

69 Universal love is glorious.

70 Love makes us Sons of God and Spiritual Kings.

71 A new topic—'To sit in the Throne of GOD'.

72 What the Throne of God is.

73 The soul conforms to its objects whether 'a sand' or infinity.

74 The glory of created man: quotation from Pico.

75 Pico on the creation of man, continued.

76 Continued quotation from Pico.

77 Continued quotation from Pico.

78 Comment on Pico, and one more quotation.

79 Man, as Eusebius said, 'was first in the Intention, tho last in the Execution'.

80 Man may choose unity with God and so Love.

81 Reason can discover 'all the Mysteries of heaven'. Man is the greatest miracle. A soul is 'a fountain or a sun of Eternity.'

82 The soul as a sun or fountain.

83 It shines by Love, whether the soul itself or God in the soul.

84 This subject continued. The soul is a mirror of God.

85 Yet the soul also 'shineth of it self'.

86 The apostacy of souls on Earth.

87 Yet we can love the unloving.

88 Principle xxii: 'where a Benefit is fairly intended, we are equaly obliged for the Intention or Success'. This should determine our attitude to God.

89 'Riches are not to be Hated, nor Coveted.'

90 I can never be poor with God as friend.
91 Nothing else matters.
92 So I must honour God as David did.
93 Principle xxiii: 'This Life is the most precious Season in all Eternity'.
94 Value of these principles.
95 Principle xxiv: 'Practice and Exercise is the Life of all'.
96 Necessity of frequent meditation on celestial things so that they become familiar.
97 By practice we can do all things.
98 Principle xxv: 'Spiritual Things are the Greatest'.
99 Extent of the soul's powers.
100 Wonderful consequences of their unlimited extent.

These sections may be grouped as follows:

1–44 Twenty principles of Felicity.
45–53 Chiefly on Free Will (but also other matters), including one more principle.
54 Summary so far.
55–70 Love and self-love and their reconcilement.
71–87 The Glory of Created Man.
88–99 Three more principles.
100 Second Summary.

Heading, 'The Fourth Centurie', the word 'Fourth' being over an erasure which looks life 'Fifth'.

1. lines 1–3 *Having spoken . . . enjoy it*: the opening of this Century originally ran as follows:
    'Since the Author in the last centurie hath spoken so much concerning his Enterance and Progress into the Study of Felicity, and all He hath there said pertaineth only to the Contemplativ Part of it I will in this Centurie supply his Place and Speak of the Principles with which he endued Himself to enjoy it.'
    It is difficult to understand why Traherne at first adopted this transparent fiction of not being 'the Author'. There is no suggestion in the recast section that 'your friend' is other than Traherne himself, but the dichotomy has been left in some later sections, e.g. 20 *ad init.*
    line 3 *enjoy it*: above is a deleted interlinear addition, 'in the [?]'.
    line 4 *consisteth*, followed by 'much in' deleted.
    line 5 *som things*, preceded by 'there are' and followed by 'that', all deleted.
    line 6 *fitting*, changed from 'that fitt'.

2. line 1 *see*, substituted for 'have', itself substituted for an original 'see'.
    line 2 *Books*, followed by 'unless he did see them: and a vain thing to see them buried there' deleted.
    line 4 *by . . . exercise*, substituted for 'with . . . Practice'.

3. line 2 *World*, preceded by 'whole' deleted.
   line 8 *true*, an addition.
   line 9 *Perfect*, an addition,
   Divine, followed by 'Philosopher' deleted.

4. line 2 *vain*, followed by 'by St Paul' deleted.
   line 5 *St Paul*: Colossians 2[8], 'philosophy and vain deceit'.
   lines 10-11 *Changed . . . Image*, 2 Corinthians 3[18]
   into, substituted for 'by'.
   lines 11-12 *Express . . . Person*, Hebrews 1[3].
   lines 12-13 *made . . . Invisible*, Nicene Creed.
   line 20 *as*, preceded by 'nor' deleted.
   line 22 *Christ is the Wisdom of the father*, 1 Corinthians 1[24].
   line 23 *Life . . . GOD*, Colossians 3[3].
   line 25 *Heaven*, followed by 'nay His' deleted.
   line 26 *that they are hid in him*, substituted for 'that In Him are hid all' deleted.
   lines 26-27 *In Him . . . Knowledg*, Colossians 2[3].

5. line 2 *Intelligent*, preceded by 'or rather' deleted.
   line 9 *Is . . . Wisdom?*, shortened from 'What is a Philosopher; is it not a Lover of Wisdom?'
   line 11 *or very near it*, an addition.
   Wisdom, followed by 'at least an Appendix, and som property pertaining to his Essence' deleted.
   be, an addition.
   line 13 *Imperfection*, substituted for 'it'.
   line 15 *he may*, preceded by ''Tis true' deleted.
   defectiv, followed by 'and ignorant' deleted.
   line 16 *a Christian* (first time), substituted for 'he'.
   line 17 *Nor*, preceded by 'But som say' deleted.
   line 18 *Ignorances*, substituted for 'Blemishes'.
   Wisdom, substituted for 'Excellencies'.

6. lines 1-2 *in understanding to be Men*, 1 Corinthians 14[20].
   line 3 *but*, followed by 'Dreams and Shadows' deleted.
   line 4 *Shels: OED* quotes Carlyle, 'Mere effigies and shells of men'.
   lines 5-8 *Hearts . . . Christ*, Colossians 2[2].
   line 9 *desirable*, followed by 'he should be Assured' deleted.
   line 13 *Heaven*, followed by 'becaus the Word of God has told him so' deleted.
   line 17 *Assurance*, followed by 'of Understanding' deleted.
   lines 17-19 *i.e. those . . . all Things*, an addition.
   line 22 *see*, followed by 'and Know' deleted.
   line 23 *Reality*, followed by 'and verity' deleted.
   Beams, followed by 'then of those things' deleted.

7. line 7 *Shall . . . despised*, cf. § 13, lines 5-6.
   despised, preceded by 'always' deleted.

line 8 *of*, followed by 'all' deleted.

line 9 *the*, followed by a redundant 'the' deleted, and then by 'most, and' separately deleted.

Time, followed by 'allowed her' deleted.

line 10 *Divine*, followed by 'and Angelical' deleted.

lines 11–12 *We . . . silver*, Proverbs 2⁴, modified.

lines 14–19 *Wisdom . . . to Thee*, Proverbs 4⁷⁻⁹.

line 15 *yet all neglect her*, an addition (not from Proverbs).

line 30 *Temple of Honor, Temple of Virtue*, if this is an allusion, I have not identified it.

8. line 6 *Pleasures*, preceded by 'Pleas' deleted.

line 8 *bears*, preceded by 'break' deleted.

line 11 *lives by Rule*: for Susanna Hopton's living by rule (i.e. methodism) see Wade, p. 82, and the quotation there from Spinckes.

9. line 1 *There*, preceded by 'A' deleted.

line 4 *one*, preceded by 'form' (beginning of 'former') deleted.

line 16 *certainly*, followed by 'that' deleted.

line 21 *Conversation*, way of life. The reference is to Philippians 3²⁰.

lines 22–23 *ye . . . Bowels*, 2 Corinthians 6¹²

With this section compare and contrast § 60. Compare and contrast also Wordsworth, *Prelude*, xi. 142–4:

> . . . the world
> Of all of us,—the place where, in the end,
> We find our happiness, or not at all!

Also Blake's disapproval of Urizen in *Vala* for his over-concern with 'futurity'.

10. line 1 *Exchange*, substituted for 'forsake'.

now, followed by 'for Happiness' deleted.

line 2 *but*, preceded by 'forsake them' and followed by 'he', all deleted.

line 4 *Dishonors*, followed by 'will' deleted.

line 5 *Stage*, followed by 'of this World' deleted.

line 6 *Riches* (second time), shortened from 'All Riches indeed'.

line 7 *to*, shortened from 'unto'.

line 9 *incompitable*, followed by 'with it are' deleted.

line 10 *endeavored*, followed by 'but our Happiness' deleted.

11. line 3 *more*, followed by 'time' deleted.

line 6 *contented*, followed 'with having it' deleted.

line 8 *none*, followed by 'afterwards' deleted.

that, preceded by 'Nay as' deleted.

line 10 *toil*, followed by 'and Sweat' deleted.

they, followed by 'are so abundantly satisfied that they' deleted.

lines 11–12 *Their pretence . . . of it*, an addition.
line 12 *So*, followed by 'doth' deleted.
line 13 *lost*, substituted for 'mist'.
line 14 *if*, preceded by 'that' deleted.
line 15 *precious*, followed by 'a Commodity' deleted.
line 19 *as . . . seeking it*, an addition.

12. line 1 *enjoyed*, followed by 'Therfore' deleted.
lines 6–7 *Tacitus si*: the metre requires the order of these two words to be transposed.
The hexameters seem to belong to the moral at the end of some version of Aesop's fable of the Fox and the Crow.
line 16 *Miscarriage*, misbehaviour, cf. § 30, line 12.

13. lines 3–5 *alone . . . Wilderness*, Psalm 102[6, 7], inaccurately quoted from memory.
lines 5–6 *Prais . . . despise*, cf. § 7, line 7.
line 10 *persuaded to*, followed by 'be' deleted.
line 12 *men*, substituted for 'they'.
line 13 *Gold*, followed by 'and Silver' deleted.
for, followed by 'to hav them discovered' deleted.
line 14 *Known*, preceded by 'they are' deleted.
be, shortened from 'hav been'.
line 21 *forbidden*, preceded by 'long after' deleted.
then . . . common, an addition.
line 24 *our*, written above 'the' which is not deleted.
Addresses, followed by 'to her' deleted.

14. line 1 *he*, i.e. your friend, as in § 1.

15. line 2 *Principle*, followed by 'to reciev' deleted.
line 3 *Mornay* (1549–1623), a leading French Protestant and founder of the Protestant Academy at Saumur to which Marvell accompanied his pupil William Dutton in 1656. Traherne may have known his *Concerning the trunesse of Christian Religion*, of which Sir Philip Sidney began and Arthur Golding completed the translation (4th edn., 1617).
line 4 *a saw*, substituted for 'it'.
line 4–5 *but a Thing with Teeth*, shortened from 'but a Saw—that is a Thing with ['D' deleted] Teeth, and that cuts with Drawing'.
line 9 *Error*, followed by 'and of Greater Consequence' deleted.
line 10 *he that*, preceded by 'And' deleted.
line 11 *impertinent*, irrelevant.
line 12 *what*, followed by 'Instruments' deleted.
line 14 *Nor*, followed by 'can we' deleted.

16. line 4 *serv us*, an immediate addition over a caret.

17. line 1 *Tho*, substituted for 'If'.

    line 8 *A Common Joy*, cf. Wordsworth, *The Recluse*, 773, 'joy in widest commonalty spread'.

18. lines 3–4 *Conversation*, social life, not quite the same sense as in § 9, line 21.

    lines 5–6 *it is . . . receiv*, Acts 20³⁵.

20. Dobell compares the poem *Mankind is sick*.

    line 1 *He, I* are both Traherne. Cf. § 1 and notes.

    line 2 *Generation of Vipers*, Matthew 3⁷, but John the Baptist's point was that his audience were like snakes escaping from a reaping or a combustion.

    line 14 *savior Witnesseth*, presumably a reference to Christ's unfavourable comparison with Sodom and Gomorrah, Matthew 10¹⁵.

    line 15 *folly*, substituted for 'Sodom'.

    line 18 *Beauty of Holiness*, Psalms, e.g. 29².

21. line 1 *He . . . himself*, Traherne.

    line 6 *Royal Chymist*, perhaps an allusion to Charles II, who took consider‑ able interest in the Royal Society and 'had a laboratory and knew of many Empyrical Medicines' (Evelyn, *Diary*, 6 February 1685).

    line 13 *that*, substituted for 'which' (or possibly vice versa).

§§ 21, 22, 23 all bring in a comparison with Paradise.

23. line 16 *Refuge*, Psalm 46¹ 'God is our refuge and strength'.

24. line 10 *Lands*, substituted for 'Earth'.

    line 13 *whence*, just below this is '25' deleted.

    So this last sentence is an immediate addition or continuation.

25. The figure '5' is corrected from something else.

    line 3 *shining*, an immediate addition over a caret.

    line 11 *Deordination*: *OED* quotes Jeremy Taylor, *Dissuas. Popery*, i. 99, 'excess of riot and deordination'. The word as used here looks back to 'Order' in line 1.

28. line 4 *Dwell*, substituted for 'liv'.

    lines 11–13 *Inasmuch . . . unto me*, Matthew 25⁴⁰.

30. line 9 *clothed in the Righteousness*, cf. Psalm 132⁹ 'clothed with righteousness', and perhaps 2 Corinthians 5² 'clothed upon with our house which is from heaven'.

    line 12 *Miscarriage*, cf. § 12, line 16.

    line 13 The original ending was 'erre again'. The change was immediate.

31. line 2 *coated*, quoted: *OED* reports this spelling (and pronunciation?) in the sixteenth and seventeenth centuries.

    lines 2–3 *her ways . . . Peace*, Proverbs 3¹⁷.

33. At the end there is a later note in very small writing beginning 'l. of 2 [? a] specious' and with about as much more which I cannot decipher.

    Phocion, written sideways. Phocion (fourth century B.C.) is the subject of one of Plutarch's *Lives* which contains several stories about his contempt of riches.

34. line 1 *Luther: Tischreden* I, 87 (Weimar, 1912), 'ego sum liber ab avaritia'.
lines 4–6. As often, Traherne quotes inexactly. Clough's translation of Phocion's reply is: 'If my son returns to a right mind, his patrimony is sufficient; if not, all supplies will be insufficient.'

36. line 1 *befall*, substituted for 'shake'.
line 5 *the*: above is written 'His'.
Nakedness, preceded by 'very' deleted.

37. lines 4–5 *from the Centre . . . Hills*; cf. V. 6, lines 5–6.

38. line 1 *lov*, preceded by 'Do but' deleted.
line 6 *celestial*, substituted for 'your'.
lines 6–7 *delight . . . above*, substituted for 'here'. The text shows some uncer‐
tainty in composition.
line 10 *Extent*, followed by 'and unlimited Endlessness' deleted.

39. line 3 *Virtues*, preceded by 'his' deleted.

40. line 10 *God*, duplicated by inadvertence, here printed once only. It is followed by 'within' deleted.
be sure, preceded by 'wish' deleted.
line 11 *things*, preceded by 'all other' deleted.
without, an addition.
God. for he, originally 'Him. For God'.
line 12 *faithfull . . . promised*, Hebrews 10²³.
that had promised, substituted for 'and perfect in all on his part'.
line 13 *God was perfect*, an addition made when the above change was made.
line 14 *pertain*, substituted for 'belong'.

41. line 5 *Friend of God*, cf. Presentation Quatrain, line 1, where 'my best friend' means God. Cf. also James 2²³, 'Abraham . . . was called the Friend of God.'
lines 11–12 *Keep . . . Life*, Proverbs 4²³, modified.

42. line 7 *salved*: see *OED*. Here it seems to be *OED* verb² 2 'to clear up' (a difficulty), a normal seventeenth‐century use.

44. Ignorance of this Principle (lines 1–2) leads to desire to please men and the consequent evils.

45. line 2 *Orient*, brilliant; cf. III. 3, line 1.
lines 8–9 *It is . . . receiv*, Acts 20³⁵; cf. § 18, lines 5–6.
line 16 *that is*, substituted for 'of all'.
line 17 *Kingdoms*, followed by 'given to us' deleted.
line 18 *Earth*, followed by 'and all Worlds' deleted.
line 20 *soul*, preceded by 'living' deleted.

line 21 *Dead Things*, substituted for 'these'.
Good, followed by 'wholy inexpressible' deleted.

47. line 22 *improportionable*, disproportioned.
Beauty, substituted for 'Method'.

48. lines 24-25 *and your self abominable*, an addition.

49. line 13 *infinitly*, an addition.
line 14 *and to lov him*, an addition.
line 28 *and . . . Power*, an addition.

50. line 7 *in it with a*, originally 'with the'.
line 11 *Occupations*, deleted: over it is 'Affairs' also deleted.
line 14 *and crowning*, an addition.
line 16 *Impertinent*, irrelevant.

52. lines 10-11 *find in*, substituted for 'the Rubbish of'.

53. line 2 *now*, an addition.
line 3 *superadded Treasures*; cf. I. 76, lines 1-4.

54. line 4 *fragments*: this almost suggests Blake, *Jerusalem*, 27: 'Man anciently
contain'd in his mighty limbs all things in Heaven & Earth. . . . But now
the Starry Heavens are fled from the mighty limbs of Albion.'
line 9 *upon . . . appearance*, an addition.

55. line 7 *ten yeers*: perhaps 1653-63, i.e. from going to the University to shortly
after settling in at Credenhill. It is clear from this that the *Centuries* are
fairly late, perhaps written about 1670. Cf. note on I. 80, line 11.
line 14 *Stonish*, stony, chiefly figurative. *OED* quotes from Robinson's
More's *Utopia* (1551).

56. line 11 *Moses*, Leviticus 19[18], 'thou shalt love thy neighbour as thy self'.
S. Paul, e.g. 1 Corinthians 13.
line 14 *impart*: the manuscript has 'imp^t', the 't' being, as commonly, uncrossed.
Dobell read it as 'l' and expanded to 'imperil' and it is very possible that he
was right.
ones own, substituted for 'our' and 'Souls' left, but I print 'Soul'.

57. lines 12-13 *By loving . . . receiv it*, just possibly an addition.

58. lines 7-8 *What . . . unto me*, Matthew 25[40]
line 9 *Crown*, preceded by 'half' deleted.
being, substituted for 'and were'.
line 11 *all*, an addition.
line 12 *relief*, substituted for 'my Supper'.
line 16 *End of*, followed by 'another' deleted.
line 18 *Noble*, substituted for 'universal'.

59. line 3 *unless . . . of His*, Romans 8[9].
lines 3-4 *Lov in him*, changed from 'His Lov'.
line 6 *adventure*, followed by 'and expose himself' deleted.

lines 6–7 *he, Whose Lov is like*, originally 'his Lov, Whose is like'.

line 9 *Measures*, followed by 'and how to be saving of its Costs' deleted.
Cf. Wordsworth's Sonnet, *Inside of King's College Chapel, Cambridge*:

> . . . high Heaven rejects the lore
> Of nicely-calculated less or more.

60. line 4 *Vail*, the common use, perhaps derived from the veil of the Temple,
and cf. Blake's *Vala*, the phenomenal world which is a veil between man
and reality.
There, in Heaven.
line 11 *necessities to reliev*, an addition.
line 21 *expect it after Death*: compare and contrast § 9.

61. line 9 Another reminiscence of Shirley's lyric, cf. *The Review* ii** 12.

64. line 8 *his Glory*, originally 'True Glory', then 'His Glory', finally as printed.

66. line 1 *He, I*, the same person, i.e. Traherne, as is clear from §§ 1, 20, 30. But
had he some idea of a double self, an ordinary and an inspired?
line 10 *Sphere*, cf. *My Spirit*.
line 11 *som say*: contrast *The Circulation* 65–68.
line 13 *Persons*, substituted for 'its Dimensions'.

67. line 5 *Act . . . Power*: Traherne's doctrine that perfection is the actualization
of all potentialities is summarized in *The Anticipation* 91, 'His Essence is all
Act'.
Daemon, spirit, as usual with this spelling.

69. lines 15–16 *Guided to the same Ends*, an addition.

72. line 9 *Greatest*: 'est' may be an addition.
lines 18–19 *Alpha . . . last*, Revelation 1[8, 11].
line 19 *Amen*, Revelation 1[6, 7, 18].
the faithfull Witness, Revelation 1[5].
lines 19–21 *The Glory . . . are one*, John 17[22].
lines 21–22 *In Him . . . Bodily*, Colossians 2[9].
line 22 *Bodily*, followed by 'It Dwelleth in Him for our sakes. But' deleted.
If, changed from 'if'.
lines 23–24 *His Church . . . in all*, Ephesians 1[22, 23].

73. line 1 *remaineth*, followed by 'behind' deleted.
line 9 *All*, written over something else beginning with 'T'.

74. lines 5–8 *How Precious . . . unto Thee*, a conflation, not exact; cf. Psalm
139[17, 18] and 40[5].
line 17 *Picus Mirandula* (1463–94): his *Oratio* (*De Dignitate Hominis*) was
first published in 1496 at Bologna and was available to Traherne in several
later editions. In Pico's *Opera Omnia* (Basel, 1601) it begins on p. 207.
The passage here quoted comes from the beginning (*Legi* to *invidiosam*), p. 102

of the modern edition, ed. Garin, Florence, 1942. In lines 27–31 Traherne puts Pico's accusatives (*internuntium,* &c.) in the nominative. In line 40 he interposes 'And so he goeth on'.

line 18 *read,* followed by 'that' deleted.

line 22 *his,* Abdala's.

line 23 *Mercurius Trismegistus,* Milton's 'thrice great Hermes', supposed author of the Hermetic writings. The quotation here is Pico's. Wade (p. 218, footnote) is mistaken in thinking that Traherne is here using Hermes direct. The quotation is from *Asclepius* (i. 294 of the modern edition, ed. Scott, 1924).

line 23 *Magnum,* an addition, but part of the latin text.

line 29 *Stabilis,* preceded by 'tam' [?] deleted.

line 31 *Hymenaeus,* corrected from 'Hymenaus' [?].

line 35 *link or,* an addition.

lines 37–38 *little . . . Angels,* Psalm 8⁵, a favourite quotation of Traherne's; here Pico's.

line 39 *Principal,* preceded by 'cheif or' deleted.

75. All from Pico (p. 104 of 1942 edition: *Iam summus* to *alloquutus*).

line 2 *the World,* an addition.

　　most, an addition.

line 8 *that might,* preceded by 'who should' deleted.

line 9 *lov,* preceded by 'and' deleted.

line 24 *dari,* this reading of Traherne's is found in the 1601 edition: the 1942 edition reads 'dare'.

76. All from Pico (pp. 104–6: *Nec certam* to *effinges*), following immediately on the preceding.

line 4 *only,* an addition.

　　all, followed by 'prescribed Bounds' deleted.

77. All from Pico (p. 106: *O summam* to *caligine*). One sentence is omitted between it and the preceding, and there are one or two other small omissions.

line 4 *brought forth,* substituted for 'born'.

　　bring . . . what, changed from 'bring that . . . which'.

line 7 *omnigena:* 1601 and 1942 editions both read 'omnigenae'.

line 14 *he,* preceded by 'becoming' deleted.

78. line 2 *university,* Traherne must mean Rome.

lines 7–10 *Neither doth . . . Intelligence,* from Pico (p. 108: *Neque enim plantam* to *angelum facit,* with one short omission). The rest of the section is Traherne's comment.

79. line 1 *neither,* preceded by 'So' deleted.

line 2 *Fable,* is written right over another word beginning with 'F'.

line 4 *Eusebius* (*c.* 260–*c.* 340), the historian of the Church. I have not been able to identify the passage in spite of Traherne's indication.

line 5 *tho*, substituted for 'being'.

line 17 *Reasons*, followed by '(and all assignable)' deleted.

line 20 *Almighty*, followed by 'Thus you see the Rindes and Shells of Verity, but the living Waters flow in Liquid Reason' deleted.

80. line 8 *Divaricated*, preceded by 'feet' deleted. The word means 'spread wide apart': Marvell, *Rehearsal Transpros'd* (1672), p. 160, uses it of a woman's fingers spread apart in an insulting gesture.

81. line 1 *Nazianzen*: see III. 65 and 98. I have failed to locate this reference.

lines 2–3 *Even so ... And what*, an addition. 'Our', with capital 'O', originally began a sentence.

line 4 *Author*, Pico: see § 77, lines 13–16.

line 7 *Dialogue*, see § 74, line 23 and note. *Asclepius* is a dialogue between Asclepius and Hermes.

line 15 *So*, preceded by 'The' (not 'Yᵉ') deleted.

line 17 *are*, substituted for 'is'.

line 18 *as ... knowing*, substituted for 'being made of Nothing'.

lines 20–21 *being ... Nothing*, an addition.

line 22 *Rivers*, substituted for 'Streams'.

82. line 12 *fatness*, preceded by 'Pleasure o' deleted. Note the characteristic catalogue, and again in § 85.

84. line 13 *in it*, followed by 'so the Soul' deleted. This suggests that this section is a fair copy, the phrase being copied a line too soon. The same thing happened in §§ 86, 87.

85. lines 8–9 *a Spring ... sealed*, Song of Solomon 4¹².

line 10 *Contents*, preceded by 'Secret' deleted.

line 31 *it can desire*, preceded by 'All this Good' deleted.

86. line 6 *but*, followed by 'the Lid of Ig' deleted.

line 11 *a*, substituted for 'the'.

87. line 9 *Shine*, preceded by 'lov' deleted (copied too soon).

88. line 2 *or*, substituted for 'and'.

line 20 *God*, preceded by 'my' deleted.

89. line 10 *unseasonable*, substituted for 'Troublesom'.

92. lines 3–4 *At Midnight ... Judgements*, Psalm 119⁶².

lines 4–5 *Seven times ... Mercy*, Psalm 119¹⁶⁴, but with 'Glorious Mercy' deliberately substituted by Traherne for 'righteous judgments'.

line 6 *Triumph*, substituted for 'Delight'.

I will Triumph in thy Works, Psalm 92⁴.

lines 6–7 *I will Delight in thy Law*, Psalm 119⁷⁰.

lines 7–8 *I will ... Acts*, Psalm 9¹, not at all exact.

line 9 *Glorious ... Kingdom*, Psalm 145¹².

lines 11–12 *I will Boast . . . Long*, Psalm 44[8].
line 12 *be Glad in the Lord*, Psalm 104[34].
line 14 *sing and be Glad*, Psalm 67[4] ('be glad and sing').
line 15 *Earth . . . sheild*, cf. Psalm 47[9], 'the shields of the earth'.
This section is mainly a cento of quotations, not very exact, from the Psalms. Even where there is no recognizable quotation, the language tends to be psalmodic.

95. lines 5–6 *cannot rest, till it be employd*: for paradox cf. *Eden* 1.

96. line 8 *Propriety*, appropriateness, not, as more often in Traherne, property.

97. line 5 *upon*, substituted for 'by'.
line 14 *may*, preceded by 'it' deleted.
   overcom, followed by 'but many things are too Great, and many things are too heavy for it to rule or bear' deleted.

98. line 2 *Divine*, followed by 'Honorable or Holy, Noble or Blessed' deleted.
   Principle, followed by 'among all other as one of the most Soveraign' deleted.
line 4 *Usefull . . . Delightfull*, both adjectives preceded by 'most' deleted.
line 7 *which . . . contemplat*, an addition.
line 8 *Power*, preceded by 'Almighty' deleted.
   Wisdom (second time), preceded by 'Eternal' deleted.
   Goodness (with *ss*), preceded by 'Endless' deleted.
line 10 *Contemplating*, changed from 'as Contemplat'.
   freely, followed by 'and Manage them as volubly' deleted. An intermediate stage was 'Managing them as volubly'.
line 13 *them*, followed by 'entirely' deleted.
line 14 *a*, shortened from 'any'.
line 18 *follow*, an immediate insertion over a caret.
line 21 *tho*, preceded by 'To which we return, that' deleted.
lines 22–23 *it can . . . Object*, substituted for 'that in Wisdom and Goodness is possible'.
line 26 *contemplation*, followed by 'unless it be Perfect' deleted.

99. line 3 *till*, preceded by 'not [?]' deleted.
line 10 *by it*, an addition.
line 13 Between *following* and *therupon* is '100' deleted. This suggests that this section, or at any rate the end of it, is not a fair copy.

THE FIFTH CENTURY

Summary

V. 1 The Objects and Way of Enjoying Felicity are two themes, but both are God.
2 'The Infinity of God is our Enjoyment.'
3 Illimitability of the Soul.
4 Thus God's infinite ability is answered by the Soul's infinite capacity.
5 The visible world consists of pictures made by God.
6 Infinite space is multiplied by infinite time, always present.
7 Eternity is an 'infinit immovable Duration'.
8 'Eternitie magnifies our Joys exceedingly.'
9 God's omnipresence makes everything infinite.
10 Thus 'our Bliss and Happiness' is perfected and completed.

In these last ten sections Traherne displays Felicity as a union of God and the Soul in Eternity and Infinity.

The heading of this *Century*, as of the other three, is fully capitalized in this edition, but the manuscript reads 'The fifth Centurie'. This comes at the top of the recto, but half-way down the recto of the previous leaf Traherne had written, and left, 'The fifth Century', but he cut off the bottom part of the leaf. The reason may merely have been to start a new *Century* on a new page.

1. lines 11–12 *Particulars* is the middle word of the line in the manuscript: it has a premature '2' in and below it.

2. line 2 *Barely*, merely, i.e. even for this reason.
   line 12 *the Measure*, preceded by 'and' deleted.
   and the . . . Souls, immediate addition over a caret.
   line 15 *and*, an immediate addition.
   line 16 *then*, followed by 'while' deleted.
   lines 21–22 *unless . . . us*, an addition.
   line 23 *feel*, followed by 'it' deleted.
   line 26 *but*, preceded by a redundant 'but' deleted.
   removed, followed by 'from us' deleted.
   lines 27–29 *It is impossible . . . Being*: this last sentence is an addition, but, as the writing shows, an immediate addition, crammed into the space before the figure '3'. Before 'within' (line 27) the word 'be' has been omitted.
   line 29 *is inevitably fatal to*, is the inevitable fate of. For 'fatal' meaning 'destined', cf. *Christian Ethicks*, p. 144, 'Dead Agents that are made to act by a *Fatal* Necessity, without sence or Desire.'

3. The figure '3' has been put in brackets to mark it off from 'is' and 'inevitably', between which it comes.
   line 1 *can*, preceded by 'and' deleted.

line 3 *such*, an addition.

line 5 *Souls*, substituted for 'Thoughts'.

lines 5-8 *We see . . . Angels*; cf. Blake's two views of the senses, (1) as 'the chief inlets of soul in this age', and (2) as shutting us out from reality.

line 10 *realy and*, an addition.

lines 17-18 *Evry Man . . . of it*; cf. Blake's creative solipsism as in *Jerusalem*, 77, 'Imagination . . . in which we shall live in our Eternal or Imaginative Bodies.'

4. line 2 *Goodness*, followed by 'and' deleted.
    want a, followed by 'Place and' deleted.
    its, substituted for 'their'.
line 4 *enough*, followed by 'and' deleted.
line 8 *is*, substituted for 'was'.
line 12 *Treasure*, followed by 'infinit' deleted.

5. line 1 *Table*, 'a board or other flat surface on which a picture is painted' (OED).
line 9 *Penicill*, brush (Latin *penicillum*): this form is not quoted in OED.

6. line 2 *Treasure*, originally 'Treasures'.
    yet, preceded by 'And' deleted.
lines 3-4 *a more Wonderfull Region*, an addition.
lines 5-6 *from the Centre . . . Hills*; cf. IV. 37, lines 4-5 and § 9, line 20, below.
line 9 *that is*, substituted for 'the only Space'.
line 10 *only present*, an addition.

8. line 2 *began*, followed by 'continu but a Time' deleted.
line 4 *leav us*, substituted for 'vanish'.
line 15 *all*, substituted for 'both'.
    our selvs, an addition.
line 18 *Blessedness*, followed by 'together' deleted.
lines 22-23 *us . . . while*, an addition.
line 24 *the shores*, preceded by 'and' deleted.
    seeming, changed from 'seem'.
    tho, an addition.
line 27 *them in*, an addition.
line 28 *Light*, preceded by 'our' deleted.
line 29 *not*, followed by 'yet' deleted.

9. line 5 *fame*, preceded by 'our' deleted.
line 6 *infinit*, followed by 'Extent and' deleted.
line 8 *evry where*, an addition.
line 21 *his Endless Infinitie*, substituted for 'Immensity'.

10. line 5 *Delights*, preceded by 'And' deleted.
    line 6 *preparing*, changed from 'prepared'.

11. In spite of this numerical heading for another section and in spite of Traherne's obvious idea of writing 'The fifth Centurie' I cannot but look on V. 10 as a triumphant and perfect conclusion. How could Traherne have gone beyond it? The *Centuries* are not unfinished.